THE INTEGRITY OF THE QUR'AN

Edinburgh Studies in Islamic Scripture and Theology

Published and forthcoming titles

Hadith Commentary: Continuity and Change
Edited by Joel Blecher and Stefanie Brinkmann

Transcendent God, Rational World: A Māturīdī Theology
Ramon Harvey

The Integrity of the Qur'an: Sunni and Shi'i Historical Narratives
Seyfeddin Kara

Tawātur *in Islamic Thought: Transmission, Certitude and Orthodoxy*
Suheil Laher

edinburghuniversitypress.com/series/esist

THE INTEGRITY OF THE QUR'AN

Sunni and Shi'i Historical Narratives

SEYFEDDIN KARA

EDINBURGH
University Press

Edinburgh University Press is one of the leading university presses in the UK. We publish academic books and journals in our selected subject areas across the humanities and social sciences, combining cutting-edge scholarship with high editorial and production values to produce academic works of lasting importance. For more information visit our website: edinburghuniversitypress.com

Edinburgh University Press Ltd
13 Infirmary Street
Edinburgh EH1 1LT

First published in hardback by Edinburgh University Press 2024

Typeset in 11/13 Minion 3 by
IDSUK (DataConnection) Ltd

A CIP record for this book is available from the British Library

ISBN 978 1 4744 6223 5 (hardback)
ISBN 978 1 4744 6224 2 (paperback)
ISBN 978 1 4744 6225 9 (webready PDF)
ISBN 978 1 4744 6226 6 (epub)

Contents

Acknowledgements vi
Note on Transliteration and Dates viii
Preface ix

Part I *Isnād-cum-matn* Analysis in the Study of Early Islam

Introduction: Re-evaluating Methodological Trajectories in the Study of Early Islam 3

1 ʿĀʾisha's Legal Debate on the Boundaries of Breastfeeding 38

Part II Searching for the Stoning Penalty in 'the Book of God'

2 The Litigation of the Two Men according to 'the Book of God' 77

3 The Prophet, the Jews and the Stoning Penalty 103

4 Caliph ʿUmar's Sermon on the 'Missing Stoning Verse' 139

Part III Distortion Narratives in Shiʿi Hadith

5 Transition of the Distortion Narrative into Shiʿi Reports 173

6 Distorting the Book of God 206

7 The Return of the Avenger and Teaching the Correct Qur'an 228

Conclusion: Rethinking Narratives and Shaping Historical Discourse 250

Bibliography 255
Index 267

Acknowledgements

I would like to express my sincere gratitude to the individuals and organisations whose support and contributions have been invaluable in the creation of this monograph. Foremost, I am deeply grateful to the Marie Skłodowska-Curie Global Fellowship, whose support facilitated my research journey across the UK, Germany, Canada and Sweden. Their assistance has been instrumental in bringing this project to fruition.

Special appreciation goes to Walid Saleh and Jens Scheiner for their instrumental role in supporting my application for the Global Fellowship, and to the former for his generous mentorship during my tenure at the University of Toronto. I extend my heartfelt thanks to Marie S. Curie Project Officer Marta Mauleon Villanueva for her unwavering support during the challenging periods of the Global Fellowship. My time at the University of Toronto was enriched by the guidance and assistance of Pamela Klassen, Natalie Rothman, Suleyman Dost, Karen Ruffle, Michael Twamley, Fereshteh Hashemi and the dedicated staff and colleagues at the Department for the Study of Religion, the Department of Historical and Cultural Studies and the Department of Historical Studies. Their support, along with the provision of workspaces across three of the university's campuses, significantly contributed to the progress of this book alongside my teaching responsibilities on early Islam.

I am indebted to Suleyman Dost, whose support extended beyond professional collaboration to genuine friendship. Mohammed Rustom and his wife, Nosheen Mian, provided unwavering friendship and invaluable feedback during our time in Canada. I am particularly grateful for Rustom's comprehensive comments and editing of the initial hundred pages of the book.

I extend my thanks to Oliver Scharbrodt and Alexander Maurits, head of department at the Centre for Theology and Religious Studies, Lund University, for their generous support during my tenure at Lund. Gratitude is also due to Mairaj Syed for his insightful feedback on the first three chapters of the book. Special thanks to Maroussia Bednarkiewicz for her invaluable assistance in designing the *isnād* maps using her 'isnalyser' programme. Her exceptional work has significantly enhanced the visual representation of the data, and also helped identify and rectify certain errors during the process.

I am grateful to John S. Kloppenborg for the knowledge gained from his course on redaction criticism and for allowing me to attend. Furthermore, I appreciate Samuel Byrskog's assistance in providing essential literature on current trends in biblical studies. My gratitude extends to Mohammad Saeed Bahmanpour and Abbas Di Palma for their invaluable assistance in navigating challenging Arabic texts. I am grateful to David Powers and Juan Cole for generously sharing their relevant works with me. I would also like to acknowledge Afzal Sumar, Sayyed Ali Reza Sadr and Mohammad Sadr, as well as the Shiʿa Research Institute, for their support and funding.

I am sincerely appreciative of the feedback provided by the anonymous reviewers via Edinburgh University Press, whose insightful comments significantly improved the quality of this work. Special thanks are due to Series Editor Ramon Harvey for his thoughtful and erudite contributions, along with his meticulous attention to detail. I am also thankful to Nicola Ramsey for her support and to Rachel Bridgewater for overseeing the publication of this monograph. I would like to extend my special thanks to Managing Desk Editor Eddie Clark for his patience in performing the final checks and making the finishing touches during the production stage. Aatif Bokhari and Noah H. Taj deserve acknowledgement for their proofreading of the final manuscript, and likewise Muhammad Ridwaan for copy-editing it.

I express gratitude for the open access funding provided by the Libraries of the Joint Faculties of Humanities and Theology and the Centre for Theology and Religious Studies, both at Lund University.

Finally, I am deeply grateful to my wife, Emmi, and my sons, Yusuf, Yakob and Isak, for their unwavering support and understanding during the demanding process of writing this book, which took us across multiple countries.

Note on Transliteration and Dates

I followed the Arabic transliteration guidelines set forth in the *Journal of Qur'anic Studies*. In the text, I avoided using the definite article 'al-' for renowned and oft-cited names like Zuhrī and Bukhārī. I did not transliterate well-known words like 'Kaaba'. Moreover, I used double dates for the classical era.

Preface

The inception of this project originated from the exploration of my monograph on ʿAlī b. Abī Ṭālib's codex, which ignited a profound curiosity within me regarding distortion narratives. Consulting the late Harald Motzki, whose wisdom and guidance remain an enduring influence, further emboldened my pursuit of this line of scholarly enquiry. While the preliminary findings of this research offer promising insights, I approach the reception from the academic community with both anticipation and humility. My aspiration is for this work to serve as a catalyst, sparking further engagement and discourse within the realm of hadith, the early history of Islam and *isnād-cum-matn* analysis.

The journey of this book has been one filled with challenges and unexpected turns, reflecting the ups and downs of life's unpredictable path. It led me across various countries and continents. Commencing during my tenure as an assistant professor at Hartford Seminary (Hartford International University) in 2018, its evolution coincided with a period of significant personal and professional transitions. Despite facing obstacles, including the unforeseen loss of my position due to visa restrictions imposed by the then-US government, the vision for this work endured.

During a transformative phase marked by my temporary engagement as a delivery driver in Durham and Gateshead, the captivating landscapes of northern England became both my inspiration and solace. Amid my travels, I diligently crafted the initial chapters, driven by a profound commitment to this project. Despite moments of doubt, the unwavering essence of this manuscript sustained my determination. Persevering through numerous challenges, I sought the Marie Skłodowska-Curie Global Fellowship, which granted me invaluable international exposure and resources. This pivotal opportunity not only facilitated the revision of existing chapters but also enabled the timely completion of the remaining segments, culminating in my appointment to a permanent position at the University of Groningen.

In memory of Harald Motzki,
A scholar whose contributions will forever inspire

PART I

Isnād-cum-matn Analysis in the Study of Early Islam

Introduction

Re-evaluating Methodological Trajectories in the Study of Early Islam

Objectives and Results: Exploring the Integrity of the Qur'an

From the outset, allow me to clarify my objectives and accomplishments in writing this book. The book has thematic, conceptual and methodological motivations. The thematic motivation is to have an open-minded study and debate on the textual integrity of the Qur'an. The preferred source for the study is hadith, or Muslim oral reports, about the distortion of the Qur'an through the alleged omission of some verses. In accordance with this intention, the book examines some relevant Sunni and Shiʿi reports that play a central role in distortion narratives. These narratives include the so-called missing verses on stoning and breastfeeding from the Qur'an, distorting the Book of God, the return of al-Mahdī (a messianic figure who is expected to return before the end of time to fill the earth with justice) and teaching the correct Qur'an.

The conceptual motivation is related to studying both Sunni and Shiʿi reports. The central conviction that informs my conceptual approach is that a comprehensive examination of Sunni and Shiʿi Muslim reports will provide a detailed landscape of the early history of Islam. Such a comparative study will not only provide a deeper understanding of the early history of Islam but also shed light on the nature of the interaction, influence and rivalry between the two denominations during the phases of their nascent formation. Therefore, I maintain that hadiths have historical source value, and that it is possible to reconstruct the early history of Islam if they are studied by a rigorous method.

My methodological motivation is related to the use of *isnād-cum-matn* analysis. To achieve the thematic and conceptual objectives, the book employs *isnād-cum-matn* analysis of the relevant hadiths. Each hadith consists of two parts: a chain of transmission (*isnād*), attesting to the veracity of a particular report, and the text (*matn*), which is considered the verbal utterance of the Prophet. The author of this book defends the position that *isnād-cum-matn* analysis is the most methodologically sound means through which we can study the hadith corpus, despite some of its shortcomings. By employing *isnād-cum-matn* analysis on Sunni and Shi'i hadiths to investigate a controversial phenomenon about the textual history of the Qur'an, this book will test the limits of *isnād-cum-matn* analysis in dating and reconstructing the early history of Islam. When these motivations are combined, this study coalesces into three central goals:

1. To discover the historical origins of the notion of distortion of the Qur'an.
2. To identify the interaction and influence between Sunni and Shi'i traditionalists who advocated this notion from the second/eighth to fifth/eleventh centuries.
3. To make methodological advances in the study of early Islam by testing the boundaries of *isnād-cum-matn* analysis.

Given the diversity of the narratives, the study will also investigate some related matters in relation to the early history of Islam, such as the crystallisation of the Qur'anic codex, the role of the Prophet Muhammad in the early Medinan community, his relations with the Jews, the connection between Islamic law and rabbinic law, the redaction of prophetic hadith to align it with the position of Muslim legal schools, the scholarly debate about the breastfeeding of minors and adults to form non-biological family ties in Islamic tradition, the formation of Shi'i identity and the redaction, editing and forgery culture in the written transmission of Shi'i reports. While examining these crucial topics, the book will make the following claims:

- Based on the study of the reports attributed to 'Umar, the Qur'anic codex was crystallised before the reign of 'Umar. This is the earliest dating of the Qur'anic codex based on the study of hadith.
- The Prophet Muhammad possibly implemented the stoning penalty as an arbitrator between Jewish factions, not as a lawmaker.
- Because the narratives about the missing Stoning Verse attributed to 'Umar also include the account of the succession of Abū Bakr, these reports became well known in the Shi'i communities in Iraq. Therefore, most probably, the existence of such reports gave the idea of distortion of the Qur'an to sectarian Shi'is who were desperate to establish the presence of hard textual evidence (*naṣṣ*) for the succession and imamate in the Qur'an.

- There is strong evidence that Sunni legal schools redacted prophetic reports to align them with their legal views. For example, Mālik promoted the concept of abrogation (*naskh*) by editing the prophetic reports. However, this interference was not in the form of fabricating brand-new reports and projecting them back to the Prophet. There is only an isolated incident in which a Sunni transmitter interpolated to the report attributed to ʿĀ'isha, the element of a domestic animal eating the verses of the Qur'an. Therefore, it refutes the Schachtian position of widespread systematic fabrication in the Muslim hadith corpus.
- Shiʿis followed suit to edit and combine some Sunni reports. They plagiarised the texts of some Sunni reports and forged new chains to attribute them to the Imams as a part of their identity-building process. Therefore, it demonstrates that *isnād-cum-matn* analysis is not only an important tool for dating hadiths, but it is crucial for uncovering forgeries.
- By identifying the individuals responsible for the forgeries, the book better explains the forgery culture in the early Muslim tradition.

In sum, the book thematically sheds light on the textual integrity of the Qur'an and its crystallisation, as well as the early history of Islam. Methodologically, it demonstrates the efficacy of *isnād-cum-matn* analysis in discovering and uncovering complex and problematic issues in the study of early Islam. These thematic and methodological achievements lead to broader conceptual conclusions that the early history of Islam still remains a mystery, and unconventional and comprehensive approaches are needed to reconstruct it.

Background: Distortion (*taḥrīf*) and the Textual History of the Qur'an

The Qur'an is the central text of Islam and Muslims worldwide strive to shape their lives according to its principles and rulings. Yet the textual integrity of the Qur'an has largely been taken for granted, and some aspects of it have not been investigated fully, especially the idea of the distortion (*taḥrīf*) of the Qur'anic text. There are different meanings and understandings of the distortion in Muslim sources.[1] However, it may be possible to obtain the meaning of the word *taḥrīf* from the Quran itself, as it is the most important source of Muslims as well as the Arabic language. The root of the word *taḥrīf* is trilateral, namely, *ḥā'-rā'-fā'*. The original acceptation of the term is to change the meaning of words. The Qur'an contains four

1 Muhammad Hadi Maʿrifat offers the most comprehensive analysis of *taḥrīf* and its diverse meanings and applications in connection with the science of the Qur'an (Maʿrifat, *Introduction to the Science of the Qur'an*, pp. 274–379; and *Ṣiyānat al-Qur'ān min al-taḥrīf*).

verses in which the word *taḥrīf* is mentioned. These verses are used in the form of present tense. On these four occasions, it refers to the Jews' distortion of the meaning or interpretation of the Torah thrice:

> Are you then eager that they should believe you, though a part of them would hear the word of God and then distort it, after they had understood it and they knew what they were doing. (Q. 2:75)

> Among the Jews are those who distort words from their meanings. (Q. 4:46)

> and then, because of their breaking their covenant, We cursed them and made their hearts hard: they distorted the words from their meanings and have forgotten a part of what they were reminded. (Q. 5:13)

Additionally, it refers to their distortion of the text of the Torah once:

> They distort words beyond their [proper] usages, saying, 'If you are given this, take it; but if you are not given it, then beware.' (Q. 5:41)

The term *taḥrīf* can pertain to either the meaning of the verses or the actual wording of the verses themselves. However, as per the study of relevant traditions, it is generally accepted that it signifies the distortion of the wording of the Qur'an, specifically through the omission of certain verses or words. The Qur'anic verses evince that this distortion was a result of deliberate meddling by later Jews. Consequently, within the Islamic context, it is comprehended as the deliberate exclusion of verses or alterations in the wording of the Qur'an following the time of the Prophet Muhammad, who recited and dictated the Qur'anic verses to his followers. Hence, he possessed the authority and legitimacy to include or exclude verses or words in/from the Qur'an. Nevertheless, any intentional modifications to the text and its intended meaning subsequent to the Prophet's era are deemed as distortions of the Qur'anic text. This research will specifically focus on reports concerning the omission of Qur'anic wordings, rather than investigating alterations in meaning.

Since the second/eighth century, a group of Muslim traditionalists have claimed that certain verses were removed from the Qur'anic text after the death of the Prophet, making the present Qur'anic text incomplete.[2]

2 The debate around the distortion refers to the omission of certain verses of the Qur'an. Other than the Khawārij, no other Muslim groups endorsed any form of interpolation in the Qur'an. The Maymūniyya, which was a splinter group of the Khawārij, contended that Sūrat Yūsuf was not a part of the Qur'an (Modarressi, 'Early Debates on the Integrity of the Qur'ān', p. 23).

In other words, the present Qur'an does not include the complete set of verses believed to be revealed to the Prophet Muhammad. It is believed that at the time of revelation, Muslims memorised the verses of the Qur'an, and Muhammad appointed four main scribes, 'Alī b. Abī Ṭālib (d. 40/661), Ubayy b. Ka'b (between 19/640 and 35/656), 'Abdullāh b. Mas'ūd (d. 32/653) and Zayd b. Thābit (d. 45/665–6), to record the Word of God in writing on loose folios. Finally, when Muhammad died in 11/632, Muslims compiled these loose folios into a unified codex. Zayd b. Thābit, the most junior scribe of the Prophet, led two initiatives to compile the Qur'an at the time of the first caliph, Abū Bakr, and the third caliph, 'Uthmān.[3] However, it is well known in Muslim sources that the remaining three scribes of the Prophet compiled their own notes on the Qur'an into codices.[4] According to the sources, 'Alī did not come out of his house until he had collated his own copy of the Qur'an.[5] 'Abdullāh b. Mas'ūd and Ubayy b. Ka'b followed suit. Consequently, it must have been infuriating for the most senior Companions of the Prophet for a much younger and junior companion, Zayd b. Thābit,[6] to oversee such an important task.

It is probable that given the significance and prestige that one could attain from the official collection of the Word of God, the first (and the second caliph, who was also involved in this project) and third caliphs might have made conscious decisions to task Zayd b. Thābit with the official collection of the Qur'an. Because the Qur'an was accepted as the Word of God by the early Muslims, its compilation required delicate care to not upset the balance of power in the nascent Muslim community. 'Alī b. Abī Ṭālib, 'Abdullāh b. Mas'ūd and Ubayy b. Ka'b were among the earliest Muslims who endured many difficulties with the Prophet and had already attained an esteemed status in the eyes of the Muslim community. Honouring them the special status of a compilation of the Qur'an would further enhance their status and upset the existing balance of power and authority. The fact that 'Uthmān commissioned Zayd to compile the Qur'an again in the presence of Ḥafṣa's codex, which was basically the codex of Abū Bakr and 'Umar, shows that the collection of the Qur'an was considered a caliphal tradition. To achieve the important task of collating the Word of God and making it available to Muslims yielded prestige and authority.

Nevertheless, Muslim sources unanimously agree that Zayd did an exceptional job completing the task on both occasions. The codex that he collated for 'Uthmān, which was based on the codex that he had collated

3 Motzki, 'The Collection of the Qur'ān', p. 6.

4 Jeffery, *Materials for the History of the Text of the Quran.*

5 Kara, *In Search of Ali Ibn Abi Talib's Codex*, p. 177 and *passim.*

6 Lecker, 'Zayd B. Thābit', p. 262 and *passim.*

for Abū Bakr (through Ḥafṣa's codex),[7] became the official codex, otherwise known as the 'Uthmānic codex. 'Alī's codex was rejected, 'Abdullāh b. Mas'ūd and Ubayy b. Ka'b's codices were destroyed and the 'Uthmānic codex became the unrivalled standard Qur'an for Muslims. By and large, Muslims, including the two rival denominations, Sunnis and Shi'is, have maintained that this codex genuinely preserves Muhammad's preaching.

Despite the initial opposition from Western academic circles, especially from the so-called revisionist school,[8] the Muslim narrative of early closure of the Qur'an's canon before the first/seventh century has gained significant traction.[9] In this regard, Holger Zellentin notes that

> even before the discovery of early manuscripts of the Qur'an that now strongly suggests the closure of the Qur'an's canon before the end of the seventh century, Wansbrough's radical questioning has eventually helped the case for the plausibility of locating the Qur'an in a Meccan and Medinan context.[10]

Zellentin refers to the discovery of the Ṣan'ā' palimpsests. The groundbreaking studies on these palimpsests further solidified the view about the closure of the Qur'an's canon before the end of the first/seventh century. In their pioneering study, Sadeghi and Goudarzi published edited folios of the Ṣan'ā' palimpsests.[11] Earlier discoveries revealed that the Ṣan'ā' palimpsests, besides the main writings, also contained a secondary layer of erased writings, which were believed to represent the earliest non-standard recension of the Qur'an.[12] Through X-ray fluorescence imaging of the four folios, the study managed to recover the lower writings. Additionally, the study employed the radiocarbon dating method and dated the parchments to

7 I have already discussed the reasons why Zayd b. Thābit might have been commissioned to collate the Qur'an on two occasions; see Kara, *In Search of Ali Ibn Abi Talib's Codex*, pp. 37–74.

8 See, Donner, 'The Qur'ān in Recent Scholarship', pp. 29–50; Motzki, 'The Collection of the Qur'ān', pp. 1–34; Stewart, 'Reflections on the State of the Art in Western Qur'anic Studies', pp. 4–68.

9 See also, Sinai, 'When Did the Consonantal Skeleton of the Quran Reach Closure? Part I', pp. 273–92; Sinai, 'When Did the Consonantal Skeleton of the Quran Reach Closure? Part II', pp. 509–21.

10 Zellentin, *The Qur'an's Reformation of Judaism and Christianity*, p. 5. Zellentin also highlights pertinent scholarly works, delivering a comprehensive summary of the recent discoveries surrounding the early manuscript of the Qur'an: Déroche, *Qur'ans of the Umayyads*; Hilali, *The Sanaa Palimpsest*; Sadeghi and Goudarzi, 'Ṣan'ā' 1 and the Origins of the Qur'ān'.

11 Sadeghi and Goudarzi, 'Ṣan'ā' 1 and the Origins of the Qur'ān', pp. 1–129.

12 Sadeghi and Bergmann, 'The Codex of a Companion of the Prophet and the Qur'ān of the Prophet', pp. 343–436.

the period between AD 614 and 656 with a 68 per cent probability. Furthermore, the study found a 95 per cent probability that they 'belong to the period between AD 578 and AD 669'.[13] According to these findings, Sadeghi and Bergmann concluded that 'it is highly probable, therefore, that the Ṣanʿā' 1 manuscript was produced no more than 15 years after the death of the Prophet Muḥammad'.[14]

Although the radiocarbon dating method can determine the approximate date of the animal's slaughter for the parchment, it cannot precisely ascertain when the actual writing took place. Sadeghi and Bergmann, however, express confidence that the date of the parchment gives an approximate date of the lower writing, as they consider it unlikely that the parchment is significantly older than the writing.[15]

Sadeghi and Goudarzi's study of all the palimpsests yielded even more ground-breaking results. Both the radiocarbon dating method and textual analysis of the different layers indicated an earlier date. The radiocarbon method applied to the parchments found that the lower codex is from 'the period before AD 671 with a probability of 99%' (before AD 661 with a probability of 95.5 per cent, and before AD 646 with a probability of 75 per cent).[16] This discovery of the lower text is particularly crucial for the research as it represents, along with the standard 'Uthmānic codex, the earliest known extant copy of the Qur'an.[17] A tentative textual analysis, based on a comparison of the lower layer, the 'Uthmānic codex, and the companion codices, suggested an even earlier date, as the comparison indicated that the lower layer is older than the 'Uthmānic codex. Hence, the authors argued that the text of the Qur'an could be dated as early as the Prophet's lifetime and that he himself standardised the Qur'an:

> 'Uthmān was charged with the task of standardizing the Qur'ān. Some other early reports however indicate that this was done already by the Prophet himself. This last view is now found to be better supported. It follows from the fact that the 'Uthmānic Qur'ān, C-1, and the Companion codices generally have the same passages within the *sūras*, that the *sūras* were fixed before these various textual traditions branched off, in particular before the spread of the 'Uthmānic version. With only a few exceptions, the differences among the codices

13 Sadeghi and Bergmann, 'The Codex of a Companion of the Prophet and the Qur'ān of the Prophet', p. 348.

14 Sadeghi and Bergmann, 'The Codex of a Companion of the Prophet and the Qur'ān of the Prophet', p. 358.

15 Sadeghi and Bergmann, 'The Codex of a Companion of the Prophet and the Qur'ān of the Prophet', p. 354.

16 Sadeghi and Goudarzi, 'Ṣanʿā' 1 and the Origins of the Qur'ān', p. 8.

17 Sadeghi and Goudarzi, 'Ṣanʿā' 1 and the Origins of the Qur'ān', p. 8.

are at the level of morphemes, words, and phrases – not at the level of sentences or verses.[18]

One of the most significant findings of the Ṣanʿāʾ palimpsests was the minor differences between the ʿUthmānic codex and the Companion codices. This finding is pertinent to the study of the narratives on the distortion of the Qur'an. Furthermore, there have been subsequent studies of the Ṣanʿāʾ palimpsests but nevertheless they did not fundamentally challenge the findings of Sadeghi and Goudarzi about the early closure of the Qur'anic canon.[19]

Though this finding appears plausible, confirming it proves challenging due to the limitations of the carbon dating method and the information found in Muslim sources.[20] Muslim sources contain numerous accounts regarding the compilation of the Qur'an following the Prophet's death.[21] Furthermore, paleographical evidence strongly suggests that the canon was likely finalised within the initial fifteen years following the Prophet's death. While further research is necessary to narrow down the exact closure of the canon, it seems the current palaeographical studies offer limited assistance.

Nevertheless, the findings presented in this book could potentially resolve the current stalemate as they affirm with certainty that the closure occurred before the death of the second caliph, ʿUmar (d. 23/644), and strongly indicate the presence of an authoritative canon during the reign of Abū Bakr (d. 13/634) or within two years after the Prophet's death.

The Distortion Narratives in Muslim Sources

The idea of the Qur'an's distortion nevertheless crept into Sunni and Shiʿi sources,[22] due to the claim that certain verses of the Qur'an were omitted from the original Qur'an which the Prophet preached. Sunni traditionalists and legal schools advocated the existence of this distortion – in the form of omission of some Qur'anic verses – within a legal framework. In contrast, Shiʿi traditionalists perpetuated the concept to support the succession of the Prophet by their Imams and the sanctity of the Twelver Shiʿi Imams.

There are three main opposing narratives on the genesis of the distortion of the Qur'an. Two of these are held by scholars of Shiʿism, while the third position has found a place in the Sunni orthodoxy. The first Shiʿi stance

18 Sadeghi and Goudarzi, 'Ṣanʿāʾ 1 and the Origins of the Qurʾān', p. 8.

19 Déroche, *Qur'ans of the Umayyads*; Hilali, *The Sanaa Palimpsest;* Cellard, 'The Ṣanʿāʾ Palimpsest'.

20 I offer an analysis of these findings and the surrounding debates in Kara, *In Search of Ali Ibn Abi Talib's Codex*, pp. 53–7.

21 Motzki, 'Collection of the Qur'an'; Kara, 'Suppression of ʿAlī b. Abī Ṭālib's Codex'.

22 Modarressi, 'Early Debates on the Integrity of the Qurʾān', p. 22.

was represented by Modarressi, who echoed the Twelver Shiʿi orthodoxy view advocated by some of the most prominent twentieth-century Twelver scholars, such as Husayn Ali Borujerdi (d. 1961) and Abu al-Qasim al-Khoei (d. 1992).[23] Modarressi argued that the genesis of the distortion of the Qur'an can be found in the various Sunni reports which thereby gave sectarian Shiʿis the idea to use the narrative in advocacy of their Shiʿi cause. The distortion narrative was adopted into the Shiʿi theology in the third/ninth century when an 'extremist' group, the Mufawwiḍa,[24] gained a strong foothold in the Shiʿi community.[25]

On the other hand, Amir-Moezzi represented the other end of the spectrum. Echoing the views of al-Sayyārī[26] (d. mid- or late third/ninth century) and Muḥaddith Nūrī[27] (d. 1902), Amir-Moezzi argues that the origin of the distortion is based on accurate historical events, namely, that the 'Umayyad's distorted the Qur'an to remove textual evidence about the succession of the family of the Prophet and the sanctity of the Shiʿi Imams. His argument is based on existing Shiʿi sources and the interpretation of some recent developments in Qur'anic studies that seemingly fit well in his distortion theory. He claimed that the idea of distortion was the orthodox Shiʿi position until the influential Buyid scholar Ibn Bābawayh (d. 381/991) single-handedly changed the course of Shiʿi theology by adopting the Sunni view on the textual integrity of the 'Uthmānic codex.[28] Shiʿis thus historically positioned themselves in various places between these opposing spectrums on the issue. In this vein, Rainer Brunner's study[29] is a key survey[30] that provides a detailed overview of the position of Shiʿi scholars on distortion in pre-modern and modern times.[31]

Sunni orthodoxy has tried to explain the existing narrative with concepts such as abrogation (*naskh*). John Burton studied Sunni reports on the subject, focusing specifically on the 'abrogation' of Qur'anic verses.[32] Sunni orthodoxy has also accepted the view that the existing narrative on the distortion in Sunni sources relates to abrogation, and not distortion,

23 Burūjardī, *Nihāyat al-uṣūl*, pp. 481–5.
24 Ali, 'The Rational Turn in Imāmism Revisited'.
25 Modarressi, 'Early Debates on the Integrity of the Qur'ān', pp. 32–6; Modarressi, *Crisis and Consolidation in the Formative Period of Shīʿite Islam*, pp. 33–48.
26 al-Sayyārī, *Revelation and Falsification.*
27 Nūrī, *Faṣl al-khiṭāb.*
28 al-Sayyārī, *Revelation and Falsification*, pp. 26–7.
29 Brunner, *Die Schia und die Koranfälschung*.
30 Saleh, 'Review of *Die Schia und Die Koranfälschung*'.
31 Brunner in his excellent research discusses the significance of the integrity of the Qur'an in the Sunni–Shiʿi ecumenical discussions in the twentieth century. Brunner, *Islamic Ecumenism in the 20th Century*.
32 Burton, *The Collection of the Qur'ān*; Burton, 'The Penalty for Adultery in Islam'.

and thus blamed the origins of the distortion of the Qur'an on Shiʿis.[33] Joseph Eliash,[34] Todd Lawson,[35] Meir M. Bar-Asher,[36] David Powers[37] and Shady H. Nasser[38] hence also conducted studies on this topic. These sources provide a meticulous study of the primary and secondary sources on the subject, which I do not intend to duplicate. In this book, I strive to achieve what they have not done, which is to test their views based on the study of primary Sunni and Shiʿi sources, in order to investigate the origins of the distortion narrative.

Consequently, the primary objective of this book is to determine the exact timeframe wherein the notion of the Qur'an's distortion came into existence and to define the further transmission of these traditions, thereby revealing an interaction between Sunni and Shiʿi traditionalists. If the origins of the distortion narrative are discovered, it may be possible to trace the interactions and influences which proliferated the idea of the Qur'an's distortion. The central theory of this monograph posits that due to the shared characteristics of the concept of distortion in both Sunni and Shiʿi narratives, it may become plausible to identify potential intersections that gave rise to the narratives of distortion in both Sunni and Shiʿi traditions.

Studying the Sources: The Trauma of the 'Projecting Back' Theory and *isnād-cum-matn* Analysis

The study of the existing literature points out that the origins of the distortion narrative are traced back to several reports that exist in both Sunni and Shiʿi sources. To analyse these hadiths, I employed *isnād-cum-matn* analysis. Furthermore, examining the background of this method and its significance in hadith studies is crucial in terms of understanding the achievement of this study.

Since the influential works of Ignác Goldziher (d. 1921) and Joseph Schacht (d. 1969), many studies and debates have been conducted on the historical value of hadiths. Goldziher, in his *Muhammedanische Studien*,[39]

33 Modarressi, 'Early Debates on the Integrity of the Qur'ān', pp. 22–3.

34 Eliash, 'The Shiʿite Qur'an'.

35 Todd, 'Note for the Study of a "Shīʿī Qur'ān"'.

36 Bar-Asher, 'Variant Readings'.

37 Differently from the others, Powers studied the concept within the framework of the Qur'anic term *kalāla* and Qur'anic proclamation of Muhammad's sonlessness and his status as the seal of prophets. Powers, *Muḥammad Is Not the Father of Any of Your Men*, p. xiii and *passim*; Powers, 'Sinless, Sonless and Seal of Prophets'.

38 In addition to discussing the sectarian debate surrounding the distortion of the Qur'an, Shady Nasser also sheds light on its contemporary relevance. Nasser, *The Transmission of the Variant Readings of the Qur'ān*, pp. 31–3.

39 Goldziher, *Muslim Studies*.

argued that the Muslim hadith corpus does not narrate the actual events attributed to the Prophet and his Companions. Rather, later Muslims fabricated these reports, especially during the Umayyad era's political disputes, to make a case for political parties such as the Umayyads (41/661–132/750), Zubayrids (64/683–73/692) and ʿAlids, in order to legitimise their right to rule.[40] Their goal was to have the support of the Messenger of God on their side long after he died, through these fabricated reports. The Umayyads were especially successful in their endeavour by sponsoring the early hadith collectors in Syria and western Arabia, the birthplace of Islam. Later, the Abbasids (132/750–1258/656) continued with the precedent set by the Umayyads to legitimise their uprising against the Umayyads and their rule over Muslims. The ʿAlids countered this propaganda campaign by forging their own hadiths to justify the succession of ʿAlī and his merits over the caliphs and the divine right of the Prophet's family to lead the Muslims. One of the main pieces of evidence that Goldziher put forward for his theory was the oral transmission of hadiths. Because they were orally transmitted over several generations, they could have easily been forged or manipulated along the way.

Schacht fully embraced Goldziher's thesis and further developed it with a greater focus on the inherent deficiency of oral transmission and the (mis)use of hadith by Muslim legal schools. In a way, Schacht shifted the focus from the propaganda of political groups to the legal schools' efforts to legitimise their way of law-making, as well as moving away from textual analysis and to an analysis of the chains of transmission. Schacht's influential 'projecting-back' theory, which expanded on Goldziher's thesis, claimed that Muslim oral reports were constructed much later than the events that they claim to narrate,[41] hence, they were fabricated because of disputes between the Muslim political and legal factions. This projecting-back theory argued that Muslim scholars also forged chains of transmission to legitimise their legal or political views. Hence, instead of verifying the transmission of Muslim narrations that are reportedly derived from the Prophet himself, the hadith chains go backwards, or grow backwards, from newer transmitters to older ones. This is in order to establish a so-called authenticity for certain narrations and thereby strengthen the particular view of any given legal school.[42]

The approach and theories of these two hadith studies' giants made a long and lasting impact on the study of Islam in Europe and North America. Their theories deeply influenced the academic study of Islam and steered the direction that hadith studies would take. Hadiths were no longer considered a historical source for studying the life of Muhammad

40 Goldziher, *Muslim Studies*, pp. 90–7.

41 Schacht, *The Origins of Muhammadan Jurisprudence*, p. 163.

42 Schacht, *The Origins of Muhammadan Jurisprudence*, pp. 146–8.

and early Islam, even when studied critically. They had no function other than being the literary productions of later Muslim generations. This led to the trauma of a lack of trust and obscurity in hadith studies, which continues to plague the field till today. Without methodological robustness and sophistication to overcome the inherent weakness of oral transmission, as articulated by Goldziher and Schacht, hadith studies stagnated in academia for several decades thereafter.

That being the case, methodological developments in biblical studies came to the aid of hadith studies. The effective use of form criticism, combined with a meticulous study of the chains of transmission in conjunction with the text, helped in making this breakthrough.

The investigation of both the chains and texts of hadiths was initially emphasised by Jan Hendrik Kramers in his 1953 article, 'Une tradition à tendance manichéenne (La "mangeuse de verdure")',[43] and further expounded upon by Joseph van Ess in his 1975 work, *Zwischen Hadit und Theologie.*[44] This method has emerged partially in response to dissatisfaction with the existing chain of transmission analysis, which is perceived as 'a too artificial interpretation of the *isnād* bundles'.[45] It is inspired by developments in biblical studies, but the elaborate study of transmitters emerged under the influence of Schacht and G. H. A. Juynboll (d. 2010). Juynboll furthered the study of the chains of transmission based on Schacht's large-scale hadith fabrication theory and made a compelling case for the historical value of the widely attested chains of transmission.[46] Conversely, he discarded non-widely circulated reports and considered them to be outright forgeries. The problem with this approach was that only a couple of hundred hadith could fulfil the stringent criteria set by Juynboll.

Iftikhar Zaman in his study undertook a preliminary form of *isnād-cum-matn* analysis.[47] However, Harald Motzki (d. 2019) and Gregor Schoeler took the lead in adopting the historical-critical method into hadith studies and forming its foundational principles. Motzki and Schoeler independently invented *isnād-cum-matn* analysis to demonstrate that it is viable to adopt the historical-critical method for the purposes of studying hadith.[48] Motzki was at the forefront of this methodology in terms of its scholarly promotion and advocacy. He accepted the proposition that the oral transmission process exposes the text to possible manipulation and

43 An English translation of the article was published as Kramers, 'A Tradition of Manichaean Tendency', pp. 245–57.

44 van Ess, *Zwischen Hadit und Theologie.*

45 Motzki, 'Dating Muslim Traditions', p. 250.

46 Juynboll, 'Nāfi''; Juynboll, 'Some *Isnād*-Analytical Methods'; Juynboll, *Muslim Tradition.*

47 Zaman, 'The Evolution of a Hadith'.

48 Motzki, 'Quo Vadis, *Ḥadīṯ*-Forschung?'; Schoeler, *Charakter.*

forgery, but not on a large scale, as Schacht and Michael Cook suggested.[49] He argued that it was still possible to trace the origins of hadith, detect manipulations and, in some cases, reconstruct the original text in the way Muhammad or the earliest transmitters uttered it. This can be achieved by analysing different variants for a literary comparison according to shared plots, motifs and wordings. In other words, both Motzki and Schoeler argued for the historical source value of hadith.

To make a stronger case for the method, Harald Motzki delved into a comprehensive examination of various methods to early Islamic sources. He categorised these methods into four distinct groups, meticulously assessing their reliability:

1. Methods employing the *matn* (the textual content of traditions).
2. Dating methods based on the collections in which traditions are found.
3. Dating based on the *isnād* (the chain of transmitters within traditions).
4. Approaches that incorporate both *matn* and *isnād*.[50]

Motzki proceeds to conduct an elaborate survey of representations of the first three methods, pinpointing their inherent limitations. His critique primarily centres on their reliance on unsubstantiated assumptions,[51] heavy dependence on *argumentum e silentio* and exclusive utilisation of form criticism.[52]

Consequently, Motzki contends that these methods erroneously led scholars to infer the existence of a widespread and organised hadith forgery process perpetrated by Muslim scholars. He vehemently rejects this allegation, asserting that such a claim lacks substantiation. In his response to Michael Cook, he elucidates his stance:

> However, in view of the reservations against his arguments, these are not the only positions which can be chosen. Neither Schacht nor Cook have convincingly shown that 'spread of *isnād*s' was really practised on a significant scale. They have only shown that there were several possible ways how *isnād*s could be forged and that Muslim scholars could have had different motives to do so. Apart from possibilities, Schacht and Cook produced only scarce evidence that *isnād* forgery really happened. On the basis of mere possibilities and a few instances of real forgery, it makes no sense to abstain completely from using the *isnād*s for dating purposes.[53]

49 Motzki, 'Dating Muslim Traditions', p. 235.
50 Motzki, 'Dating Muslim Traditions', pp. 205–6.
51 Motzki, 'Dating Muslim Traditions', p. 214.
52 Motzki, 'Dating Muslim Traditions', p. 215.
53 Motzki, 'Dating Muslim Traditions', p. 235.

It is essential to highlight that the primary purpose of this methodology is not necessarily the authentication of traditions; instead, its central aim revolves around tracing these traditions back to specific points in time. This is based on the understanding that whether authentic or not, traditions 'have a history'.[54] Furthermore, while engaged in the dating process, there exists the remote possibility – albeit exceedingly rare – of authenticating certain traditions.[55]

In this method, the abundance of variant narrations within a tradition assumes paramount importance. A richer diversity of variants enhances the robustness of the analytical outcome.[56] However, it is crucial to note that this variation should not be confined solely to the *isnāds*; for the authentication of a tradition to be feasible, there must also exist textual variations of the same tradition. This premise is grounded in the idea that reports handed down from one generation to another are bound to change.[57]

This phenomenon becomes more pronounced in the context of oral transmission. The alterations or distortions of the text tend to diminish when the tradition is documented in written form or 'standardised'. In Islamic history, the standardisation of transmission gradually evolved during the initial three Islamic centuries. Consequently, variations in the text were likely more substantial in the early periods but would have diminished in later periods.

This method consists of five steps, which are listed here in order:

- Variants of the hadith in question are exhaustively located in the hadith collections.
- Based on studying the chains of transmission of the gathered variants, chains of transmission diagrams are made to document the transmission process and identify Common Links and Partial Common Links. In case of discord among the textual variants, the geographical and generational proximity of the transmitters is investigated to verify their connections, integrity and motivations.
- The researcher then seeks to establish whether the previously identified Common Links were the real collectors or professional disseminators of the hadith. To achieve this, it is necessary to conduct a detailed synoptic comparison of the already compiled texts of hadith variants with one another.
- Having completed synoptic analyses of the texts in question, the objective is to establish a correlation between them. Therefore, a comparison is made between the chains of transmission and the texts themselves.

54 Motzki et al., *Analysing Muslim Traditions*, p. 235.
55 Motzki et al., *Analysing Muslim Traditions*, p. 235.
56 Motzki, 'Dating Muslim Traditions', p. 251.
57 Motzki et al., *Analysing Muslim Traditions*, p. 91.

- If the research can establish such a correlation, it can help reconstruct the original wording as uttered by the source or transmitted by the Common Link. At this stage, researchers can also identify the individuals who changed the original text in the transmission process after the Common Link.

Among the more recent practitioners of *isnād-cum-matn* analysis is Najam Haider,[58] who, rather than analysing a small number of hadiths in great detail, has focused on a large volume of hadiths and drawn broader observations from them. Although he does not employ traditional *isnād-cum-matn* analysis, his approach has been successful in deriving comprehensive conclusions about various sources of hadith.[59] Jens Scheiner applied the method to the reports concerning the annexation of Damascus,[60] while Nicolet Boekhoff-van der Voort utilised it for analysing the events of the Raid of the Hudhayl.[61] Mairaj Syed also demonstrates the use of this method in dating the hadiths on the torture of ʿAmmār b. Yāsir.[62] Pavel Pavlovitch adopts a version of the method which remains within the parameters set by Schacht and, under Juynboll's heavy influence, assumes a large-scale forgery in the Muslim hadith corpus.[63] Pavlovitch, also implemented it with Powers on Saʿd b. Abī Waqqāṣ traditions.[64]

Finally, Sean Anthony most recently[65] attempted to implement *isnād-cum-matn* analysis to date ʿUrwa b. al-Zubayr's letters in his interesting and ambitious work.[66] Among other methods, such as the study of material and written evidence, coupled with *isnād-cum-matn* analysis, he dates the origins of the letters of ʿUrwa b. al-Zubayr and compares them with non-Islamic sources written between the sixth and eighth centuries. Due to its recent implementation of the method, this work warrants a more thorough examination.[67]

58 Haider, *The Origins of the Shīʿa.*

59 Kara, 'Review of *The Origins of the Shīʿa*'.

60 Scheiner, *Die Eroberung von Damaskus.*

61 Motzki et al., *Analysing Muslim Traditions*, pp. 305–81.

62 Syed, 'The Construction of Historical Memory', p. 106.

63 Pavlovitch, *The Formation of the Islamic Understanding of Kalāla*, pp. 29–31.

64 Pavlovitch and Powers, '"A Bequest May Not Exceed One-Third"'.

65 To my knowledge he first implemented it in Motzki et al., *Analysing Muslim Traditions*, pp. 385–463.

66 Anthony, *Muhammad and the Empires of Faith.*

67 David Powers has already written a highly critical essay on the book. Although Powers's criticism is stern, some of his criticism is well grounded, especially regarding Anthony's propensity to go with his gut feelings instead of following sound evidence. Powers, 'Review of *Muhammad and the Empires of Faith*', p. 29. It must be noted that Anthony seems to have been adversely affected by editorial mishaps, for which his scholarship should not be questioned.

The book is a well-researched contribution to the field, especially the detailed bibliographical evaluations through which Anthony provides valuable information about the forefathers of hadith transmission. This is not the appropriate place to give a full overview of the book, but there is a pertinent issue that I want to draw attention to, which Powers appeared to have chosen not to pursue further.

Powers's criticism of Anthony is accurate in regard to the speculative nature of the work, along with the lack of clarity in Anthony's perception of early Islam. The lack of clarity seems to emanate from Anthony's effort to find a middle ground between the 'revisionist school' represented in its persistent form by Stephen Shoemaker and the 'critical school' by Harald Motzki, Gregor Schoeler and Andreas Görke. These are two irreconcilable schools of thought simply because they argue for two diametrically opposing approaches to the study of early Islam. In any case, the 'critical school' already prevailed against the persistent revisionism in an acrimonious debate,[68] which I will discuss below. Anthony's attempts to make the impossible possible render him incoherent, thereby exposing him to Powers's unforgiving criticisms.

The very fact that Anthony cites the work[69] of individuals – Shoemaker versus Motzki, Schoeler and Görke – involved in this bitter debate throughout his book, yet fails to mention the debate itself, comes across as suspicious. This debate marked a significant turning point in the acceptance of *isnād-cum-matn* analysis as a viable method of analysing hadith texts, while rejecting extreme revisionism. Moreover, the debate represented a triumph for the idea that the Muslim hadith corpus could serve as a valuable historical source, instead of being wholly rejected as ahistorical. What I mean by 'extreme revisionism' is the persistent attachment to the idea of denouncing the historical nature of the early Islamic sources. It is also misleading to ignore the significance of the debate because it provides crucial background information on how the field of hadith studies reached its current state and the negative role that extreme revisionism has played in the unnecessary stagnation of hadith studies for several decades.

In this vein, I have no objection to curious and open-minded academic enquiries like that which Patricia Crone, Michael Cook and John Wansbrough undertook. They seemed to be driven by their insatiable curiosity. The same open-mindedness led Crone and Cook to change their position on the origins of Islam and accept the existence of historical Muhammad.[70]

68 See the debate: Shoemaker, 'In Search of 'Urwa's *Sīra*'; Görke et al., 'First Century Sources for the Life of Muḥammad?'.

69 Shoemaker, 'In Search of 'Urwa's *Sīra*'; Görke et al., 'First Century Sources for the Life of Muḥammad?'.

70 See Crone, 'What Do We Actually Know about Mohammed?'; Rabb, 'Simplicity, Creativity, Lucidity as "Method" in the Study of Islamic History'.

Navigating Misunderstandings and Breaking the Perpetual Cycle

The adherents of the method defended and elucidated *isnād-cum-matn* analysis, and in the interest of advancing the field of hadith studies, I initially wanted to avoid rehashing these previously settled debates. Continuously reworking unproductive debates and having to re-explain the same concepts impedes our ability to advance genuine scholarship. Instead, it keeps us stuck in a perpetual cycle, preventing us from gaining a deeper historical understanding of early Islam. Therefore, I advocate for a shift in focus towards more constructive and progressive avenues of research within the field. When scholarly disputes arise, each party presents its arguments, and resolution occurs when one argument convincingly prevails. Motzki, Schoeler and Görke have essentially concluded these discussions, which effectively countered the arguments of scholars like Shoemaker, who echoed Juynboll's and Christopher Melchert's concerns. Considering the absence of significant recent developments in these critiques, I find no necessity to reconsider them. However, not everyone holds identical perspectives and has followed these discussions closely. Hence, I want to provide a synopsis of the debate between its proponents and opponents based on a summary of my earlier works.[71]

Application of isnād-cum-matn *Analysis to Hadiths with Limited Variations*

Before entering into the methodological debate, it is important to mention some contentious aspects of *isnād-cum-matn* analysis. One of which is that the method is more effectively applied to traditions that possess numerous variants. However, this can often lead to the mistaken assumption that the method can only be employed with traditions that have an abundance of variants. This misconception may arise due to the relative complexity of this method, and consequently, the field of Islamic studies is not always well-acquainted with it. Nevertheless, this does not alter the fact that *isnād-cum-matn* analysis can be applied to traditions with fewer variants.[72]

In this vein, Motzki conducted a meticulous study of Mālik b. Anas's *Muwaṭṭa'*, in response to Norman Calder's assertions.[73] Calder argued that the book is not the work of Mālik b. Anas (d. 179/795) but was produced at a much later date, around 270 AH.[74] Calder reached this conclusion by

71 Kara, *In Search of Ali Ibn Abi Talib's Codex*, pp. 75–94; Kara, 'The Collection of the Qur'ān in the Early Shī'ite Discourse', pp. 379–81.

72 Motzki, 'The Prophet and the Cat'.

73 Calder, *Studies in Early Muslim Jurisprudence.*

74 Calder, *Studies in Early Muslim Jurisprudence*, p. 37.

presenting various arguments, one of which involved a comparison of two works attributed to Mālik. In his comparative analysis of Mālik's works, the *Muwaṭṭa'* and *Mudawwana*, Calder noted that a tradition narrated from the Prophet regarding the purity of cats and water that comes into contact with them is included in the *Muwaṭṭa'* but not in the *Mudawwana* when a similar issue arises. Therefore, he speculated that if the tradition is absent in the *Mudawwana*, it can be inferred that the tradition emerged later than the *Mudawwana*. Calder, thus, concluded that the idea that Mālik 'is personally responsible for the *Muwaṭṭa'* in its present form is unlikely. For him, the book clearly represents the product of organic growth, requiring time to develop.'[75]

To challenge Calder's assertion, Motzki embarked on a comprehensive examination of the tradition concerning the purity of cats attributed to Mālik. Employing *isnād-cum-matn* analysis, he initiated his analysis by identifying a total of sixteen variants of this tradition. Subsequently, Motzki undertook a comparison of both the chains of transmission and their texts and arrived at the conclusion that Mālik was the source of the version he narrated. Motzki also addressed Calder's assertion that the tradition evolved from an 'anecdote' detailing the actions of the Companion Abū Qatāda regarding water in contact with a cat. Examining eight different variants of this tradition, Motzki investigated to ascertain whether these variants predated the narration attributed to the Prophet.[76] Consequently, Motzki demonstrated that employment of *isnād-cum-matn* analysis is possible even with fewer variants.

However, the ability to select any tradition, establish its dating, detect potential revisions, and identify its authors depends on specific conditions. When a tradition enjoys extensive attestation and appears in numerous sources, the research outcomes undoubtedly gain more credibility.[77] Nonetheless, even if a tradition has fewer variants but offers substantial textual evidence, it remains possible to draw reasonable conclusions about its historical authenticity. Furthermore, the capacity to draw meaningful conclusions from a comparison of a few traditions primarily hinges on their precise content and phrasing. Such assessments can only be made through thorough, case-by-case examinations of these traditions in detail.[78]

Single-strand Hadiths: Outright Forgery or a Reliable Historical Source?

However, misconceptions persist regarding *isnād-cum-matn* analysis, specifically the notion that it can only be effectively applied when a tradition possesses three key attributes: (1) a substantial number of versions, (2) a

75 Calder, *Studies in Early Muslim Jurisprudence*, pp. 35–6.
76 Motzki, 'The Prophet and the Cat', p. 58.
77 Görke, 'Eschatology, History, and the Common Link', pp. 184–6.
78 Personal communication with Görke.

profusion of divergent *isnād*s and (3) widespread geographical dissemination. While it would indeed be ideal for scholars of early Islam to encounter such scenarios, the reality of scarce historical sources demands a more pragmatic approach.

This misconception largely arises from the belief that *isnād-cum-matn* analysis relies exclusively on the analysis of chains of transmission. However, Motzki, Schoeler and Görke have consistently emphasised that this is not the case. In response to Stephen J. Shoemaker's critique of *isnād-cum-matn* analysis' utilisation of single strands,[79] Görke and Schoeler addressed this issue.[80] They pointed out that Shoemaker's fixation on the chains prevents him from recognising that while a robust analysis of chains may necessitate a dense network of transmitters when exclusively dealing with chains, the method also considers various versions of the text. Consequently, a dense network of transmitters is not a prerequisite. By taking into account the textual variants, one can already draw secure conclusions about the interdependence of texts with a less extensive network of transmitters.[81]

Motzki questioned Juynboll's observation, which suggests that Common Links are typically not found among the Successors (*tābiʿūn*) but rather one or more generations later. Furthermore, the general conclusion that Common Links must be the fabricators of their respective single strands, and therefore, these strands are historically unreliable.[82] Motzki further expounds on his first point by contending that if one accepts Juynboll's premise that *isnād*s only began to emerge around the third quarter of the Islamic calendar, and thus single strand *isnād*s containing transmitters earlier than this date must be later fabrications, then Common Links immediately preceding these single strands should logically belong to the Successors. Nevertheless, studies have demonstrated that, in such instances, Common Links are not typically found among the Successors but rather emerge one or more generations later.[83] Moreover, Juynboll's inability to accurately identify the genuine Common Links leads him to erroneous conclusions.[84]

Regarding Juynboll's second point, Motzki contends that the emergence of *isnād*s in the third quarter of the first century does not necessarily imply that early transmissions were invented.[85] In fact, Motzki believes that single strands result from the fact that early collectors, unlike their later counterparts, typically cited only one source (and consequently, one chain)

79 Shoemaker, 'In Search of ʿUrwa's *Sīra*'.
80 Görke et al., 'First Century Sources for the Life of Muḥammad?'.
81 Görke et al., 'First Century Sources for the Life of Muḥammad?', p. 41.
82 Motzki et al., *Analysing Muslim Traditions*, p. 51.
83 Motzki et al., *Analysing Muslim Traditions*, pp. 50–1.
84 Motzki et al., *Analysing Muslim Traditions*, p. 51.
85 Motzki et al., *Analysing Muslim Traditions*, p. 51.

for a tradition. This may have been due to their practice of transmitting only those traditions deemed most reliable or the absence of a requirement to cite multiple authorities and their informants at that time.[86]

However, acknowledging the possibility that single-strand traditions might be authentic, albeit with the caveat that they could also be products of a fabrication process, raises a fundamental question: was there any transmission prior to the Common Link? Motzki answers affirmatively, suggesting the existence of actual or alleged informants.[87] This perspective aligns with Motzki's broader view of the science of hadith, which posits that hadiths should be initially considered credible historical sources, and the burden of proving inauthenticity rests on scholars unless compelling evidence to the contrary is presented.[88] Therefore, in contrast to Schacht, Juynboll, Melchert and others, Motzki asserts that the transmission process extends beyond the Common Link, occurring even before it.[89]

This, in turn, raises another question: how can the existence of single-strand traditions prior to the Common Link be explained? Motzki addresses this by proposing that Common Links were the pioneering collectors who gathered material in specific regions and disseminated it in a scholarly manner. Their collections have survived, while transmissions not absorbed or further propagated by these early collectors were either lost or continued to exist as oral or written traditions outside established schools or major centres of learning, such as family traditions. The concealed existence of these transmissions allowed later collectors to identify transmission lines that did not pass through the Common Links or the scholars of major centres.[90] Furthermore, Motzki contends that it is a misinterpretation to believe that a single strand results from a process in which individual transmitters successively passed a tradition to each other until it reached a Common Link from which it branched out. Instead, it signifies that, if genuine, a later collector cites a chain of transmitters for a tradition that does not intersect with the strands of other known collectors.[91]

Motzki underscores that the inclusion of single-strand traditions should not be unconditional. They are permissible for investigation 'if these texts diverge from those of the partial common link (PCL) transmitters'.[92]

86 Motzki et al., *Analysing Muslim Traditions*, p. 52.
87 Motzki et al., *Analysing Muslim Traditions*, p. 214.
88 David Powers (Powers, 'On Bequests in Early Islam', p. 199) and Najam Haider (Haider, *The Origins of the Shīʿa*, p. 58) also adopted this approach. However, Powers changed his views over the time. Pavlovitch and Powers, '"A Bequest May Not Exceed One-Third"', pp. 136–7.
89 Motzki et al., *Analysing Muslim Traditions*, p. 214.
90 Motzki et al., *Analysing Muslim Traditions*, p. 214.
91 Motzki et al., *Analysing Muslim Traditions*, p. 58.
92 Görke et al., 'First Century Sources for the Life of Muḥammad?', p. 44.

Indeed, Juynboll asserts that PCLs are crucial for establishing the historicity of a cluster, and the absence of PCLs suggests fabrication of traditions.[93]

Furthermore, Motzki challenges Juynboll's theory, which posits that only widely transmitted traditions can be deemed authentic. Motzki argues that while the Muslim hadith corpus contains a limited number of traditions with widespread transmission (around several hundred), it also comprises thousands of other traditions. He questions whether historians can justify disregarding this substantial historical data solely for the sake of convenience. Is it genuinely practical and methodologically sound to dismiss the historical value of all single strands simply because some lack complex interconnections?[94] He proceeds to offer a brief test to assess the feasibility of Juynboll's proposal. In this hypothetical scenario, if a Common Link transmitted a tradition to five individuals belonging to the first generation, one would expect the number of transmitters to multiply in each subsequent generation. As a result, by the fifth generation, the total number of transmitters should theoretically reach 3,125, a figure that appears highly implausible.[95]

Finally, Motzki succinctly captures Juynboll's rationale for rejecting single strands. Motzki posits that Juynboll, much like Schacht, operated under the assumption that irregularities would exist in the structure of the Muslim hadith corpus if an uninterrupted process of transmitting traditions from one generation to the next occurred. In such a scenario, traditions should have branched into several streams immediately after the time of the Prophet. However, this is typically not the case; instead, they tend to diverge after forming a single strand comprising three to four transmitters. Juynboll attributes this abnormality to the Common Link, suggesting that in this situation, the Common Link fabricated the tradition. He supports this claim by referencing the naming of informants who were sought for information about the Prophet and his Companions during the third quarter of the first Islamic century (61–73/681–92). Essentially, these traditions were projected backward in time around this period due to emerging needs, and the Common Links orchestrated this manipulation. This premise forms the basis of Juynboll's overarching conclusion that single strands containing early transmitters from the third quarter of the first Islamic century are inherently unreliable.[96]

One pertinent point that requires clarification is the misunderstanding about the term 'single strand': the contested single-strand hadith in the field about those narrations that purportedly originate from the Prophet or

93 Juynboll, 'Nāfiʿ', p. 211.

94 Motzki et al., *Analysing Muslim Traditions*, p. 55.

95 Motzki et al., *Analysing Muslim Traditions*, p. 55.

96 Motzki et al., *Analysing Muslim Traditions*, p. 50.

a Companion and then pass down through a single strand for a couple of generations before branching out through individuals, often referred to as the Common Link. This is technically described as a single-strand transmission. The debate regarding single-strand hadith primarily centres on these types of narrations. Scholars like Motzki and Schoeler argue that such narrations have a traceable history leading back to a source (the individual(s) before the Common Link), while proponents of the Junbollian school believe that the Common Link is the forger.

The most rigorous critics of hadith, including Juynboll, generally do not find issues at the lower levels of the hadith, such as when several single-strand *isnāds* converge to form a PCL. The central debate hinges on whether the Common Link is a forger or a genuine transmitter because, beyond the Common Link, there exists a single strand.

An Acrimonious Debate

Juynboll's legacy of vehement criticism regarding single-strand hadiths continued reverberating in the works of Shoemaker and Melchert.[97] Central to Shoemaker's arguments, and an aspect he shares with Melchert, is their concern regarding the utilisation of single-strand traditions. In principle, Shoemaker acknowledges that *isnād* criticism could prove valuable in scrutinising Muslim traditions, provided that the traditions under examination feature 'highly dense' *isnād* clusters.[98] For Shoemaker, Juynboll's caution against using single strands serves as a crucial safeguard within *isnād* analysis. Yet, Motzki and others do not hesitate to rely on single strands and draw conclusions from their analysis, which seemingly suggests the possibility of authenticating certain Islamic sources originating in the first century. However, Shoemaker maintains that deriving definitive conclusions from single strands is not feasible, as they lack reliability. Consequently, he asserts that Motzki's reliance on them often yields questionable results, further undermining the credibility of the method.[99]

Nonetheless, Shoemaker recognises the method's effective application to some early Islamic traditions.[100] However, akin to Melchert, he contends that although Motzki's analysis convincingly identifies several traditions from the early second century, his attempts to extend beyond this limit lack the same level of persuasiveness. Melchert also strongly criticises Motzki's

97 See also Schneider, 'Narrativität und Authentizität', pp. 84–115; Berg, *The Development of Exegesis in Early Islam.*
98 Shoemaker, 'In Search of 'Urwa's *Sīra*', p. 292.
99 Shoemaker, 'In Search of 'Urwa's *Sīra*', p. 266.
100 Shoemaker, 'In Search of 'Urwa's *Sīra*', p. 267.

work in 'Quo vadis *Ḥadīt*-Forschung'[101] and disparages *isnād-cum-matn* analysis for its use of single strands, asserting that investing significant effort in authenticating a tradition he deems devoid of historical value is a worthless pursuit.[102] Motzki disagrees with this evaluation, as he demonstrates that the tradition conveys at least three historical facts and makes the case that given the scarcity of historical material concerning the early history of Islam, historians cannot afford to disregard texts even if they may initially appear to have limited value.[103]

Furthermore, Shoemaker takes issue with Motzki's attempts to establish a date for traditions that surpass the Common Link's era. He further asserts that Motzki's effort to date the traditions to an earlier period through an 'assumption' that Common Links signify a *terminus ante quem* is somewhat manipulative.[104] Shoemaker's doubts regarding *isnād-cum-matn* analysis ultimately lead him to conclude that this method does not offer any novel insights into the life of Muhammad. Consequently, he asserts that the most valuable method for uncovering the earliest traditions within early Islamic tradition remains the critical examination of the text.[105]

In their thorough rebuttal, Motzki, Görke and Schoeler mounted a robust defence of their positions while also offering a detailed critique of Shoemaker's work. They ultimately concluded that, despite some noteworthy contributions, Shoemaker's work is marred by many misunderstandings and inconsistencies.[106] One of the most noteworthy inconsistencies underscored in Shoemaker's critique, as emphasised by Motzki, Görke and Schoeler, revolves around Shoemaker's selective faith in *isnād* criticism and his selective dependence on single strands as he deems two transmission lines adequate to attribute a tradition as probably linked to the Common Link.[107]

Another critique directed at Shoemaker pertains to his disproportionate emphasis on *isnād*s within his criticism. His conclusion that *isnād-cum-matn* analysis falls short of delivering an accurate assessment of tradition heavily relies on his focus on the chains. In response to this, Görke and Schoeler contend that Shoemaker's conclusion appears somewhat hasty and lacks comprehensive engagement with the method as a whole. Furthermore, his preoccupation with the chains hinders him from recognising that while

101 It was first published in German under the title 'Quo vadis *Ḥadīṯ*-Forschung?' and then translated into English and re-published under the title 'Whither *Ḥadīth* Studies?' in Motzki et al., *Analysing Muslim Traditions*, pp. 47–122.

102 Melchert, 'The Early History of Islamic Law', p. 303.

103 Görke et al., 'First Century Sources for the Life of Muḥammad?', p. 43.

104 Görke et al., 'First Century Sources for the Life of Muḥammad?', p. 43.

105 Shoemaker, 'In Search of 'Urwa's *Sīra*', p. 269.

106 Görke et al., 'First Century Sources for the Life of Muḥammad?', p. 2.

107 Görke et al., 'First Century Sources for the Life of Muḥammad?', p. 5.

Juynboll's assertion, which suggests that a reliable analysis of chains necessitates a dense network of transmitters, may be accurate when solely dealing with chains. *Isnād-cum-matn* analysis considers various versions of traditions, thus, a less extensive network of transmitters can already yield secure conclusions about the interrelationships between texts when considering the textual variants.[108]

Shoemaker's critique of the method revolves around its dependence on single strands. However, as previously mentioned, these criticisms appear to echo Juynboll's perspectives against the use of single strands. These contentions, however, have not been adapted to accommodate the nuances of *isnād-cum-matn* analysis, thereby overlooking a critical aspect of the method's efficacy.

Furthermore, in his response within the same article, Motzki elaborates that in his various works, he has provided a comprehensive rationale for his decision to modify Juynboll's *isnād* analysis and incorporate single strands into his method. Motzki identifies significant misunderstandings in Shoemaker's comprehension of *isnād-cum-matn* analysis. While Shoemaker's concise description of the method is accurate, his ability to discern its practical implementation is lacking as he confuses *isnād-cum-matn* analysis with 'the source reconstruction method'. This error carries significant weight as it underscores Shoemaker's challenge in grasping the practical application of the method.[109]

Regarding Shoemaker's presumption that all Common Links fabricated the names of the reporters they mentioned, as well as his assertion that unknown individuals circulated all the Islamic traditions he regards as rumours and legends, Motzki reaffirms his perspective that this approach lacks coherence. While he acknowledges that some Common Links may not have known the precise source of certain traditions and consequently attributed them to the most likely origin, he believes that others retained knowledge of the initial source from whom they had heard the tradition. In such cases, he views the Common Link as a *terminus ante quem*.[110] Motzki also acknowledges the possibility that some Common Links may have fabricated elements of the text or chains of traditions themselves. He acknowledges that 'it might be difficult to ascertain the actual sequence of events, but there are instances where the evidence points to one of these possibilities.'[111] His methodology is designed to investigate this evidence and determine the most plausible scenario.

108 Görke et al., 'First Century Sources for the Life of Muḥammad?', p. 41.
109 Görke et al., 'First Century Sources for the Life of Muḥammad?', p. 44.
110 Görke et al., 'First Century Sources for the Life of Muḥammad?', p. 45.
111 Görke et al., 'First Century Sources for the Life of Muḥammad?', p. 45.

Motzki further addresses Shoemaker's criticism regarding his attempt to trace the source of narratives concerning the murder of the Jew Ibn Abī al-Ḥuqayq. Through a meticulous examination of various versions of the story, Motzki identifies Zuhrī as the Common Link who circulated one of these narratives.[112] Due to the complex transmission history of the chains in these variants, Shoemaker reluctantly concedes Motzki's findings. However, Shoemaker passionately rejects Motzki's subsequent effort to uncover the source of Zuhrī's account. Following a comparative analysis of the variants of this lengthy and detailed tradition, Motzki concludes that Zuhrī's source was Kaʿb b. Mālik's children.[113] Motzki justifies his conclusion with two key pieces of evidence: firstly, it is evident that Zuhrī's chain is deficient in most of the variants, often concluding with his informant's name(s) rather than naming an eyewitness or, at the very least, a Companion of the Prophet who could have heard the story from an eyewitness. Secondly, historical information from Islamic sources indicates that the Kaʿb b. Mālik family belonged to the same clan as the murderers of Ibn Abī al-Ḥuqayq, namely, the Banū Salima.[114]

Shoemaker contests this conclusion by pointing out that the names of the sources differ in various variants, suggesting that this might indicate later transmitters' attempts to extend the chain back to Zuhrī's source. Regarding the connection between the Kaʿb family and Ibn Abī al-Ḥuqayq's murder, Shoemaker posits that the authors of Islamic history may have fabricated the story.[115] In response, Motzki poses some straightforward questions that reiterate his stance on similar allegations put forth by proponents of the Schachtian and Wansbrough school: who exactly are these 'later transmitters' and the 'early authors' of Islamic history? Are they Zuhrī's students, subsequent transmitters, or the compilers of anthologies containing variant traditions? Are Shoemaker's vague conjectures reasonable in light of the names attested in multiple versions of the tradition?[116] Once again, Motzki identifies a noteworthy inconsistency in the arguments presented by these types of approaches to Islamic sources. In the face of well-conducted research and substantial evidence, these approaches tend to offer speculations without specifying names or providing additional historical data to support their claims.

Motzki highlights more discrepancies in Shoemaker's criticism, yet these points should suffice to comprehend the nature of the criticism

112 Motzki, 'The Murder of Ibn Abī l-Ḥuqayq', p. 195.
113 Motzki, 'The Murder of Ibn Abī l-Ḥuqayq', p. 231.
114 Görke et al., 'First Century Sources for the Life of Muḥammad?', pp. 46–7.
115 Görke et al., 'First Century Sources for the Life of Muḥammad?', p. 47.
116 Görke et al., 'First Century Sources for the Life of Muḥammad?', p. 47.

directed at *isnād-cum-matn* analysis and Motzki and its proponents' response. In sum, one of the primary criticisms of the method revolves around its use of single strands. According to Motzki, this critique stems from the presumption that Muslim traditions were fabricated. However, Motzki justifies using single strands by considering their emergence as a natural outcome of transmission. The second criticism arises from the misconception that the method solely relies on *isnād* analysis. This notion is unjustified since the method also involves textual analysis and derives its conclusions from the correlation between chain and text. Nonetheless, Motzki concedes that the lack of early Muslim sources and the inclusion of an element of 'assumption' in dating early sources pose significant challenges for the method. Motzki acknowledges that while assumptions are inevitable, the issue may be mitigated by relying on more substantial data to inform these assumptions. However, he notes that the first issue, the scarcity of early sources, cannot be rectified. As I suggested previously,[117] examination of Shiʿi sources could potentially aid in addressing the first issue.

Finally, Pavlovitch, similar to Juynboll, adopts a sceptical outlook towards single-strand chains of transmission.[118] Similarly, Pavlovitch works with the assumption that single-strand hadiths are likely the result of forgeries.[119] He disregards the above-mentioned arguments of Motzki and others that justify a positive approach to single strands and the need to work with them. Furthermore, Pavlovitch considers variations as a sign of forgery and alleges that in some problematic instances, Common Links or PCLs are responsible for forgeries without providing any clear evidence as to why.[120] Pavlovitch's studies produced some interesting and important results,[121] which will be referenced in this book, yet his Juynbollian approach defeats the very purpose of the method as Motzki and Schoeler developed it. In this vein, Scheiner explicitly countered Pavlovitch's critique concerning single-strand hadiths. He emphasised its lack of originality and referred to the relevant literature where proponents of *isnād-cum-analysis* had already addressed similar criticisms.[122]

117 Kara, *In Search of Ali Ibn Abi Talib's Codex*, p. 94.

118 Pavlovitch, *The Formation of the Islamic Understanding of Kalāla*, pp. 29–31.

119 Pavlovitch, *The Formation of the Islamic Understanding of Kalāla*, p. 31. See also Scheiner, '*Isnād-cum-matn* Analysis and *Kalāla*', pp. 483–4.

120 For a more detailed analysis of Pavlovitch's methodological problems, see Scheiner '*Isnād-cum-matn* Analysis and *Kalāla*'.

121 Pavlovitch, 'The Islamic Penalty for Adultery'; Pavlovitch, 'The Stoning of a Pregnant Adulteress from Juhayna'; Pavlovitch, 'Early Development of the Tradition of the Self-confessed Adulterer in Islam'.

122 Scheiner, '*Isnād-cum-matn* Analysis and *Kalāla*', p. 484.

The Future of Islamic Historiography

There is a seismic shift in the academic study of early Islam, which has recently become more open to the idea of a 'historical Muhammad' and his role in the advent of Islam, after decades of revisionism. The pioneering studies in hadith methodologies, mentioned above, and palaeographical studies on the textual history of the Qur'an[123] have challenged the dominant view concerning the value of Muslim sources and narratives by demonstrating concurrence between palaeographical evidence and Muslim sources. The ground in Islamic studies has thus shifted since a wholesale rejection of the Muslim historical narrative is no longer considered viable;[124] these wider shifts in the study of Islam have enabled researchers to be more receptive to alternative methods and approaches.

As noted above, *isnād-cum-matn* analysis has gained traction in the study of hadith. Motzki showed the potential of the *isnād-cum-matn* method but, by and large, he deliberately avoided applying it to central issues relating to early Islam. More often than not, he found himself on the defensive, carefully attending to the minute details of his arguments so as not to expose himself to the criticism of prominent scholars who had earned a significant following in top universities in European and North American academia. For example, in his article 'The Murder of Ibn abī l-Ḥuqayq: On the Origin and Reliability of Some Maghāzī Reports', Motzki explains why he chose a peripheral topic, the killing of an insignificant figure in early Islam. He notes that one of the most important biases held against Muslim sources is that '[their] background is theological, in that the traditions tried to create a specific theology of history, or in that the Muslims simply tended to put a halo around the founder of their religion'.[125] To evade this kind of biased criticism, he often studied peripheral events that had no direct relevance to the formation of Islam. Thus, although he was equipped with a capable methodology, he refrained from studying the most pressing question in the field: 'what really happened in first/seventh-century Arabia?'.[126] It is no surprise, therefore, that Motzki was criticised precisely for avoiding central issues and focusing on peripheral matters,[127] even though he[128] and Schoeler[129] did study a few important episodes in the formation of Islam.

123 Sadeghi and Goudarzi, 'Ṣanʿāʾ 1 and the Origins of the Qurʾān'; van Putten, '"The Grace of God" as Evidence for a Written Uthmanic Archetype'; Cellard, 'The Ṣanʿāʾ Palimpsest'.

124 Donner, *Muhammad and the Believers*, pp. 51–3.

125 Motzki, 'Murder of Ibn Abi l-Huqayq', p. 171.

126 Motzki et al., *Analysing Muslim Traditions*, p. 287.

127 Melchert, 'The Early History of Islamic Law', p. 303.

128 Motzki, 'The Collection of the Qurʾān'.

129 Schoeler, *The Biography of Muḥammad.*

Motzki and others could also have stretched the boundaries of *isnād-cum-matn* analysis by focusing not only on dating and reconstruction but also on the transmitters and redactors' political, theological and ideological objectives, as had been done in the redaction criticism in biblical studies. But he did not have the opportunity to make such amendments to the method, because he spent most of his energy on making a case for the historical source value of hadith and fending off relentless criticism of the old guards of academia.

New Testament scholars also dealt with the issue of 'projecting back' or 'retrojection' in redaction criticism. Retrojection is a similar concept used in redaction criticism to identify the local elements that influenced the Gospel editors/redactors when authoring the Gospels.[130] For example, when Matthew, who lived in Antioch of Syria and flourished between 85 and 90 CE, was editing his Gospel, he must have been swayed by the local context, which was not only fellow Christians but also Jewish inhabitants of the city. Therefore, there was comparatively more emphasis on Jewish beliefs in his Gospel.

On the other hand, Luke, who resided in the Greco-Roman world, considered the local culture when he redacted his Gospel by relating the teachings of Jesus to Greco-Roman culture and values. Naturally, redactors considered local context or sometimes asserted their assumptions on the nature of Jesus and his relations with the disciples. By examining these redactions, Gospel scholars can sometimes uncover a segment of the historical Jesus's life[131] and, often, the historical context in which the Gospel editors lived and what their priorities and thought processes were.[132] The oral tradition of the hadith corpus is different from the redaction of the Gospels, but transmitters and collectors would have inevitably taken the local elements – whether political, theological, legal or customary – into consideration during the oral reproduction of hadith. As Brian Stock succinctly articulated, 'in oral as written culture, memory functions within the social group, which, with its particular conventions, traditions, and institutions, acts as a conceptual filter for image formation and recollection . . . The past, whether conceived abstractly or concretely, can be present, if relevant to ongoing cultural needs.'[133]

Furthermore, the last chain of the transmission process of hadith involves written recording or editing/redaction. The use of redaction criticism, together with form criticism, could reveal the reasons for using specific terminologies or avoiding the use of certain words. For example, as I

130 Meier, 'John the Baptist in Matthew's Gospel'.
131 Kloppenborg, 'Hirte Und Andere Kriminelle'; Kloppenborg, *Q, the Earliest Gospel.*
132 Hock, 'Lazarus and Micyllus'.
133 Stock, *The Implications of Literacy*, p. 15.

discuss in the following chapters, we are still unable to decipher the reasons for the basic terminology of hadiths: why certain transmitters or redactors refer to Muhammad as *al-Nabī* (the Prophet) while some others refer to him as *Rasūl Allāh* (the Messenger of God). This could be a simple stylistic choice, relating to local trends, or due to the transmitters' or redactors' theological and legal assumptions.

While hadith studies stagnated, New Testament scholars continued to debate and improve the historical-critical method to make historical sense of their sources. In addition to form and redaction criticism, they move into new areas, such as the dynamic field of research concerning mnemonic negotiations, whether memorisation or social, collective and cultural memory.[134] They argue that the historical reconstruction of, for instance, Rabbinic Judaism[135] and Christian origins[136] has very much to do with how people lived and negotiated with the past in the present, even when writings from and about the past existed.

Be that as it may, form and chain of transmission criticism could be combined with redaction criticism in *isnād-cum-matn* analysis, which disarms one of the criticisms against it, namely, that it does not deal with the historical context in which the transmission occurred. In this book, I have tried to incorporate redaction criticism into *isnād-cum-matn* analysis to some extent. There must be more systematic and concerted efforts to unlock the full potential of *isnād-cum-matn* analysis in future studies.

While Andrew Rippin, in reflecting on John Wansbrough's writings, claimed that it is impossible to answer the question 'what really happened' in the early period of Islam,[137] recent scholarship has shown that there is much to discover about its early history. Many studies, including the present, demonstrate that there is a historical kernel in Muslim sources that can be reconstructed through rigorous and verifiable methods. It is also possible to uncover the manipulation that occurred in these sources,[138] intentionally or unintentionally, because of political, theological, legal and sectarian strife.[139] This includes the forgery[140] and manipulation of hadiths,

134 Byrskog, *Story as History – History as Story.*

135 Gerhardsson, *Memory and Manuscript.*

136 Kelber, *The Oral and the Written Gospel.*

137 Rippin, 'Literary Analysis of Quran, *Tafsīr* and *Sīra*'.

138 For some of the examples, see Kuzudişli, 'Sunnī–Shīʿī Interaction'; Kara, 'The Collection of the Qurʾān in the Early Shīʿite Discourse'; Brown, *Hadith*, pp. 73–4.

139 Husayn adeptly demonstrated that another form of interference with hadiths is the erasure of the history of anti-ʿAlid sentiment from the Sunni sources. Husayn, *Opposing the Imām.*

140 Qutbuddin's approach to the topic of forgery culture in the Muslim oral tradition is not only intriguing but also illuminating. Qutbuddin, *Arabic Oration*, p. 16.

which was introduced into both Sunni and Shi'i collections.[141] By digging deeper, we can uncover the historical kernel that exists in Muslim sources and separate it from the outer layers of manipulation that have been added over time.

Finally, unlike what Goldziher and Schacht have argued with respect to hadith, the possibility of 'retrojection' did not prompt New Testament scholars to abandon the study of the Gospels altogether. However, it is peculiar that the same problem has prompted Islamicists to abandon studying hadith for several decades. This prolonged break in hadith studies can be attributed to a deep-seated colonial and ideological bias against Islam and Muslims. However, there have been promising recent developments in the field. The approach established by Motzki and Schoeler has shown progress, and there is a renewed focus on hadith studies, which is likely to lead to advancements in the field over the next decade. This progress may parallel the achievements in Qur'anic studies observed in the previous decade.[142]

The Nature of the Hadiths

I have examined some of the earliest Sunni and Shi'i sources to investigate the relevant hadiths. Sunni reports found in Mālik b. Anas's (93/711–179/795) *Muwaṭṭa'*, 'Abd al-Razzāq al-Ṣan'ānī's (d. 211/826) *Muṣannaf*, Ibn Abī Shayba's (d. 235/849) *Muṣannaf*, Bukhārī's (d. 256/870) *Ṣaḥīḥ*, Ibn Mājah's (d. 209/824) *Sunan*, Tirmidhī's (209/824–279/892) *Jāmi'*, Muslim's (d. 261/875) *Ṣaḥīḥ*, Abū Dāwūd's (d. 275/889) *Sunan* and Nasā'ī's (d. 303/915) *Sunan*.

Shi'i reports are found in later sources such as Aḥmad b. Muḥammad al-Sayyārī's *Kitāb al-qirā'āt* (third/ninth century) and Muḥammad b. Ya'qūb al-Kulaynī's *al-Kāfī* (d. 329/941), Sulaym b. Qays al-Hilālī's (d. mid-second/eighth century) *Kitāb*, 'Alī b. Ibrāhīm al-Qummī's (d. 307/980) *Tafsīr*, al-Shaykh al-Ṣadūq's (d. 381/991) *Kitāb man lā yaḥḍuruhu al-faqīh and 'Ilal al-sharā'i*, al-Shaykh al-Ṭūsī's (d. 460/1067)*Tahdhīb al-aḥkām* and finally

141 Unguarded and uncanonised religious scriptures are inherently vulnerable to corruption by those tasked with protecting and teaching them. As custodians of these texts, they may come to believe that their authority supersedes the text itself and that it is their divine duty to redact it according to their own contextual understanding. This presents a significant problem, as the interpretation of these texts can become heavily influenced by personal biases and societal norms, leading to a distorted representation of the original message. Furthermore, unguarded scripture can be easily manipulated for personal gain or political purposes, creating further distortion and undermining the authenticity of the text. To understand how this occurred in the New Testament, see Ehrman, *The Orthodox Corruption of Scripture*.

142 Stewart, 'Reflections on the State of the Art in Western Qur'anic Studies'.

al-Qāḍī al-Nuʿmān's (d. 363/973) *Daʿāʾim al-islām*. I analyse Sunni reports in the first four chapters, and then Shiʿi reports in the remaining three.

Most reports on the distortion are related to narratives on the stoning penalty.[143] The stoning penalty (*rajm*) is one of the thorniest subjects of Islamic law and Qur'anic exegesis and plays a crucial role in the Sunni narrative on the distortion of the Qur'an. These narrations, which are recorded in the canonical and pre-canonical Sunni sources, claim that the prescribed punishment in the 'Book of God', seemingly referring to the Qur'an, is the stoning penalty. While Q. 24:2 prescribes a hundred lashes to adulterers and fornicators alike,[144] classical Muslim jurists and exegetes such as Mālik (d. 179/795), Shāfiʿī (d. 204/820), Ṭabarī (d. 310/923) and Suyūṭī (d. 911/1505), among others, maintained the validity of stoning.

Mālik offered three justifications: the Torah, the sunna of the Prophet Muhammad and the Qur'an. Shāfiʿī extensively studied the traditions of stoning and based his argument on the abrogation (*naskh*) of Qur'anic verses by the sunna. In their commentaries on the Qur'an, Muslim exegetes employed the arguments developed by these legal scholars. As a result, the validity of the stoning penalty has been nearly taken for granted in Islamic legal traditions, from the classical period until the modern.[145]

Considering the dire implications this has, modern Islamic legal scholarship has attempted to explain Muslim scholars' support for stoning. According to some, it is brutal, even by medieval standards of punishment, and has no place in modern societies.[146] However, many Muslim scholars have avoided addressing it because there are numerous reports from the Prophet and the Companions in favour of stoning, and they have been unable to develop consistent and sound methodologies to disallow the stoning penalty without abandoning the corpus of reports altogether.[147] Some hold on to Nöldeke's argument that early Muslim traditions and

143 Kecia Ali Provides a comprehensive evaluation of the topic with reference to modern views of Muslim legal schools. Ali, *Sexual Ethics and Islam*, ch. 4.

144 'The woman and the man guilty of adultery or fornication (*zinā*), flog each of them with a hundred lashes: Let not compassion move you in their case, in a matter prescribed by God, if you believe in God and the Last Day: and let a party of the Believers witness their punishment' (Q. 24:2).

145 See Nöldeke et al., *The History of the Qurʾān*, pp. 198–204; Burton, *The Collection of the Qurʾān*; Burton, 'The Penalty for Adultery in Islam', pp. 269–84; Pavlovitch, 'The Islamic Penalty for Adultery', pp. 473–97; Melchert, 'Qurʾānic Abrogation across the Ninth Century', pp. 75–98.

146 See Eltantawi, *Shari'ah on Trial.*

147 See Scott Lucas's introduction on the reformist approaches to the Muslim traditions and reports. Lucas, '"Perhaps You Only Kissed Her?"', pp. 399–415.

reports prescribing stoning are forgeries.[148] However, as Scott Lucas points out, there are simply too many traditions to support such a proposition.[149]

Alternatively, some have opted for a selective reading of the sources that trace the origins of this punishment to the Companions.[150] There are, however, notable exceptions to these studies. For example, Pavel Pavlovitch has studied the variants of the tradition of the stoning of Māʿiz b. Mālik using *isnād-cum-matn* analysis and dated it to the death of Zuhrī (d. 124/742). In his second study of the variants of the tradition about a pregnant adulteress, he traces them to a much later period, namely, the death of ʿAbd al-Razzāq (d. 211/826).[151] Syed Atif Rizwan's study also analyses some of these traditions about stoning, including those attributed to ʿUmar in regard to the Stoning Verse. Rizwan's approach, however, lacks a systematic methodology and, despite his commendable command of early Muslim sources, only speculates that the variants originated at the end of the first/seventh century.[152]

What is common to the studies above is their approach to the stoning penalty from a legal perspective. Scholars have yet to consider the relevance of these reports to the history of the Qur'anic text, particularly those narratives about the missing verses attributed to ʿUmar b. al-Khaṭṭāb.[153] Because of their intimate connection to the distortion of the Qur'an, this book approaches the narratives on the stoning penalty in relation to their relevance to distortion. Chapters 2, 3 and 4 study the three different reports on the stoning penalty, two of which are attributed to the Prophet and one to ʿUmar.

Chapter 1 focuses on a report related to breastfeeding. The report is attributed to ʿĀ'isha and contains a legal debate on the possibility of breastfeeding adults, whereby they would be prohibited from marriage due to a non-biological kinship being established. The debate took place between ʿĀ'isha and the other widows of the Prophet, who are led by Umm Salama. In the debate, the widows of the Prophet refer to another event that took place at the time of the Prophet. ʿĀ'isha presents the event as a precedent for her legal view, while Umm Salama and others maintain that it was an exception. The debate is interesting, but what makes these variants important for our

148 Nöldeke et al., *The History of the Qur'ān*, pp. 198–204.

149 Lucas, '"Perhaps You Only Kissed Her?"'.

150 Eltantawi's research is important for giving an alternative perspective to the subject. However, it does not engage in sufficient detail with prophetic traditions on the stoning penalty. Eltantawi, 'Mysterious Legislation', pp. 288–313.

151 Pavlovitch, 'Early Development of the Tradition of the Self-confessed Adulterer in Islam', pp. 371–410; Pavlovitch, 'The Stoning of a Pregnant Adulteress from Juhayna', pp. 1–62.

152 Rizwan, 'The Resurrection of Stoning as Punishment', p. 322.

153 I must acknowledge John Burton's analysis of the texts of some of the relevant traditions, but his perspective was their relevance to the concept of 'abrogation'. Burton, *The Collection of the Qur'ān*.

purposes is that they also refer to an event according to which a domestic animal ate the relevant verses of the Qur'an after the death of the Prophet. Therefore, it suggests that a form of distortion of the Qur'an took place shortly after the Prophet's death.

Chapter 2 analyses the prophetic hadith where two men came to the Prophet to settle a case. The plaintiff's son and the defendant's wife were apparently caught during the act of sexual indecency, and according to the initial settlement that took place in the absence of the Prophet, the defendant had to pay a substantial ransom to save his son from harsh punishment. At the same time, the wife was not given any penalty. They asked the Prophet to review the case and judge between them according to the Book of God. Accordingly, the Prophet reviewed the case according to the 'Book of God' and ordered the return of the ransom to the plaintiff and the stoning of the defendant's wife. This chapter, thus, focuses on the textual implications of the use of the 'Book of God' and whether it refers to the Qur'an or the Old Testament. The close comparison of the variants of the report goes beyond the intended aim of focusing on the origins of the idea of distortion of the Qur'an. The chapter makes interesting discoveries about the editing of hadith by the transmitters in order to insert their linguistic marks, which may be related to their stylistic choices or positions.

Chapter 3 examines the variants of the hadith that a group of Jews came to the Prophet with the request of arbitration to establish the correct punishment for adultery. The numerous variants provide conflicting narratives of the episode, and the chapter tries to reconstruct the original report, along with whether it can be dated back to the Prophet's lifetime. Again, there is the use of the 'Book of God' in the variants of this hadith which thus provides important information about what this phrase actually refers to. Furthermore, the chapter focuses on the attitude of the Prophet on the use of the stoning penalty and whether he employed it as an Islamic punishment or as an application of Jewish law. Chapter 3 delves into an interesting debate about the use of dual punishment in Islamic law, as well as 'Abdullāh b. Salām, a Jewish convert who supposedly helped the Prophet uncover the true punishment for adultery in the Torah. This also includes theorising about the role of the Prophet in the early Medinan community along with the existence of the so-called Constitution of Medina.

Chapter 4, which is arguable the most controversial, studies the report relating to the existence of the Stoning Verse in the Qur'an along with its subsequent removal after the death of the Prophet. The report is attributed to 'Umar, who takes an uncompromising stance on the Stoning Verse which he claims to have been revealed to the Prophet, but not included in the codex. The chapter traces the origins of the report attributed to 'Umar and makes a considerable effort in establishing whether the report can be dated back to 'Umar or not. This chapter is crucially important for this book because there are textual similarities between the reports attributed to ʿUmar and the sixth Imam, Jaʿfar al-Ṣādiq, the latter of which are examined in Chapter 5. The chapter, therefore, looks for potential interactions between Sunnis and Shiʿis during those periods. ʿUmar's statements also indicate the crystallisation of the Qur'anic codex before his reign. This is because, despite his political power and religious authority, he was not able to interfere with the Qur'anic codex to add the missing Stoning Verse. The chapter thus also explores the possibilities of extracting information to the closure of the Qur'anic canon.

Chapter 5 moves from studying Sunni reports to analysing Shiʿi ones. Following the results obtained from the previous chapter, Chapter 5 delves deeper into whether the reports attributed to the sixth Imam, Jaʿfar al-Ṣādiq, are genuine. Furthermore, how far back can they be dated in comparison to the Sunni reports attributed to ʿUmar? The textual similarities indicate similar origins, but the chapter also investigates geographical connections to attain further evidence. If the evidence relates solely to textual similarities, there is the risk of labelling it as simply circumstantial evidence. At this point, the study becomes similar to solving a murder mystery: detectives notice a pattern, identify the motivation and then have the material evidence pointing at a particular suspect. However, without substantiating that the suspect had a connection to the victim or the crime scene, it would be difficult to convince a jury beyond a reasonable doubt. Chapter 5 focuses on assessing the available evidence and deliberating if it is possible to reach definitive conclusions about the origins of the distortion narrative.

In the remaining two chapters (Chapters 6 and 7) the focus is on the dating of two Shiʿi hadiths on the literal mentioning of the distortion of the Qur'an and the return of the twelfth Imam, al-Mahdī, who will supposedly teach the correct Qur'an.[154]

How to Read This Book

I suggest two ways of reading this book:

1. Readers who are curious about Islam, the Qur'an, Islamic law and Islamic history, while having a basic understanding of Islam and the

154 I struggled to find Shiʿi reports about distortion because most Shiʿi reports directly related to distortion do not have variants, making them difficult to work with. The reports that are studied in Chapters 6 and 7 have enough variants, so I was able to work with these reports to extract information. It is therefore impossible to work with the Shiʿi reports regarding the variant readings of the Qur'an due to the fact that the texts do not have any structural changes, rather only interpolations of the names of the Shiʿi Imams in the Qur'anic verses. I provide my reasons for not focusing on these types of reports in the relevant chapters.

Muslim hadith tradition, can skip the sections which analyse the chains of transmission and the texts. Instead, identify the chapters that interest you, and read the sections under the main title of the chapters that serve as a brief introduction to the plot of each chapter. Each chapter includes a summary and a conclusion, which can be read and understood on their own.

2. The second type of reader, who is familiar with the Muslim hadith tradition but not an expert in hadith or *isnād-cum-matn* analysis, should start with the Introduction and read the sections under the main title of the chapters that serve as a brief introduction to the plot of each chapter. You can skip the sections which analyse the chains of transmission, but should focus on the textual analysis section, the latter of which is easier to follow and less technical. It would be helpful to study the *isnād* maps, which provide relevant information about the locations, dates, individual connections and transmissions of these reports. This group of readers is recommended to peruse the chapter summaries and conclusions, even though there may be some overlap relating to content. These sections are intentionally designed to be self-contained, allowing the first group of readers to acquire knowledge without having to read the entire book.

CHAPTER 1

'Ā'isha's Legal Debate on the Boundaries of Breastfeeding

One of the central narratives on the distortion of the Qur'an after the death of the Prophet consists of a group of reports attributed to 'Ā'isha, the widow of the Prophet. She was the most prominent widow of the Prophet after Khadīja bint Khuwaylid (d. 619).[1] 'Ā'isha was the daughter of the first caliph, Abū Bakr, and inherited a prestigious legacy, both because of her husband and father. She was known to be very young when she got married. Therefore, she lived for a long time after the Prophet's death and played a crucial role in the political and religious affairs thereafter. Her crucial role in the Battle of the Camel in 36/656 was one of the defining chapters of early Islamic history. When 'Alī defeated the rebels, led by 'Ā'isha and her relative Zubayr b. al-'Awwām (d. 36/656) and Ṭalḥa b. 'Ubaydullāh (d. 36/656), he sent 'Ā'isha to Medina unharmed, and she remained in her house until the end of her life.[2]

Establishing a Legal Bond between Opposite Genders through Breastfeeding

During this period, she narrated many prophetic reports to her companions and students, who were mostly her relatives. Most of these reports were related to legal issues and the Prophet's interaction with his wives. In one of these reports, she narrated an episode in which the Prophet advised Sahla bint Suhayl to breastfeed Sālim b. Abī Ḥudhayfa, a non-biological family member, to render him *maḥram* or unlawful to marry.[3] This would

1 On the wives of the Prophet, see Ali, *The Lives of Muhammad.*

2 Kennedy, *The Prophet and the Age of the Caliphates*, pp. 75–6.

3 *Maḥram* is a close family member of the opposite gender, either biologically or through wedlock.

establish a legal bond[4] between Sahla bint Suhayl and Sālim, like mother and son. The report suggests that Sālim was an adult at the time, which makes it appear to be an unconventional situation. Yet, it is clear from the text that the Prophet did not suggest direct breastfeeding but 'the form of putting drops of the mother's milk into a dish or a drink'.[5]

The report is significant in relation to Islamic law as it regulates an artificial way to forge a family-like bond between females and males. It also contains information about the removal of some verses on breastfeeding from the Qur'an after the death of the Prophet. Therefore, it is related to studying the distortion of the Qur'an. The central characters involved in the episode are Sālim, a client of Abū Ḥudhayfa, Abū Ḥudhayfa himself and his wife, Sahla bint Suhayl. It appears that Sahla bint Suhayl encountered a problem with the presence of Sālim in their private space, who was not her biological son, thus conceivably able to marry Sahla bint Suhayl. Nevertheless, he lived with them in the same small house. When Sahla bint Suhayl questioned the Prophet for advice, the Prophet suggested that breastfeeding would solve the problem.

'Ā'isha then used this event as a legal precedent to make Sālim b. 'Abdullāh b. 'Umar, the grandson of the second caliph, 'Umar, *maḥram* through breastfeeding to be able to see him without hassle. Around this chief theme, there seem to be several variants that emerged to state the number of necessary breastfeedings that turn a person from non-*maḥram* to *maḥram*. They also stated that the number of required breastfeeding to make a male *maḥram* was five, and then changed it to ten distinct breastfeedings. Furthermore, the variants claim that the Qur'an had included these specific numbers (five and ten breastfeedings) at the time of the Prophet, and that it was then removed from the Qur'an. Here is a sample variant:

> It was reported to us by 'Abd al-Razzāq, who said, it was reported to us by Ibn Jurayj, who said: I have heard from Nāfi', who narrated from Sālim b. 'Abdullāh, who said: 'Ā'isha, the wife of the Prophet, sent him

4 On milk kinship in Muslim tradition, see Altorki, 'Milk-Kinship in Arab Society'. Altorki quotes Coulsun's definition of milk kinship: 'Relationship by blood, affinity or fosterage creates a bar to marriage. As regards blood relatives, a person is prohibited from marrying any lineal descendant, any lineal ascendant, any descendant of his or her parents, and the immediate child of any grandparent. Relationship through marriage, or affinity, raises the bar to marriage between a person and the spouse of any ascendant, the spouse of any descendant, any ascendant of his or her spouse and any descendant of his or her spouse. Foster relationship arises when a woman breast-feeds someone else's child. It creates a bar to marriage not only between foster brothers and sisters but also between the foster mother and all her relatives on the one side and her foster children, their spouses and their descendants on the other side.' Also in Coulson, *Succession in the Muslim Family*, p. 14.

5 Motzki et al., *Analysing Muslim Traditions*, p. 39.

> (Sālim) to her sister Umm Kulthūm bint Abī Bakr to have him nursed ten breastfeedings to enable him to visit her when he grows up. She breastfed him three times then she got ill. Sālim could not visit her, thus saying: that they claimed that 'Ā'isha said: 'The Book of God Almighty and Glorified used to have ten breastfeedings. It was then changed to five. However, the number of [five] breastfeedings went away with [the death of] the Prophet from the Book of God.'[6]

Be that as it may, neither of the verses related to the required number of breastfeedings are included in the Qur'anic text, either in the past or present. For this reason, there were elaborate discussions in early legal works, and many conflicting reports exist on the subject. It is important to state that the main subject of enquiry is not the so-called removal of the five or ten breastfeedings, but the non-existence of these verses in the present Qur'anic codex. According to some of the variants, these verses were extant in the Qur'an at the time of the Prophet, but then removed or lost after the death of the Prophet.

Consequently, the subject of the query is the relevance of these reports to the distortion of the Qur'an. However, since the topics are interrelated, this study is also relevant to legal matters on breastfeeding and the concept of abrogation. Schacht briefly studied this report to argue how rival schools forged reports to invalidate each other's arguments.[7]

For the study of the variants in relation to the breastfeeding narrative, I found twenty-six variants in eight Sunni collections: three variants in Mālik's *Muwaṭṭa'*, five variants in 'Abd al-Razzāq al-Ṣan'ānī's *Muṣannaf*, one variant in Ibn Abī Shayba's *Muṣannaf*, ten variants in Muslim's *Ṣaḥīḥ*, four variants in Ibn Mājah's *Sunan*, two variants in Abū Dāwūd's *Sunan* and one variant in Nasā'ī's *Sunan*. These reports represent almost all the traditions involving 'Ā'isha, who reportedly narrates a tradition related to the Prophet's judgement on breastfeeding and the so-called missing Breastfeeding Verse.

The twenty-six variants indicate that the report spreads from 'Ā'isha to individual transmitters, who were Nāfi', al-Qāsim, Sālim, Umm Salama, 'Urwa b. al-Zubayr and 'Amra bint 'Abd al-Raḥmān. Therefore, it appears

6 al-Ṣan'ānī, *Muṣannaf*, vol. 7, p. 466.

7 Schacht, *The Origins of Muhammadan Jurisprudence*, p. 48. However, Motzki, in his lengthy analysis of several variants of the report, refutes Schacht's argument and makes a strong case that it is possible to date them back to 'Ā'isha's date of death, or even an earlier date at the time of the Prophet. I will further examine Motzki's argument in due course. Still, it must be noted that Motzki implemented a source-critical method in his study and examined a limited number of these reports. I will expand on Motzki's study by employing *isnād-cum-matn* analysis on all the relevant reports. Motzki et al., *Analysing Muslim Traditions*, pp. 43–4.

that 'Ā'isha was both a source and Common Link for the report. Furthermore, Nāfiʿ, Zaynab bint Umm Salama, 'Urwa b. al-Zubayr, 'Amra bint 'Abd al-Raḥmān and al-Qāsim spread the tradition to multiple individuals. Therefore, they are Partial Common Links (PCLs). From the PCLs, the variants were further spread by prominent hadith collectors such as Zuhrī, Mālik, Nāfiʿ and Yaḥyā b. Saʿīd. They were then eventually recorded in the major Sunni hadith collections. I will study the variants in six groups, organised according to the five PCL groups and the remaining miscellaneous variants in a separate group.

The Nāfiʿ Cluster

Chain of Transmission Analysis

There were three variants that spread from Nāfiʿ. Of these variants, one reaches back to 'Ā'isha directly, and two reach 'Ā'isha via Sālim b. 'Abdullāh b. 'Umar. It is peculiar that while two chains in the Nāfiʿ cluster reach 'Ā'isha via Sālim, one reaches 'Ā'isha directly without Sālim. It is possible that Nāfiʿ either added Sālim to the chain because he was the central character of the report, or Sālim's name was dropped from the chain. The third possibility is that the chain is original, meaning Nāfiʿ heard this report from 'Ā'isha. The *isnād* analysis will shed further light on this issue.

The first variant was recorded in Mālik's (d. 179/795) *Muwaṭṭa'*,[8] who received it from Nāfiʿ (d. 118/736 or 119/737).[9] The sound relationship between Mālik and Nāfiʿ is well established.[10] Nāfiʿ received the report from Sālim b. 'Abdullāh. The sound relationship between Nāfiʿ and Ibn 'Umar, who is the father of Sālim b. 'Abdullāh, is also well established.[11] Since Nāfiʿ was Ibn 'Umar's client, it is likely that he heard the variant from Sālim b. 'Abdullāh, and that Sālim b. 'Abdullāh received it from 'Ā'isha (d. 58/678).

Sālim b. 'Abdullāh was born during the caliphate of 'Uthmān.[12] It is almost certain that Sālim must have been a toddler when this episode occurred. 'Uthmān's caliphate began in 23/644 when 'Ā'isha was around thirty or thirty-one years old and ended in 36/656 when 'Ā'isha was around forty-two or forty-three. Sālim b. 'Abdullāh was born around this period and died in 106/725, in his sixties. If he died in 106/725, the event might have occurred towards the end of 'Uthmān's caliphate, possibly

8 Mālik, *Muwaṭṭa'*, vol. 1, p. 453.

9 Although sources provide various dates for Nāfiʿ's date of death, Motzki makes a good case for this date; see Motzki et al., *Analysing Muslim Traditions*, p. 68.

10 Motzki et al., *Analysing Muslim Traditions*, pp. 47–122. See also Juynboll, 'Nāfiʿ', pp. 207–44, in which Juynboll considers Nāfiʿ a fictional person.

11 Motzki et al., *Analysing Muslim Traditions*, pp. 47–122.

12 al-Dhahabī, *Siyar aʿlām al-nubalā'*, vol. 4, p. 458.

Diagram 1 Available online at: https://edin.ac/4agw5Lu

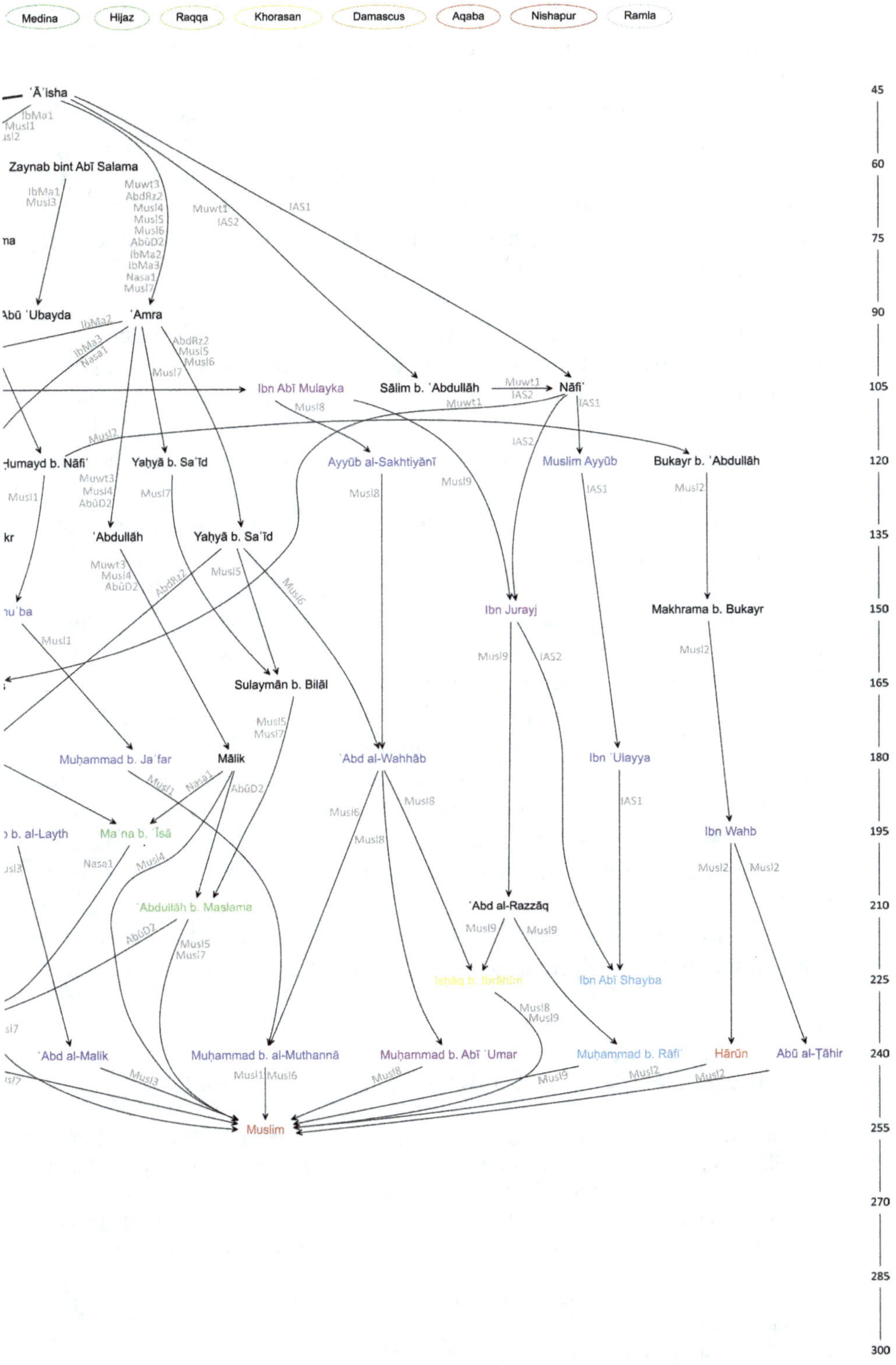

Medina
Hijaz
Raqqa
Khorasan
Damascus
Aqaba
Nishapur
Ramla
ʿĀʾisha
Zaynab bint Abī Salama
Abū ʿUbayda
ʿAmra
Ibn Abī Mulayka
Sālim b. ʿAbdullāh
Nāfiʿ
Ḥumayd b. Nāfiʿ
Yaḥyā b. Saʿīd
Ayyūb al-Sakhtiyānī
Muslim Ayyūb
Bukayr b. ʿAbdullāh
ʿAbdullāh
Yaḥyā b. Saʿīd
Ibn Jurayj
Makhrama b. Bukayr
Sulaymān b. Bilāl
Muḥammad b. Jaʿfar
Mālik
ʿAbd al-Wahhāb
Ibn ʿUlayya
Maʿna b. ʿĪsā
Ibn Wahb
ʿAbdullāh b. Maslama
ʿAbd al-Razzāq
Isḥāq b. Ibrāhīm
Ibn Abī Shayba
ʿAbd al-Malik
Muḥammad b. al-Muthannā
Muḥammad b. Abī ʿUmar
Muḥammad b. Rāfiʿ
Hārūn
Abū al-Ṭāhir
Muslim
45
60
75
90
105
120
135
150
165
180
195
210
225
240
255
270
285
300

just before 36/656 when Sālim was a toddler. This is based on the Qur'anic legal ruling that 'Mothers breastfeed their children for two whole years' (Q. 2:233), because of which the age for weaning children off breastmilk is two. Of course, some circumstances might change the age of weaning, but there is no indication of an anomaly in the variant about Sālim's age. Therefore, at the time of the episode, Sālim was a toddler and already being breastfed by his mother or nurse, which means he was not a direct witness to the event. It was hence impossible for him to remember the details of the narrative. It is probable that his family members later narrated to him what had happened when he was an infant as a good memory. This could be considered an irregularity in the chain of transmission because Sālim was not an eyewitness to it. Nevertheless, it is possible that his family accurately narrated the episode to him later. Therefore, it is probable that this chain is sound, but it must be kept in mind that Sālim's account of the episode is indirect; consequently, it could be considered hearsay.

The second variant was recorded in Ibn Abī Shayba's (d. 235/849–50) *Muṣannaf*.[13] Ibn Abī Shayba received it from (Ismāʿīl b. Ibrāhīm) Ibn ʿUlayya (d. 193/809–10), a prominent scholar of Basra.[14] Ibn ʿUlayya received it from a second-generation Muslim named Ayyūb [b. Abī Tamīma al-Sakhtiyānī] (d. 131/748–9) of Basra. There seems to be a considerable age difference between the informants as Ayyūb died sixty-two years before Ibn ʿUlayya. However, it is possible for Ibn ʿUlayya to receive it from Ayyūb.[15] Ayyūb received it from his favourite source, Nāfiʿ.[16] Nāfiʿ, among many other prominent figures of early Islam, also reported from ʿĀ'isha. Given that after the Battle of the Camel in 36/656, ʿĀ'isha gave up her political ambitions and resided in Medina for twenty-two years, it was plausible that Nāfiʿ received the report from ʿĀ'isha directly. ʿĀ'isha died in 58/678, and Nāfiʿ died in 118/736, some sixty years apart from each other. Since Nāfiʿ lived for eighty-five years,[17] it is technically possible that he received it from ʿĀ'isha, but considering the evidence that there are two more chains

13 Ibn Abī Shayba, *Muṣannaf*, vol. 3, pp. 385–6.

14 al-Dhahabī, *Siyar aʿlām al-nubalā'*, vol. 9, pp. 198–220; Juynboll, *Encyclopaedia of Canonical Ḥadīth*, pp. 226–9.

15 Motzki draws attention to Juynboll's suspicion of this kind of age difference. For Juynboll, the significant age difference is a major red flag for the fabrication of tradition, which he called 'age tricks'. Motzki refuted Juynboll's presupposition based on the biographical sources and common sense, hence making a solid case for the pupil and teacher relationship between Ibn ʿUlayya and Ayyūb. Motzki et al., *Analysing Muslim Traditions*, pp. 78–80.

16 Motzki evaluates various dates and settles on this date. Motzki et al., *Analysing Muslim Traditions*, p. 64.

17 Motzki et al., *Analysing Muslim Traditions*, p. 64.

in which Nāfiʿ received the same report via Sālim, it may not have been the case. The textual analysis may reveal Nāfiʿ's source for the variant.

The third variant was recorded in Ibn Abī Shayba's *Muṣannaf*.[18] He received it from Ibn Jurayj (d. 150/767–8) of Mecca. Ibn Jurayj received it from Nāfiʿ, and like the first variant, Nāfiʿ received the variant from Sālim b. ʿAbdullāh, who received it from ʿĀ'isha. There seems to be no issue with the chain of transmission in the first group of variants as three of them return to ʿĀ'isha. There is a minor problem with the second chain, which might be resolved in the textual analysis.

Textual Analysis

The text of the first variant recorded in Mālik's *Muwaṭṭa'* appears to purport that ʿĀ'isha wanted to meet with Sālim b. ʿAbdullāh privately after he had grown up. However, since ʿĀ'isha and Sālim were not *maḥram*, there would be certain legal preventative measures to the extent of their interactions. To remove the barrier of being non-*maḥram*, ʿĀ'isha sent Sālim b. ʿAbdullāh to her sister Umm Kulthūm bint Abī Bakr so that she may breastfeed him. She needed to do it at least ten times to establish the bond, thus, rendering Sālim an unlawful person to marry (*maḥram*) for ʿĀ'isha through this artificial way of breastfeeding. Unfortunately for Sālim, during the process of breastfeeding, Umm Kulthūm got ill after the third breastfeeding. Perhaps during this time, her child had weaned off breastmilk too, meaning she had no milk to continue the course of the required breastfeedings. Therefore, Sālim was not able to visit ʿĀ'isha in private.

The text of the second variant opens with a general statement that 'when ʿĀ'isha wanted to meet a male person, she would order him to be breastfed', instead of the direct account of Sālim b. ʿAbdullāh who was sent to Umm Kulthūm for breastfeeding. The reason for the difference is obvious, for in the first instance Nāfiʿ receives the information from Sālim b. ʿAbdullāh while in the second instance, he receives the information directly from ʿĀ'isha. Since the general statement in the second text is in the third person, it gives the impression that somewhere along the transmission process, either Nāfiʿ or others paraphrased this sentence. The text then moves on to ʿĀ'isha's order to Umm Kulthūm to breastfeed Sālim b. ʿAbdullāh ten times. This information differs from the first text in which ʿĀ'isha orders Sālim b. ʿAbdullāh to go to Umm Kulthūm for breastfeeding. Again, this occurrence may be explained: in the first text, Sālim b. ʿAbdullāh gives the account of the episode from his perspective and he perhaps was not aware of the initial conversation that took place between ʿĀ'isha and Umm Kulthūm.

18 al-Ṣanʿānī, *Muṣannaf*, vol. 7, p. 466.

However, like the information provided in the first variant, Umm Kulthūm got ill after the third breastfeeding, and the effort yielded no result. There is also a piece of extra and puzzling information provided at the end of the second text: 'Ā'isha ordered Fāṭima bint 'Umar, who was the stepdaughter of Umm Kulthūm, to breastfeed 'Āṣim b. Sa'īd. Fāṭima bint 'Umar acted accordingly and breastfeed 'Āṣim b. Sa'īd ten times. There seems, however, to be some intermixing between two thematically similar reports. Although the central character of this episode is Sālim, the focus of this variant seems to be rendering a male as unlawful to marry with ten breastfeedings. This proposition rests upon the fact that after giving the summary of the Sālim episode which was interrupted after three breastfeedings, the attention shifts to the breastfeeding of 'Āṣim b. Sa'īd by Fāṭima bint 'Umar ten times.

Furthermore, the context of the tradition, especially the opening statement, 'when 'Ā'isha wanted to meet a male person, she would order him to be breastfed', suggests that, unlike the first unsuccessful episode, this episode seems to be providing a successful practice of 'Ā'isha's use of the method of breastfeeding adults in order to render them unlawful to marry. Since 'Ā'isha is the sister of Umm Kulthūm, who is the stepmother of Fāṭima bint 'Umar, through a successful course of breastfeeding by Fāṭima bint 'Umar, 'Ā'isha would have automatically become the foster step-aunt of 'Āṣim b. Sa'īd, thus rendering her unmarriageable for him. Therefore, he could visit her without observing the legal restrictions that marriageable persons would have to observe.

The chain of this variant could be the same as the chain of the second variant in which 'Ā'isha ordered Fāṭima bint 'Umar to breastfeed 'Āṣim b. Sa'īd ten times. The summary style of the text, with a third-person narrative, supports this position. It is possible that one of the transmitters combined the two reports, meaning Nāfi' received the second report, namely, that 'Ā'isha ordered Fāṭima bint 'Umar to breastfeed 'Āṣim b. Sa'īd ten times, from 'Ā'isha and used this chain in the report.

The text of the third variant provides some additional information that may help to make better sense of this group of variants. Like the first variant, it reaches Nāfi' through Sālim, therefore, the text is similar to the first variant: 'Ā'isha wanted Sālim to visit her privately and she sent Sālim to her sister Umm Kulthūm to breastfeed him ten times. However, after the third time she got ill, and the process was interrupted. There is, however, an important piece of information that suggests Sālim was a toddler when the episode occurred, namely, that the variant clearly states that Sālim was a minor when he was urged to be breastfed by Umm Kulthūm. The variants state: "'Ā'isha, the wife of the Prophet, sent him [Sālim] to her sister Umm Kulthūm bint Abū Bakr to have him breastfeed ten times to enable him to visit her when he grows up (*li-yalij 'alayhā idhā kabira*).' It seems

'Ā'isha was thinking ahead; she liked the infant Sālim and wanted to be able to enjoy his company as an adult, too. Therefore, she took a proactive measure to have him breastfed by a close relative while he was still a toddler. This information makes it clear that Sālim did not witness the episode, but rather heard it from his close relatives. Because this information is only included in one of the variants, however, it is not possible to verify it.

After this point, the most pertinent information about distortion is given:

> They claimed that 'Ā'isha said: 'The Book of God Almighty and Glorified used to have ten breastfeedings. It was then changed into five. However, the number of breastfeeding has gone with [the death of] the Prophet from the Book of God.'[19]

Together with the above-mentioned elements about Sālim's age, this version provides the information that the Qur'an contained verses about the number of breastfeedings required to make a person unlawful to marry. However, these verses were removed from the Qur'an with the death of the Prophet. It appears that one of the transmitters felt obliged to make such an explanation to justify the reason why as an infant, he was supposed to be breastfed ten times, but because he was breastfed three times only, he was not able to visit 'Ā'isha privately.

Given that this is the only variant which informs us about the removal of the verse after the death of the Prophet, it cannot be verified. Because the section about the missing Breastfeeding Verse starts with 'they *claimed* that 'Ā'isha said:' it means that Nāfi' had his doubts about this additional part. The fact that he nevertheless included it in the report, seems to support my view. It is probable that either Ibn Jurayj, 'Abd al-Razzāq or Nāfi' interpolated this information into the text. The text suggests that this was a separate report and the two separate reports were combined to provide extra information, and the intent was therefore not malicious. The individual wanted to provide an explanation from other available sources. At this point, some elements in these variants can be dated back to Nāfi''s date of death, which is 117/832–3. These elements include the fact that 'Ā'isha wanted to render Sālim unlawful to marry to meet him privately in the future, and she therefore asked her sister Umm Kulthūm to breastfeed him. The process, as we know, was interrupted, thus failing the required ten breastfeedings. If I can find these same elements in the remaining variants, it may be possible to date them to an earlier date.

19 al-Ṣan'ānī, *Muṣannaf*, vol. 7, p. 466.

The Zaynab Cluster

Chain of Transmission Analysis

The fourth variant was recorded in Ibn Mājah's *Sunan.*[20] Ibn Mājah (d. 273/887) received the variant from Muḥammad b. Rumḥ (d. 242/857).[21] Muḥammad b. Rumḥ received it from ʿAbdullāh b. Lahīʿa (d. 174/790), both of whom resided in Egypt. Ibn Lahīʿa[22] was a prominent scholar whose influence in Egypt was compared to that of Mālik in Medina or al-Awzāʿī in Damascus.[23] He received the variant from Yazīd b. Abī Ḥabīb (d. 128/745) and ʿUqayl [b. Khālid] (d. 141/758–9 or 144/761) of Kufa.[24] Yazīd b. Abī Ḥabīb also resided in Egypt. He lived during the era of Muʿāwiya and was a second-generation Muslim.[25]

Yazīd b. Abī Ḥabīb received the variant from another second-generation hadith collector, Ibn Shihāb (al-Zuhrī).[26] It appears that Yazīd b. Abī Ḥabīb was responsible for spreading the variant from Medina to Egypt. Alternatively, he received it from Zuhrī when the latter stayed in Egypt. Zuhrī received it from Abū ʿUbayda b. ʿAbdullāh b. Zamʿa, who was the great-grandson of Umm Salama, the wife of the Prophet, and transmitted a limited number of reports.[27] There is no date of death for Abū ʿUbayda, but it is possible for him to have reported the variant from his mother, Zaynab bint Abī Salama (d. circa 74/693–4),[28] to Zuhrī. Zaynab bint Abī Salama was the stepdaughter of the Prophet and reported the variant from all the widows of the Prophet, including her mother, Umm Salama (d. 62/681–2). There is no problem with this transmission line.

The fifth variant was recorded in Muslim's *Ṣaḥīh*[29] and reported from Muḥammad b. al-Muthannā (d. 252/866), who was active in Basra.[30] He received the variant from Muḥammad b. Jaʿfar (Ghundur) (d. 193/809), who was a well-known hadith collector in Basra and the most prominent

20 Ibn Mājah, *Sunan*, p. 626.

21 al-Dhahabī, *Siyar aʿlām al-nubalāʾ*, vol. 11, pp. 499–500.

22 See Brockopp, 'Ibn Lahīʿa'.

23 al-Dhahabī, *Siyar aʿlām al-nubalāʾ*, vol. 8, p. 14.

24 See Schoeler, *The Biography of Muḥammad*, pp. 43–45. See also Juynboll, *Encyclopaedia of Canonical Ḥadīth*, p. 400.

25 al-Dhahabī, *Siyar aʿlām al-nubalāʾ*, vol. 6, pp. 32–3.

26 Schoeler briefly discusses the relation between ʿUqayl and Zuhrī; see Schoeler, *The Biography of Muḥammad*, pp. 45–6.

27 Ibn Saʿd, *al-Ṭabaqāt*, vol. 7, pp. 402–3; al-Mizzī, *Tahdhīb al-kamāl fī asmāʾ al-rijāl*, vol. 34, pp. 58–9.

28 al-Dhahabī, *Siyar aʿlām al-nubalāʾ*, vol. 3, p. 201.

29 Muslim, *Ṣaḥīh*, vol. 2, p. 1077.

30 al-Dhahabī, *Siyar aʿlām al-nubalāʾ*, vol. 12, pp. 124–6; al-Mizzī, *Tahdhīb al-kamāl fī asmāʾ al-rijāl*, vol. 26, pp. 359–65.

student of Shuʿba[31] [b. al-Ḥajjāj] (d. 160/776–7) of Basra.[32] From him, Muḥammad b. Jaʿfar received this variant. Shuʿba received the variant from Ḥumayd b. Nāfiʿ. He lived and died in Medina and narrated reports from Zaynab bint Umm Salama.[33] There is no date of death for Ḥumayd b. Nāfiʿ, but given that he was a second-generation Muslim, he may have received it from Zaynab bint Umm Salama. Finally, Zaynab bint Umm Salama narrated the variant from both ʿĀʾisha (d. 58/678) and Umm Salama (d. 62/682–3).

The sixth variant was recorded again in Muslim's *Ṣaḥīh*,[34] who received it from Abū al-Ṭāhir and Hārūn b. Saʿīd al-Aylī. Bukhārī stated that he recorded the utterance of Hārūn. Therefore, I will study Hārūn b. Saʿīd al-Aylī (d. 253/867), who was from the city of Aqaba. He was known to be a student of Ibn Wahb,[35] from whom he reported this variant. Ibn Wahb received it from Makhrama b. Bukayr (d. 159/775–6), a resident of Medina who often reported from his father Bukayr b. ʿAbdullāh's collection.[36] He reported this variant from his father, Bukayr b. ʿAbdullāh (d. 127/744–5), who was a prominent hadith collector and active in Medina and Egypt. He was counted among the late second-generation Muslims.[37] Similar to the previous variant, he received the variant from Ḥumayd b. Nāfiʿ. He then received it from Zaynab, and she received it from Umm Salama and ʿĀʾisha. As stated above, Yazīd b. Abī Ḥabīb transmitted the variant from Medina to Egypt, but it appears that Bukayr b. ʿAbdullāh also transmitted it to Egypt, and both did so around the same time.

The seventh variant was also recorded in Muslim's *Ṣaḥīḥ*,[38] who received it from ʿAbd al-Malik b. Shuʿayb b. al-Layth (d. 248/863), an Egyptian collector and grandson of the prominent Egyptian scholar Layth b. Saʿd (d.175/791–2).[39] He received it through a family chain: his father, Shuʿayb b. al-Layth (d. 199/814–15), and his grandfather, Layth b. Saʿd, both of whom were based in Egypt. Layth b. Saʿd received it from the Egyptian ʿUqayl b. Khālid (d. between 141/758 and 144/761), who also transmitted one of the other variants in the Zaynab clusters. He was a client of descendants of the

31 al-Dhahabī, *Siyar aʿlām al-nubalāʾ*, vol. 9, pp. 99–101; al-Mizzī, *Tahdhīb al-kamāl fī asmāʾ al-rijāl*, vol. 25, pp. 5–9.

32 al-Baghdādī, *Tārīkh Baghdād*, vol. 10, pp. 353–67; al-Dhahabī, *Siyar aʿlām al-nubalāʾ*, vol. 7, pp. 203–9.

33 al-Mizzī, *Tahdhīb al-kamāl fī asmāʾ al-rijāl*, vol. 18, pp. 400–1.

34 Muslim, *Ṣaḥīh*, vol. 2, p. 1078.

35 al-Mizzī, *Tahdhīb al-kamāl fī asmāʾ al-rijāl*, vol. 18, pp. 90–2.

36 al-Mizzī, *Tahdhīb al-kamāl fī asmāʾ al-rijāl*, vol. 27, pp. 324–7.

37 al-Dhahabī, *Siyar aʿlām al-nubalāʾ*, vol. 6, pp. 171–3; al-Mizzī, *Tahdhīb al-kamāl fī asmāʾ al-rijāl*, vol. 4, pp. 242–6.

38 Muslim, *Ṣaḥīh*, vol. 2, p. 1078.

39 al-Mizzī, *Tahdhīb al-kamāl fī asmāʾ al-rijāl*, vol. 18, pp. 329–32.

third caliph, ʿUthmān, and had a well-established connection to Zuhrī, from whom he reported extensively.[40] He also reported this variant from Zuhrī (d. 124/742), possibly hearing it when the latter was in Egypt. Like the fourth variant, Zuhrī received the variant from Abū ʿUbayda b. ʿAbdullāh b. Zamʿa and the rest of the chain is the same as the fourth variant. Having studied the Zaynab cluster, I can affirm that all four variants could be traced back to Umm Salama and ʿĀ'isha without interruption. The reports were spread from Medina to Basra and Egypt by various transmitters.

Textual Analysis

At first sight, the Zaynab cluster suggests that the three variants give an account of a legal debate between the widows of the Prophet. ʿĀ'isha, the most prominent wife of the Prophet after Khadīja bint Khuwaylid (d. 619), permitted Sahla bint Suhayl to breastfeed Sālim to make him unlawful to marry when he was an adult (i.e. when he reached the age of puberty) as the Prophet practised. She maintained that the Prophet legalised breastfeeding adult males indirectly to make them unlawful to marry for the convenience of being able to live together under the same roof or meeting them in private. On the other hand, Umm Salama, the third most prominent widow of the Prophet, along with the other widows of the Prophet, held that this was an exception that the Prophet only granted to Sahla bint Suhayl to appease her husband Abū Ḥudhayfa's discontent. The texts seem to provide valuable information about the context of the report on the breastfeeding of Sālim. It appears that this report was presented as a piece of evidence in a legal debate between the widows of the Prophet regarding the legal consequences of breastfeeding infants and grown-up males who did not have any biological bond to nursing females.

In the text of the fourth variant recorded in Abū Dāwūd's *Sunan*, Zaynab, the daughter of Umm Salama, does not mention her mother's name. Instead, she makes a general statement that the remaining widows of the Prophet, which includes her mother, Umm Salama, objected to ʿĀ'isha's legal verdict on rendering adults unlawful to marry by way of breastfeeding. Aside from ʿĀ'isha, the remaining widows were not sure if the Prophet granted an exception to Sahla bint Suhayl or not. They therefore were cautious, implying that they did not practise it. In this variant, there is no reference to the so-called missing verse that provides the prescribed number of breastfeedings to make someone unlawful to marry:

> All the wives of the Prophet objected to ʿĀ'isha and refused any man to visit them, similar to the breastfeeding of Sālim, a client of Abū

40 al-Dhahabī, *Siyar aʿlām al-nubalā'*, vol. 6, pp. 302–3.

Ḥudhayfa. They said, 'we do not know; perhaps this permission was granted to Sālim alone.'[41]

The topic is focused on whether the breastfeeding of Sālim can be used as a precedent to render non-familial infants unlawful to marry by way of breastfeeding. There is a direct quote in the text from the widows of the Prophet, but Zaynab probably gave the account of her mother's opinion from her mouth.

The text of the fifth variant recorded in Muslim's *Ṣaḥīḥ* provides additional details about the conversation that took place between Umm Salama and 'Ā'isha. It seems that the conversation commenced with Umm Salama, who wanted to express her concern about the possible peril of infringing on Islamic law. The text states that Umm Salama warned 'Ā'isha about the child who was about to reach puberty, which, according to Islamic law, makes a person an adult, and they thus must observe modesty in their dealings with the opposite sex. Yet he could still enter the house of the Prophet's widows unannounced. In response, 'Ā'isha reminded Umm Salama about the report of the Prophet, wherein he permitted Sahla bint Suhayl to breastfeed Sālim, the client of Abū Ḥudhayfa, who had already reached puberty and was considered an adult. Although the statement implies that 'Ā'isha pre-empted the problem by getting the child breastfed, it is unclear when or through whom she took care of the situation. It is almost certain, however, that 'Ā'isha had the boy breastfed beforehand, meaning when he was an infant.

At this point, it seems there was no further discussion between the two widows of the Prophet and the response of Umm Salama to 'Ā'isha's argument is not clear. However, the other variants and the tone of Umm Salama, who explicitly stated that she dislikes the arrangement, makes it clear that there was a debate or tension between the widows of the Prophet about their interpretation of the prophetic report. 'Ā'isha believed she could make non-*maḥram* male family members unlawful to marry by way of breastfeeding. All the others, however, led by Umm Salama, opposed her on this. In this sense, it seems to be a genuine report because it notes a discord among the wives of the Prophet on a legal matter.

The text of the variant at hand further indicates that 'Ā'isha had the boy breastfed already. Thus, she was not concerned about him reaching the age of puberty. It indirectly gives credence to Nāfi''s clusters that provide the account of 'Ā'isha's practice of breastfeeding as an artificial way of rendering males unlawful to marry. She justified her view through the practice of the Prophet. The objection of Umm Salama, however, indicates that this was not an established view at the time. Based on this textual analysis, the

41 Ibn Mājah, *Sunan*, p. 626.

two transmission lines which come through Zaynab have three common elements: (1) There was a disagreement between 'Ā'isha and the other widows of the Prophet, led by Umm Salama, about breastfeeding adult strangers; (2) Umm Salama and the other widows of the Prophet interpreted the verdict of the Prophet on the episode of Sahla bint Suhayl's breastfeeding of Sālim differently from 'Ā'isha; and (3) the event in which the Prophet advised Sahla to breastfeed Sālim had indeed occurred. Aside from 'Ā'isha, the other widows of the Prophet also acknowledged it, albeit the lack of additional details provided in the 'Urwa cluster.

These elements are paraphrased in both texts significantly, which may be explained by the fact that the fourth variant travelled to Egypt while the fifth variant remained in Medina and Basra. This indicates a healthy and coherent process of transmission. In the text of the sixth variant, the tone of Umm Salama's objection to 'Ā'isha seems to be the same as the fifth variant: 'By God! I do not want to be seen by a young boy who has passed the age of breastfeeding.' Furthermore, instead of implying that the child is about to reach puberty, the variant states that the child has passed the age of breastfeeding, meaning he is over two years old. After this point, Zaynab gives 'Ā'isha's prolonged account of the episode of the Prophet's warrant for Sahla bint Suhayl to breastfeed Sālim. Unlike the fourth variant, the fifth and sixth variants do not mention an explicit disagreement between the widows of the Prophet regarding the interpretation of Sahla bint Suhayl's breastfeeding of Sālim. It is presented as a conversation rather than disagreement. Given that there is a more detailed account of the episode of breastfeeding Sālim, however, there is some collaboration between it and the difference in transmission lines after Ḥumayd b. Nāfi'.

The transmission line of the seventh variant is similar to that of the fourth variant. Therefore, these two variants should have similar elements in the them. A comparison of both texts indeed shows striking similarities between the texts. There is an acute clarity in the objection of Umm Salama and the other widows of the Prophet regarding breastfeeding adults. They were certain that the Prophet granted an exception to Sahla bint Suhayl to breastfeed Sālim, and it was not a general dispensation. There are two points to ponder. There is a certain interdependence between the fourth and seventh variants as they share each of the elements, and perhaps more clarity is present in the seventh variant rather than the fourth, which is, 'we do not know perhaps this permission was granted to Sālim alone'. The seventh variant states:

> They said to 'Ā'isha: 'By God, we see this kind of breastfeeding nothing but a warrant by which the Messenger of God permitted her (Sahla bint Suhayl) [to see] Sālim alone. It is not [a warrant] for anyone to visit us through the same breastfeeding; neither do we see it [as a general warrant].'

The first statement could be given the same kind of negative meaning based on the context. It is clear from the context of the fourth variant that the same meaning may be extracted: 'All of the wives of the Prophet objected to 'Ā'isha and refused any man to visit them as in the example of breastfeeding of Sālim.'

The seventh variant was reported through Abū 'Ubayda b. 'Abdullāh b. Zam'a, who was Umm Salama's son, and the fourth variant was reported through Zaynab, who was Umm Salama's daughter. They may have understood a similar meaning from what they heard but uttered it slightly differently. This explains that, despite the similarity between the elements, there is extensive paraphrasing. The second point is that there seems to be an inconsistency between variants four, seven, five, and six, namely, that the texts of the latter two seem to be incomplete, in the sense that they do not mention the response of Umm Salama to 'Ā'isha's argument, which is stated explicitly in variants four and seven. It is possible that information regarding the interpretation of the Prophet's widows may have been excluded from these variants. Or, the transmitters might have thought that such a disagreement may bring disrepute to the widows of the Prophet, since it implies that 'Ā'isha inadvertently breached Islamic law in her interpretation.

I reach this conclusion because of the overall theme of disagreement in all four variants between 'Ā'isha and Umm Salama. It would be naive to assume that Umm Salama, who was one of the most learned wives of the Prophet, along with the other widows of the Prophet, had been unaware of Sahla bint Suhayl's breastfeeding of Sālim. It is also clear from the variants that despite being aware of it, they considered it an exception granted exclusively to Sahla bint Suhayl. Thus, it is peculiar that in the two variants, Umm Salama did not respond to 'Ā'isha's argument, which gives the impression that the last part of the report was omitted in these two variants. In any case, textual interdependencies in the Zaynab cluster correspond with the transmission lines. Therefore, they can be dated back to Zaynab bint Abī Salama's death, which was around 74/693–4.

The 'Urwa Cluster

Chain of Transmission Analysis

The eighth variant was recorded in Mālik's *Muwaṭṭa'*.[42] It seems Yaḥyā [b. Yaḥyā al-Laythī] (d. 234/848–9 or 236/850–1) received this variant from Mālik and included it in his recension of the *Muwaṭṭa'*. Mālik in turn received it from Zuhrī and the relationship between Mālik b. Anas (d. 179/795) and Zuhrī (d. 124/742) is well documented by Harald Motzki

42 Mālik, *Muwaṭṭa'*, vol. 1, p. 454.

in *Analysing Muslim Traditions*, which is a collection of some of his most important essays on hadith analysis. Motzki, in the same book, draws attention to Joseph Schacht's erroneous conclusions on the chains of transmission in which Mālik in his *Muwaṭṭa'* reports from Zuhrī. Schacht, in his monumental study *The Origins of Muhammadan Jurisprudence* argues[43] that only particular types of chains of transmission in which Mālik reports from Zuhrī may be authentic.[44] Motzki, in this study, disagrees with Schacht on such an arbitrary classification and challenges Schacht by attesting to the veracity of these reports.[45]

Zuhrī received the variant from 'Urwa b. al-Zubayr (d. 94/712–13), who received it from his aunt 'Ā'isha. Andreas Görke, in his detailed study on the sources of 'Urwa, notes 'Urwa's notorious reputation for not indicating his sources in the historical accounts he transmitted. Despite this, 'Urwa indicates his sources in the legal or exegetical traditions, such as the tradition at hand.[46] It appears that the variant is an exception to Görke's finding as it is a legal tradition,[47] yet 'Urwa did not explicitly spell out his source in the chain of transmission. Given that 'Urwa was a nephew of 'Ā'isha and the text of the variant mentions 'Ā'isha's name and account of the episode, it is likely that he received it directly from her. I will delve further into this analysis in the following pages. Up to this point, there has been no problem with the chain of transmission. The variant emerged in Medina and remained there, and it can be traced back to 'Ā'isha.

The ninth variant is recorded in 'Abd al-Razzaq's *Muṣannaf*.[48] He received the variant from the prominent Ma'mar of Basra. Ma'mar received the variant from Ibrāhīm b. 'Uqba, who was the brother of the Medinan Mūsā b. 'Uqba. There is no date of death for Ibrāhīm b. 'Uqba,

43 Schacht, *The Origins of Muhammadan Jurisprudence*, pp. 246–7.

44 Harald Motzki explains Schacht's criteria in detail: 'To start with, one can ask: Where does he derive the certainty that, on the one hand, Zuhrī's legal opinions which Mālik reports he asked Zuhrī about or heard from him (for example with the formula "*'an Ibn Shihāb annahu sami'tuhu yaqūl*", i.e., from Ibn Shihāb, that he heard him say) are really authentic, whereas, on the other hand, ra'y which Mālik introduces with, for example, "*'an Ibn Shihāb annahu qāla: sami'tu Abū Bakr ibn 'Abd al-Raḥmān yaqūl*" (from Ibn Shihāb, that he said: "I heard Abū Bakr ibn 'Abd al-Raḥmān say) do not derive from Ibn Shihāb and by no means from his authorities?' (Motzki et al., *Analysing Muslim Traditions*, p. 3.)

45 Motzki et al., *Analysing Muslim Traditions*, pp. 2–4.

46 Görke, 'The Relationship between *Maghāzī* and *Ḥadīth* in Early Islamic Scholarship', pp. 171–85.

47 Having said that, it appears the lines between legal and historical accounts are blurry and this tradition may well be included in the historical accounts category.

48 al-Ṣan'ānī, *Muṣannaf*, vol. 7, p. 466.

but he was older than his brother Mūsā b. 'Uqba and died before him.[49] In any case, it is possible that he received the variant from 'Urwa b. al-Zubayr. 'Urwa finally received the variant from his aunt 'Ā'isha without a problem. This variant spread from Medina to Iraq.

The tenth variant was recorded in Abū Dāwūd's (d. 275/889) *Sunan*,[50] and he received it from the Egyptian Aḥmad b. Ṣāliḥ (d. 247/862). Aḥmad b. Ṣāliḥ was active in Iraq, the Hijaz and Syria and mainly transmitted reports from Zuhrī.[51] He received this report from 'Anbasa [b. Khālid al-Aylī] (d. 198/814), who was a client of the Banū Umayyad and active in Egypt and the Hijaz.[52] He received the variant from his uncle Yūnus [b. Yazīd] (d. 159/775–6 or 160/776–7), who was a client of Mu'āwiya (d. 60/680), the first Umayyad caliph. He was a Kufan and known to be well versed with Zuhrī's reports and reported from him.[53] He also reported this variant from Zuhrī and, like the eighth variant, Zuhrī reported it from 'Urwa b. al-Zubayr, who reported it from 'Ā'isha. In the eighth variant, 'Urwa b. al-Zubayr's source was not explicitly mentioned but 'Ā'isha's name was. However, in this variant, 'Ā'isha's name was explicitly mentioned in the chain of transmission along with Umm Salama since the text gives the narrative of the debate between two of them. This variant also spread to Egypt. Although all three variants can be dated back to 'Ā'isha, it must be noted that Motzki, in his analysis of these reports, initially made the point that 'Ā'isha might not have been the direct narrator of these variants, as they were not reported in the first person but in the third person.[54] I will keep this in mind in the textual analysis of the reports.

Textual Analysis

The 'Urwa b. al-Zubayr cluster continues to provide a detailed account of the Prophet's permission to Sahla bint Suhayl – the wife of Abū Ḥudhayfa, who was a veteran supporter of the Prophet – to breastfeed their adopted son Sālim to render him unlawful to marry. This is a key piece of evidence for 'Ā'isha's legal opinion, and it appears there is no dispute among the wives of the Prophet about its occurrence. However, they did debate about its interpretation due to its implications. The text of the eighth variant provides one of the longest accounts of the episode. It provides a context which prompted Sahla bint Suhayl to go to the Prophet to seek a solution

49 Ibn Sa'd, *al-Ṭabaqāt*, vol. 7, p. 519.
50 Abū Dāwūd, *Sunan*, vol. 2, p. 223.
51 al-Dhahabī, *Siyar a'lām al-nubalā'*, vol. 12, pp. 160–77.
52 al-Mizzī, *Tahdhīb al-kamāl fī asmā' al-rijāl*, vol. 22, pp. 404–5.
53 al-Dhahabī, *Siyar a'lām al-nubalā'*, vol. 6, pp. 298–301.
54 Motzki et al., *Analysing Muslim Traditions*, pp. 39–40.

to their problem. The text states that the problem emerged after the revelation of 'call them (adopted children) after their [biological] fathers, that is more just in the eyes of God. If you do not know their fathers' [names, call them] your brothers in religion and your clients (*mawālīkum*)' (Q. 33:5). The revelation of this verse made it clear that, as opposed to the pre-Islamic practice that adopted children had rights similar to biological children, Islamic law considered adopted children outside the bond of kinship. Therefore, the Qur'an urges Muslims to associate adopted children with their biological parents.

Alarmed by the legal implications of the verse, Sahla bint Suhayl rushed to the Prophet to ask him for a solution to her quandary. They had already adopted Sālim, a client of Abū Ḥudhayfa, and considered him their son. They also had him married and he had been enjoying a loving familial relationship. However, unlike the Umm Salama cluster, there is no mention of Abū Ḥudhayfa's discontent about Sālim's presence, which supposedly prompted Sahla bint Suhayl to visit the Prophet. Furthermore, the variant indicates that Sālim was married at the time. Thus it is not only him but his wife, Fāṭima bint al-Walīd b. 'Utba b. Rabīʿa, who also lived with them under the same roof. It may have been the case that Abū Ḥudhayfa became concerned about the arrangement upon the revelation of the verse. Therefore, there may be no inconsistency between the variants. The narrations may simply be narrations of the transmitters' own perspectives, and they may or may not have been aware of the context fully.

Perhaps one of the most striking aspects of the text at hand is that, in his response to the question, the Prophet utters: 'breastfeed him five times, and he will be unlawful to marry by doing so.' In the variants I have studied so far, the Prophet did not utter 'five times', which is understood here as the amount of required breastfeedings to make a person unlawful to marry. He did not mention any number, but 'Ā'isha stated that the breastfeedings should complete a course of ten times to make a person unlawful to marry. In this report, there is an explicit mention of five times which was previously mentioned in one of the variants in Nāfiʿ's clusters as one of the elements of 'the missing verses'. In the previous variants, the Prophet did not mention a specific number; rather, he simply stated to 'give him milk'. 'Ā'isha also stated that the required number of breastfeedings was ten. In any case, the text states that 'Ā'isha took this episode as precedent for enabling her to see visiting non-*maḥram* men. Thus, 'she would ask her sister Umm Kulthūm bint Abī Bakr and the daughters of her brother to give milk to the men who come to see her.' While there is a discrepancy with the number of required breastfeedings, the opposition of the wives of the Prophet to 'Ā'isha's interpretation of the episode is clear:

> The rest of the wives of the Prophet refused if a man wanted to see them through the same way of giving milk, and they would say: 'by God, no! We do not see the matter this way. The Messenger of God permitted only Sahla Bint Suhayl to nurse Sālim alone. By God, no! No one can visit us by way of such nursing!' This was what the Prophet's wives thought about breastfeeding adults.[55]

Given that these two elements are included in both the Zaynab and 'Urwa clusters, it appears that the legal dispute between the wives of the Prophet may be dated back to the lifetimes of the Prophet's widows. These elements are (1) there was a disagreement between 'Ā'isha and the other widows of the Prophet about breastfeeding adults; (2) the other widows of the Prophet interpreted the verdict of the Prophet on the episode of Sahla bint Suhayl's breastfeeding of Sālim differently from 'Ā'isha. It is possible that the widows of the Prophet witnessed the episode of Sahla bint Suhayl and the Prophet's permission to her to make Sālim unlawful to marry.[56] However, because Motzki used the source-critical method in his study and analysed several reports only, it is understandable as to why he was cautious. Considering the existence of this element both in the Zaynab and 'Urwa clusters, I have greater certainty that this event, which is the third common element, did occur at the time of the Prophet.[57]

The text of the ninth variant is significantly shorter than the eighth variant and only includes brief information stating that "'Ā'isha used to say: "Seven or five breastfeedings does not render one unlawful to marry."' The brief statement of 'Ā'isha included the previous statement of five times, but also included seven times. The varying figures about the required number of breastfeedings indicates some uncertainty. Furthermore, in this variant, Ibrāhīm b. 'Uqba seems to not be satisfied with 'Ā'isha's response that 'Urwa narrated. He also asks Saʿīd b. al-Musayyab about the traditions, to which the latter states: 'I say neither what 'Ā'isha says nor what Ibn 'Abbās says. But if a drop of milk entered his stomach, after he knew that it had entered his stomach, it would make it unlawful [to marry].'[58] This element, which contains Ibn al-Musayyab's disagreement with both 'Ā'isha and Ibn 'Abbās, is only included in this variant. Therefore, I cannot verify it.

55 Mālik, *Muwaṭṭa'*, vol. 1, pp. 454–5.

56 Motzki et al., *Analysing Muslim Traditions*, p. 44.

57 I arrived at this conclusion independently from Motzki. After finishing this chapter, I came across Motzki's comments on this issue, which concur with my findings, and then revised this chapter.

58 Motzki, based on the report in Mālik's *Muwaṭṭa'* and 'Abd al-Razzāq's *Muṣannaf*, cites the opinion of Ibn al-Musayyab that he 'disapproved of the suckling of adults and denied that it had any legal consequences'. However, this report seems to be contradicting them.

Despite that, the verifiable evidence that the number of breastfeedings to render a person unlawful to marry diverges to five, seven and ten, suggesting that there was an ongoing debate on the matter. Consequently, it is highly unlikely that there was a revealed verse of the Qur'an which explicitly stated that the required numbers were five or ten. There seems to be confusion due to the conflicting legal views on the matter, which may stem from confusion on whether the Qur'an included a verse on it or not, or that legal scholars felt a need to attribute their views to the Qur'an. The second possibility might further reinforce John Burton's views on the wide use of the notion of abrogation by Islamic legal schools to substantiate their positions on legal matters.

The text of the tenth variant is lengthy but contains a similar yet discernibly paraphrased version of the eight variant which was studied in the 'Urwa b. al-Zubayr cluster. Both variants contain the shared elements, which are nine in total:

1. The connection between Zayd's adoption by the Prophet and Abū Ḥudhayfa's adoption of Sālim.
2. Abū Ḥudhayfa married Sālim with his niece Hind bint al-Walīd.
3. Background information about pre-Islamic traditions indicating that foster children enjoyed the same rights and privileges as biological children.
4. The inclusion of Q. 33:5.
5. Sahla bint Suhayl's plea for a solution to the Prophet.
6. The Prophet's advice for Sahla bint Suhayl to indirectly breastfeed Sālim (while in variant eight, the Prophet explicitly instructs Sahla bint Suhayl to breastfeed Sālim five times to make him unlawful to marry. In the tenth variant, however, the Prophet utters 'breastfeed him' and then she breastfeeds him five times).
7. Sahla bint Suhayl's compliance with the Prophet's instructions.
8. 'Ā'isha taking this episode as precedence for rendering men unlawful to marry.
9. The other widows of the Prophet, including Umm Salama, objected to 'Ā'isha's legal opinion.

Despite containing all the textual elements, both textual variants are heavily paraphrased, which perhaps took place after Zuhrī. Some of the differences include that in the eighth variant, the Prophet explicitly instructed Sahla bint Suhayl to breastfeed Sālim five times to make him unlawful to marry, whereas in the tenth variant, the Prophet utters 'breastfeed him'. She then breastfeeds him five times. Additionally, there is no mention of the term 'unlawful to marry' (*maḥram*) in the tenth variant. Instead, it states 'give him milk'. She gave him milk five times, and he became like her foster son.

Also, in the eighth and tenth variants, the widows of the Prophet clearly objected to 'Ā'isha's legal opinion. They refused to meet any man in this way, and the tenth variant stated that they only allowed this to happen if the person was an infant at the time of breastfeeding. However, in the eighth variant, the objection of the widows is more vocal. In contrast, in the tenth variant, they object to the idea of making a grown man unlawful to marry through breastfeeding because the Prophet granted an exception to Sahla bint Suhayl alone. Therefore it cannot serve as a precedent. In other words, the point of dispute was not about rendering a male unlawful to marry when he was breastfed while a minor but rendering an adult male unlawful to marry by means of indirect breastfeeding. Finally, the eighth variant does not have a specific reference to Umm Salama. Instead, it states 'the rest of the wives of the Prophet refused'. On the other hand, the tenth variant specifically mentions Umm Salama's name: 'But, Umm Salama and the rest of the wives of the Prophet refused.'

Motzki analysed this group of reports on breastfeeding narrated through 'Urwa and made an important discovery. In his study of these variants, Motzki noticed that the report consists of four independent stories: (1) The story about Abū Ḥudayfa and his adopted son Sālim, (2) the conversation between Sahla and the Prophet, (3) 'Ā'isha's legal opinion and practice and (4) the legal opinion and practice of the widows of the Prophet including Umm Salama.

Motzki found that these four separate stories are skilfully weaved into one story. He argued that Zuhrī is responsible for combining them.[59] It is not certain what section of the report was transmitted through the chain provided, but because there are other clusters to compare it with, it is possible to reconstruct what was narrated from 'Ā'isha. Upon the study of both sections of the 'Urwa b. al-Zubayr cluster, it becomes clear that there is convincing evidence of a genuine transmission process supported by textual congruity. Therefore, the common elements in these variants can be dated back to 'Urwa b. al-Zubayr's date of death, which was 94/712–13.

The 'Amra Cluster

Chain of Transmission Analysis

A group of variants transmitted through the PCL 'Amra bint 'Abd al-Raḥmān (d. circa 98/716–17 or 106/724–5) will be studied in this section. Like the eighth variant, the eleventh variant was recorded in Mālik's *Muwaṭṭa'* through Yaḥyā [b. Yaḥyā al-Laythī].[60] Mālik (d. 179/795) received

59 Motzki et al., *Analysing Muslim Traditions*, p. 43.
60 Mālik, *Muwaṭṭa'*, vol. 1, p. 456.

it from 'Abdullāh b. Abī Bakr b. Ḥazm (d. 135/752–3) of Medina, who was known as Abū Bakr al-Madanī.[61] He received the variant from his paternal aunt 'Amra bint 'Abd al-Raḥmān (d. 103/721–2 or 108/726–7), one of the prominent early female scholars of Islam. 'Amra spent a considerable time with 'Ā'isha and reported many traditions from her.[62] She reported this variant from 'Ā'isha as well.

The twelfth variant was recorded in 'Abd al-Razzāq's (d. 211/826) *Muṣannaf*,[63] who reports it from (Sufyān) Ibn 'Uyayna (d. 198/813–14), who was active Iraq and the Hijaz. 'Abd al-Razzāq was also active in Yemen, Mecca, Medina, Syria and Iraq. Therefore, there is no issue with the fact that he received the variant from Ibn 'Uyayna. Ibn 'Uyayna received it from Yaḥyā b. Sa'īd (d. 143/760–1). Yaḥyā b. Sa'īd received it from 'Amra, and she again reported it from 'Ā'isha.

The thirteenth variant was recorded in Muslim's (d. 261/875) *Ṣaḥīh*.[64] The rest of the chain is the same as that of the eleventh variant: Yaḥyā b. Yaḥyā ← Mālik ← 'Abdullāh b. Abī Bakr ← 'Amra ← 'Ā'isha. It seems Muslim recorded the variant from Yaḥyā b. Yaḥyā's recension of the *Muwaṭṭa'*. The fourteenth variant was also recorded in Muslim's *Ṣaḥīh*.[65] He received it from 'Abdullāh b. Maslama al-Qa'nabī (d. 221/836–7), who was active in Medina, Mecca and Basra. Al-Qa'nabī received this variant from Sulaymān b. Bilāl (d. 172/788–9 or 177/793–4), who was active in Medina. He received it from Yaḥyā [b. Sa'īd] (d. 143/760–1) of Medina, who received it from 'Amra, who then finally received it from 'Ā'isha.

The fifteenth variant was recorded in Muslim's *Ṣaḥīh*.[66] He received it from Muḥammad b. al-Muthannā (d. 252/866) of Basra,[67] who received it from 'Abd al-Wahhāb (al-Thaqafī) (d. 194/809–10) of Basra.[68] 'Abd al-Wahhāb received it from Yaḥyā b. Sa'īd (d. 143/760–1), and similar to the thirteenth variant, he received it from 'Amra ← 'Ā'isha. The sixteenth variant was recorded in Abū Dāwūd's *Sunan*.[69] He reported it from 'Abdullāh b. Maslama al-Qa'nabī (d. 221/836–7,) who also transmitted the fourteenth

61 al-'Asqalānī, *Tahdhīb al-tahdhīb*, vol. 5, p. 144; al-Dhahabī, *Siyar a'lām al-nubalā'*, vol. 5, p. 314.

62 al-Dhahabī, *Siyar a'lām al-nubalā'*, vol. 4, p. 508; al-Mizzī, *Tahdhīb al-kamāl fī asmā' al-rijāl*, vol. 12, p. 389.

63 al-Ṣan'ānī, *Muṣannaf*, vol. 7, p. 467.

64 Muslim, *Ṣaḥīh*, vol. 2, p. 1075.

65 Muslim, *Ṣaḥīh*, vol. 2, p. 1075.

66 Muslim, *Ṣaḥīh*, vol. 2, p. 1075.

67 Motzki et al., *Analysing Muslim Traditions*, p. 405.

68 al-Dhahabī, *Siyar a'lām al-nubalā'*, vol. 9, pp. 238–9; al-Mizzī, *Tahdhīb al-kamāl fī asmā' al-rijāl*, vol. 18, pp. 503–9.

69 Abū Dāwūd, *Sunan*, vol. 2, pp. 223–4.

variant from Sulaymān b. Bilāl. However, he reported this variant on the authority of Mālik (d. 179/795), who, like the eleventh variant, received it from 'Abdullāh b. Abī Bakr b. Ḥazm (d. 135/752–3) ← 'Amra ← 'Ā'isha.

The seventeenth variant was recorded in Ibn Mājah's (d. 273/887) *Sunan.*[70] He reported the variant from 'Abd al-Wārith b. 'Abd al-Ṣamad b. 'Abd al-Wārith (d. 252/866–7) of Basra, who reported the variant from his father, 'Abd al-Ṣamad b. 'Abd al-Wārith (d. 207/822–3) of Basra.[71] 'Abd al-Ṣamad reported it from Ḥammād b. Salama (d.167/783), who was a client and prominent narrator and grammarian of Basra.[72] He received the variant from 'Abd al-Raḥmān b. al-Qāsim (d. 126/743–4 or 131/748–9)[73] of Medina, and he received it from his father, Qāsim b. Muḥammad b. Abī Bakr (d. between 106/724 and 108/727), a prominent jurist of Medina as well as nephew and student of 'Ā'isha from whom he transmitted many narrations. His father, Muḥammad b. Abī Bakr, was the son of the first caliph, Abū Bakr.[74] He received the variant from 'Amra (d. circa 98/716–17 or 106/724–5).

The eighteenth variant was recorded by Ibn Mājah (d. 273/887),[75] who received it from Abū Salama Yaḥyā b. Khalaf (d. 242/856–7). Abū Salama appears to be based in Basra, and Muslim also received narrations from him.[76] He transmitted it from 'Abd al-A'lā [b. 'Abd al-A'lā b. Muḥammad] (d. 189/805) of Basra. He was known to be trusted but he has been accused of lying.[77] 'Abd al-A'lā received it from the famous historian Muḥammad b. Isḥāq (d. 151/769), who was from Baghdad and also travelled to the Hijaz, Syria and Egypt. Muḥammad b. Isḥāq received it from two different chains: 'Abdullāh b. Abī Bakr b. Ḥazm (d. 135/752–3) ← 'Amra ← 'Ā'isha; and 'Abd al-Raḥmān b. al-Qāsim ← Qāsim b. Muḥammad b. Abī Bakr ← 'Ā'isha.

It is more probable that the wording belongs to the first chain. The nineteenth variant was recorded in Nasā'ī's *Sunan* (d. 303/915),[78] who received it from Hārūn b. 'Abdullāh (d. 243/858) of Baghdad.[79] There appears to be some gap between Nasā'ī and Hārūn b. 'Abdullāh, but Nasā'ī was born in 214/829. Therefore, he was able to receive the variant as a young scholar.

70 Ibn Mājah, *Sunan*, vol. 1, p. 625.
71 al-Dhahabī, *Siyar a'lām al-nubalā'*, vol. 9, p. 517; al-Mizzī, *Tahdhīb al-kamāl fī asmā' al-rijāl*, vol. 18, pp. 99–102.
72 al-Dhahabī, *Siyar a'lām al-nubalā'*, vol. 7, pp. 445–56.
73 'Uṣfūrī, *Kitāb al-ṭabaqāt*, vol. 4, p. 446.
74 al-Dhahabī, *Siyar a'lām al-nubalā'*, vol. 5, pp. 54–9.
75 Ibn Mājah, *Sunan*, pp. 625–6.
76 al-Mizzī, *Tahdhīb al-kamāl fī asmā' al-rijāl*, vol. 31, pp. 292–3; Ibn Khalaf, *al-'Ulūm bi-shuyūkh al-Bukhārī wa-Muslim*, vol. 1, pp. 572–3.
77 al-Dhahabī, *Siyar a'lām al-nubalā'*, vol. 9, p. 243.
78 Nasā'ī, *Sunan*, vol. 1, p. 625.
79 al-Dhahabī, *Siyar a'lām al-nubalā'*, vol. 12, pp. 115–16.

He received the variant from Ma'na (d. 198/814), who was a resident of Medina and a prominent student of Mālik. He also received this variant from Mālik (d. 179/795) and Ḥārith b. Miskīn. Mālik received it from 'Abdullāh b. Abī Bakr (d. 135/752–3) ← 'Amra ← 'Ā'isha. The twentieth variant is recorded in Muslim's *Ṣaḥīḥ*,[80] and he received it from Yaḥyā b. Yaḥyā's recension of the *Muwaṭṭa'*.

The chain of transmission of the twenty-first variant was recorded in Muslim's *Ṣaḥīḥ*.[81] The chain of transmission is identical to the fourteenth variant recorded in Muslim's *Ṣaḥīḥ*: 'Abdullāh b. Maslama al-Qa'nabī ← Sulaymān b. Bilāl ← Yaḥyā b. Sa'īd ← 'Amra ← 'Ā'isha. The twenty-second variant's chain of transmission is again recorded in Muslim's *Ṣaḥīḥ*,[82] along with a duplication of the fifteenth variant recorded in Muslim's *Ṣaḥīḥ*: Muḥammad b. al-Muthannā ← 'Abd al-Wahhāb ← Yaḥyā b. Sa'īd ← 'Amra ← 'Ā'isha. Upon studying the chain of transmission of the twelve variants – two of which are duplicates – I can state that the 'Amra bint 'Abd al-Raḥmān cluster can be traced back to 'Ā'isha. The variants originated in Medina and spread mostly to Iraq and Syria.

Textual Analysis

The text of the eleventh variant is short and consists of three sentences:

> It was among what was sent down in the Qur'an that ten clear breastfeeding renders [one] unlawful [to marry]. It was later abrogated with the five clear [breastfeedings]. When the Messenger of God passed away, it was recited in the Qur'an.

These three short sentences inform us about a verse of the Qur'an that included the ruling 'ten clear breastfeeding renders unlawful [to marry]'. However, the number of necessary breastfeeding to render a person unlawful to marry was abrogated and replaced by five breastfeedings. When the Prophet Muhammad died, the Muslims still recited this verse. Finally, it implies that it eventually did not make it to the Qur'anic codex, therefore indicating the distortion of the Qur'an.

Mālik's Redaction of the Narrative

The text of this report is curious, and it appears to support the earlier finding that the third variant of the Nāfi' cluster consists of two separate

80 Muslim, *Ṣaḥīḥ*, vol. 2, p. 1075.
81 Muslim, *Ṣaḥīḥ*, vol. 2, p. 1075.
82 Muslim, *Ṣaḥīḥ*, vol. 2, p. 1075.

reports, because this particular report is strikingly similar to the second section of the Nāfiʿ report.

Transmitted by Nāfiʿ: They claimed that 'Ā'isha said: 'The Book of God Almighty and Glorified used to have ten breastfeedings. It was then **changed** to five. However, the number of [five] breastfeedings went away with [the death of] the Prophet from the Book of God.'[83]	Transmitted by Mālik: It was among what was sent down in the Qur'an that ten clear breastfeedings render unlawful [to marry]. It was later **abrogated** with the five **clear** [breastfeedings]. When the Messenger of God passed away, it was recited in the Qur'an.

The fact that the third variant of the Nāfiʿ cluster does not include legal jargon such as 'abrogated' (*nusikha*) or 'clear' (*maʿlūmātin*) suggests that Mālik redacted these elements in accordance with his legal views and most probably adopted the number of required breastfeedings which are mentioned in this report and the other reports that he narrated. This is because Mālik was a student of Nāfiʿ, yet Nāfiʿ, in his narration of this report, does not mention these elements. It is unclear who Nāfiʿ's source was, but given that these elements were only mentioned in the 'Amra clusters, it is probable that Nāfiʿ also received this report from 'Amra but did not think of it as genuine. Therefore, he did not even bother mentioning the chain to give it legitimacy; he rather provided it as an unreliable anecdote.

The text of the twelfth variant is even shorter than the eleventh variant. It includes only the first two elements, namely, the revelation of the ten breastfeedings and then its abrogation by five breastfeedings to render a person unlawful to marry. There are signs of major paraphrasing in both texts. Despite the shortness of the texts, the major linguistic differences can be explained by the differing transmission line after 'Amra. The text of the thirteenth variant is very similar to the eleventh variant and the identical chain of narration up to Yaḥyā b. Yaḥyā may explain this similarity. The eleventh variant was recorded in Yaḥyā b. Yaḥyā's recension of the *Muwaṭṭa'*, thus it ends with him. However, the thirteenth variant was recorded in Muslim's *Ṣaḥīh* who seems to have copied it from Yaḥyā b. Yaḥyā's recension of the *Muwaṭṭa'*. Due to the identical nature of the chains of transmission and texts, it is impossible to extract additional historical information from this text.

83 al-Ṣanʿānī, *Muṣannaf*, vol. 7, p. 466.

Similar to the text of the twelfth variant, the text of the fourteenth variant includes two common elements: the revelation of the ten breastfeedings in the Qur'an and then the revelation of five breastfeedings. Even in such concise details, there are clear linguistic differences. In the fourteenth variant, there is no mention of the word '*ṣirna*' or 'became' which states that the initial ten breastfeedings became five breastfeedings. The fourteenth variant states, 'There was revealed in the Qur'an ten clear breastfeedings which rendered one unlawful to marry, then it was abrogated by five clear breastfeedings which rendered one unlawful to marry.' Furthermore, almost every word of the two texts has been paraphrased, yet they contain textual affinity by way of including the two common elements.

The fifteenth variant does not have a text. Like the fourteenth variant, it was recorded in Muslim's *Ṣaḥīh*, and the fifteenth variant's text notes that "Amra heard 'Ā'isha saying the same', thus indicating that both texts are similar. I suspect this text contained the two elements alone. Therefore, Muslim considered them to be one and did not include this text separately, but this remains unclear. Similar to the eleventh and thirteenth variants, the text of the sixteenth variant was reported through Mālik and contained all three elements. This text is recorded in Abū Dāwūd's *Sunan*, and 'Abdullāh b. Maslama al-Qa'nabī reported it to Abū Dāwūd from Mālik, and there are slight signs of paraphrasing. This may be justified by the fact that al-Qa'nabī heard it from Mālik directly.

The text of the seventeenth variant was recorded in Ibn Mājah's *Sunan* and transmitted through 'Abdullāh b. Abū Bakr. This variant includes two elements, meaning it does not mention that the breastfeeding verses were recited after the death of the Prophet. Furthermore, this text was heavily paraphrased. Unlike the other variants, it does not mention in the opening sentence whether the required number of breastfeedings was five or ten. Instead, it opens with 'God had revealed this [verse] in the Qur'an, but then it fell away (*saqaṭa*)'. It then states: 'It does not render it unlawful to marry except for ten breastfeedings or five clear [breastfeedings].' There is an important linguistic distinction in the variants of the tradition to refer to the removal or the change of the verse about the number of breastfeedings. For example, the variant at hand uses the phrase 'it fell away' (*saqaṭa*) to state that the verse was removed from the Qur'an.

However, in the eleventh, thirteenth and sixteenth variants, there is the explicit use of the word 'abrogated' (*nusikha*). The twelfth variant uses the word 'became' ('became (*ṣirna*) five [breastfeeding]'). The third variant used the word 'changed' (*rudda*). These linguistic differences provide the impression of a genuine oral transmission because there is a clear corroboration between the transmission lines and the linguistic differences. The common figure who transmits the reports with the wording of abrogation or *naskh* is Mālik. The word 'abrogation' was also used in the nineteenth and twentieth reports, likewise transmitted by Mālik. Most importantly, the word 'abrogation' is only used in the texts which Mālik transmitted. This finding leads to the conclusion that Mālik redacted the texts of these variants to change the original word. The original report might have been *saqaṭa*, *ṣirna* or *rudda*. This was in accordance with Mālik's linguistic and legal, or even theological, views. He seemed to try to make sense of the report and justified it with the concept of abrogation. This was then picked up by his student Shāfiʿī and heavily used in his legal theory.

Domestic Sheep Eating the Qur'anic Folio

The eighteenth text was also recorded in Ibn Mājah's *Sunan* and contained the most controversial text among the variants:

> The Verses of Stoning and Breastfeeding of an adult ten times had been revealed. The folios [upon which the verses were written] were kept under my bed. When the Messenger of God died, we were occupied with his death. So, a tame sheep entered [into the room] and ate it.[84]

In addition to the Breastfeeding Verse, this tradition also includes the Stoning Verse. However, the Stoning Verse element is not included in any other variants. It was interpolated into the text during the transmission process. Initially, it may seem that Muḥammad b. Isḥāq was the culprit for this interpolation; because he transmitted this chain alone, and as a hadith collector, he most probably was aware of the reports of the Stoning Verse and redacted the text to provide further information. Nevertheless, Muḥammad b. Isḥāq's involvement is not certain.

According to the text, 'Ā'isha provided further details about the fate of the folios in which the verse of breastfeeding was recorded and the exact time when it was lost. It appears that the folios were kept under 'Ā'isha's bed, and they were eaten by a domestic sheep when she was occupied with the burial of the Prophet. Because this information was included only in this variant, it was interpolated in the text and not part of the original narration. Furthermore, there is no historical information that the Prophet kept written folios under his bed. The official scribes of the Prophet recorded the Qur'an, and they kept their recordings in their possession. In addition, many Muslims memorised the verses of the Qur'an. 'Ā'isha was never involved in this process. Therefore, it is unlikely for her to have had preserved the folios under her bed.

84 Ibn Mājah, *Sunan*, vol. 1, pp. 625–6.

Finally, no other variant includes such information and there are no apparent problems with the chain of transmission. Therefore, it is almost certain that one of Ibn Mājah's informants, either Abū Salama or ʿAbd al-Aʿlā, heavily tampered with the variant. The accusation of lying directed at ʿAbd al-Aʿlā could imply his involvement as the culprit. Nevertheless, either of them could have interpolated the information about the Stoning Verse in the variant, rather than Ibn Isḥāq. We know that it cannot be Ibn Mājah because he recorded the other variants which do not contain this information. Be that as it may, the element that the Qur'anic folios were kept under ʿĀ'isha's bed and that they were eaten by a domestic sheep could only be dated back to Ibn Mājah's date of death with certainty, which was 273/887.

The nineteenth variant includes all three elements. At this point, it becomes clear that the ʿAmra cluster was transmitted through two main lines: Yaḥyā b. Saʿīd and Qāsim b. Muḥammad b. Abī Bakr. The line that goes through Yaḥyā b. Saʿīd only contains the information that there was a verse of five breastfeedings which was then replaced by the verse of ten breastfeedings. On the other hand, the line that goes through Qāsim b. Muḥammad b. Abī Bakr, in addition to these two elements, includes the element that this verse was still being recited as a part of the Qur'an when the Prophet died. Therefore, this additional element could only be dated back to Qāsim b. Muḥammad b. Abī Bakr's date of death, which was between 106/724 and 108/727. The texts of the remaining three variants, the twentieth, twenty-first and twenty-second, also show these characteristics.

Bringing our study of the ʿAmra cluster to an end, it can be concluded that among twelve variants, only one variant mentions the alleged eating of the Qur'anic folio by a domestic animal in which the Breastfeeding and Stoning Verses were written. Since these elements were not included in other variants, it is clear that this resulted from a forgery carried out by either Abū Salama or ʿAbd al-Aʿlā. Additionally, the removal of the five breastfeedings followed by ten, from the Qur'an, could be dated back to ʿAmra's date of death, which is circa 98/716–17 or 106/724–5. All the variants of ʿAmra's clusters contain this information, but because no other cluster includes it, it cannot be dated back to ʿĀ'isha. A variant in the Nāfiʿ cluster contains this element, but Nāfiʿ expressed his doubt about it. Furthermore, the chain of transmission was not given as the variant is a combination of two separate reports. It was also clear that Mālik redacted the text of the report to interpolate the word 'abrogation' into the text. However, the element that by the time the Prophet died these verses were recited as a part of the Qur'an can be dated back to Qāsim b. Muḥammad b. Abī Bakr's date of death, which was between 106/724 and 108/727.

The Qāsim Cluster

Chain of Transmission Analysis

The twenty-third variant was recorded in Ibn Mājah's *Sunan*,[85] who reported it from Hishām b. 'Ammār (d. 245/859) of Damascus, a prominent scholar of his time.[86] Hishām b. 'Ammār received it from Sufyān b. 'Uyayna (d. 198/813–14), who was active in Iraq and the Hijaz. Hishām b. 'Ammār probably received this variant when he visited the Hijaz for pilgrimage. Sufyān b. 'Uyayna received it from 'Abd al-Raḥmān b. al-Qāsim (d. 126/743–4 or 131/748–9)[87] and he heard it from his father, Qāsim b. Muḥammad b. Abī Bakr. A considerable difference from the 'Amra cluster is that Qāsim b. Muḥammad b. Abī Bakr received it directly from 'Ā'isha instead of 'Amra. This is possible, since Qāsim b. Muḥammad b. Abī Bakr was 'Ā'isha's nephew and student.

The twenty-fourth chain was recorded in Muslim's *Ṣaḥīh*[88] from 'Amr al-Nāqid (d. 232/842) of Raqqa[89] and Ibn Abī 'Umar (d. 243/858) of Mecca,[90] both of whom received it from Sufyān b. 'Uyayna (d. 198/813–14). After this point, similar to the previous chain of transmission, Sufyān received it from 'Abd al-Raḥmān b. al-Qāsim ← Qāsim b. Muḥammad b. Abī Bakr ← 'Ā'isha. The twenty-fifth variant reported in Muslim's (d. 261/875) *Ṣaḥīh* was received from both Isḥāq b. Ibrāhīm al-Ḥanẓalī and Muḥammad b. Abī 'Umar.[91] Isḥāq b. Ibrāhīm al-Ḥanẓalī, also known as Isḥāq b. Rāhwayh (d. 238/ 852–53), was a resident of Khorasan and one of the greatest jurists of his time. He was also a friend and classmate of Ibn Ḥanbal.[92] Muḥammad b. Abī 'Umar (d. 243/858) was from Mecca.[93] The two of them received it from 'Abd al-Wahhāb al-Thaqafī (d. 194/809–10), who was a prominent hadith scholar in Basra.[94] He received it from Ayyūb al-Sakhtiyānī (d. 131/748), also a reliable and pious scholar of Basra.[95] Ayyūb received it from Ibn Abī Mulayka (d. 117/735–6), a respected resident of Mecca who received it from Qāsim b. Muḥammad (d. 101/719 or 112/731). The fourth caliph and first Shi'i Imam, 'Alī, adopted Qāsim as his son, and he became

85 Ibn Mājah, *Sunan*, vol. 1, pp. 625–6.
86 al-Dhahabī, *Siyar a'lām al-nubalā'*, vol. 11, pp. 421–35.
87 'Uṣfūrī, *Kitāb al-ṭabaqāt*, vol. 4, p. 446.
88 Muslim, *Ṣaḥīh*, vol. 2, p. 1076.
89 al-Dhahabī, *Siyar a'lām al-nubalā'*, vol. 11, pp. 147–8.
90 al-Dhahabī, *Siyar a'lām al-nubalā'*, vol. 12, pp. 97–8.
91 Muslim, *Ṣaḥīh*, vol. 2, p. 1076.
92 al-Dhahabī, *Siyar a'lām al-nubalā'*, vol. 11, pp. 359–71.
93 al-Dhahabī, *Siyar a'lām al-nubalā'*, vol. 12, pp. 97–8.
94 al-Dhahabī, *Siyar a'lām al-nubalā'*, vol. 9, pp. 208–40.
95 al-Dhahabī, *Siyar a'lām al-nubalā'*, pp. 6–26.

a prominent Shi'i figure,[96] who was also well regarded by Sunni scholars. He was one of the most prominent jurists of Medina, and he transmitted reports from his aunt 'Ā'isha.[97] The connection between 'Ā'isha and Qāsim remains irrefutable. The variants emerged in Medina, and then travelled to Mecca and Khorasan.

Finally, the twenty-sixth variant was recorded in Muslim's (d. 261/874–5) *Ṣaḥīh*.[98] He received the report from both Isḥāq b. Ibrāhīm and Muḥammad b. Rāfi', but Muslim notes that he recorded the utterance of Muḥammad b. Rāfi' (d. 245/860). He was a prominent hadith collector, client and contemporary of Aḥmad b. Ḥanbal and 'Abd al-Razzāq.[99] He was active in Nishapur and Khorasan but travelled to the Hijaz and Kufa in the pursuit of knowledge and hadith. He spent time together with 'Abd al-Razzāq, possibly in Kufa, and transmitted this report from 'Abd al-Razzāq (d. 211/827). 'Abd al-Razzāq reported five variants of this report but did not record this chain in his *Muṣannaf*. Instead, he recorded similar chains, such as the report he received from Ibn Jurayj (d. 150/767–8), but Ibn Jurayj's informant in this variant was different, as it was Ibn Abī Mulayka. In the variant that he recorded in his book, however, he reports it from Nāfi'. It is curious that 'Abd al-Razzāq did not record this variant in his book. There may have been various reasons for this, but it is difficult to speculate. There is an anecdote in the text of the variant that notes Ibn Abī Mulayka's hesitation in narrating this variant:

> Ibn Abī Mulayka said: 'I refrained from [reporting this narration] for a year or so as I was fearful. I then met Qāsim and told him: "you have narrated a narration to me, but I have not narrated it afterwards." He said: "what is that I narrated to you?"' Ibn Abī Mulayka said [which narration it was]. Qāsim then told him: 'Narrate it on my authority from 'Ā'isha.'

It may have been that the note included in the variant stopped 'Abd al-Razzāq from recording it in his *Muṣannaf*; however, this is impossible to ascertain. In any case, Ibn Abī Mulayka received it from Qāsim b. Muḥammad and Qāsim from his aunt 'Ā'isha. There seems to be no problem tracing these reports back to 'Ā'isha. The only minor issue is that 'Abd al-Razzāq did not record this variant in his *Muṣannaf*. Nevertheless, he did record five other variants of this report, and the following textual analysis of the variants may provide further information.

96 al-Khoei, *Mu'jam rijāl al-ḥadīth*, vol. 15, p. 49.
97 al-Dhahabī, *Siyar a'lām al-nubalā'*, vol. 5, pp. 54–60.
98 Muslim, *Ṣaḥīh*, vol. 2, p. 1076.
99 al-Dhahabī, *Siyar a'lām al-nubalā'*, vol. 12, pp. 215–18.

Textual Analysis

There are four texts under the Ibn Abī Mulayka cluster. There is no doubt that these variants are slightly paraphrased versions of the same report, especially as it relates to the twenty-third and twenty-fourth reports, which are verbatim. There is an exception in the twenty-fourth variant, where the word 'displeasure' (*al-karāhiyya*) was omitted. This was probably a result of an editorial mishap because the rest of the sentence is intact, and it is the same as the twenty-third variant, meaning it was not transmitted orally, but rather when the volume was copied. Furthermore, the last sentence of the twenty-fourth variant is missing: 'She did it and came to the Messenger of God and said: "I have never seen any signs of displeasure on the face of Abū Ḥudhayfa after this and he was then present at [the Battle of] Badr."' Instead, it included the information that, "Amr added to this narration that [Abū Ḥudhayfa] participated in the Battle of Badr. Ibn Abī 'Umar, in his narration [reported that]: the Messenger of God laughed [instead of smiled].'

It becomes clear that 'Amr al-Nāqid narrated the element of Abū Ḥudhayfa's participation in the Battle of Badr. However, Ibn Abī 'Umar, who also narrated the same variant to Muslim, had likewise mentioned this piece of information. Additionally, in his narration, Ibn Abī 'Umar mentioned that the Prophet laughed instead of smiling. The almost identical nature of the two texts can be explained by the fact that these two variants were transmitted through Qāsim's son, 'Abd al-Raḥmān. However, the remaining two variants in the Qāsim cluster were transmitted through Ibn Abī Mulayka, and they are distinctly different from the variants transmitted through 'Abd al-Raḥmān b. al-Qāsim. These two variants, the twenty-fifth and twenty-sixth, have similar elements, including the central point that Sahla bint Suhayl came to the Prophet and explained their problem in relation to Sālim. But this explanation also contained two separate elements: (1) Sālim has just reached the age of puberty; and (2) he had become aware of himself, meaning he had already reached the age of puberty.

These two elements can only be found in these two variants, because of their point of connection, which is Ibn Abī Mulayka. With a certain degree of confidence, it is possible to conclude that Ibn Abī Mulayka interpolated these elements into the text as an explanatory gloss. Since it was obvious that Sālim was an adult at the time of the event, as it was also mentioned in the variants of the 'Urwa cluster, he did what redactors usually do and gave context to better convey the text's meaning to the audience.

The second common element is that the Prophet suggested that she breastfeed Sālim to resolve the issue (*arḍi'īhi taḥrumī 'alayhi*). This part of the narration is the same in both texts. The twenty-sixth variant ends with this information and provides an anecdote about Ibn Abī Mulayka's hesitation to transmit this report. On the other hand, the twenty-fifth variant provided some details and embellishments which are in accordance with the transmission line since the two variants reach Muslim in two different lines after Ibn Abī Mulayka. These are signs of a healthy and natural oral transmission for this group of variants. Compared to the other groups, all the variants include the information that Sālim was an adult and had thus reached the age of puberty. Other common elements make it possible to date these elements back to Qāsim, such as when Sahla bint Suhayl came to the Prophet and explained their problem in relation to Sālim, the Prophet suggested for her to breastfeed him. Qāsim's date of death is 101/719 or 112/731. Because these elements were also included it in the other variants, they can be dated back to 'Ā'isha's date of death, which is 58/678. In light of the 'Urwa, Zaynab and Nāfiʿ clusters, which all affirm the event, this event could even be dated back to the Prophet's lifetime.

There is a correlation between the transmission process and the textual development of the variants. Certain points of information are added to the text as an explanatory gloss, which was most probably related to the judgement of the transmitters who wanted the audience to make more sense of the report that they transmitted. At this point, there is no need to scrutinise the text further. The necessary information has been extracted from the textual variants and the final analysis will be given below.

Summary and Conclusion

In studying the variants in the Nāfiʿ cluster, there were no problems with the chains of transmission. The report emerged from Medina and travelled to Mecca and Iraq without interruption. The textual analysis signified that the third text contained the most pertinent information about the distortion of the Qur'an, suggesting that 'the number of breastfeedings has gone with [the death of] the Prophet from the Book of God'.[100] This element was only included in the third variant. As it was not included in the previous two variants of the cluster, it cannot be dated back to Nāfiʿ. Despite that, some other common elements could be dated back to Nāfiʿ's date of death. One of these elements was that 'Ā'isha wanted to meet Sālim privately. To do so, she wanted to make him unlawful to marry by asking her sister Umm Kulthūm to breastfeed him; however, the process was interrupted and this fell short of the required ten breastfeedings.

The study of the Zaynab cluster provided the information that the chain of transmission of these reports could be dated back to Zaynab bint Umm Salama without any problem. They originated from Medina and travelled

100 al-Ṣanʿānī, *Muṣannaf*, vol. 7, p. 466.

to Basra and Egypt through various transmitters. Textual analysis specified the presence of variants reflecting a legal dispute between 'Ā'isha and Umm Salama. This debate centred on whether the Prophet's permission for Sahla bint Suhayl to breastfeed Sālim established a legal precedent for allowing the breastfeeding of adult males (without physical contact), thereby rendering them ineligible for marriage. The study of the textual variants revealed three common elements:

- There was a disagreement between 'Ā'isha and the other widows of the Prophet led by Umm Salama about breastfeeding adults.
- Umm Salama and the other widows of the Prophet interpreted the verdict of the Prophet differently from 'Ā'isha.
- 'Ā'isha and the other widows of the Prophet acknowledged the event in which the Prophet advised Sahla to breastfeed Sālim.

These elements can be safely dated back to Zaynab bint Abī Salama's date of death, which was around 74/693–4.

The group of variants in the 'Urwa cluster emerged from Medina and spread to Iraq and Egypt. The chain of narrations did not have any major problems and all three variants could be dated back to 'Ā'isha. The textual analysis of the 'Urwa b. Zubayr cluster revealed that three common elements mentioned above existed in the 'Urwa, Zaynab and Nāfi' clusters. Therefore, the three common elements could be dated back to 'Ā'isha's date of death. It is also probable to date the third element to the Prophet, because 'Ā'isha and Umm Salama had access to the Prophet, and most probably witnessed the event.

However, the texts of the reports also present some discord between them, such as the number of required breastfeedings. The texts of the eighth variant in the 'Urwa cluster mentioned the number of the required breastfeedings to make a person unlawful to marry for the first time. In the texts of the previous variants the Prophet only uttered 'give him milk' without mentioning any specific number. Only in one of the texts in the Nāfi' clusters is the element of five breastfeedings mentioned as 'the missing verses', rather than as the utterance of the Prophet.

I then concluded that, in light of the verifiable evidence, the number of required breastfeedings to make a person unlawful to marry fluctuates between five, seven or ten, as per the different variants. This suggests that there was an ongoing debate on the matter. The early Muslims had differing views on the number of breastfeedings to make a person unlawful to marry. Therefore, it is highly unlikely that there was a revealed Qur'anic verse explicitly stating the required numbers. The misunderstanding probably emerged due to conflicting legal views on the matter, which may stem from the confusion that the Qur'an included a verse on the matter, or that legal scholars felt the need to attribute their views to the Qur'an. The second possibility may seem to reinforce John Burton's view on using the notion of abrogation by Islamic legal schools to substantiate their positions on legal matters. But given that, so far, only one variant contained the element of abrogation, it seems that such interferences were exceptions rather than the norm.

A group of variants spread by ʿAmra were also free of defects in their chains of transmission. They spread from Medina to Iraq and Syria and they can be traced back to ʿĀ'isha. The textual analysis noted the similarity between the eighth variant of the Nāfiʿ cluster and the ʿAmra cluster transmitted by Mālik. The textual study discovered Mālik's proclivity to redact the prophetic report in accordance with his legal view on abrogation. In the eleventh, thirteenth and sixteenth variants, all of which Mālik transmitted, there was an explicit preference for the word 'abrogated' (*nusikha*). The twelfth variant, not transmitted by Mālik, used the word 'became' (*ṣirna*), and the third variant, again not transmitted by Mālik, used the word 'changed' (*rudda*). The word abrogation was also used in the nineteenth and twentieth reports, which Mālik likewise transmitted. This offers a conclusion that Mālik redacted the texts of these variants in accordance with his linguistic, legal and even theological views.[101] This was then picked up by his student Shāfiʿī and heavily adopted in his legal theory. Hence, it is safe to conclude that Mālik utilised abrogation as a legal concept before Shāfiʿī, and it is likely that Shāfiʿī adopted it from Mālik and then formulated and extensively employed it.

The eighteenth variant of the ʿAmra clusters included the element of the Stoning Verse together with the Breastfeeding Verse. According to the variant, the folios that included both verses were eaten by a tame sheep after the death of the Prophet. However, because this element did not exist in the other variants, it could only be dated back to Ibn Mājah's date of death, which was 273/887. During the study of the nineteenth variant, it became clear that the ʿAmra cluster was transmitted through two main lines: Yaḥyā b. Saʿīd and Qāsim b. Muḥammad b. Abī Bakr. The line that went through

101 A familiar situation to what Erhman described in the Christian context: 'And they were copied by warm-blooded scribes who were intimately familiar with the debates over doctrine that made their scribal labors a desideratum. It was within this milieu of controversy that scribes sometimes changed their scriptural texts to make them say what they were already known to *mean*. In the technical parlance of textual criticism – which I retain for its significant ironies – these scribes "corrupted" their texts for theological reasons.' Ehrman, *The Orthodox Corruption of Scripture*, xxi. As per John S. Kloppenborg's explanation in his lectures at University of Toronto, these interventions in the text are not meant to deceive or manipulate, but rather to make the text more relatable to the audience, particularly within the context of redaction of the Gospels. I believe the motivation was the same in Muslim hadith transmission and recording tradition.

Yaḥyā b. Sa‘īd only contained the information that there was a verse of five breastfeedings which was then replaced by the verse of ten breastfeedings.

On the other hand, the line that went through Qāsim b. Muḥammad b. Abī Bakr, in addition to these two elements, included the element that this verse was still being recited as a part of the Qur’an when the Prophet died. Therefore, this additional element could only be dated back to Qāsim b. Muḥammad’s date of death, which was between 106/724 and 108/727.

The chain of reports from the Qāsim cluster were transmitted uninterruptedly. The variants emerged in Medina, then travelled to Mecca, Khorasan and perhaps to Nishapur. The Qāsim cluster focused on the event between the Prophet and Sahla bint Suhayl about breastfeeding Sālim. The analysis found that the twenty-fifth and twenty-sixth variants had the same common elements, including the information that Sahla bint Suhayl came to the Prophet and explained their problem in relation to Sālim.

Other common elements make it possible to date these elements back to the first Qāsim, such as when Sahla bint Suhayl came to the Prophet and explained their problem in relation to Sālim, the Prophet suggested for her to breastfeed him. Because these elements were also included in the other variants, they can be dated back to ‘Ā’isha’s date of death (d. 58/678). In light of the ‘Urwa, Zaynab and Nāfi‘ clusters, which all affirm the event, this event could even be dated back to the Prophet’s lifetime, because all individuals had access to the Prophet and possibly witnessed the event.

PART II

Searching for the Stoning Penalty in ‘the Book of God’

CHAPTER 2

The Litigation of the Two Men according to 'the Book of God'

The topic of the stoning penalty in Muslim reports is vast and has been extensively documented by numerous sources, including reports attributed to the Prophet, Companions and Imams. In my review of Sunni sources, I found a total of 196 variants divided into nine groups that give an account of the stoning penalty during the time of the Prophet and the caliphs 'Umar and 'Alī. These variants are found in various collections of hadith, including Mālik's *Muwaṭṭa'*, 'Abd al-Razzāq al-Ṣan'ānī's *Muṣannaf*, Ibn Abī Shayba's *Muṣannaf*, Bukhārī's *Ṣaḥīḥ*, Muslim's *Ṣaḥīḥ*, Ibn Mājah's *Sunan*, Tirmidhī's *Jāmi'*, Abū Dāwūd's *Sunan*, and Nasā'ī's *Sunan*.

While only two of the nine groups are related to the so-called Stoning Verse, which is the subject of controversy, it is important to study all the accounts of the stoning penalty to understand its overall implementation by the early Muslims. The other seven groups are indirectly related to the stoning penalty and provide valuable insights into how the penalty was understood and practised by the early community. Therefore, it is crucial to examine and analyse all these variants to gain a comprehensive understanding of the stoning penalty in Islamic law, along with its historical context. By doing so, we can gain a deeper appreciation of the development and evolution of Islamic legal thought and practice.

When I reviewed the 196 hadiths regarding Islam and the stoning penalty, I found that 24 of them pertained to a case between two men who came to the Prophet Muhammad to litigate their dispute over an adulterous relationship. The plaintiff's son worked for a brief period of time in the defendant's home as a paid worker. During this period, the son had an affair with the defendant's wife. When the defendant found out about the affair, he informed the plaintiff that the son's punishment was that he must receive the stoning penalty. The plaintiff, however, ransomed his son for a hundred sheep and a slave girl.

After the initial settlement of the dispute, it seems the plaintiff was troubled by the unfavourable outcome and made further enquiries to 'the people of knowledge'. They informed him that the initial settlement was disproportionate and severely unfavourable to the plaintiff. Since his son was unmarried, he did not deserve the stoning penalty. The son's punishment was supposed to be a hundred lashes and exile for a year. They also informed him that the defendant's wife committed adultery as she was the one married. Therefore, her penalty was that she must be stoned.

This case becomes further complicated since, at the beginning of the report, both the defendant and plaintiff urged the Prophet to judge between them according to 'the Book of God', a reference to the Qur'an given the Islamic context. Having listened to the plaintiff, the Prophet confirmed that he would, in fact, judge between them according to the Book of God. He then affirmed the revised ruling, which the plaintiff had also learned from 'the people of knowledge', and thus had the plaintiff's sheep and slave girl returned to him. The Prophet then ruled that the son must receive a hundred lashes and be exiled for a year. As for the adulteress wife, the Prophet ordered Unays al-Aslamī to go to her, and if she confessed, to then stone her. She subsequently confessed to having committed adultery, and Unays al-Aslamī stoned her.

> Mālik b. Anas, on the authority of Ibn Shihāb, 'Ubaydullāh b. 'Abdullāh b. 'Utba b. Mas'ūd, Abū Hurayra and Zayd b. Khālid al-Juhanī, narrates that two men came before the Prophet to settle a dispute. One of the men said: 'O Messenger of God! Judge between us according to the Book of God (*Kitāb Allāh*).' The other man, who was the wiser of the two, said: 'Yes, O Messenger of God! Judge between us according to the Book of God and permit me to speak.' The Prophet said, 'Speak.' The man said, 'This man hired my son, and my son fornicated with his wife. The man [husband] informed me that my son's punishment was stoning. I ransomed my son for a hundred sheep and a slave girl. I then asked the people of knowledge, and they informed me that my son's punishment is a hundred lashes and exile for a year. They also informed me that the punishment for his wife was stoning.' The Messenger of God said: 'By God, in whose hands is my soul, I judge between you according to the Book of God. As for your sheep and slave girl, [they] are to be returned to you. Flog his son a hundred times and exile him for a year.' The Prophet then ordered Unays al-Aslamī to go to the man's wife, [saying that] if she confesses, [to then] stone her. She confessed, and Unays al-Aslamī stoned her.

What may seem to be a purely legal matter turns into one of the most important justifications for distortion of the Qur'an in the Sunni hadith.

Although there is no direct reference in the report to the distortion of the Qur'an, the explicit reference to the Book of God by the plaintiff, defendant and the Prophet gives the impression that there was a ruling in the Qur'an that prescribed a stoning penalty for the adulterers. However, there is no such ruling found in the 'Uthmānic codex. Therefore, proponents of the Qur'an's distortion concluded that the verse containing the relevant ruling must have been expunged from the Qur'an, possibly after the death of the Prophet. Consequently, there is a basis for the idea of the distortion of the Qur'an through the omission of its verses. From such a perspective, the report serves both purposes: a justification for the stoning penalty for adulterers as well as a justification for believing in distortion of the Qur'an.

Out of twenty-four variants, one was mentioned in Mālik's *Muwaṭṭa'*, one in Ibn Abī Shayba's *Muṣannaf*, sixteen in Bukhārī's *Ṣaḥīḥ*, one in Ibn Mājah's *Sunan*, two in Tirmidhī's *Jāmi'*, one in Abū Dāwūd's *Sunan* and two in Muslim's *Ṣaḥīḥ*.

I will proceed with the chain of transmission analysis of the variants. To make the reading more manageable, I will sub-group the variants based on the Partial Common Links (PCLs), or the transmitters who receive the report from an authority and first spread it to more than one transmitter. If a variant is transmitted through a single chain of transmission, I will then include it into the textually most similar sub-group, or evaluate it independently.

An initial observation of the chain of transmission map suggests that although there are twenty-four chains, they are not all original. Rather, ten of them are duplicated, especially the chains of transmission recorded in Bukhārī's *Ṣaḥīḥ*. Although there are sixteen variants given in Bukhārī's *Ṣaḥīḥ*, each chain transmits two texts. Thus, Bukhārī's variants include eight separate chains of transmission. The chains of transmission of the variants go down from the Prophet as a single line through Abū Hurayra and Zayd b. Khālid (al-Shiblī also reports from the Prophet), 'Ubaydullāh b. 'Abdullāh and Zuhrī. From Zuhrī, the chains of transmission fan out into six separate transmission lines, through which they reach the canonical Sunni collections.

Upon initial observation, Ibn Shihāb Zuhrī (d. 124/742), who was one of the most prominent scholars in Medina during the second/eighth century,[1] seems to be the Common Link of the variants. From him, through a single line, the chain of transmission goes back to 'Ubaydullāh b. 'Abdullāh, and from him to Abū Hurayra and then Zayd b. Khālid. However, in three variants, recorded in Ibn Mājah's *Sunan*, Tirmidhī's *Jāmi'* and Ibn Abī Shayba's *Muṣannaf*, al-Shiblī is mentioned alongside Abū Hurayra and Zayd b. Khālid who reported from the Prophet. Furthermore, in two variants

1 Motzki et al., *Analysing Muslim Traditions*, p. 1.

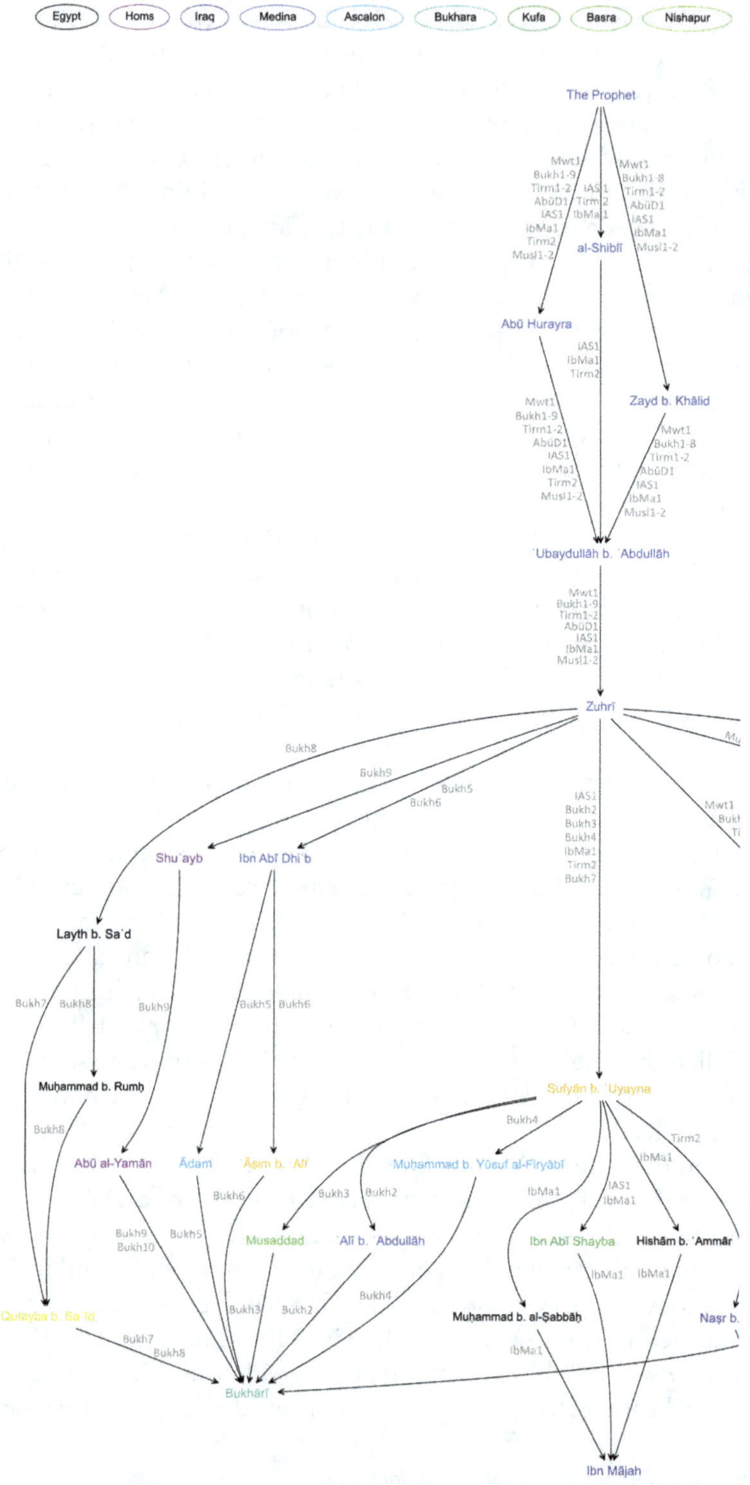

Diagram 2 Available online at: https://edin.ac/3IGr6rI

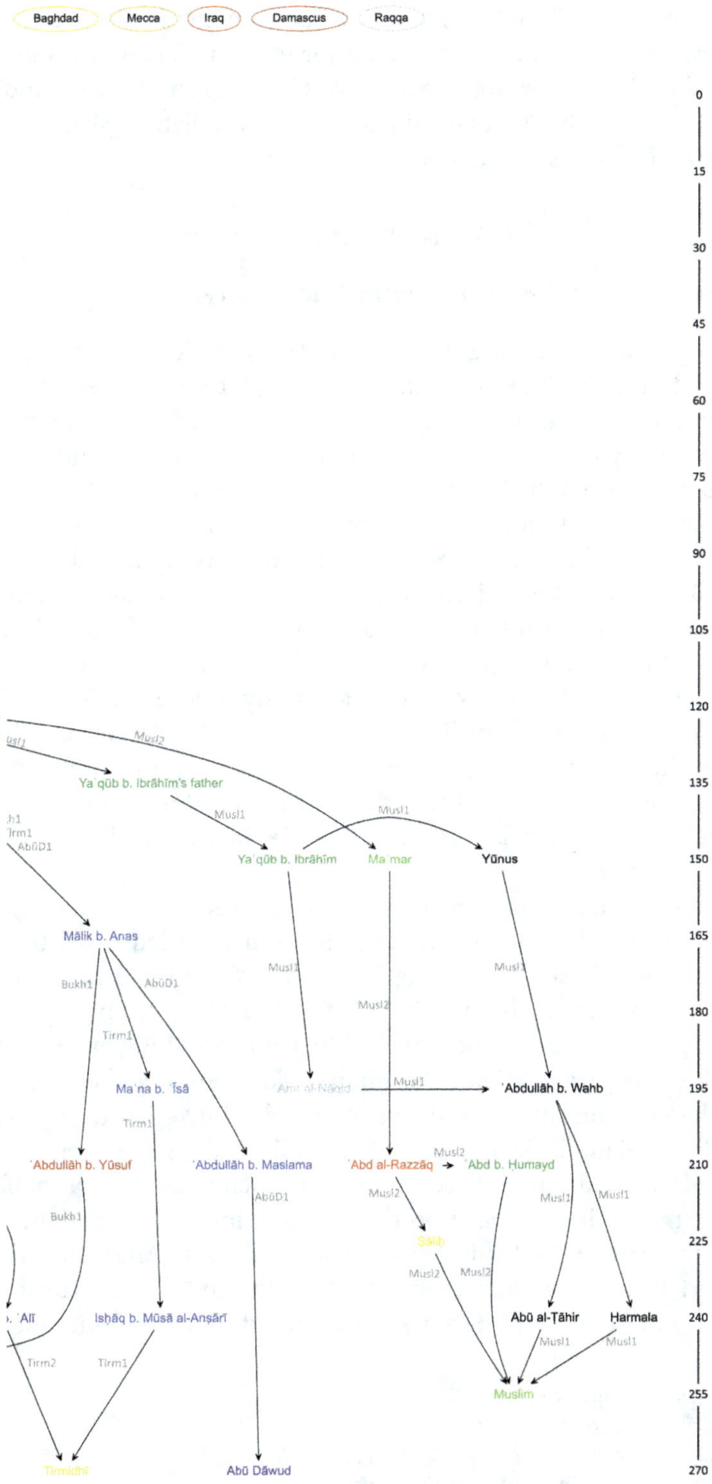
Baghdad
Mecca
Iraq
Damascus
Raqqa
0
15
30
45
60
75
90
105
120
135
150
165
180
195
210
225
240
255
270
Ya'qūb b. Ibrāhīm's father
Ya'qūb b. Ibrāhīm
Ma'mar
Yūnus
Mālik b. Anas
Ma'na b. 'Īsā
'Abdullāh b. Wahb
'Abdullāh b. Yūsuf
'Abdullāh b. Maslama
'Abd al-Razzāq
'Abd b. Ḥumayd
Abū al-Ṭāhir
Ḥarmala
Isḥāq b. Mūsā al-Anṣārī
Muslim
Tirmidhī
Abū Dāwud
Musl1
Musl2
Bukh1
Tirm1
Tirm2
AbūD1

recorded in Bukhārī's *Ṣaḥīḥ*, Zayd b. Khālid's name is omitted and only Abū Hurayra's name was mentioned prior to 'Ubaydullāh b. 'Abdullāh. As illustrated in Diagram 2, Mālik, Sufyān b. 'Uyayna, Ibn Abī Dhi'b and Layth are the PCLs. Lastly, Ma'mar, Shu'ayb and 'Abdullāh b. Wahb transmit single-strand variants of the report.

The Mālik b. Anas Cluster

Chain of Transmission Analysis

I shall begin with analysing the chain of transmission of the first variant mentioned in Mālik b. Anas's *Muwaṭṭa'*.[2] Mālik receives the variant from Zuhrī, whose date of death was 124/742, around a decade before the end of the Umayyad dynasty. Zuhrī was one of the most prolific hadith transmitters, and he received the reports from 'Ubaydullāh b. 'Abdullāh (d. 94/71–213), both of whom received the reports from Abū Hurayra (d. 59/681) and Zayd b. Khālid (d. 68/687–8). Both Abū Hurayra and Zayd were identified as having heard it from the Prophet. 'Ubaydullāh b. 'Abdullāh's grandfather was the brother of 'Abdullāh b. Mas'ūd, the famous Companion of the Prophet. 'Ubaydullāh b. 'Abdullāh was himself a well-known hadith collector and taught Zuhrī for a lengthy time. Therefore, although it may be possible to trace the report back to 'Ubaydullāh b. 'Abdullāh, based on the principles of *isnād-cum-matn* analysis, it is best to date the circulation of this variant to the year 124/742, the aforementioned date of Zuhrī's death. The circulation place was Medina, where both Mālik and Zuhrī were active.

The second chain of transmission is recorded in Bukhārī's *Ṣaḥīḥ*.[3] Bukhārī was an itinerant hadith collector and travelled to all the major centres of the Abbasids: including Syria, Iraq, Yemen and Egypt. He narrated this report from 'Abdullāh b. Yūsuf (d. 217/832–3), a highly regarded scholar from Damascus,[4] who travelled to Tunisia and Egypt. He is known to have reported from Mālik, and Bukhārī later reported from him. He is thus included as one of the reporters of Mālik's *Muwaṭṭa'* and reported this variant from Mālik b. Anas (d. 179/795).[5] Given the shared temporal and geographical proximity between these three scholars, it is probable that they transmitted it from each other. At this point, with confidence, I can identify the first PCL of this report, who is Mālik b. Anas, who received the report from Zuhrī and then reports it to 'Abdullāh b. Yūsuf and at least two other collectors. From Zuhrī, through the same link, the report

2 Ibn Anas, *Muwaṭṭa'*, vol. 5, p. 822.
3 Bukhārī, *Ṣaḥīḥ*, vol. 8, pp. 172–3.
4 al-Dhahabī, *Siyar a'lām al-nubalā'*, vol. 10, pp. 357–8.
5 al-Khaṭīb al-Baghdādī, *Tārīkh Baghdād*, vol. 10, pp. 333–6.

reaches back to the Prophet. A third chain of transmission was recorded in Bukhārī's *Ṣaḥīḥ*,[6] which is identical to this variant, thus there is no need to analyse it on its own.

The fourth chain of transmission was recorded in Tirmidhī's (d. 279/892) *Jāmi'*,[7] and reported from Isḥāq b. Mūsā al-Anṣārī (d. 244/858–9), who resided in Medina, Samarra and Nishapur. Isḥāq b. Mūsā al-Anṣārī was one of Tirmidhī's favourite informants, and there is no reason to suggest that Tirmidhī fabricated the variant. Isḥāq b. Mūsā al-Anṣārī received the variant from Ma'na b. 'Īsā al-Qazzāz (d. 98/814), who lived in Medina and primarily reported from Mālik and Ibn Abī Dhi'b.[8] He was one of Mālik's most trusted students.[9] Ma'na received the variant from Mālik. Despite this, there is some uncertainty as to how Isḥāq b. Mūsā al-Anṣārī received it from Ma'na.

The fifth chain of transmission is recorded in Abū Dāwūd's *Sunan*,[10] one of the six canonical Sunni hadith collections. Abū Dāwūd (d. 275/889) travelled widely across the Muslim world to collect reports in such far locations as Iraq, Egypt, Syria, the Hijaz, Nishapur and Merv. He received the variant from 'Abdullāh b. Maslama (al-Qa'nabī) (d. 221/836–7), who was a reputable scholar of hadith. He was initially from Medina, and later lived in Basra and Mecca. He is reputed for narrating reports in the canonical Sunni collections.[11] He received the variant from Mālik, who transmitted it from Zuhrī, who received it through the same single strand.

Textual Analysis

In general, there is an unmistakable resemblance between the variants of the texts, which may be explained by the fact that Zuhrī, as the Common Link, transmitted them. In this vein, Mālik's version,[12] which I quoted above, has strong resemblances to other variants. It provides a direct reference to the Prophet in the form of the title Messenger of God (*Rasūl Allāh*), which is used by both the plaintiff and defendant. Despite this, some other variants do not refer to the Prophet as the Messenger of God, but as *al-Nabī* (the Prophet).[13] It also includes the term 'the Book of God' (*Kitāb Allāh*). The text of the second variant recorded in Bukhārī's *Ṣaḥīḥ*[14] is identical

6 Bukhārī, *Ṣaḥīḥ*, vol. 8, pp. 172–3.
7 Tirmidhī, *Sunan*, vol. 2, p. 91.
8 Bukhārī, *al-Tārīkh al-kabīr*, vol. 8, pp. 390–1.
9 al-Dhahabī, *Siyar a'lām al-nubalā'*, vol. 9, pp. 305–7.
10 al-Dhahabī, *Siyar a'lām al-nubalā'*, vol. 4, p. 153.
11 al-Dhahabī, *Siyar a'lām al-nubalā'*, vol. 10, pp. 257–8.
12 Mālik, *Muwaṭṭa'*, vol. 5, p. 822.
13 For example, see Ibn Abī Shayba's variant below.
14 Bukhārī, *Ṣaḥīḥ*, vol. 8, pp. 172–3.

to the text recorded in Mālik's *Muwaṭṭa'*. It is almost certain that it was recorded from Mālik's *Muwaṭṭa'* as 'Abdullāh b. Yūsuf, who is mentioned in the chain of transmission, states that he heard it from Mālik. The text of the third variant[15] is a duplicate of the second variant. Tirmidhī's *Sunan* records the fourth variant,[16] which comes through a different chain of transmission; however, the text is not given. The author states that the text is similar to Mālik's text. The fifth variant[17] is included in Abū Dāwūd's *Sunan* and reported through al-Qa'nabī ← Mālik ← Zuhrī. This variant is identical to the variant recorded in Mālik's *Muwaṭṭa'*. It is fairly certain that al-Qa'nabī also copied it from the *Muwaṭṭa'*. At this stage, I consider the subtle difference in this set of variants as indicative of a sound transmission process.

The Sufyān b. 'Uyayna Cluster

Chain of Transmission Analysis

The sixth variant was recorded in the pre-canonical collection Ibn Abī Shayba's *Muṣannaf*.[18] Scott C. Lucas, in his study of Ibn Abī Shayba's (d. 235/849–50) *Muṣannaf*, concludes that it certainly contains the reports that are transmitted through Ibn Abī Shayba.[19] Furthermore, Lucas notes that the collection mostly consists of only one in eleven reports as a prophetic hadith; most of the reports are attributed to the Companions and Followers of the Companions of the Prophet.[20] Upon giving detailed information about the textual history of the *Muṣannaf*, Lucas notes that Ibn Abī Shayba 'collected his narrations from a wide array of second/eighth century religious authorities, nearly all of whom lived in Iraq'.[21] Ibn Abī Shayba was based in Kufa and thus, it is normal that he mostly heard reports from Iraqi transmitters.

Furthermore, Lucas points out two exceptions to this: Sufyān b. 'Uyayna (d. 198/813–14) and Jarīr b. 'Abd al-Ḥamīd. The former is the person of interest for this variant, as Ibn Abī Shayba received the variant from Sufyān b. 'Uyayna, a third-generation Muslim who was born in Kufa. Although, at some point, he moved to Mecca, he later returned to Kufa,[22] and was

15 Bukhārī, *Ṣaḥīḥ*, vol. 8, pp. 172–3.
16 Tirmidhī, *Sunan*, vol. 2, p. 91.
17 Abū Dāwūd, *Sunan*, vol. 4, p. 144.
18 Ibn Abī Shayba, *Muṣannaf*, vol. 5, p. 540.
19 Lucas, 'Where Are the Legal "Ḥadīth"?', p. 290.
20 Lucas, 'Where Are the Legal "Ḥadīth"?', pp. 285–6.
21 Lucas, 'Where Are the Legal "Ḥadīth"?', p. 290.
22 See al-Dhahabī, *Tadhkirat al-ḥuffāẓ*, pp. 262–5.

primarily active in Iraq.[23] Lucas further contends that Ibn Abī Shayba acquired Sufyān b. ʿUyayna's narrations along with the others 'through listening to their lectures and/or copying their lecture notes rather than from actual books'.[24] Lucas does not state his reasoning for such an assertion, but historical sources give credence to this argument, at least in regards to Sufyān b. ʿUyayna.

According to Ibn al-Nadīm's *al-Fihrist*, Sufyān b. ʿUyayna was a Zaydi[25] scholar who never wrote a book, nor gathered his collections in written form.[26] It is most probable that he transmitted them through delivering lectures or through individual interactions. This chain of transmission then reaches Zuhrī,[27] one of the top authorities cited in Ibn Abī Shayba's *Muṣannaf*.[28] Aside from Medina, the report was circulated in Kufa, wherein Sufyān b. ʿUyayna was responsible for its spreading. When he visited Mecca, he must have also visited Medina for pilgrimage, recorded this report and transmitted it to Ibn Abī Shayba thereafter.

The seventh variant[29] recorded in Bukhārī's *Ṣaḥīḥ* reaches Sufyān b. ʿUyayna through the renowned scholar of hadith ʿAlī b. ʿAbdullāh [b. Jaʿfar al-Madanī] (d. 234/849) with slight textual variations. He narrates reports that are found in the canonical Sunni hadith collections, and is known to be one of the most influential scholars who lived in Basra and Medina. He was a student of Sufyān b. ʿUyayna and taught Bukhārī.[30] The period in which these three scholars lived further supports the possibility that Bukhārī received the variant from ʿAlī b. ʿAbdullāh, who received it from Sufyān b. ʿUyayna, from Zuhrī, from ʿUbaydullāh, and finally from both Abū Hurayra and Zayd b. Khālid. Hence, this report was also circulated in Basra through ʿAlī b. ʿAbdullāh.

23 Lucas considers Sufyān b. ʿUyayna as an exception to Ibn Abī Shayba's sources as he argues that Sufyān b. ʿUyayna moved to Mecca upon having lived in Kufa, thus he was a Meccan scholar. However, Sufyān b. ʿUyayna, having lived in Mecca for more than a decade, returned to Kufa, hence he was rather a Kufan scholar and was not an exception to other sources of Ibn Abī Shayba. See Lucas, 'Where Are the Legal "Ḥadīth"?', pp. 291–2.

24 Lucas, 'Where Are the Legal "Ḥadīth"?', p. 291.

25 It must be acknowledged that, at this point, the sectarian identities were fluid as the crystallisation took place after another century (Haider, *The Origins of the Shīʿa*, 207–74). Nevertheless, I use this kind of information to detect possible motivation to interfere with the reports when there is anomaly.

26 Ibn al-Nadīm, *Kitāb al-fihrist*, vol. 1, p. 227.

27 Motzki provides a study on the relationship between Sufyān b. ʿUyayna and Zuhrī; see Motzki et al., *Analysing Muslim Traditions*, pp. 70–9.

28 Lucas, 'Where Are the Legal "Ḥadīth"?', p. 293.

29 Bukhārī, *Ṣaḥīḥ*, vol. 8, pp. 167–8.

30 See al-Mizzī, *Tahdhīb al-kamāl fī asmāʾ al-rijāl*, vol. 22, pp. 5–35.

The eighth chain of transmission is recorded in Bukhārī's *Ṣaḥīḥ* through Musaddad [b. Musarhad] (d. 228/843).[31] Musaddad was a major hadith collector who narrated reports from the third generation of Muslims and is recorded in the collections of Abū Dāwūd, Tirmidhī and Nasā'ī. He was active in the city of Basra and a student of Sufyān b. 'Uyayna.[32] The ninth variant was recorded in Bukhārī's *Ṣaḥīḥ*,[33] who reported it from Muḥammad b. Yūsuf al-Firyābī (d. 212/827), who was a disciple of Sufyān al-Thawrī (d. 161/778) and resident of Ascalon, Palestine.[34] Muḥammad b. Yūsuf al-Firyābī was a student of Sufyān b. 'Uyayna (d. 198/813–14) and reported from him extensively when he accompanied him in Kufa and Mecca.[35]

The tenth chain of transmission recorded in Bukhārī's *Ṣaḥīḥ* is reported through Muḥammad b. Yūsuf and is identical to the ninth chain of transmission given in the same book. The eleventh chain of transmission was recorded in Bukhārī's *Ṣaḥīḥ*,[36] reported through 'Alī b. 'Abdullāh from Sufyān b. 'Uyayna from Zuhrī. It is identical to the chain of transmission that I have discussed above; therefore, it does not merit further discussion. The twelfth chain of transmission[37] was recorded in Bukhārī's *Ṣaḥīḥ* reported from Musaddad ← Sufyān b. 'Uyayna ← Zuhrī. I have also discussed the identical chain above.

The thirteenth chain of transmission[38] in this group of variants was recorded in Ibn Mājah's (d. 273/887) *Sunan* and reported through Ibn Abī Shayba. Ibn Mājah travelled to significant learning centres throughout Muslim lands in order to seek knowledge and collect reports, including Iraq, the Hijaz and Egypt.[39] He was a student of Ibn Abī Shayba and included many reports from his teacher in his *Sunan*.[40]

Given the evidence mentioned throughout historical works, it would be highly imaginative to assume that Ibn Mājah fabricated his narrations from Ibn Abī Shayba. In addition, Ibn Mājah received this variant from Hishām b. 'Ammār (d. 245/859) and Muḥammad b. al-Ṣabbāḥ (d. 227/841). There is no need to investigate all these transmitters as the sound connection between Ibn Abī Shayba and Sufyān b. 'Uyayna, and between Sufyān b. 'Uyayna and Zuhrī, has been established. From Zuhrī,

31 Bukhārī, *Ṣaḥīḥ*, vol. 9, p. 92.
32 al-Mizzī, *Tahdhīb al-kamāl fī asmā' al-rijāl*, vol. 10, pp. 443–8.
33 Bukhārī, *Ṣaḥīḥ*, vol.8, p. 176.
34 al-Dhahabī, *Siyar a'lām al-nubalā'*, vol. 10, p. 114.
35 al-Dhahabī, *Siyar a'lām al-nubalā'*, vol. 10, p. 115.
36 Bukhārī, *Ṣaḥīḥ*, vol. 8, pp. 167–8.
37 Bukhārī, *Ṣaḥīḥ*, vol. 9, p. 92.
38 Ibn Mājah, *Sunan*, vol. 1, p. 852.
39 al-Dhahabī, *Siyar a'lām al-nubalā'*, vol. 13, pp. 277–80.
40 Ibn al-Dhahabī, *Tadhkirat al-ḥuffāẓ*, vol. 2, p. 636.

the chain of transmission goes back to ʿUbaydullāh b. ʿAbdullāh ← Abū Hurayra, Zayd b. Khālid and al-Shiblī ← the Prophet. This is the second chain that includes al-Shiblī's name.

The fourteenth chain of transmission was recorded in Tirmidhī's *Jāmiʿ*.[41] Muḥammad b. ʿĪsā Tirmidhī (d. 279/892) was a highly respected scholar who lived in the Surxondaryo Region in Uzbekistan, and travelled to Transoxiana, Iraq and the Hijāz.[42] Tirmidhī reported the variant from Naṣr b. ʿAlī (d. 250/864), who was one of the eminent scholars of this time.[43] He was from the city of Basra but also travelled to Baghdad.[44] According to these reports, Naṣr b. ʿAlī angered the Abbasid caliph Mutawakkil (d. 247/861) when he recited a prophetic report praising ʿAlī b. Abī Ṭālib, Fāṭima, Ḥasan and Ḥusayn. In response, Mutawakkil ordered Naṣr b. ʿAlī to be punished with a thousand lashes, under the assumption that he was a Shiʿi. However, upon hearing that he was a Sunni, he retracted the punishment.[45] The biographical evaluation (*rijāl*) works also note that Naṣr b. ʿAlī received reports from Sufyān b. ʿUyayna.[46] Tirmidhī and Naṣr b. ʿAlī were contemporaneous and therefore, there is no reason to suspect that the former received the variant from the latter. Naṣr b. ʿAlī received the variant from his usual informant Sufyān b. ʿUyayna, who then received the report from Zuhrī. Sufyān b. ʿUyayna, as I have discussed previously, was active in Iraq and the Hijaz. Therefore, it is possible that he reported the variant to Naṣr b. ʿAlī.

Textual Analysis

Ibn Abī Shayba's sixth variant[47] strongly resembles the Mālik b. Anas cluster; they narrate the same incident, while using slightly different utterances, which is consistent with the differences in the chain of transmission. Unlike the Mālik b. Anas cluster, Ibn Abī Shayba's variant, which is in the Sufyān b. ʿUyayna cluster, does not use the title Messenger of God (*Rasūl Allāh*). Instead, the transmitters of the variant referred to the Prophet as the

41 Tirmidhī, *Sunan*, vol. 2, p. 91.

42 al-Dhahabī, *Siyar aʿlām al-nubalāʾ*, vol. 13, p. 271.

43 al-Dhahabī, *Siyar aʿlām al-nubalāʾ*, vol. 12, p. 144.

44 al-Khaṭīb al-Baghdādī, *Tārīkh Baghdād*, vol. 12, p. 389.

45 al-Khaṭīb al-Baghdādī, *Tārīkh Baghdād*, vol. 12, p. 390.

46 Chase Robinson and Michael Cooperson provide essential information about the formation of the *rijāl* genre and Islamic historiography. Robinson, *Islamic Historiography*; Cooperson, *Classical Arabic Biography*. Liyakat Takim's work is crucial for understanding the formation and evolution of Shiʿi *rijāl* genre. Takim, 'The Origins and Evaluations of Hadith Transmitters in Shiʿi Biographical Literature'.

47 Ibn Abī Shayba, *Muṣannaf*, vol. 5, p. 540.

Prophet (*al-Nabī*). Furthermore, in Ibn Abī Shayba's version, neither the plaintiff nor defendant explicitly refer to the Prophet by his title:

> We were with the Prophet (*al-Nabī*), and a man stood up and said: 'I implore you by God! Will you not judge between us according to the Book of God?' The other plaintiff, who was wiser than him, said: 'Judge between us according to the Book of God! Allow me to speak [about it].'[48]

Although both clusters use the expression 'the Book of God' (*Kitāb Allāh*), there are subtle differences and paraphrases in the construction of the preceding sentences. Both the Mālik b. Anas cluster and Ibn Abī Shayba's version end with the confession of the adulteress wife, who was eventually stoned under the supervision of Unays al-Aslamī. The emphasis on judgement between the two parties is noticeable. The two plaintiffs come to the Prophet for litigation and ask the Prophet to 'judge' between them. However, the words used are different: while Mālik's text uses the word *aqḍi* in both sentences, which is the imperative form,[49] in Ibn Abī Shayba's text[50] the first sentence features the word *qaḍayta* (literally, 'you [have] decided'), a second-person singular masculine past active verb. The second sentence features the verb *aqḍi*. Both Arabic words are derived from the root *qāf-ḍād-yā'* and share a similar meaning and both versions of the tradition display important evidence of paraphrasing.

It is plausible that the original text included the word *aqḍi* in both sentences, including the second-person masculine imperative form. Grammatically speaking, if the imperative form is used to refer to a higher authority, then the meaning changes to one of pleading. This style is used in the Qur'an on many occasions for the purposes of supplication, and thus, this usage makes more sense in the context. The fact that the texts come through two PCLs, Sufyān b. 'Uyayna and Layth both of whom use *qaḍayta* in the first sentence and *aqḍi* in the second sentence, while the remaining three PCLs use *aqḍi* in both sentences, gives further credence to the idea that the version as spread by Zuhrī contained *aqḍi* in both sentences.

The reason for this paraphrasing may have been an intentional interference. This is because there is a relevant verse in the Qur'an that reads, 'But no, by your Lord, they will not truly believe until they make you [Muhammad] judge between them in all matters of dispute and find

48 Ibn Abī Shayba, *Muṣannaf*, vol. 5, p. 540.

49 'Yā Rasūl Allāh aqḍi baynanā bi-Kitāb Allāh' and 'ajal yā Rasūl Allāh fa-aqḍi baynanā bi-Kitāb Allāh'.

50 'Unshiduka Allāh 'alā qaḍayta baynanā bi-Kitāb Allāh' and 'aqḍi baynanā bi-Kitāb Allāh'.

within themselves no discomfort from what you have judged (*qaḍayta*) and submit totally' (Q. 4:65). The exact expression *qaḍayta* as used in this verse may have been the reason for its use in Ibn Abī Shayba's text. Since the verse refers to the role of the Prophet as the ultimate judge between Muslims, the report corroborates with this verse. Hence, both Sufyān b. 'Uyayna and Layth might have intentionally edited the text to establish its conformity with the relevant verse of the Qur'an.

However, this textual editing could have also been employed due to an unintentional mix-up. They had likely memorised the verses of the Qur'an before learning this hadith and thus uttered it under the influence of the Qur'anic verse. Given that both Layth and Sufyān b. 'Uyayna were active in and around Medina and Mecca, it is probable that Sufyān b. 'Uyayna's reading was influenced by Layth, who was from the prior generation. Another possibility is that it might have been a coincidence. Both of these options are plausible, but regardless, the extent of the redaction is minor.

In addition, both variants refer to the common element of the 'people of knowledge', with some variations; however, where Mālik's text uses the expression 'I asked the people of knowledge' (*sa'altu ahla al-'ilmi*), Ibn Abī Shayba's text states, 'I asked men from the people of knowledge' (*sa'altu rijālan min ahli al-'ilmi*). Again, these textual variations are indications of paraphrasing, hence a possible healthy verbal transmission. Both variants mention that initially, the father of the fornicator's son ransomed his son for a hundred sheep and a slave or servant. However, Mālik's version included a piece of additional information, that the husband informed the father that his 'son's punishment is stoning'. In both texts, upon listening to the case, the Prophet confirms that he 'will judge between you according to the Book of God'. In a way, he grants the wishes of both sides. The Prophet then issues his verdict, which is that one hundred sheep and a slave or servant are to be returned to the father, and the fornicating son is to be flogged a hundred times and exiled for a year. Finally, he dispatched Unays al-Aslamī to the adulteress wife, instructing him that if she confesses, she is to be stoned. Because both texts reached back to Zuhrī via different chains of transmission, it is possible to state at this early stage that these common elements, which possibly make up the original text, can be dated back to Zuhrī. In other words, these common elements were likely part of the original report that Zuhrī distributed. The study of the remaining texts may provide further evidence in terms of the common and differing elements.

Bukhārī's version,[51] which is the seventh variant of this group, is identical to Ibn Abī Shayba's. Like Ibn Abī Shayba's text, there is no direct reference to Muhammad, and instead the reference *al-Nabī* was adopted.

51 Bukhārī, *Ṣaḥīḥ*, vol. 8, pp. 167–8.

The PCL in both chains is Sufyān b. 'Uyayna; due to the identical nature of both variants and given that Sufyān b. 'Uyayna never wrote a book,[52] we can assume that he dictated both variants. The note which was included most probably by 'Alī b. 'Abdullāh at the end of Bukhārī's version requires a closer look: 'I asked Sufyān: "Did he not say: my son should be stoned?" Sufyān replied: "It is doubtful on the side of Zuhrī. He may have said it, or he may have been silent."'[53] In both Mālik and Ibn Abī Shayba's variants, the plaintiff states that the defendant called for the stoning punishment be due upon the adulterer's son.

All of this may indicate that the defendant played a trick to increase the pressure on the father, so that he may pay the requested ransom. When the father learned from the Prophet that his son would not be stoned, he was relieved and not as concerned about the lashes and exile. This missing sentence is what 'Alī b. 'Abdullāh seems to be asking Sufyān b. 'Uyayna about, and Sufyān replies saying that he was unsure. This small anecdote further indicates that it is probable that Sufyān heard the report from Zuhrī and could not remember if he uttered the missing section or not. It would be self-defeating for a forger to include such an anecdote in a report to draw suspicion.

The eighth variant was recorded in Bukhārī's *Ṣaḥīḥ*[54] and the text is identical to the previous variant recorded in the same book, but it is an abridged version reported through Sufyān – therefore, the identical nature of the version is justified. The variant only mentions the statement given by the Prophet 'I am going to judge between you according to the Book of God', which is pertinent to this study. There is an explicit reference to 'the Book of God', which I assume, at this point of our study, refers to the Qur'an.

The text of the ninth variant[55] is again similar to Ibn Abī Shayba's variant, with a minor difference in the opening sentences. The similarity and minor difference may be explained by the fact that Ibn Abī Shayba reported it through Sufyān b. 'Uyayna ← Zuhrī. This variant is also reported through Sufyān b. 'Uyayna ← Zuhrī, but only after Sufyān b. 'Uyayna and Muḥammad b. Yūsuf transmitted it to Bukhārī. There are minor differences in the variants. In Ibn Abī Shayba's variant, the account of the event begins with 'We were with the Prophet, [when] a man stood up and said...' (*Kunnā 'inda al-Nabī fa-qāma rajulun, fa-qāla* ...). However, the variant that is transmitted through Muḥammad b. Yūsuf from Sufyān b. 'Uyayna begins with 'A man came to the prophet and said: "I implore you by God,

52 Bukhārī, *Ṣaḥīḥ*, vol. 8, p. 282.
53 Bukhārī, *Ṣaḥīḥ*, vol. 8, pp. 167–8.
54 Bukhārī, *Ṣaḥīḥ*, vol. 9, p. 92.
55 Bukhārī, *Ṣaḥīḥ*, vol. 8, p. 176.

judge between us with the Book of God!" The man's opponent (plaintiff) who was wiser, stood up and said …' (*Jā'a rajulun ilā al-Nabī, fa-qāla: anshuduka Allāh illā qaḍayta baynanā bi-Kitāb Allāh. Fa-qāma khaṣmuhu wa-kāna afqaha minhu …*), so Ibn Abī Shayba's version gives the impression that the two men had already been in the presence of the Prophet and the defendant stood up and opened the discussion.

The above differs from other variants, in which the defendant arrives in the presence of the Prophet and discussed the case. Aside from this minor difference, it is interesting that, just as was the case with Ibn Abī Shayba's version, this variant also refers to the Prophet as *al-Nabī*. Thus, giving the impression that it may have been Sufyān b. 'Uyayna's personal choice to refer to the Prophet as *al-Nabī*; since the Prophet is referred to as *Rasūl Allāh* in all of the other variants. There may have been extraneous reasons why he insisted on referring to the Prophet as *al-Nabī*; it could be related to a theological significance or a stylistic choice. Nevertheless, I cannot comment further on this as it requires a more comprehensive enquiry.

The text of the tenth variant[56] is a replica of the ninth variant, thus there is no need to analyse it. The eleventh variant[57] is identical to the eighth variant recorded in Bukhārī's *Ṣaḥīḥ* both in terms of transmission and text, thus I exclude it from the study as well. The twelfth variant recorded in Bukhārī's *Ṣaḥīḥ* is a shortened version of the report 'We were with the Prophet, and he said: "I am going to judge between you according to the Book of God."'[58] There is not much to say about the variant since it is very brief, but the text carries the distinct textual signature of Sufyān b. 'Uyayna, who prefers to refer to the Prophet as *al-Nabī*. Furthermore, it includes the most relevant part of the variant, which is the reference to 'the Book of God'.

The thirteenth variant[59] is recorded in Ibn Mājah's *Sunan* and has an almost identical text to the variant recorded in Ibn Abī Shayba's *Muṣannaf*. There are only two slight differences. First, instead of *al-Nabī*, Ibn Mājah's *Sunan* refers to the Prophet as *Rasūl Allāh*, which is different from the usual reference of Sufyān b. 'Uyayna, who is also included in the chain of this version. Second, at the end of the variant, Hishām states that, 'Unays went to the woman the following day, she confessed and then he stoned her.'[60] The similarities may be explained by the fact that Ibn Mājah directly copied this variant from Ibn Abī Shayba's *Muṣannaf*. This is because the chain of transmission states that Ibn Mājah received the variant from three

56 Bukhārī, *Ṣaḥīḥ*, vol. 8, p. 176.
57 Bukhārī, *Ṣaḥīḥ*, vol. 8, pp. 167–8.
58 Bukhārī, *Ṣaḥīḥ*, vol. 9, p. 92.
59 Ibn Mājah, *Sunan*, vol. 1, p. 852.
60 Ibn Mājah, *Sunan*, vol. 1, p. 852.

informants, namely, Ibn Abī Shayba, Hishām b. 'Ammār and Muḥammad b. al-Ṣabbāḥ, who received it from Sufyān b. 'Uyayna. Ibn Mājah copied this report directly from Ibn Abī Shayba's *Muṣannaf* and redacted the title of the Prophet from *al-Nabi* to *Rasūl Allāh*, which was perhaps in more use at the time. Ibn Mājah also added the last sentence to the variant that he had heard from Hishām.

The fourteenth variant was recorded in Tirmidhī's *Sunan*. The text reaches us through Naṣr b. 'Alī ← Sufyān b. 'Uyayna ← Zuhrī and multiple informants whom Tirmidhī mentions at the end of the text. The text is similar to the other variants that come through Sufyān b. 'Uyayna, and there is an interdependency between the variants.

The Ibn Abī Dhi'b Cluster

Chain of Transmission Analysis

The fifteenth chain of transmission[61] recorded in Bukhārī's *Ṣaḥīḥ* was transmitted through Ādam, referring to Ādam b. Abī Iyās (d. 220/836). Although initially from Khorasan, Ādam b. Abī Iyās lived in Ascalon, Palestine.[62] He travelled to the learning centres of Syria, Iraq and the Hijaz,[63] where he met various scholars and collected reports. Ādam b. Abī Iyās was a well-known hadith collector and one of Bukhārī's teachers, thus there is no reason to suspect that he narrated the report to Bukhārī. Ādam b. Abī Iyās received the variant from Ibn Abī Dhi'b (d. 159/775–6), who was a student of Zuhrī. Ibn Abī Dhi'b was a highly regarded scholar of hadith and contemporaneous to Mālik b. Anas. Ibn Abī Dhi'b lived in Medina and was well travelled as a student and collector of hadiths.[64] Therefore, it is possible that he passed this report to Ādam b. Abī Iyās when he travelled to Palestine or when Ādam b. Abī Iyās visited the Hijaz, as both possibilities are plausible. Ibn Abī Dhi'b received the report from his teacher Zuhrī. This chain indicates that the report did not remain in Medina and Iraq but rather also travelled to Palestine. The sixteenth chain of transmission[65] is recorded in Bukhārī's *Ṣaḥīḥ* and reported from 'Āṣim b. 'Alī (d. 221/836–7), who is known to be a disciple of Shu'ayb. He was a famous Qur'an reciter and renowned transmitter of one of the seven canonical readings (*qirā'āt*) of the Quran. He was based in Mecca and met 'Ikrima b. 'Ammār (d. 159/775–6).[66] Given that Zuhrī is the Common Link for the variants,

61 Bukhārī, *Ṣaḥīḥ*, vol. 9, p. 75; this report is duplicated in vol. 3, p. 184.
62 Bukhārī, *al-Tārīkh al-kabīr*, vol. 2, p. 39.
63 al-Khaṭīb al-Baghdādī, *Tārīkh Baghdād*, vol. 7, p. 484.
64 al-Mizzī, *Tahdhīb al-kamāl fī asmā' al-rijāl*, vol. 8, pp. 188–94.
65 Bukhārī, *Ṣaḥīḥ*, vol. 8, p. 171.
66 al-Dhahabī, *Siyar a'lām al-nubalā'*, vol. 9, p. 262.

it is probable that 'Āṣim b. 'Alī also heard the variant through 'Ikrima b. 'Ammār despite naming Ibn Abī Dhi'b as his informant. As I have already noted, Ibn Abī Dhi'b (d. 159/775–6) was a student of Zuhrī. Ādam b. Abī Iyās (d. 220/836) also narrated a variant found in Bukhārī's *Ṣaḥīḥ* through Ibn Abī Dhi'b who reported it directly from Zuhrī. Given this information, I can also identify Ibn Abī Dhi'b as one of the PCLs.

The seventeenth chain of narration[67] recorded in Bukhārī's *Ṣaḥīḥ* is reported from Ādam, again referring to Ādam b. Abī Iyās, whose chain is as follows: Ibn Abī Dhi'b ← Zuhrī ← 'Ubaydullāh b. 'Abdullāh ← Abū Hurayra and Zayd b. Khālid al-Juhanī. This is identical to the fifteenth chain of transmission in this cluster.

Textual Analysis

The fifteenth textual variant mentioned in Bukhārī's *Ṣaḥīḥ*[68] has some similarities to the previous versions: two men come to the Prophet to settle their dispute, triggered by the affair of the plaintiff's son and the defendant's wife, along with the subsequent ransom that consisted of a hundred sheep and a slave girl. There is also the 'Book of God' as a reference point and the stoning of the adulteress wife under the supervision of Unays. Another shared element is the plaintiff's initial settlement, after which he enquires further with 'the people of knowledge' (*ahl al-'ilm*) and is then informed that he got the short end of the stick, since the requisite punishment was not stoning.

'The People of Knowledge'

At this point it may be justified to ask if it would be possible for these nomadic Arabs to come to the Prophet for arbitration and not know about the difference between the Qur'an and Torah, if there was any? Could they have asked for a judgement according to the Torah, believing it was the Book of God? They asked the Prophet to judge according to the Book of God, meaning they wanted a religious verdict to be implemented on the defendants. What religious verdict would they, or 'the people of knowledge', know about as it pertains to fornication and adultery? Who were 'the people of knowledge'? Scholars of early Islam do not provide answers to these questions. They could have been Muslim or Jewish scholars, but it would be unlikely to have a scholarly group among Muslims in such an early period, especially those who can be designated as 'the people of knowledge'.

67 Bukhārī, *Ṣaḥīḥ*, vol. 9, pp. 75–6.

68 Bukhārī, *Ṣaḥīḥ*, vol. 9, p. 75; this report is duplicated in vol. 3, p. 184.

It seems more plausible that they were referring to Jewish scholars, who are mentioned as *rabbāniyyūn* (sing. *rabbān*) and *aḥbār* (sing. *ḥabr*) in Q. 5:44, 5:63, 9:31 and 9:34,[69] and that the Book of God referred to the Torah. Until the change in the Muslims' direction of prayer, there was not much of an independent[70] Muslim identity.[71] The scholarly Muslim community especially emerged only much later, towards the end of the Umayyad era and the beginning of the Abbasid.[72] The separation and creation of an independent Muslim identity came with the change in the direction of prayer:

> We see you turning your face about in the sky. We will surely turn you to a *qibla* (direction of prayer) of your liking: so turn your face towards the Holy Mosque, and wherever you may be, turn your faces towards it! Indeed, those who were given the Book surely know that it is the truth from their Lord. And God is not oblivious to what they do. (Q. 2:144)

The verse informs us about the Muslim belief that the direction of prayer (*qibla*) was changed from Jerusalem to the Kaaba at the request of the Prophet: 'We will surely turn you to a *qibla* of your liking.' This refers to how the Prophet was once sure that the majority of Medinan Jews would disapprove of his prophecy, which led to the issue wherein Muslims would

69 To delve into an interesting discussion about the scholarly Jewish class in Medina, see Mazuz, *The Religious and Spiritual Life of the Jews of Medina*, pp. 21–3.

70 Kister also linked the change in the direction of prayer to Muhammad's efforts in establishing an independent identity; Kister, *Concepts and Ideas at the Dawn of Islam*, pp. 355–6.

71 In this sense, Donner's 'Believer Movement Thesis' can further support this argument or vice versa. For Donner, Islam did not emerge as a fully formed religion with a fixed set of beliefs and practices. Donner argues that this movement was characterised by a belief in one God, rejecting traditional Arabian polytheism and a sense of social and economic justice. It was led by charismatic figures known as 'believers', who sought to create a more egalitarian society in which the wealthy were held accountable for their actions and the poor were given greater opportunities for advancement. Over time, this movement merged into a more formal religion with structured beliefs, practices and institutions. The role of the Prophet Muhammad in this process, for Donner, was to provide a unifying vision for the movement and to codify its beliefs and practices into a coherent system. Donner, *Muhammad and the Believers*; Webb also echoed similar views. Webb, *Imagining the Arabs*, 135. While there is certainly room for debate and alternative interpretations, I can see how one might find Donner's 'Believer Movement Thesis' to be an insightful perspective on the early history of Islam. Especially, in terms of early Muslims interaction with the non-Muslims. Nevertheless, the Qur'an seems to be more straightforward about the role of the Prophet as the Messenger of God, not simply a leader who coordinated various factions under a unified umbrella.

72 Hallaq, *An Introduction to Islamic Law*.

follow the Jews in praying towards Jerusalem. It may be that before the Muslims' identity had crystallised, people used a general term for the scriptures of Muslims and Jews, hence referring to them both as the Book of God. The Qur'an also refers to the scriptures of Jews and Christians as the same Book: 'The Jews say, "The Christians stand on nothing," and the Christians say, "The Jews stand on nothing," though they follow the [same] Book' (Q. 2:113). Furthermore, Q. 2:144 states that 'those who were given the Book' refer to the Jews. So, there is ample reason to think that the 'Book of God' in the context of the report refers to the Torah, and that the Prophet passed a judgement based on the Torah in the initial period of Muslim presence in Medina.

A deliberate response from the Prophet that he would rule according to the Book of God affirms this position. However, at this point, such a view remains a theory as I could only trace the variants back to Zuhrī's date of death, 124/742.

In addition, there are subtle differences in this variant. Firstly, this variant refers to the Prophet both as *Rasūl Allāh* and *al-Nabī*, therefore giving the impression that both titles could be used interchangeably. Furthermore, this variant gives the identity of the plaintiff as 'a nomadic Arab' who, in contrast to the previous variants, begins the conversation with the Prophet first. In the earlier variants, the defendant made the opening statement. Additionally, although the plaintiff referred to 'the Book of God' as the reference, in this variant, the defendant only said, 'judge between us by reference to God' (*fa-aqḍi baynanā bi-Allāh*). However, in his response, the Prophet reassures both parties that he would judge between them according to the Book of God. The final variance is at the end of the transmission. As opposed to previous variants, the Prophet did not give a conditional instruction to Unays, 'if she confesses, stone her'. Rather, it states that 'go to this man's wife in the morning and stone her', an order which Unays duly executed. Given that this variant is reported through Ādam ← Ibn Abī Dhi'b ← Zuhrī, instead of through Unays who was involved in the episode, these textual differences are natural in the oral transmission process. The story's kernel remains the same, giving the impression of a healthy transmission process. Some differences in the narration may be due to paraphrasing, as there are two main differences:

- In the sixteenth variant recorded in Bukhārī's *Ṣaḥīḥ*,[73] which is similar to the previous variant where Ibn Abī Dhi'b report from Zuhrī, the defendant makes the opening statement, which is in concurrence with the rest of the variants.

73 Bukhārī, *Ṣaḥīḥ*, vol. 8, p. 171.

- There is no mention of the title *al-Nabī* in this variant, and it rather refers to the Prophet as *Rasūl Allāh.*

There are two possibilities, since Ibn Abī Dhi'b reports this variant from Zuhrī and ʿĀṣim b. ʿAlī reports the narration from Ibn Abī Dhi'b. Either Ādam, who reported the fifth variant from Ibn Abī Dhi'b, made an error when he recorded the variant, or both the plaintiff and defendant were nomadic Arabs. Either way, such a difference strengthens the evidence for a genuine transmission process. Aside from the difference, the variant includes all the main themes mentioned in the previous variants, including the reference to 'the Book of God'. The seventeenth variant's[74] chain of transmission and text are identical to the fifteenth variant,[75] which was recorded in Bukhārī's *Ṣaḥīh.* I, therefore, have decided not to examine this variant.

The Layth b. Saʿd Cluster

Chain of Transmission Analysis

The eighteenth chain of narration was recorded in Bukhārī's *Ṣaḥīḥ*,[76] and transmitted through Qutayba b. Saʿīd (d. 240/854–5), who reported extensively from Layth, Mālik, Ḥammād b. Zayd and others. Qutayba b. Saʿīd was originally from Balkh and left the city to pursue knowledge at an early age. Reports suggest that he earned the praise of Aḥmad b. Ḥanbal.[77] Qutayba b. Saʿīd moved to Baghdad in the year 216/831–2, during which time Ibn Abī Shayba was also active in Baghdad.[78] Qutayba b. Saʿīd received the variant from the prominent Egyptian scholar Layth b. Saʿd (d.175/791–2), who was a contemporary and friend of Mālik. Harald Motzki already established a firm connection between Qutayba b. Saʿīd and Layth b. Saʿd in his response to Juynboll's allegation of forgery in chains wherein both transmitters appear.[79] Finally, Layth received the variant from Zuhrī. This chain indicates that the report emerged in Medina and then spread to Iraq, Palestine and Egypt, which were some of the main learning centres in the Muslim world. The nineteenth chain of transmission[80] recorded in Bukhārī's *Ṣaḥīḥ* was again reported from Qutayba b. Saʿīd ← Layth b. Saʿd[81] ← Zuhrī. This

74 Bukhārī, *Ṣaḥīḥ*, vol. 9, pp. 75–6.
75 Bukhārī, *Ṣaḥīḥ*, vol. 9, pp. 75–6.
76 Bukhārī, *Ṣaḥīḥ*, vol. 3, p. 191.
77 al-Dhahabī, *Siyar aʿlām al-nubalā'*, vol. 11, pp. 13–16. For a slightly more detailed account on Qutayba b. Saʿīd, see Lucas, *Constructive Critics*, p. 190.
78 al-Dhahabī, *Siyar aʿlām al-nubalā'*, vol. 9, p.16.
79 Motzki et al., *Analysing Muslim Traditions*, pp. 85–9.
80 Bukhārī, *Ṣaḥīḥ*, vol. 3, p. 191.
81 Ibn Saʿd, *Kitāb al-ṭabaqāt al-kabīr*, vol. 9, p. 383.

chain indicates that the report emerged in Medina and then spread to Iraq, Palestine and Egypt.

The twentieth chain of transmission was recorded in Muslim's *Ṣaḥīḥ* (d. 261/874–5).[82] He lived in Nishapur, but travelled widely in Iraq, the Hijaz, Syria and Egypt. He received the variant from Qutayba b. Saʿīd, who was active primarily in Iraq. He narrated reports extensively from Layth b. Saʿd (d. 175/791–2),[83] whose narrations can be found in the canonical hadith collections.

There is another informant between Qutayba b. Saʿīd and Layth b. Saʿd: Muḥammad b. Rumḥ (d. 242/857), who was a well-respected scholar of hadith.[84] He was from Egypt and was also one of Ibn Mājah's teachers. Muḥammad b. Rumḥ narrated mainly from Layth b. Saʿd and he reported this report from Layth as well, who in turn received the variant from Zuhrī. At this point, it is possible to confirm Layth as one of the PLCs, although he was not as prolific as Mālik and Sufyān, having transmitted the report to only two individuals.

Textual Analysis

The text of the eighteenth variant[85] recorded in Bukhārī's *Ṣaḥīh* resembles variants found in works by Mālik, Ibn Abī Shayba and Bukhārī, as it contains certain elements from each variant. The text itself is more similar to Ibn Abī Shayba's variant, yet it refers to the Prophet as *Rasūl Allāh* instead of *al-Nabī*. It also refers to the defendant as a nomadic Arab, unlike Bukhārī's version. Despite this, the main narrative is the same; the Prophet's instruction to Unays is conditioned to the wife's confession. Layth, who heard this report from Zuhrī and transmitted it to Qutayba b. Saʿīd, was a contemporary of Mālik and Ibn Abī Shayba. This means that they might have also heard the report from each other, so it is normal that certain elements mentioned in the reports are similar. It could also mean that their sources were the same. The nineteenth variant[86] is identical to the variant[87] recorded in Bukhārī's *Ṣaḥīh*; therefore, I have chosen to not analyse this variant.

The twentieth variant[88] is similar to previous variants in general and includes all the elements mentioned in them. There is only a minor difference between this and the Layth b. Saʿd cluster, which is that at the end

82 Muslim, *Ṣaḥīḥ*, vol. 2, pp. 1324–5.
83 Ibn Saʿd, *Kitāb al-ṭabaqāt al-kabīr*, vol. 9, p. 383.
84 al-Dhahabī, *Tahdhīb al-kamāl fī asmāʾ al-rijāl*, vol. 8, pp. 100–1.
85 Bukhārī, *Ṣaḥīḥ*, vol. 3, p. 191.
86 Bukhārī, *Ṣaḥīḥ*, vol. 3, p. 191.
87 Bukhārī, *Ṣaḥīḥ*, vol. 3, p. 191.
88 Muslim, *Ṣaḥīḥ*, vol. 2, pp. 1324–5.

of all three variants, the text includes the sentence 'She confessed and in accordance with the instruction of the Messenger of God, she was stoned'. In the rest of the variants, it states that 'she confessed and Unays al-Aslamī stoned her'. Given that this sentence was added in all three variants that come through Layth, it is probable that Layth added this sentence to give more clarification to the variant to explain that Unays initiated the stoning on the order of the Prophet. Therefore, it was not part of the original text. There is a clear correlation between the chain of transmission and text sections of the variants as the text corresponded to the variations in the chain of transmission. There is also a clear pattern of certain individuals leaving their linguistic marks on the texts.

Miscellaneous Variants

Chain of Transmission Analysis

There are four variants which reach the hadith collections through single transmission lines and do not form clusters; therefore, I will study them separately below. The twenty-first chain of transmission was recorded in Bukhārī's (d. 256/870) *Ṣaḥīḥ*.[89] Bukhārī often reported from Abū al-Yamān al-Ḥakam b. Nāfiʿ (d. 222/837), who was from the city of Homs, and so there is a geographical proximity between the two. This is also further corroborated by the fact that they lived in the same period. Therefore, Bukhārī could have reported the narration from Abū al-Yamān.

Abū al-Yamān reported the hadith from Shuʿayb b. Abī Hamza (d. 162/779–80), who hailed from the city of Homs. There is a lengthy discussion about whether Abū al-Yamān received it from Shuʿayb;[90] however, since there are several other chains of transmission, there is no need to indulge in the debate at the moment. It is evident that there is a connection between the two scholars, and there is a reasonable possibility that Abū al-Yamān received the report from Shuʿayb b. Abī Hamza, the latter of whom was a well-regarded hadith collector from Homs.[91] He travelled to Islamic centres of learning and reported extensively from Zuhrī, Nāfiʿ and ʿIkrima.

Shuʿayb then received the report from Zuhrī. Nicolet Boekhoff-van der Voort provided a detailed analysis of the chain of transmission which includes Abū al-Yamān ← Shuʿayb ← Zuhrī.[92] In her study, she establishes the connection between these three scholars, paying special attention to the fact that Shuʿayb was tasked with writing the dictations of Zuhrī.[93] From

89 Bukhārī, *Ṣaḥīḥ*, vol. 9, pp. 88–9.
90 al-Mizzī, *Tahdhīb al-kamāl fī asmāʾ al-rijāl*, vol. 10, pp. 320–4.
91 al-Dhahabī, *Siyar aʿlām al-nubalāʾ*, vol. 9, pp. 188–91.
92 Motzki et al., *Analysing Muslim Traditions*, pp. 361–80.
93 Motzki et al., *Analysing Muslim Traditions*, p. 366.

Zuhrī, the chain goes to 'Ubaydullāh b. 'Abdullāh b. 'Utba b. Mas'ūd, who received it from Abū Hurayra. Contrary to the other chains of transmission, this one does not mention the name of Zayd b. Khālid al-Juhanī, receiving the report together with Abū Hurayra from the Prophet. Rather, only Abū Hurayra's name was mentioned.

The twenty-second chain of transmission is recorded in Bukhārī's *Ṣaḥīḥ*.[94] Bukhārī reported it from Abū al-Yamān, and it is identical to the previous variant mentioned above. It also does not include the names of Khālid al-Juhanī or Abū Hurayra, both of whom heard the variant from the Prophet. The twenty-third chain of transmission[95] is recorded in Bukhārī's *Ṣaḥīḥ* through 'Āṣim b. 'Alī (d. 221/836–7) and is identical to the sixteenth chain of transmission found in the same book.

The twenty-fourth chain of transmission was recorded in Muslim's *Ṣaḥīḥ* and reported from Abū al-Ṭāhir and Ḥarmala.[96] Abū Ṭāhir b. al-Sarḥ (d. 250/864) was a reputable scholar who often reported from ['Abdullāh] Ibn Wahb.[97] Ḥarmala (d. 243/858) was a client of Banū Zumīla from Egypt, and also reported it from Ibn Wahb.[98] Ibn Wahb (d. 197/813) was a prominent Egyptian Mālikī jurist. He first studied in Egypt, then moved to Medina and became Mālik b. Anas's most prominent student. He was instrumental in spreading the Mālikī school in Egypt and left a massive thirty-volume book which comprised what he heard from Mālik. He also studied with many of Zuhrī's students.[99]

At this point, the chain of transmission spreads into two branches between Ibn Wahb and Zuhrī with multiple transmitters.[100] There is no point in studying all these transmitters as the evidence of there being a sound link between the two men is highly likely. With the study of the last variant, I can now safely conclude that based on the analysis of the chains of transmission, all twenty-four variants can be traced back to Zuhrī, who is the Common Link for these variants. It could be possible that Zuhrī genuinely received this report from 'Ubaydullāh b. 'Abdullāh, or he forged it.

Furthermore, the analysis of the chains confirmed my initial observation that Mālik, Sufyān b. 'Uyayna, Ibn Abī Dhi'b and Layth were the real PLCs of these variants. In terms of the spread of the variants in different geographical locations, the reports originated in Medina and then

94 Bukhārī, *Ṣaḥīḥ*, vol. 9, pp. 88–9.
95 Bukhārī, *Ṣaḥīḥ*, vol. 8, p. 171.
96 Muslim, *Ṣaḥīḥ*, vol. 2, pp. 1324–5.
97 al-Dhahabī, *Siyar a'lām al-nubalā'*, vol. 12, pp. 62–3.
98 al-Dhahabī, *Siyar a'lām al-nubalā'*, vol. 11, p. 389.
99 al-Dhahabī, *Siyar a'lām al-nubalā'*, vol. 9, pp. 223–4.
100 See Diagram 2.

spread through the Common Link, PCLs and other transmitters to Iraq, as well as to other Muslim lands, including Palestine, Egypt, Syria, Tunisia, Transoxiana and Surxondaryo.

Textual Analysis

The text of the twenty-first variant recorded in Bukhārī's *Ṣaḥīḥ* begins with a different expression than the previous ones. This version starts with 'the Messenger of God was among us', while the previous variants began with either 'two men came before the Prophet' or 'we were with the Prophet'. This is a clear sign of paraphrasing. Aside from this difference, it contains certain elements from the previous variants, while also being interdependent. The twenty-second variant recorded in Bukhārī's *Ṣaḥīh* is identical to the twenty-first, and the twenty-third variant is identical to the sixteenth. Thus, there is no need to analyse both variants. The twenty-fourth variant only contains the chain of transmission along with a note from the author alluding to the fact that the text is similar to that of the twentieth.

While studying the reports related to the litigation of the two men, I have examined the variants related to the implementation of the stoning penalty. Upon completing the analysis of both chains of transmissions and textual variants, I can now conclude with confidence that all these variants can be traced back to the Common Link, Zuhrī, whose date of death is 124/742. Both chains of transmissions and texts hence correspond to each other.

That the variants were narrated from Zuhrī to several transmitters, who then passed the variants to various individuals, is indicative of a healthy transmission process. They were then eventually recorded in the Sunni hadith collections. All these variants are interdependent, yet they contain linguistical differences related to the Prophet litigating the dispute between the two men. The dispute was related to a man's overpaying the ransom to an adulteress woman's husband to save his son from a stoning penalty. Upon learning that the stoning penalty was not due on the son, the man brought the case before the Prophet for judgement. They both pleaded with the Prophet that he should judge according to the Book of God. In return, the Prophet reassured them that he would judge them according to the Book of God. He then corrected the previous settlement and passed the judgement of stoning for the adulteress. These common elements make up the original report and can be dated back to Zuhrī's date of death, 124/742. It is also likely that Zuhrī genuinely received this report from 'Ubaydullāh b. 'Abdullāh. Although he did not have a motive to forge it, it can only be dated back to 124/742. This is due to the absence of supporting evidence to date it back to 'Ubaydullāh b. 'Abdullāh.

Summary and Conclusion

The textual analysis of the variants confirms the findings in the chain of transmission analysis. The correlation between the transmission chains and the texts of the variants is clearly noticeable. The textual analysis also detects that the individual transmitters inserted their linguistic marks on the variants, such as the preference of the title 'the Prophet' instead of 'the Messenger of God'. I also pointed out one of the PCLs, Sufyān b. 'Uyayna, who deliberately edited the text and referred to Muhammad as *al-Nabī* (the Prophet). In all the other variants, Muhammad is referred to as *Rasūl Allāh* (Messenger of God).

I also tried to make sense of the linguistic variations between the use of the root *qāf-ḍād-yā'* in the form of the past active (*qaḍayta*, literally, 'you [have] decided') used by Sufyān b. 'Uyayna, Layth and Mālik. Conversely, 'Ubaydullāh b. 'Abdullāh and Ibn Abī Dhi'b used the imperative form (*aqḍī*, literally, 'judge!'). Both Arabic words are derived from the root *qāf-ḍād-yā'*, thus sharing similar meanings. I suggested that it was possible that the original form of the word was *aqḍī*, the imperative form which Zuhrī spread. The people went to the Prophet and pleaded with him to adjudicate the matter. The reason for the paraphrasing was either an unintentional mix-up or realigning the hadith with the relevant verse of the Qur'an.

There is a relevant verse in the Qur'an regarding this discussion and the exact expression *qaḍayta* as used in this verse may have been the real cause of the change to *qaḍayta*. Because the verse refers to the role of the Prophet as the ultimate decision-maker or judge among Muslims, the report goes hand in hand with this verse. Hence, the transmitters might have intentionally edited the hadith to establish its conformity with the relevant verse of the Qur'an. On the other hand, the textual editing could have been an unintentional mix-up.

As discussed previously, aside from its jurisprudential implementations, the report gives the impression that there was a stoning penalty in the Qur'an which was withdrawn later since no such verse is present in the Qur'anic codex. If this is correct, then the notion of distortion of the Qur'an becomes viable – even though the verse was withdrawn from the Qur'an, the ruling remained the same. John Burton examined this position in great detail and considered the idea of removal of verses from the Qur'an and preservation of their rulings as an invention of the legal schools to justify their viewpoints. Given the lack of compelling evidence for large-scale hadith forgery, such an assertion may seem far-fetched. Despite that, we need to deal with the idea that there is a group of reports attributed to the Prophet that support the claim that the Stoning Verse was originally in the Qur'an and that the Prophet judged accordingly. The next chapters will delve further into this idea. The alternative option may be that what was referred to in these variants as the Book of God is not the Qur'an but rather the Torah. Burton also articulated this theory. Unfortunately, there are few studies about using 'the Book of God' in early Islamic sources.

Nevertheless, it is probable that these nomadic Arabs came to the Prophet for arbitration and did not know much about the difference between the Qur'an and the Torah. They might have asked for a judgement according to the Torah or the divine law that the Prophet implemented, believing it was the Book of God. They asked the Prophet to judge according to the Book of God, meaning they wanted a religious verdict to be implemented on the defendants. Given that this was during the advent of Islam, it is unlikely that there were a group of Muslims entitled 'the people of knowledge' – whom the plaintiff asked for the correct judgement. It seems more plausible that they were referring to Jewish scholars, and that the Book of God referred to the Torah. A deliberate response from the Prophet that he would rule according to the Book of God reaffirms this view. However, at this point, such a view remains a theory as I could only trace the variants back to Zuhrī's date of death, 124/742.

Prior to examining the remaining variants, we may consider the possibility that the idea of distortion came into existence in the late first and early second Islamic centuries, and Zuhrī, through spreading the relevant reports, played a role in this process. A definitive conclusion may only be reached upon examining all the relevant evidence in the following chapters.

CHAPTER 3

The Prophet, the Jews and the Stoning Penalty

Of the reports related to the stoning penalty, one tradition is about an encounter between the Prophet and a group of Medinan Jews who came to him to ask for help with the litigation of a case involving two Jewish adulterers. During the episode, the Prophet questions the Jews regarding the ruling on adultery in the Torah, but they apparently misinform him. Thanks to the interference of ʿAbdullāh b. Salām,[1] who had converted to Islam from Judaism most probably eight years after the Prophet's emigration to Medina, the truth was revealed to the Prophet that the Torah included the stoning penalty for adulterers. Consequently, the Prophet ordered the two adulterers to be stoned to death. Here is a sample variant:

> Narrated to us by Mālik, on the authority of Nāfiʿ, on the authority of ʿAbdullāh b. ʿUmar, who said: The Jews came to the Messenger of God and asked the Prophet about a Jewish man and woman who committed adultery. The Messenger of God responded: 'What do you have about the issue of stoning in the Torah?' The Jews replied: 'We shame them and lash them.' ʿAbdullāh b. Salām then said: 'You have lied! Indeed, there is the stoning in the Torah.' They brought the Torah and spread it out. One of the Jews put his hand on the Stoning Verse, and then he read the verses before and after it [the Stoning Verse]. ʿAbdullāh b. Salām told the Jew: 'Raise your hand!' He raised his hand, and there was the Stoning Verse. The Jews said: 'He is truthful, O Muhammad! There is the Stoning Verse in the Torah.' The Messenger of God then ordered for them both to be stoned. ʿAbdullāh b. ʿUmar said: 'I saw the man was leaning over the woman to protect her [from the stones].' Yaḥyā said, I heard Mālik

1 Lecker, "Abdallāh b. Salām'.

> commenting: 'By "leaning over" 'Abdullāh b. 'Umar meant that the man threw himself over the woman, so the stones fell on him.'[2]

Aside from its significance in the implementation of the stoning penalty at the time of the Prophet, this chapter will further investigate the tentative findings of Chapter 2, namely, it could be that early Muslims referred to both the Torah and the Qur'an as the 'Book of God' interchangeably. Although I could not date the previous report back to the Prophet, there seems to be some confusion about what the Book of God referred to. This confusion did not seem to occur at the time of Zuhrī, who is the earlier transmitter to whom I could date the report. At the turn of the second/eighth century, the distinction between the Qur'an and the Torah was clear, yet at the time of the Prophet, such clarity may have been absent.

Since the report is about Muhammad's investigation to discover the censored 'Stoning Verse' in the Torah, it might further support the idea that when the two nomads came to Muhammad to adjudicate their case, they were referring to the Torah as the Book of God, and there was no clear distinction made at such a time.[3] Because I could not date the previous reports back to the Prophet, I cannot make a compelling case for this thesis. Yet, if I could date these variants back to the Prophet, I would prove that the Prophet initially ruled according to the Torah, at least amongst the Jews of Medina. It could be possible that he also judged between the Muslims according to this rule, especially in the case of implementing the stoning penalty. If this was the case, there was no missing Stoning Verse in the Qur'an in the first place. The Stoning Verse was in the Torah, but because both were referred to as the 'Book of God', the confusion emerged later on.

There is a precedence in the Qur'an that Muhammad implemented Jewish practices in the absence of Qur'anic injunctions or permissions, as it was in the case of praying towards Jerusalem as the Jews prayed. The direction of prayer was later changed towards Mecca, but the Qur'an made a specific reference to this instance because of the symbolic significance of the event, as it was a breaking point between the Jews and Muslims and the turning point of the emergence of an independent Muslim identity. However, the stoning penalty had no significance, and there was no need to make such a grand announcement. It was perhaps implemented only a handful of times, as per Jewish tradition, and when the Prophet announced the relevant verses of the Qur'an, the punishment was regulated according to the Qur'an in the form of lashing or confinement (Q. 4:15, 24:2,

2 Mālik, *Muwaṭṭa'*, vol. 5, pp. 1195–6.

3 Wegner, 'Islamic and Talmudic Jurisprudence'; Liebesny, 'Comparative Legal History'.

24:4–5).[4] Such a thesis is probable and depends on dating the reports back to the Prophet, along with the corroboration of textual evidence that I will try to assess.

Aside from shedding light on the issue of the stoning penalty and the notion of the distortion of the Qur'an, tracing the variants back to the Prophet would also provide some crucial information related to the biography of the Prophet (*sīra*), especially his dealings with the Jewish community of Medina. According to Muslim sources, one of Muhammad's first achievements upon his emigration to Medina was to form the so-called the Constitution of Medina, which brought the long-awaited peace and harmony to the inhabitants of Medina, where Jewish tribes had accumulated significant influence and power. One of the articles of the document allowed the Jews to refer to the Prophet for their unresolved disputes, which granted the Prophet authority for adjudication. In this sense, studying these variants will make it possible to further investigate the so-called Constitution of Medina, along with the Prophet's, and early Muslims', relations with the Jews of Medina.

There are twenty-nine variants of this report which are ascribed to the Prophet. The variants were recorded in seven canonical hadith collections: one in Mālik's *Muwaṭṭa'*, three in 'Abd al-Razzāq's *Muṣannaf*, five in Bukhārī's *Ṣaḥīḥ*, three in Ibn Mājah's *Sunan*, two in Tirmidhī's *Sunan*, ten in Abū Dāwūd's *Sunan* and five in Muslim's *Ṣaḥīḥ*. Unlike the other variants, Ibn Abī Shayba's *Muṣannaf* did not record any variants of this report. However, Ibn Abī Shayba's name is mentioned in one of the chains of transmission recorded in Muslim's *Ṣaḥīḥ*. The variants reached the written form through six different transmission lines. These lines go through Jābir b. Samūra and Jābir b. 'Abdullāh ← al-Barā' b. 'Āzib ← Ibrāhīm and al-Sha'bī ← 'Abdullāh b. 'Umar ← Abū Hurayra ← the Prophet.

Three transmission lines spread out of these six strands immediately after 'Abdullāh b. 'Umar, Ibrāhīm and al-Sha'bī and Jābir b. 'Abdullāh. Therefore, the Prophet Muhammad appears to be the source and Common Link of this report. In the remaining three transmission lines, the strands continue as single lines until they arrive at later generations. Nāfi', Mālik, Zuhrī, Mūsā b. 'Uqba, 'Ubaydullāh b. 'Umar, al-A'mash and Sharīk further spread the report to various transmitters, in which Nāfi' and Mālik seem to be playing an essential role. Out of these transmitters, 'Abdullāh b. 'Umar, al-A'mash, Zuhrī, Sharīk and Jābir b. 'Abdullāh, Ibrāhīm and al-Sha'bī seem to be the Partial Common Links (PCLs).

4 Juan Cole provides a detailed examination of the Qur'anic penalty for adultery and its relevance to Roman law. Cole, 'Late Roman Law and the Qur'anic Punishments for Adultery'; Holger Zellentin compares the Qur'anic penalty on sexual indecency with the biblical penalties. Zellentin, 'Gentile Purity Law from the Bible to the Qur'an'.

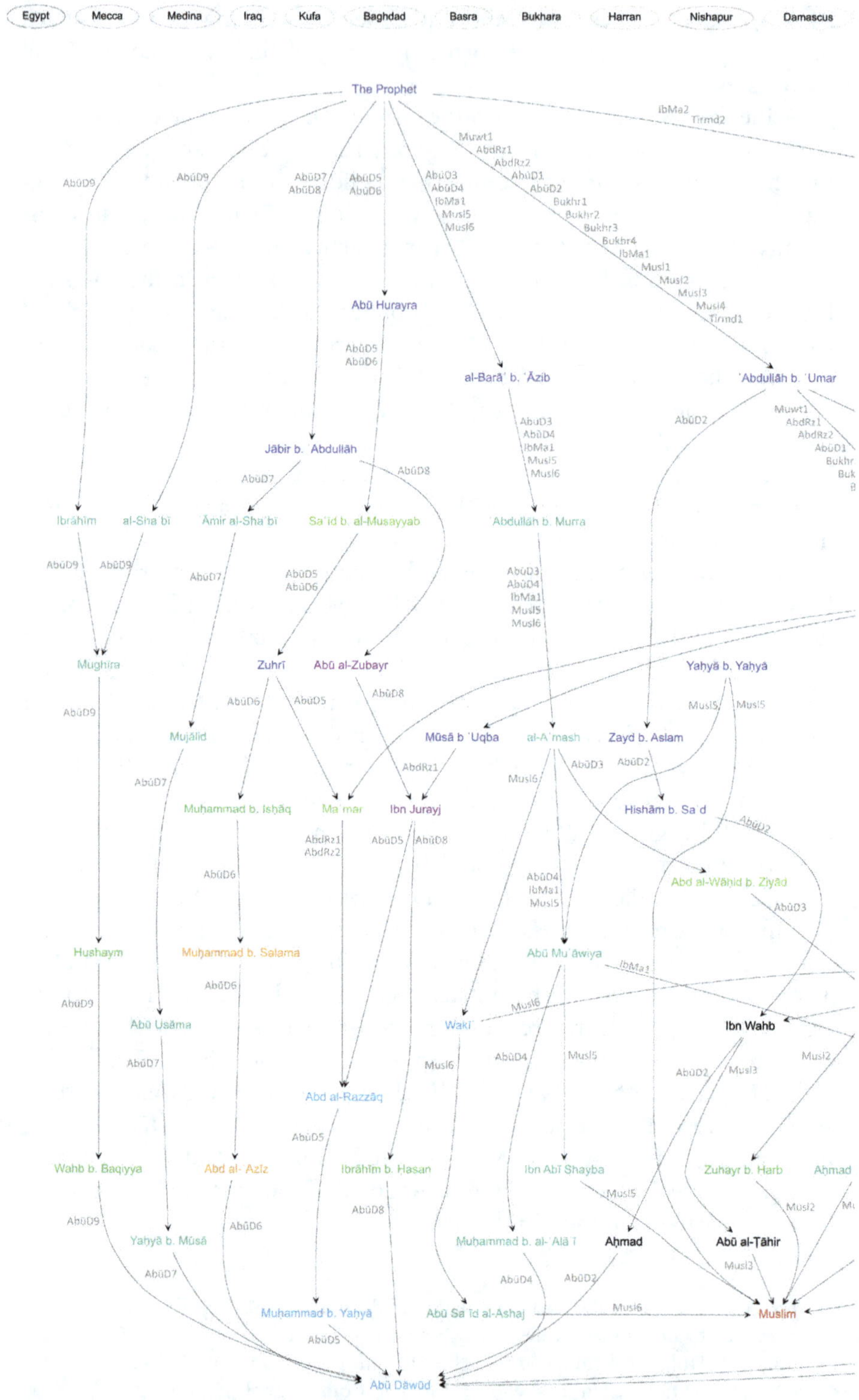

Diagram 3 Available online at: https://edin.ac/3PreUyS

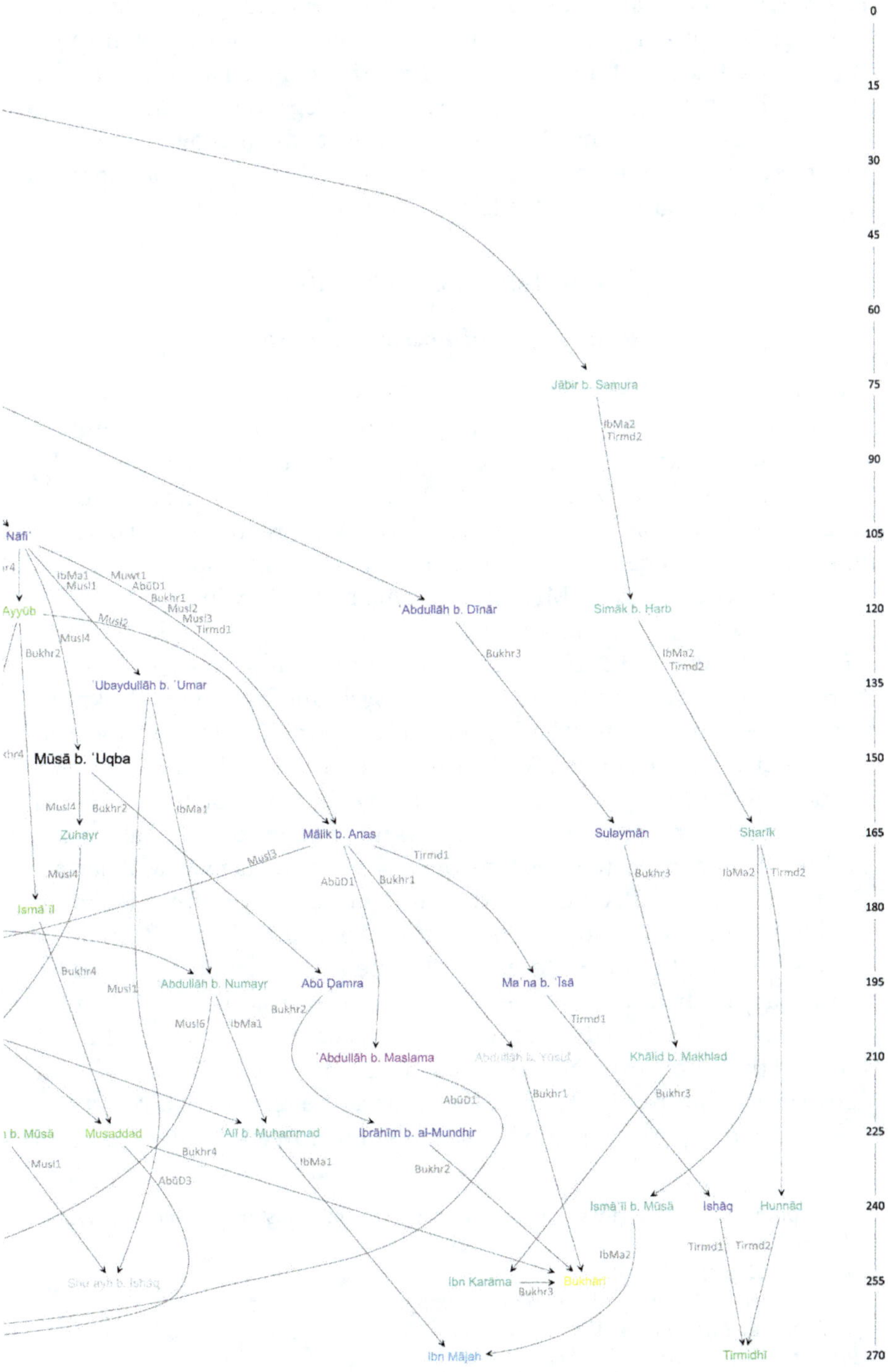

0
15
30
45
60
75
90
105
120
135
150
165
180
195
210
225
240
255
270
Jābir b. Samura
IbMa2
Tirmd2
Nāfi'
'Abdullāh b. Dīnār
Simāk b. Ḥarb
IbMa1
Musl1
Muwt1
AbūD1
Bukhr1
Musl2
Musl3
Tirmd1
Ayyūb
Musl4
Bukhr2
Bukhr3
'Ubaydullāh b. 'Umar
Mūsā b. 'Uqba
Zuhayr
Mālik b. Anas
Sulaymān
Sharīk
Ismā'īl
'Abdullāh b. Numayr
Abū Ḍamra
Ma'na b. 'Īsā
'Abdullāh b. Maslama
Khālid b. Makhlad
Musaddad
'Alī b. Muhammad
Ibrāhīm b. al-Mundhir
Ismā'īl b. Mūsā
Isḥāq
Hunnād
Ibn Karāma
Bukhārī
Ibn Mājah
Tirmidhī
Bukhr4
Musl6
AbūD3

To better analyse the variants, I initially grouped the variants according to these six PCLs. However, given that the Ibrāhīm and al-Sha'bī and Jābir b. 'Abdullāh and Sharīk clusters are too brief, I will study these three clusters together, placing all the variants in four groups. Having been spread through six different strands, some transmissions immediately fan out after the Prophet, making a promising start for this report. As a rule of thumb, tracing at least two strands back to the Prophet would allow the possibility of dating the tradition back to the Prophet Muhammad, provided the chains are in congruity with the textual variants.[5]

'Abdullāh b. 'Umar Cluster

Chain of Transmission Analysis

'Abdullāh b. 'Umar distributes fifteen variants of the report. The first chain of transmission was recorded in Mālik's *Muwaṭṭa'*,[6] and was transmitted up from Mālik ← Nāfi' ← 'Abdullāh b. 'Umar ← the Prophet. The relationship between Mālik (d. 179/795), Nāfi' (d. 118/736 or 119/737), the client of Ibn 'Umar and 'Abdullāh b. 'Umar (d. 73/693) is well established.[7] Therefore, this chain reaches back to the Prophet without interruption. This variant seems to have emerged in Medina and remained in Medina.

The second chain was recorded in 'Abd al-Razzāq's (d. 211/ 826) *Muṣannaf*.[8] 'Abd al-Razzāq was an itinerant hadith collector. He was born in Yemen but travelled to the Hijaz, Syria and Iraq to pursue knowledge and collect hadith. He compiled the reports in his eleven-volume collection titled *Muṣannaf*. Motzki provides a detailed analysis of 'Abd al-Razzāq and his *Muṣannaf*.[9] In his study, Motzki notes that Ma'mar (d. 153/770) was one of the primary informants of 'Abd al-Razzāq, and he also narrated this report from his teacher Ma'mar. Ma'mar and 'Abd al-Razzāq's paths crossed when the former moved from Basra, his birthplace, to Syria in order to study under Zuhrī. When Zuhrī died, Ma'mar moved to Yemen to escape the political turmoil that engulfed the Umayyad dynasty. It is then that 'Abd al-Razzāq became a student of Ma'mar and recorded his reports. On this occasion, however, Ma'mar received the report from Nāfi', instead of his teacher Zuhrī. Nāfi', who was active in Medina, received it from Ibn 'Umar, who received it directly from the Prophet. The relationship between the individuals mentioned in this

5 According to Juynboll, these kinds of *isnād* have the most historical value; see Juynboll, 'Nāfi'', pp. 210–11.
6 Mālik, *Muwaṭṭa'*, vol. 5, pp. 1195–6.
7 Motzki et al., *Analysing Muslim Traditions*, pp. 47–122.
8 al-Ṣan'ānī, *Muṣannaf*, vol. 7, p. 318.
9 Motzki, 'The *Muṣannaf* of 'Abd al-Razzāq'.

chain has already been established.[10] This variant therefore can safely be traced back to the Prophet. It seems that this variant originated in Medina and travelled to Yemen.

ʿAbd al-Razzāq (d. 211/ 826) received the third variant from Ibn Jurayj (d. 150/767–8).[11] ʿAbd al-Razzāq received Ibn Jurayj's reports from the latter's *Sunan*,[12] which is no longer extant. However, ʿAbd al-Razzāq preserved some of his teacher's work in his own *Muṣannaf*.[13] Ibn Jurayj mainly resided in the Hijaz but moved to Yemen and Iraq towards the end of his life to teach.[14] He received the variant from his teacher Mūsā b ʿUqba (d. 136/752–3 or 141/758–9), who was based in Medina and was a client (*mawlā*).[15] He was a well-known specialist in the *maghāzī* (expeditions of the Prophet) genre.[16] Mūsā b ʿUqba received it from Nāfiʿ, who was based in Medina. According to Motzki, the reports Ibn Jurayj receives from Nāfiʿ via Mūsā b ʿUqba are not fabricated.[17] This variant has the same chain. The rest of the chain reaches the Prophet through Ibn ʿUmar. This variant also seems to have originated in Medina and then moved to Yemen through Ibn Jurayj.

The fourth variant was recorded in Bukhārī's (d. 256/870) *Ṣaḥīḥ*[18] and reached Mālik through ʿAbdullāh b. Yūsuf (d. 217/832–3), who was a well-regarded scholar from Damascus, also active in Tunisia and Egypt.[19] He was also one of the transmitters of Mālik's *Muwaṭṭa'*.[20] I studied the connection between Bukhārī, ʿAbdullāh b. Yūsuf and Mālik in Chapter 2 and concluded that given the temporal and geographical proximity between these three scholars, it is probable that they narrated the report from one another. From Mālik, the chain goes back to Mālik's usual narrators, Nāfiʿ and ʿAbdullāh b. ʿUmar, after which it finally reaches the Prophet.

The fifth variant was recorded in Bukhārī's *Ṣaḥīḥ*.[21] Bukhārī received it from Ibrāhīm b. al-Mundhir (d. 236/850), a prominent informant of

10 Motzki et al., *Analysing Muslim Traditions*, pp. 1–45.

11 al-Ṣanʿānī, *Muṣannaf*, vol. 7, pp. 318–19.

12 Motzki, *The Origins of Islamic Jurisprudence*, pp. 204–42.

13 Motzki, 'Ibn Jurayj'.

14 Motzki, 'Ibn Jurayj'.

15 In the early Islamic period, the term *mawlā* referred to a non-Arab convert to Islam who established a relationship of clientage with an Arab tribe by converting under the guidance of an Arab. Nevertheless, this meaning underwent a shift during the transition from Umayyad to Abbasid rule, and the usage of the term gradually faded away (Bulliet, 'Conversion-Based Patronage and Onomastic Evidence in Early Islam', p. 246).

16 Juynboll, 'Mūsā b. ʿUqba'.

17 Motzki et al., *Analysing Muslim Traditions*, p. 74.

18 Bukhārī, *Ṣaḥīḥ*, vol. 2, p. 206.

19 al-Dhahabī, *Siyar aʿlām al-nubalā'*, vol. 10, pp. 357–8.

20 al-Khaṭīb al-Baghdādī, *Tārīkh Baghdād*, vol. 10, pp. 333–6.

21 Bukhārī, *Ṣaḥīḥ*, vol. 2, p. 37.

Bukhārī who resided in Medina.[22] Ibrāhīm b. al-Mundhir received the variant from another eminent scholar of Medina, Abū Ḍamra (d. 200/815–16), who, according to reports,[23] enjoyed a long life of ninety-six years.[24] He transmitted it from a fellow scholar of Medina, Mūsā b. ʿUqba (d. 136/752–3 or 141/758–9). From Mūsā b. ʿUqba, the chain goes up to Nāfiʿ ← ʿAbdullāh b. ʿUmar ← the Prophet. There are no issues with this chain. It seems that this variant emerged in Medina and remained there for a considerable period of time until the arrival of Bukhārī to the city in the first quarter of the third/ninth century. He then possibly spread it elsewhere.

Bukhārī received the chain of the sixth variant[25] from Ibn Karāma (d. 256/870), a hadith collector from Kufa.[26] Ibn Karāma received it from Khālid b. Makhlad (d. 213/828) of Kufa, but most of his informants were from Medina. He was considered trustworthy and was known to be a Shiʿi.[27] He received the variant from Sulaymān [b. Bilāl] (d. 172/788–9 or 177/793–4), who was active in Medina.[28] Sulaymān b. Bilāl received it from ʿAbdullāh b. Dīnār (d. 127/744–5), who was a resident of Medina.[29] ʿAbdullāh b. Dīnār received the variant from ʿAbdullāh b. ʿUmar (d. 73/693), through whom the variant reached the Prophet. The chain is healthy and can be traced back to the Prophet without interruption. This variant travelled from Medina to Kufa, possibly by Khālid b. Makhlad. Bukhārī must have received it when he travelled to Kufa and recorded it. This is an important variant because although it is transmitted through ʿAbdullāh b. ʿUmar, it does not encounter Nāfiʿ, who transmits this same report to several other transmitters.

The chain of the seventh variant is recorded in Bukhārī's *Ṣaḥīh*,[30] who received it from his teacher Musaddad [b. Musarhad] (d. 228/843). He was a prominent hadith collector who narrated from the third generation of Muslims. He was active in the city of Basra and a student of Sufyān b. ʿUyayna.[31] As I studied Musaddad's connection to Bukhārī in Chapter 2, there is no need to delve further into that. Musaddad received the variant from Ismāʿīl [b. ʿUlayya] (d. 193/809–10), who initially was from Kufa and then resided in Basra.[32] He received the variant from Ayyūb [b. Abī Tamīma al-Sakhtiyānī] (d. 125/443–4 or 131/748–9), a prominent scholar

22 al-Dhahabī, *Siyar aʿlām al-nubalāʾ*, vol. 10, pp. 689–91.
23 al-Dhahabī, *Siyar aʿlām al-nubalāʾ*, vol. 9, p. 87.
24 al-Dhahabī, *Siyar aʿlām al-nubalāʾ*, vol. 9, p. 87.
25 Bukhārī, *Ṣaḥīḥ*, vol. 8, p. 165–6.
26 al-Dhahabī, *Siyar aʿlām al-nubalāʾ*, vol. 12, pp. 297–8.
27 al-Dhahabī, *Siyar aʿlām al-nubalāʾ*, vol. 10, p. 218.
28 al-Dhahabī, *Siyar aʿlām al-nubalāʾ*, vol. 7, pp. 425–6.
29 al-Dhahabī, *Siyar aʿlām al-nubalāʾ*, vol. 5, p. 253.
30 Bukhārī, *Ṣaḥīḥ*, vol. 9, p. 158.
31 al-Mizzī, *Tahdhīb al-kamāl fī asmāʾ al-rijāl*, vol. 10, pp. 443–8.
32 al-Khaṭīb al-Baghdādī, *Tārīkh Baghdād*, vol. 7, pp. 196–211.

and client from Basra. He received it from Nāfiʿ.[33] From Nāfiʿ, the chain reaches ʿAbdullāh b. ʿUmar, and then to the Prophet. This variant emerged in Medina and travelled to Basra through Ayyūb, and Bukhārī collected it from Basra.

The eighth chain[34] has the same chain as the sixth variant, therefore there is no need to delve into it. The ninth chain of transmission is recorded in Ibn Mājah's (d. 273/887) *Sunan*.[35] He was born in Qazvin, located in modern-day Iran, and travelled to the Hijaz, Iraq, Syria and Egypt. He received this variant from ʿAlī b. Muḥammad [al-Ṭanāfisī] (d. 233/847–8), who was active in Kufa and Qazvin.[36] Ibn Mājah probably received this report from ʿAlī b. Muḥammad in Kufa. ʿAlī b. Muḥammad received the variant from ʿAbdullāh b. Numayr (d. 199/814–15), who was a resident of Kufa[37] and received the variant from ʿUbaydullāh b. ʿUmar [al-ʿUmarī] (d. 147/764–5), a resident of Medina.[38] He received the variant from Nāfiʿ (d. 118/736 or 119/737), who then received it from Ibn ʿUmar and Ibn ʿUmar from the Prophet. ʿAbdullāh b. Numayr had spread this variant from Medina to Kufa, and its transmission was uninterrupted.

Tirmidhī (d. 279/892) was born in Surxondaryo, which is located in south-east Uzbekistan. He received the tenth variant from Isḥāq b. Mūsā al-Anṣārī (d. 244/858–9).[39] He resided in Medina, Samarra and Nishapur and was among Tirmidhī's favourite informants. Tirmidhī travelled widely to the Hijaz, Iraq and Khorasan; therefore, he could have received the variant directly from Isḥāq. I discussed the sound relationship between the two in Chapter 1. Isḥāq received the variant from Maʿna [b. ʿĪsā] (d. 198/814), a resident of Medina and Mālik's prominent student.[40] He received this variant from his teacher Mālik (d. 179/795) and then from Nāfiʿ ← Ibn ʿUmar ← the Prophet. This variant travelled from Medina to Samarra and Nishapur through Maʿna.

Abū Dāwūd (d. 275/889) recorded the eleventh variant from ʿAbdullāh b. Maslama [al-Qaʿnabī] (d. 221/836–7),[41] who was a reputable second-generation scholar of hadith. He was initially from Medina and lived in Mecca and Basra. Abū Dāwūd was born in Sistan and travelled to Iraq, Syria, the Hijaz, Egypt, Nishapur and Merv to collect hadith. It is possible

33 Motzki discussed the veracity of this chain in Motzki et al., *Analysing Muslim Traditions*, pp. 79–80.
34 Bukhārī, *Ṣaḥīḥ*, vol. 8, p. 172.
35 Ibn Mājah, *Sunan*, vol. 1, p. 854.
36 al-Dhahabī, *Siyar aʿlām al-nubalāʾ*, vol. 11, p. 460.
37 al-Dhahabī, *Siyar aʿlām al-nubalāʾ*, vol. 9, p. 244.
38 al-Mizzī, *Tahdhīb al-kamāl fī asmāʾ al-rijāl*, vol. 19, pp. 124–9.
39 Tirmidhī, *Sunan*, vol. 2, p. 95.
40 al-Dhahabī, *Siyar aʿlām al-nubalāʾ*, vol. 9, p. 305.
41 al-Dhahabī, *Siyar aʿlām al-nubalāʾ*, vol. 4, p. 154.

that he received the report from ʿAbdullāh b. Maslama in Basra or the Hijaz. Like the variant that he transmitted in Chapter 1, he received it from Mālik and transmitted it to Abū Dāwūd. However, in this variant, Mālik's source is not Zuhrī, but rather Nāfiʿ, who received it from Ibn ʿUmar ← the Prophet. There is no interruption in this chain, and ʿAbdullāh b. Maslama spread this report in Basra at the turn of the third/ninth century, and after him, Abū Dāwūd spread it elsewhere.

Abū Dāwūd recorded the twelfth chain from Aḥmad b. Saʿīd al-Ḥamdānī (d. 253/867),[42] who was a resident of Egypt.[43] Aḥmad b. Saʿīd al-Ḥamdānī received the variant from [ʿAbdullāh] Ibn Wahb (d. 197/812–13), a prominent scholar in Egypt.[44] He received it from Hishām b. Saʿd (d. 160/867–8), who was based in Medina. Ibn Wahb likely received the variant from him during one of his numerous visits to the holy sites in Medina. Hishām b. Saʿd received it from his teacher Zayd b. Aslam (d. 136/753–4), a scholar from Medina whose father was a client of ʿUmar b. al-Khaṭṭāb. Zayd b. Aslam received it from Ibn ʿUmar (d. 74/693), who heard it from the Prophet.[45] This chain also seems to be sound and indicates that in addition to Mecca, Basra, Kufa and Yemen, the variant was also spread to Egypt via Ibn Wahb.

Muslim (d. 261/874–5) received the thirteenth variant from al-Ḥakam b. Mūsā (d. 232/847), a prominent hadith collector from Baghdad.[46] Muslim was born in Nishapur, and travelled to the Hijaz, Iraq, Syria and Egypt to collect hadith. Therefore, Muslim must have received the report from al-Ḥakam b. Mūsā when he was in Baghdad. Al-Ḥakam b. Mūsā received it from Shuʿayb b. Isḥāq (d. 264/877–8), who was born in 190/805–6 and resided in Damascus.[47] He received the variant from ʿUbaydullāh b. ʿUmar (d. 147/764–5), a resident of Medina.[48] He received it from Nāfiʿ (d. 118/736 or 119/737), who also transmitted the eleventh variant of this report through the same chain. Therefore, this chain is also uninterrupted.

Muslim received the fourteenth variant through two different lower transmission lines reconnecting at Mālik b. Anas, one of which started with Zuhayr b. Ḥarb (d. 234/849), who was born in Khorasan and moved to Baghdad.[49] He received the variant from the Basran Ismāʿīl b. ʿUlayya (d. 193/809–10),[50] who received it from a prominent scholar of Basra, Ayyūb

42 al-Dhahabī, *Siyar aʿlām al-nubalāʾ*, vol. 4, p. 155.
43 al-Dhahabī, *Siyar aʿlām al-nubalāʾ*, vol. 12, pp. 232–3.
44 al-Dhahabī, *Siyar aʿlām al-nubalāʾ*, vol. 9, pp. 224–34.
45 al-Dhahabī, *Siyar aʿlām al-nubalāʾ*, vol. 5, pp. 316–17.
46 al-Dhahabī, *Siyar aʿlām al-nubalāʾ*, vol. 11, pp. 5–6.
47 al-Dhahabī, *Siyar aʿlām al-nubalāʾ*, vol. 12, pp. 304–5.
48 al-Mizzī, *Tahdhīb al-kamāl fī asmāʾ al-rijāl*, vol. 19, pp. 124–9.
49 al-Dhahabī, *Siyar aʿlām al-nubalāʾ*, vol. 11, pp. 490–3.
50 al-Dhahabī, *Siyar aʿlām al-nubalāʾ*, vol. 9, pp. 108–21.

[b. Abī Tamīma][51] (d. 131/748–9 or 132/749–50).[52] The second line starts with Abū al-Ṭāhir [b. al-Sarḥ] (d. 250/864) of Egypt.[53] He reported it from his teacher Ibn Wahb. From this point, both lines reconnect at Mālik b. Anas ← Nāfiʿ ← ʿAbdullāh b. ʿUmar ← the Prophet.

Muslim received the fifteenth variant from his Kufan informant Aḥmad b. Yūnus (d. 227/842), who received the variant from another Kufan scholar, Zuhayr [b. Muʿāwiya][54] (d. circa 173/789–90), who received it from the Medinan hadith collector Mūsā b. ʿUqba (d. 136/752–3 or 141/758–9). Mūsā b. ʿUqba received it from Nāfiʿ, from whom the chain of transmission passes through Ibn ʿUmar until the Prophet. In addition to the three strands reaching Ibn ʿUmar, the reinforcement of this finding is strengthened by the view of classical hadith critics regarding the iconic nature of Nāfiʿ's association with Ibn ʿUmar.[55] The transmission lines of ʿAbdullāh b. ʿUmar's cluster are healthy, meaning they reach back to the PCL ʿAbdullāh b. ʿUmar without interruption. Therefore, based on the chain of transmission analysis, this group of variants can be traced back to the date of ʿAbdullāh b. ʿUmar's death, 73/693.

Textual Analysis

The texts of the variants narrate a curious encounter between the Prophet and a group of Jews who seemingly asked the Prophet's help in settling a dispute among the Jews of Medina. A Jewish man and woman who committed adultery were brought before the Prophet for arbitration. Some of the variants hint that Jewish scholars were in dispute regarding the harshness of the intended punishment and sought the arbitration of the Prophet. The textual evidence suggests that the Prophet sought to resolve the matter according to the Torah; he did not try to impose Islamic rulings on the Jews. As a result of his investigation, Muhammad found out that according to the Torah, the correct punishment for adulterers was the stoning penalty.

However, some variants state that the Jews did not come to the Prophet, but rather that the Prophet approached them upon witnessing the alternative punishment the Jews implemented on the adulterating man and woman. The Prophet took it upon himself to revive the true punishment, which was the stoning penalty. In at least one of the variants, the episode takes place when the Prophet visits a Jewish seminary. In some of the

51 Juynboll, *Encyclopaedia of Canonical Ḥadīth*, pp. 144–8.

52 Motzki established the veracity of the reports transmitted through this chain; Motzki et al., *Analysing Muslim Traditions*, pp. 78–81.

53 al-Dhahabī, *Siyar aʿlām al-nubalāʾ*, vo. 12, pp. 62–3.

54 al-Dhahabī, *Siyar aʿlām al-nubalāʾ*, vol. 8, pp. 182–7.

55 I express my gratitude to the anonymous reviewer for this valuable insight.

variants, the name of 'Abdullāh b. Salām was mentioned as a knowledgeable former Jew who had converted to Islam and informed the Prophet about the correct punishment in the Torah, while some other variants omitted his involvement.

According to the initial analysis, there seem to be two major elements of discord in the variants. I will be paying particular attention to these elements in the textual analysis. As mentioned in the sample report above, one of the elements of the variants is that a group of Jews came to the Prophet to urge him to arbitrate their dispute about the punishment for adultery. Out of all variants, nineteen include this information, and three note that the Prophet witnessed a group of Jews who were implementing an alternative punishment on two adulterers. Therefore, he enquired about the punishment related to adultery in Jewish scripture. The remaining seven variants are too short and do not include information about the matter. The second significant element is that eleventh variants state 'Abdullāh b. Salām had a decisive role in uncovering the penalty prescribed in the Torah for adulterers. However, thirteen variants ignore 'Abdullāh b. Salām's role and state that it was the Prophet who found out about the actual punishment for the adulteress in Jewish scripture. Five variants are again too short and thus omit any additional information about the matter.

Was 'Abdullāh b. Salām Involved in the Stoning Narrative?

The first text was recorded in Mālik's *Muwaṭṭa'* and narrates the event centred around 'Abdullāh b. Salām (d. circa 43/663), who was a member of the powerful Jewish Banū Qaynuqā' tribe. There are conflicting reports about the date of his conversion to Islam.[56] Based on these reports, Hirschfeld and Lecker contend that he converted to Islam eight years after the Muslim emigration to Medina.[57] According to the variant, when the Jews asked about the punishment for adultery, the Prophet directly enquired about the existence of the stoning penalty in the Torah. They responded with a dual punishment: 'We shame them and lash them.' The answer suggests that according to the Torah, shaming and lashing were the intended punishments. However, 'Abdullāh b. Salām interrupted the conversation and accused the Jews of hiding the existence of the stoning penalty in the Torah. The Jews then brought the Torah to investigate the matter further and it became apparent that the reciter concealed the Stoning Verse in the Torah. Yet, thanks to 'Abdullāh b. Salām's intervention, the existence of the stoning penalty in the Torah was exposed. Consequently, the Prophet

56 For the most detailed study on 'Abdullāh b. Salām, see Stafford, 'The Conversions of 'Abdallāh ibn Salām (d. 43/ 633)'.

57 Hirschfeld, 'Abdallah ibn Salam', pp. 43–4; Lecker, "Abdallāh b. Salām'.

ordered the two adulterers to be stoned. At this point, ʿAbdullāh b. ʿUmar, who narrated the episode from the Prophet, witnessed the actual stoning and provided dramatic detail about how the man leaned over the woman to protect her from the stones during the stoning.

Curiously, the Prophet did not seem to be concerned with establishing the existence of adultery. Rather, his focus was to establish the existence of the stoning penalty in the Torah. The Prophet did not question the number of witnesses, what they actually witnessed or if the culprits confessed to the crime. As soon as it became clear that the penalty was present in the Torah, he ordered the execution of the adulterers. This information may be a piece of crucial evidence for the role of the Prophet as an arbitrator, and not a judge, whose aim was to find out the true punishment for adultery in the Torah rather than implement an Islamic court system. Under such a circumstance, the primary aim of a judge of any legal tradition would have been to establish the existence of the offence first, not to establish the nature of the punishment.

The second text was recorded in ʿAbd al-Razzāq's *Muṣannaf* and narrated via Ibn ʿUmar. Ibn ʿUmar explicitly stated that he witnessed the event wherein Jews came to the Prophet for arbitration, and he requested a Torah reciter. When the reciter came, the Prophet questioned him about the existence of the stoning penalty in the Torah. The reciter first denied it and stated that the penalty for adulterers was 'blackening their faces and to be carried around by a donkey in public'. However, either the Prophet or someone with him asked the Jews for a reciter to recite the relevant section of the Torah. The reciter attempted to hide the existence of the stoning penalty, but ʿAbdullāh b. Salām intervened and exposed the existence of the Stoning Verse in the Torah. The Prophet immediately ordered the stoning of both adulterers. Finally, Ibn ʿUmar noted the dramatic end of the convicts; the man tried to shield the woman from the stones.

At this point, I can make several initial observations: (1) the Jews who came to the Prophet were not religious scholars; they were common Jews who neither possessed the Torah nor could recite it. Therefore, the Prophet either requested a Torah reciter or visited a Jewish seminary to enquire about the Stoning Verse (this element is included in the Zuhrī cluster, which I will study below). (2) It appears that the dispute among the Jewish group was about the execution of the stoning penalty, as one can imagine that in such a dramatic situation, the cheated husband and his family or the cheated wife's family demanded the harshest punishment. At the same time, the relatives of the adulterers pleaded for the lightest punishment. It may be for this reason that the Prophet directly asked about the possible existence of the stoning penalty in Jewish scripture. (3) The Jews came to the Prophet for arbitration, which means the people of Medina acknowledged the Prophet's role in early Medinan society as an arbitrator, and perhaps even a leader. (4) Finally, upon discovering the 'correct punishment' for the adulterers in the Torah, the Prophet decided to implement the stoning penalty. Only a leader with political authority could have the power to execute such a severe punishment. Consequently, aside from his arbitration role, the Prophet might have had political power in the early Medinan society.

The 'Constitution of Medina'

The third and fourth points inevitably lead to a crucial document related to the early history of Islam: the so-called Constitution of Medina. The document was reportedly drafted soon after the Prophet's emigration from Mecca to Medina. It was drafted in the second year of emigration to establish social cohesion in the Medinan society and perhaps even consolidate Muhammad's influence. The Medinan society was made up of Muslims, polytheists and Jews. Julius Wellhausen, W. Montgomery Watt, Michael Lecker, M. Gil, R. B. Serjeant and Saïd Amir Arjomand examined the document in detail from different perspectives.[58] The study of these major works on the Constitution indicates that there seems to be little dispute on the document's authenticity or content.[59] It was built upon the existing Arabian political patterns and customs, and assigned Muhammad the role of ultimate arbiter, as Serjeant articulated:

> Muhammad acted in accordance with Arabian political patterns in existence from the remote past. In one sense he is simply a judge-arbiter, a *ḥakam* like his series of ancestors, and he was responsible for but few modifications to Arabian law and society.[60]

According to Serjeant, the clause in the Constitution which stated 'in whatever thing you are at variance, its reference is back (*maradd*) to Allah, Great and Glorious, and to Muhammad'[61] granted the authority of arbitration to the Prophet, which is very significant as it established 'Muhammad as the ultimate arbitrator between the various groups

58 Saïd Amir Arjomand provides a detailed review of these works; see Arjomand, 'The Constitution of Medina', pp. 555–75.

59 Patricia Crone makes an unconvincing attempt to discredit the Constitution of Medina; see Crone, *Roman, Provincial and Islamic Law*, pp. 32–3; see also Hallaq, 'The Use and Abuse of Evidence', pp. 79–91.

60 Serjeant, 'The "Sunnah Jāmi'ah", Pacts with the Yat̲h̲rib Jews, and the "Taḥrīm" of Yat̲h̲rib', p. 1.

61 Serjeant, 'The "Sunnah Jāmi'ah", Pacts with the Yat̲h̲rib Jews, and the "Taḥrīm" of Yat̲h̲rib', pp. 23–5.

in Medina'. Uri Rubin further elaborates on the scope of the Prophet's authority as an arbitrator:

> This article declares that the Muslims of Quraysh and Yathrib, as well as the Jews, constitute one unity, sharing the same religious orientation, thus being distinct from all the rest of the people who adhere to other kinds of faith. It is thereby clear that the new unity is designed to be based not only on common sacred territory but also on common faith.[62]

Based on these studies, it is obvious that Islam, as a nascent faith, was in the process of forming its identity and associated itself closely with Judaism in the initial stages. The Prophet continued to implement the existing laws in Medinan society, which were not perceived as infringing on the divine will. Based on this association, the Prophet entered into agreements with local Muslim and Jewish tribes of Medina and played the role of arbitrator.[63]

Therefore, the episode of the stoning of the two Jewish adulterers may be considered within the aforementioned context. Upon ratifying the document, the Jews of Medina considered the Prophet to be an arbitrator to approach for matters of dispute. In this vein, the agitated relatives of the two adulterers came to the Prophet to seek arbitration. The episode corresponds to the historical document of the Constitution of Medina. However, it would be far-fetched to assume that the Jewish political and religious leaders had the same kind of expectation of arbitration from the Prophet in relation to the affairs of their communities, which could have granted the Prophet overarching political and religious legitimacy. The subsequent hostilities between the Jewish tribes and Muslims support this argument.

Given that the Jews who came to the Prophet for arbitration could not recite the Torah, the Prophet had to seek a reciter, making it clear that these Jews were common people. The first variant does not mention if they requested a reciter, but it implies that the reciter may have arrived together with the Torah: 'They brought the Torah and spread it out. One of the Jews put his hand on the Stoning Verse, and then he read the verses before and after it [the Stoning Verse].' Although the Jewish leaders did not acknowledge the religious authority of Muhammad, based on the study of the traditions at hand, they initially accepted his arbitration authority as he had the power to execute the two adultering Jews, even as it is related to the disputed matter of the stoning penalty. If this is the case, then the present study corroborates with the earlier dating of the Constitution of Medina,

62 Rubin, 'The "Constitution of Medina"', p. 13.

63 Ramon Harvey also offered similar analysis of the Prophet's role in this regard; Harvey, *The Qur'an and the Just Society*, pp. 102–4.

which is that it was drafted soon after the arrival of the Prophet to Medina. Therefore, it is based on this document that the Prophet arbitrated the disputed matters among the common Jews of Medina.

Furthermore, unlike the Qur'an, there is indeed a Stoning Verse in the Torah:[64]

> 22 If a man is found sleeping with another man's wife, both the man who slept with her and the woman must die. You must purge the evil from Israel. 23 If a man happens to meet in a town a virgin pledged to be married and he sleeps with her, 24 you shall take both of them to the gate of that town and stone them to death – the young woman because she was in a town and did not scream for help, and the man because he violated another man's wife. You must purge the evil from among you. (Deuteronomy: 22–24)

However, it is not clear which version of the Torah the local Jews of Medina held at the time,[65] which means the verse might have been different from the verse quoted above.[66] Nevertheless, assuming that this was the verse that existed in the Torah, upon discovering the existence of the verse, the Prophet had the offenders stoned. We can therefore state with relative certainty that Muhammad acted upon the Torah, the Book of God, to arbitrate on the matter. But does it also mean that the Prophet adopted Jewish law and implemented it on Muslims too?

So far, I have studied one tradition in the first section of the chapter, according to which the tradition can only be dated to Zuhrī's (d. 124/742) date of death. Another tradition, which I chose not to include in this book because Pavel Pavlovitch studied the report according to *isnād-cum-matn* analysis,[67] was about the stoning of Māʿiz b. Mālik. He dated the variants to Zuhrī's death.[68] In his second study[69] on the variants about a pregnant adulteress,[70] he traces the variants to a much later period: the death of ʿAbd

64 For an examination of Jewish practices related to adulterers, see Mazuz, *The Religious and Spiritual Life of the Jews of Medina*, pp. 49–51.

65 Bar-Asher's recent work provides an overview of different views on the nature of the Jews of Medina. Bar-Asher, *Jews and the Qur'an*. The most exhaustive investigation into the origins of the Jews of Medina was conducted by Haggai Mazuz in *The Religious and Spiritual Life of the Jews of Medina*. Mazuz posits that the Jews of Medina adhered to the Talmudic-Rabbinic tradition (p. 99 and *passim*). See also Gil, 'The Origin of the Jews of Yathrib'.

66 See Campbell, *Deciphering the Dead Sea Scrolls*, pp. 22–39.

67 I have located fifty variants of this tradition.

68 Pavlovitch, 'Early Development of the Tradition of the Self-confessed Adulterer in Islam'.

69 Pavlovitch, 'The Stoning of a Pregnant Adulteress from Juhayna'.

70 I have located thirteen variants of this tradition.

al-Razzāq (d. 211/826). The report that I studied in the first section and Pavlovitch studied in his two separate articles are the most important traditions for the justification of the stoning penalty by Sunni legal schools. Yet, they could only be potentially dated to a much later period than the tradition at hand, that Muhammad implemented the stoning penalty according to the Torah.

The text of the third variant again goes through the line of Nāfiʿ from Ibn ʿUmar, yet unlike the second variant, which goes through Maʿmar after Nāfiʿ, it reaches ʿAbd al-Razzāq through Ibn Jurayj from Mūsā b. ʿUqba. The astonishing interdependence of the texts is noticeable, albeit with some differences due to variances in the transmission lines after Nāfiʿ. I may include in this interdependence the text of the first variant that was also transmitted through the same Common Link, ʿAbdullāh b. ʿUmar. Similar to the first and second variants, the element of the Jews coming to the Prophet for arbitration is also present in the text of the third variant. The Prophet enquired about the ruling mentioned in the Torah for adultery. He was then misinformed by the reciter of the Torah, which was brought to his attention by ʿAbdullāh b. Salām, and when he uncovered the existence of the stoning penalty, he ordered for it to be implemented. Finally, the variant mentions the note that the adulterer man leaned over the woman to shield her from the stones.

Aside from these common elements, the text at hand provides different information. Unlike the first variant, the Prophet only asked about 'how they deal with someone who has committed adultery'. There is no mention of the Torah in the question, and neither did he refer to the stoning penalty. Furthermore, the Jews replied to his question with 'we strike them', meaning that they lash the adulterers. This information was not included in the first and second variants. After this point, Muhammad questioned them about the Torah, and they misinformed him by denying the existence of the stoning penalty. It could be possible that during the transmission process, some of the narrations of the episode were paraphrased, and some of the details were omitted and interpolated into the text. Most of these variations can therefore be explained as a natural process of oral transmission.

Islamic Legal Dispute about Dual-versus-Single-Penalty (DvSP)

However, the only problem is with the statement 'we strike them'. In the first and second variants, the Jews reply to the same question with 'we blacken the face and shame them in public by carrying them on a donkey'. While the text of the fourth variant is almost identical to the first variant – as Mālik reported it to ʿAbdullāh b. Yūsuf through the same chain – it also did not include the element 'we strike them'. The fifth variant, which contains similar elements that are mentioned in the Nāfiʿ sub-bundles, includes this element in the form 'we blacken both their faces and strike them both'. So it appears that the fifth variant combines both public shame and striking. The element of 'striking' appears only in the third and fifth variants, which suggests that the interpolation of 'striking' is the work of Mūsā b. ʿUqba (d. 136/752–3 or 141/758–9) as he is the common informant in both variants.

At this juncture, I could take two different views on the matter. On the sceptical side, Mūsā b. ʿUqba could have wilfully tampered with the variant to implement his own agenda. On the cautious side, he made a genuine mistake when transmitting the variant. If I choose to pursue the sceptical approach, I need to have supporting evidence, which in this case would be the motive to do so. In this vein, Pavlovitch's dual-versus-single-penalty (DvSP) legal dispute thesis in relation to the punishment of adulterers in the second and third centuries of Islam may provide an important motive for such an interpolation. According to the theory, until the time of Shāfiʿī[71] (d. 204/820), Muslim jurists prescribed the dual punishment: of stoning and lashing for adulterers. However, Shāfiʿī moved away from this practice and advocated either the stoning or the lashing, but not both.[72] However, Pavlovitch refers to the *Sunna* of al-Marwazī (d. 294/907), which is the earliest work of a Shāfiʿī jurist that records the DvSP dispute and notes that 'By mentioning a group of scholars from our age and its proximity', al-Marwazī indicated that 'the upholders of DPA [dual punishment for adulterers] flourished both during his lifetime and shortly before his birth in 202/817, which, incidentally, almost coincides with Shāfiʿī's death in 204/820'.[73]

It appears, however, that the existence of DvSP contentions predates Shāfiʿī. Mūsā b. ʿUqba died in 136/752–3 (or 141/758–9) and it seems that he inserted the element of 'striking' in the text deliberately to counter arguments of those who advocated the use of dual punishment. The text of the variant provided an excellent opportunity for such a motivation. The Jews had deviated from the singular punishment of the stoning penalty by implementing the dual punishment of public shaming and lashing. When the Prophet learned about the deviation from the dual punishment, he reinstated the sole punishment of stoning. Therefore, the dual punishment of stoning and lashing was also a form of deviation. However, it is also possible that Mūsā b. ʿUqba's mind was deeply immersed in these debates. Thus, he made such an interpolation without even realising it. Based on this information, in either case, it appears that the DvSP debate predates Shāfiʿī as it was already being discussed among the Medinan jurists at the turn of the second/eighth century.

71 On Shāfiʿī, see Ali, *Imam Shāfiʿī*.

72 Pavlovitch, 'The Islamic Penalty for Adultery', p. 478.

73 Pavlovitch, 'The Islamic Penalty for Adultery', pp. 479–80.

The text of the sixth variant includes the common elements mentioned in the previous variants, albeit they are slightly paraphrased: the Jews came to the Prophet for arbitration, ʿAbdullāh b. Salām confronted the information provided by the Jews on the punishment and then he pointed out the correct punishment that is stated in the Torah. Finally, the Prophet ordered the two adulterers to be stoned. The chain of the text branches out from Ibn ʿUmar separately yet confirms much of the information included in the Nāfiʿ sub-bundles. There is only one piece of information which was not available in the text of the previous variants, namely, Ibn ʿUmar states that he was present in the crowd when the two Jews were stoned, and that the man leaned over the woman to shield her from the stones. However, before this information, he states that they were stoned in *balāṭ*, referring to a place at the side of the Prophet's Mosque in Medina. His presence is a possibility, because of the detail he provided about the man leaning over the woman to shield her from the stones, but it cannot be verified at this point.

The text of the seventh variant included two peculiar textual characteristics which are different from the previous ʿAbdullāh b. ʿUmar clusters. First, there is no mention of ʿAbdullāh b. Salām in this variant as the conversation only takes place between the Prophet and the group of Jews. Second, it provides more details on the reciter of the Torah: 'They came with the Torah and asked a one-eyed man, whom they have chosen, to recite it.' The absence of ʿAbdullāh b. Salām makes the variant problematic as an ex-Jewish scholar who was fluent in Hebrew could spot the verse that the reciter was hiding under his palm from the Prophet. The Prophet did not speak Hebrew; he especially would not have been able to read an ancient Hebrew text like the Torah. Since ʿAbdullāh b. Salām has been referenced in previous variants, the omission of his name in this specific transmission could be a result of the transmission process. However, his significant involvement in uncovering the scheme of concealing the Stoning Verse in the Torah raises suspicion. It is important to note that this is an initial observation, and a more comprehensive examination of the remaining texts might lead to a deeper comprehension.

The text of the eighth variant is the same as the other Nāfiʿ sub-bundles, with minor differences that correspond with the divergence in the transmission process of the variants. However, one issue that emerges in the variants is that when the Jews came to the Prophet for arbitration, the Prophet asked them what punishment they practised. Some variants, namely, the first, which was recorded in Mālik's *Muwaṭṭaʾ*, the second, reported through Maʿmar, and the fourth and eight, reported through Mālik, contain the element that the Prophet responded to the arbitration request of the Jews with the question 'What do you have about the issue of stoning in the Torah?'. This indicates that from the beginning, the Prophet had the stoning penalty in his mind. This might support the role of the

Prophet as arbitrator since the Jews asked him to decide if it was the stoning penalty or public shaming that was due to the adulterers. However, as this information is not included in the other variants, it is likely that there was a slip or deliberate interpolation during the transmission process. Both Mālik and Maʿmar reworded this sentence to include the 'stoning penalty' in the text due to their propensity towards the stoning penalty, either inadvertently or deliberately.

The texts of the ninth and tenth variants are too short and do not include any noteworthy information. The text of the eleventh variant is included in the Nāfiʿ sub-bundle, which is transmitted through Mālik and similar to the other variants reported through Mālik. The text of the twelfth variant is included in Ibn ʿUmar's bundle, but instead of Nāfiʿ, it is transmitted through Zayd b. Aslam. In line with the differences in the transmission lines after the Common Link, who is Ibn ʿUmar, there is a piece of extra information that may be found in all of Nāfiʿ's sub-bundles: the Jews invited the Prophet to a village called al-Quff, wherein the Prophet visited a Jewish seminary or the Bayt al-Midrās.[74] At the time, al-Quff belonged to the Jewish tribe of Banū Qaynuqāʿ, who had settled in lower Medina. It appears that this is the same Jewish seminary where Zayd b. Thābit received his training on Hebrew and Jewish laws and customs.

Therefore, the variant implies that the two adulterers belonged to the Jews of Banū Qaynuqāʿ. However, this information is only mentioned in this variant and hence cannot be verified. It is possible that because ʿAbdullāh b. Salām was a member of the Banū Qaynuqāʿ, and since he seemingly played a crucial role in the episode, the transmitters assumed the Jews in question were from Banū Qaynuqāʿ. Therefore, they may have made that interpolation accordingly. However, ʿAbdullāh b. Salām's name along with the fact that he caught the Jews hiding the Stoning Verse in the Torah were also not mentioned in this variant.

Interestingly, the element of the Prophet's visit to a Jewish seminary was mentioned in the Abū Hurayra cluster. But in that variant, it states that the Jews came to the Prophet while he was sitting in the Mosque and asked him to arbitrate the case of the adulterating man and woman. The Prophet then stood up, visited a Jewish seminary and urged them to inform him about the penalty for adultery. However, in the text of the variant at hand, the Jews first invite the Prophet to al-Quff. He visited the seminary there, and

74 Based on the Muslim narratives, Lecker discusses the village called al-Quff and the Bayt al-Midrās (Lecker, 'Muhammad at Medina', pp. 37–9). Lecker provides a more detailed study in Lecker, 'Zayd b. Thābit', pp. 263–4. Samuel A. Stafford's recent study highlights that, according to Muslim sources, the Prophet would visit the Bayt al-Midrās with his followers to engage in debates with its Jewish scholars concerning biblical history, theology and prophecy (Stafford, 'The Conversions of ʿAbdallāh ibn Salām (d. 43/ 633)', pp. 252–4).

they asked him to litigate the case accordingly. Given that this information is not included in the other Ibn ʿUmar bundles, it may be possible to argue that Zayd b. Aslam or another person in the chain interpolated the element to provide more specific detail. The element of visiting the Jewish seminary might have been adopted from the Abū Hurayra cluster to emphasise that the Jews in question were members of Banū Qaynuqāʿ, as well as to provide more detail to the story.

Bukhārī recorded one of the Ibn ʿUmar clusters, which is the thirteenth variant that was transmitted from Nāfiʿ to ʿUbaydullāh b. ʿUmar, and then spread into two strands. One of those is the ninth variant, but I could not examine it due to the briefness of the text. The present variant is the second transmission line which goes through Bukhārī ← al-Ḥakam b. Mūsā ← Shuʿayb b. Isḥāq. The text is similar to the others in the Ibn ʿUmar clusters. The Prophet asked a neutral question about the punishment for adultery and was told that it involved blackening the face and public shame. Then, he ordered the Torah to be brought and a young man recited it. At this point, ʿAbdullāh b. Salām intervened and demanded the young reciter to lift his hand. The Stoning Verse was exposed when he lifted his hand, and Muhammad ordered the stoning penalty. Finally, Ibn ʿUmar confirmed that he witnessed the event and the adulterer man tried to shield the woman from the stones. The variant does not include the element of 'striking', and rather only mentions the Jewish practice of public shame. The fourteenth and fifteenth variants are too short to be compared with the other variants. They only relate that the Jews brought two adulterers to the Prophet for arbitration.

The al-Aʿmash Cluster

Chain of Transmission Analysis

There are five variants reported through the PCL al-Aʿmash. Ibn Mājah received the sixteenth chain of transmission from ʿAlī b. Muḥammad [al-Ṭanāfisī] (d. 233/847–8) of Kufa.[75] ʿAlī b. Muḥammad received the variant from Abū Muʿāwiya [al-Saʿdī] (d. 194/809–10 or 195/810–11), who was a well-known scholar from Kufa.[76] He received the variant from his teacher and prominent second-generation Kufan hadith collector, al-Aʿmash (d. 148/765).[77] He received the variant from ʿAbdullāh b. Murra (d. 100/718–19), a Kufan scholar,[78] who transmitted the variant from al-Barāʾ b. ʿĀzib (d. 72/691), a Companion of the Prophet who converted to Islam

75 Ibn Mājah, *Sunan*, vol. 1, p. 855.
76 al-Dhahabī, *Siyar aʿlām al-nubalāʾ*, vol. 9, pp. 74–8.
77 al-Dhahabī, *Siyar aʿlām al-nubalāʾ*, vol. 6, pp. 227–42.
78 al-Mizzī, *Tahdhīb al-kamāl fī asmāʾ al-rijāl*, vol. 16, pp. 115–16.

at a young age, while the Prophet was still in Mecca. He travelled around the Muslim lands and eventually retired in Kufa.[79] It is probable that when he resided in Kufa, he reported the variant to 'Abdullāh b. Murra and spread it from Medina to Kufa. Al-Barā' b. 'Āzib had also witnessed the event at the time of the Prophet. So far, I can contend that the variants of the tradition were in circulation at an initial period in Medina, and that multiple transmitters had spread it to Kufa.

Abū Dāwūd (d. 275/889) received the seventeenth variant from Musaddad (d. 228/843),[80] who also transmitted the seventh variant of the 'Abdullāh b. 'Umar cluster to Bukhārī. Musaddad was a prolific hadith collector, and both Abū Dāwūd and Musaddad were active in Basra. Given the proximity of time and location, there are no issues related to the transmission of the variant. Musaddad received the variant from another prominent Basran transmitter, 'Abd al-Wāḥid b. Ziyād (d. 177/793–4),[81] who transmitted the variant from al-A'mash (d. 148/765). Al-A'mash, who conveyed the traditions to three other transmitters, is clearly one of the PCLs and spread the variant in Kufa and Basra. Similar to the sixteenth chain, al-A'mash received the variant from 'Abdullāh b. Murra ← al-Barā' b. 'Āzib ← the Prophet.

Abū Dāwūd recorded the eighteenth chain from [Abū Kurayb] Muḥammad b. al-'Alā'ī (d. 247/861),[82] a reputable Kufan scholar.[83] Muḥammad b. al-'Alā'ī reported it from another Kufan transmitter by the name of Abū Mu'āwiya [al-Sa'dī] (d. 194/809–10 or 195/810–11). Similar to the sixteenth variant of the report, Abū Mu'āwiya received it from al-A'mash ← 'Abdullāh b. Murra ← al-Barā' b. 'Āzib ← the Prophet.

Muslim received the nineteenth variant from both Yaḥyā b. Yaḥyā [b. Bakr al-Tamīmī al-Naysābūrī] (d. 226/840) and Ibn Abī Shayba (d. 235/849–50). Yaḥyā b. Yaḥyā was a very prominent scholar from Transoxiana and collected hadith in the Hijaz, Iraq, the Levant and Egypt.[84] Both scholars reported the variant from Abū Mu'āwiya. Like the sixteenth and eighteenth variants, he transmitted it from al-A'mash ← 'Abdullāh b. Murra al-Barā' b. 'Āzib ← the Prophet.

Muslim reported the twentieth variant from both Ibn Numayr and Abū Sa'īd al-Ashaj (d. 257/870–1) of Kufa. ['Abdullāh] Ibn Numayr (d. 199/814) was a Kufan hadith collector, and he reported it from Wakī' [b. al-Jarrāḥ] (d.196/811–12), an Iraqi hadith collector.[85] He then reported the variant

79 al-Mizzī, *Tahdhīb al-kamāl fī asmā' al-rijāl*, vol. 3, pp. 195–6.
80 al-Mizzī, *Tahdhīb al-kamāl fī asmā' al-rijāl*, vol. 4, p. 154.
81 al-Mizzī, *Tahdhīb al-kamāl fī asmā' al-rijāl*, vol. 9, pp. 8–9.
82 al-Mizzī, *Tahdhīb al-kamāl fī asmā' al-rijāl*, vol. 4, p. 154.
83 al-Mizzī, *Tahdhīb al-kamāl fī asmā' al-rijāl*, vol. 11, pp. 394–8, vol. 26, pp. 243–8.
84 al-Dhahabī, *Siyar a'lām al-nubalā'*, vol. 10, pp. 512–19.
85 al-Dhahabī, *Siyar a'lām al-nubalā'*, vol. 9, pp. 141–53.

from al-Aʿmash (d. 148/765), from which the same chain follows. There appears to be no problem with these transmission lines.

Textual Analysis

The text of the sixteenth variant differs from the Ibn ʿUmar cluster as it is reported through al-Barāʾ b. ʿĀzib; therefore, there seems to be a corroboration between the transmission lines and text. According to the text, the Jews did not come to the Prophet for arbitration – instead, Muhammad passed by the Jews while they were punishing a man and woman by way of blackening their faces and lashing them. Muhammad assumed that the couple was punished for adultery and questioned their scholars about it on the spot. He implored them to reveal the true punishment of adultery in the Torah, and one of the scholars could not resist Muhammad's plea. Therefore, he revealed that they had prevented the actual punishment of stoning because it was too harsh. The Prophet was seemingly eager about reviving God's punishment and ordered the stoning of the couple immediately, based on the confession of the Jewish scholar. There is no mention of ʿAbdullāh b. Salām and his role in pointing out the Stoning Verse in the Torah. This variant also contains elements of the Ibn ʿUmar cluster. However, there is a new element that the Prophet, by chance, witnessed the punishment and took it upon himself to revive the true punishment of stoning for adultery.

It appears that this textual variant was paraphrased significantly, and its meaning was mixed up with different reports during the transmission process, given that the different parts of the text used various elements, such as blackening the face, the conversation with the religious scholar and the element of 'imploration' (*anshuduka bi-Allāh*). The last of these was a common theme in some of the variants covered in Chapter 2, which caused suspicion as to whether the narrators of this variant were failed by their memory and conflated several reports during the transmission process.

Otherwise, given the circumstances of Medina at the time, it is untenable that the Prophet would interfere in the affairs of the Jews without invitation, especially at the expense of creating additional tensions. During the initial periods of his stay in Medina, the Prophet did not have the full authority of a ruler to the extent that he could order the execution of some Jews based on his own initiative. As I have discussed above, 'the Constitution of Medina' did not grant him such a right, and it was beyond his authority to do so. It is possible that ʿAbdullāh b. Murra received the variant from al-Barāʾ b. ʿĀzib towards the end of his career. Several decades had passed by then since the occurrence of the episode, and his memory had failed him terribly. Therefore, I can only date this variant's common element back to al-Aʿmash (d. 148/765), who relates that the Prophet had a Jewish man and woman stoned for committing adultery.

The texts of the seventeenth and eighteenth variants are like the text of the thirteenth, save for the minor differences in wording. This gives credence to the earlier finding, that the transmission error occurred when ʿAbdullāh b. Murra received the variant from al-Barāʾ b. ʿĀzib towards the end of his career. This is supported by the fact that the variant spreads out from al-Aʿmash, and the three texts were almost identical. The text of the nineteenth variant is identical to the other variants in the al-Aʿmash clusters.[86] Finally, the text of the twentieth variant is too short for any significant analysis. There is no mention of ʿAbdullāh b. Salām's role in these clusters.

The Zuhrī Cluster

Chain of Transmission Analysis

There are three variants in the Zuhrī cluster. The twenty-first chain was recorded in ʿAbd al-Razzāq's (d. 211/826) *Muṣannaf*,[87] who received it through Maʿmar ← Zuhrī ← Saʿīd b. al-Musayyab ← Abū Hurayra ← the Prophet. The sound connection between Zuhrī and Saʿīd b. al-Musayyab (d. 94/712) has been studied.[88] Saʿīd b. al-Musayyab was a very prominent second-generation Muslim and an authority in hadith and Islamic law. There is a natural connection between Saʿīd b. al-Musayyab and his father-in-law, Abū Hurayra (d. 59/681) of Medina. Therefore, this chain of transmission can be traced back to the Prophet without a problem. Saʿīd b. al-Musayyab plays a crucial role in spreading the reports attributed to ʿUmar about the so-called Stoning Verse. Therefore, I will discuss him in detail in Chapter 4, which studies the reports attributed to ʿUmar. Nevertheless, Saʿīd b. al-Musayyab was active in Medina but later moved to Basra and Kufa, and therefore Zuhrī could have received the report from him either in Medina or in Basra.

The twenty-second chain was recorded in Abū Dāwūd's *Sunan*,[89] who received it from Muḥammad b. Yaḥyā (d. 258/871–2). He was active in Nishapur, Rayy, Isfahan, Basra, Kufa, Baghdad, Mecca, Medina, Yemen and Egypt.[90] He received it from ʿAbd al-Razzāq (d. 211/826), who was also an itinerant hadith collector, and was active in Yemen, Mecca, Medina,

86 There is only a piece of supplementary information about the verses of the Qur'an which were supposedly revealed when the episode occurred: Q. 5:41, 44, 45 and 47. However, this information cannot be verified as it is only mentioned in this particular variant. It seems that the narrators after Ibn Abī Shayba thought this information was relevant to the tradition and interpolated it into the text as an explanatory gloss.

87 al-Ṣanʿānī, *Muṣannaf*, vol. 7, pp. 316–18.

88 Motzki et al., *Analysing Muslim Traditions*, pp. 1–45.

89 Abū Dāwūd, *Sunan*, vol. 4, pp. 155--6.

90 al-Dhahabī, *Siyar aʿlām al-nubalāʾ*, vol. 12, pp. 273–85.

Syria and Iraq. It is not difficult to consider that their paths crossed at one of these places, and Muḥammad b. Yaḥyā received the variant from ʿAbd al-Razzāq. That ʿAbd al-Razzāq's *Muṣannaf* does not include this report may be problematic. In hadith collections, however, these kinds of problems may be explained by editorial issues or the timeframe when the authors came into possession of the tradition and penned their works. Nevertheless, ʿAbd al-Razzāq received the variant from Maʿmar ← Zuhrī ← Saʿīd b. al-Musayyab ← Abū Hurayra ← the Prophet.

Abū Dāwūd received the twenty-third variant from ʿAbd al-ʿAzīz b. Yaḥyā al-Ḥarrānī (d. 235/849–50),[91] who was a resident of Harran[92] in Anatolia.[93] He received the variant from his teacher Muḥammad b. Salama (d. 191/807 or 192/808) of Harran.[94] He received the variant from Muḥammad b. Isḥāq (d. 150/767). Muḥammad b. Isḥāq was a well-travelled hadith collector and settled in Baghdad after the Abbasids overthrew the Umayyad dynasty. He received it from his teacher Zuhrī (d. 124/742) ← Saʿīd b. al-Musayyab ← Abū Hurayra ← the Prophet. Studying the chains of transmission shows that the tradition travelled throughout Muslim lands by the third century via multiple transmission lines.

Textual Analysis

The twenty-first text was recorded in ʿAbd al-Razzāq's *Muṣannaf*, which gives Abū Hurayra's account of the episode. He noted that the event marked the Prophet's first stoning in Islamic history. He further provided the account of the supposed conversation that took place between the Jews, and that their real intention behind referring the matter to the Prophet was to test him. However, this information seems to be purely speculative as there is no way for Abū Hurayra to have witnessed the conversation that took place among the Jews before they came to the Prophet. Furthermore, this information was not mentioned in the previous clusters, thus it is most likely a later interpolation.

According to the narrative, the Jews came to the Prophet while he was at his Mosque and questioned him about the punishment for adultery. He stood up in silence, went to a Jewish seminary and urged them to inform him about the penalty for adultery in Jewish scripture. They first informed him that the punishment was that 'His face is to be blackened, and he is to be carried around by a donkey in public'. However, a

91 Abū Dāwūd, *Sunan*, vol. 4, p. 144.

92 Harran was a major city in the western part of northern Mesopotamia during the Umayyad period.

93 al-Mizzī, *Tahdhīb al-kamāl fī asmāʾ al-rijāl*, vol. 18, pp. 215–18.

94 al-Dhahabī, *Siyar aʿlām al-nubalāʾ*, vol. 9, p. 49.

young man among the Jewish students stood up and informed him that the actual punishment was the stoning penalty. He also informed the Prophet that the Jews had lightened the punishment because some noble Jews found it to be too harsh. When they did not implement it on the noble Jews, the commoners protested, so the Jewish leaders agreed on a lighter punishment, which was to blacken the faces and be carried by a donkey in public. The Prophet then passed a judgement according to the Torah, 'The Prophet said, "I indeed pass judgement according to the Torah."' The two adulterating Jews were thus to be stoned. At the end of the text, 'Abd al-Razzāq mentions that Zuhrī received the information via Sālim from Ibn 'Umar that during the stoning, the man leaned over the woman to protect her from the stones. Abū Hurayra narrated the event differently from the others and provided detailed information, which seems to be an embellishment that I will further assess while delving into the other variants.

The twenty-second text is similar to the previous text in this cluster, which was recorded in 'Abd al-Razzāq's *Muṣannaf.* The chain of the variant at hand states that Muḥammad b. Yaḥyā received it from 'Abd al-Razzāq and reported it to Abū Dāwūd, who recorded it in his *Sunan.* It is the same variant, aside from a minor difference (the insertion of the element of 'lashing' in this variant), which corresponds with the oral transmission process. In the previous variant, when the Prophet asked the Jews about the punishment for adulterers, they replied, 'His face is to be blackened, and he is to be carried around by a donkey in public.' The text of the variant also adds 'striking' to the punishments. I have also noted a similar effort in the Nāfi' bundles, where it seems that Mūsā b. 'Uqba included this element in the text. In the text of the variant, the individual responsible is either Muḥammad b. Yaḥyā (d. 258/871–2) or Abū Dāwūd (d. 275/889).[95] A similar element of 'striking' is present in the text of the twenty-third variant, which is in the Zuhrī cluster as well as Abū Dāwūd's *Sunan.* Given that the text of this variant is narrated in the third person, it is more plausible that Abū Dāwūd summarised it and included the 'striking' element like the previous text. Therefore, it is almost certain that the interpolation of the element of 'striking' in the Zuhrī cluster was the work of Abū Dāwūd. Importantly, the name of 'Abdullāh b. Salām and his role are again not mentioned in this cluster.

95 This information might be additional evidence for Pavlovitch's thesis on the dual-versus-single-penalty (DvSP) debate, as it indicates that the debate still existed in the middle of the third/ninth century. But as I have noted above, it is possible that the beginning of the debate predates Shāfiʿī and goes back to the turn of the second/eighth century.

The Sharīk, Jābir b. ʿAbdullāh, Ibrāhīm and al-Shaʿbī Clusters

Chain of Transmission Analysis

Even though there are six remaining variants – two in Sharīk's cluster, two in Ibrāhīm and al-Shaʿbī's clusters and two in Jābir b. ʿAbdullāh's clusters – I decided to study them under one section as the variants in these have very short texts. I will begin with the Sharīk cluster. The twenty-fourth chain was recorded in Ibn Mājah's *Sunan*,[96] and Ibn Mājah received it from Ismāʿīl b. Mūsā [al-Fazārī] (d. 245/859–60), who was a resident of Kufa and known to be a Shiʿi.[97] Ismāʿīl b. Mūsā received the variant from Sharīk [b. ʿAbdullāh] (d. 177/794), a prominent Kufan hadith collector and legal scholar, who had a mild propensity towards Shiʿism.[98] He received the variant from Simāk b. Ḥarb (d. 123/740–1), another Kufan scholar.[99] Finally, Simāk received it from Jābir b. Samura (d. 76/695–6), a Companion of the Prophet who resided in Kufa.[100] This Kufan, and partially Shiʿi, chain reaches the Prophet without any problems. Tirmidhī reported the twenty-fifth variant from Hunnād [b. al-Sarī] (d. 243/857), a prominent scholar of Kufa.[101] Hunnād received the variant from Sharīk [b. ʿAbdullāh] (d. 177/794) of Kufa. Sharīk received the variant from Simāk b. Ḥarb ← Jābir b. Samura ← the Prophet. Thus, there seems to be no issues with both variants included in the Sharīk cluster.

Abū Dāwūd recorded the two Jābir b. ʿAbdullāh clusters. Abū Dāwūd reported the twenty-sixth variant[102] from Yaḥyā b. Mūsā al-Balkhī (d. circa 240/855–6), who was initially from Kufa and also resided in Balkh.[103] He received it from Abū Usāma [Ḥammād b. Usāma al-Qurayshī] (d. 201/817), who was a prominent scholar from Kufa.[104] He received the variant from Mujālid [b. Saʿīd] (d. 144/762) of Kufa.[105] He received it from ʿĀmir al-Shaʿbī (d. 100/718–19), a second-generation Muslim of Hamadan. He was born during the caliphate of ʿUmar and resided in Kufa, and then travelled to Medina.[106] He received the variant from Jābir b. ʿAbdullāh (d. 78/697) of Medina. He was one of the prominent Companions of the Prophet and a

96 Ibn Mājah, *Sunan*, vol. 1, p. 855.
97 al-Dhahabī, *Siyar aʿlām al-nubalāʾ*, vol. 11, pp. 176–7.
98 al-Dhahabī, *Siyar aʿlām al-nubalāʾ*, vol. 8, pp. 201–16.
99 al-Dhahabī, *Siyar aʿlām al-nubalāʾ*, vol. 5, pp. 245–9.
100 al-Dhahabī, *Siyar aʿlām al-nubalāʾ*, vol. 4, pp. 187–8.
101 al-Dhahabī, *Siyar aʿlām al-nubalāʾ*, vol. 11, pp. 465–6.
102 al-Dhahabī, *Siyar aʿlām al-nubalāʾ*, vol. 4, p. 156.
103 al-Mizzī, *Tahdhīb al-kamāl fī asmāʾ al-rijāl*, vol. 32, pp. 6–9.
104 al-Dhahabī, *Siyar aʿlām al-nubalāʾ*, vol. 9, pp. 277–9.
105 al-Dhahabī, *Siyar aʿlām al-nubalāʾ*, vol. 6, pp. 285–7.
106 al-Dhahabī, *Siyar aʿlām al-nubalāʾ*, pp. 295–306.

devout Shiʿi who supported ʿAlī staunchly. ʿĀmir al-Shaʿbī likely received the variant from Jābir b. ʿAbdullāh when he visited Medina. Jābir is known to have taught at the Mosque of the Prophet until he died at the age of ninety-four.[107] He received it from the Prophet.

Abū Dāwūd reported the twenty-seventh variant from Ibrāhīm b. Ḥasan al-Miṣṣīṣī (d. 225/839–40) of Baghdad,[108] who received the variant from Ḥajjāj b. Muḥammad (d. 206/821) of Baghdad. He received it from the prominent Meccan scholar Ibn Jurayj[109] (d. 150/767–8), who also authored a *Sunan*. Ibn Jurayj received it directly from the Meccan Abū al-Zubayr (d. circa 127/744–5);[110] Abū al-Zubayr then heard it from Jābir b. ʿAbdullāh (d. 78/697), who heard it from the Prophet.

The first chain of the Ibrāhīm and al-Shaʿbī cluster is the twenty-eighth variant,[111] which Abū Dāwūd transmitted from Wahb b. Baqiyya (d. 239/853), who was a major hadith collector. He moved to Baghdad and resided there.[112] He received the variant from Hushaym [b. Bashīr b. Abī Khāzim] (d. 183/799–800), a renowned hadith collector from Baghdad.[113] Hushaym received the variant from the second-generation Muslim and prominent jurist Mughīra [b. Miqsam] (d. circa 133/750–1) of Kufa. He received the variant both from Ibrāhīm [al-Nakhaʿī] and al-Shaʿbī [b. Dhī Kibār]. The dates of death of both Ibrāhīm (d. 96/717) of Kufa and al-Shaʿbī (d. 103/723) indicate that this chain is problematic as the Prophet Muhammad died in 11/632. They both claimed to hear the event from the Prophet, but given the time gap, it is unlikely that they witnessed the event as al-Shaʿbī was born around ten years after the death of the Prophet.[114] They skipped their informant and mentioned the Prophet. As the chain of transmission is interrupted, I can date this variant to the earliest death of Ibrāhīm (d. 96/717). Abū Dāwūd received the twenty-ninth variant[115] again from Wahb b. Baqiyya (d. 239/853). As a matter of fact, the chain of this variant is identical to the previous one, except that this variant skips Mughīra [b. Miqsam] and includes the transmitter Ibn Shubruma

107 al-Dhahabī, *Siyar aʿlām al-nubalāʾ*, vol. 3, pp. 190–4.

108 al-Dhahabī, *Siyar aʿlām al-nubalāʾ*, vol. 10, p. 557.

109 Motzki provides detailed biographical information on Ibn Jurayj; see Motzki, *The Origins of Islamic Jurisprudence*, pp. 268–85. See also Juynboll, *Encyclopaedia of Canonical Ḥadīth*, pp. 212–25.

110 Motzki established the connection between both of these Meccan scholars; Motzki, *The Origins of Islamic Jurisprudence*, pp. 208–11.

111 Abū Dāwūd, *Sunan*, vol. 4, p. 157.

112 al-Dhahabī, *Siyar aʿlām al-nubalāʾ*, vol. 11, pp. 463–4; al-Mizzī, *Tahdhīb al-kamāl fī asmāʾ al-rijāl*, vol. 34, pp. 115–18.

113 al-Dhahabī, *Siyar aʿlām al-nubalāʾ*, vol. 8, pp. 288–94.

114 al-Dhahabī, *Siyar aʿlām al-nubalāʾ*, vol. 4, pp. 295–306.

115 al-Dhahabī, *Siyar aʿlām al-nubalāʾ*, vol. 4, p. 157.

(d. 144/761–2) of Kufa.[116] He received it from al-Shaʿbī (d. 103/723), and al-Shaʿbī heard it from the Prophet. There is again a gap between al-Shaʿbī and the Prophet.

Textual Analysis

The text of the twenty-fourth variant, included in the Sharīk cluster, is too short and does not include any meaningful information. The text of the twenty-fifth variant, which is in the Sharīk cluster, only mentions that Jābir b. Samura reported from the Prophet that 'the Prophet stoned a Jewish man and woman'. Therefore, from the Sharīk cluster, I can only extract the information that the Prophet stoned a Jewish man and woman.

The Euphemism of 'Like a Stick Penetrating into a Jar'

The text of the twenty-sixth variant, which branches out from the PCL Jābir b. ʿAbdullāh, contains different features from the clusters transmitted through the other PCLs. This Kufan variant begins with the Jews coming to the Prophet and requesting arbitration for the punishment of the two adulterers. The Prophet then asked for the two most knowledgeable Jewish scholars in order to question them. They then brought two sons of Ṣuriyā to the Prophet as their most knowledgeable men. However, in another variant which is mentioned in Ibn Hishām's *Sīra*, without a complete chain, it states that ʿAbdullāh b. Ṣuriyā, along with two other people, came to the Prophet.[117] Therefore, it would be safe to assume that the three men mentioned in the text refer to ʿAbdullāh b. Ṣuriyā, his brother and perhaps another individual with him. The Prophet then asks them to inform him about the penalty for adulterers according to the Torah. Without any resistance, they mention that the penalty was stoning. However, they also provided some interesting information which is not available in the other variants, such as, 'We find in the Torah that if four of them testify that they saw that the man's penis penetrate her vagina, like a stick penetrating into a jar, they are to be stoned.' The information lays out the conditions for implementing the stoning penalty,[118] which was missing in the other variants.

As mentioned above in the other variants, it was strange that the Prophet was not interested in establishing the offence of adultery. His attention was focused on establishing the existence of the stoning penalty in the Torah. Abū Dāwūd, or someone else in the chain, seems to have also noticed this

116 al-Dhahabī, *Siyar aʿlām al-nubalāʾ*, vol. 6, pp. 347–8.

117 Ibn Hishām, *al-Sīra al-nabawī*, vol. 2, p. 206.

118 Interestingly, in the Talmudic tradition, the euphemism used to establish the occurrence of adultery is 'as a brush in a tube' (Mazuz, *The Religious and Spiritual Life of the Jews of Medina*, p. 48).

anomaly and wanted to fix it by inserting the graphic detail for the condition of establishing the offence of adultery. I am cautiously confident that Abū Dāwūd is responsible for this interpolation because the conditions for implementing the stoning penalty are also mentioned[119] in the tradition transmitted by the man from the Banū Aslam tribe tradition.[120] I did not include the study of the tradition in this book because Pavlovitch has already analysed it elsewhere. However, I am also cautiously confident Abū Dāwūd did not forge the euphemism of 'like a stick penetrating into a jar'. It was already available to him as the variant was first recorded in 'Abd al-Razzāq's *Muṣannaf*,[121] and the chain indicates that Abū Dāwūd received the text from 'Abd al-Razzāq through al-Ḥasan b. 'Alī.

It seems that Abū Dāwūd took the 'like a stick penetrating into a jar' element from the report about the man from the Banū Aslam tribe and incorporated it into the variant at hand. By doing so, he ostensibly fixed the problem of the Prophet's disinterest in establishing the offence in the current report. He also wanted to reinforce his position on the validity of the stoning penalty as he did in the case of interpolating the element of 'striking' in the previous variant. However, the second possibility may be that he did it due to the failure of his memory. He confused similar texts, and thus inadvertently made these interpolations. The evidence for the second possibility is the Ibrāhīm and al-Sha'bī cluster, which I will soon examine. The twenty-seventh variant is included in Abū Dāwūd's *Sunan* and belongs to Jābir b. 'Abdullāh's clusters, and only states that 'the Prophet had stoned a Jewish man and woman who committed adultery'.[122] Therefore, it is not possible to extract extra information from it.

The twenty-eighth and twenty-ninth textual variants belong to the PCL's Ibrāhīm and al-Sha'bī, which failed the *isnād* analysis in terms of tracing it back to the Prophet due to their age gap. In the text of the twenty-eighth variant, Abū Dāwūd notes that the text of this variant is the same as the previous one (i.e. the twenty-sixth variant), except for the element of 'like a stick penetrating into a jar', which was not included in the twenty-eighth and twenty-ninth variants. This information indicates that Abū Dāwūd did not tamper with the text of the twenty-sixth variant deliberately. If we suppose that Abū Dāwūd was 'projecting back' his views on the prophetic traditions, he could have also included the element of 'like a stick penetrating into a jar' into the twenty-eighth and twenty-ninth variants. Therefore, among the two possibilities I discussed under the twenty-sixth variant, it is safer

119 'The Prophet then asked: "Did you penetrate in a way as an eye-liner stick disappears in the kohl jar or a rope in the well?" He replied "Yes."'

120 Abū Dāwūd, *Sunan*, vol. 4, p. 144.

121 al-Ṣan'ānī, *Muṣannaf*, vol. 7, p. 322.

122 Abū Dāwūd, *Sunan*, vol. 4, p.157.

to assume that this interpolation was probably due to failed memory or editorial mishap. The existence of the two variants supports this possibility.

Summary and Conclusion

The study of the chains of transmission has verified that the report was widely spread to Muslim centres in Medina, Kufa, Basra, Egypt, Nishapur and Khorasan. Aside from the twenty-eighth variant, there was no problem among the six clusters, which thus could be traced back to the Prophet without any issues. The ʿAbdullāh b. ʿUmar cluster, which includes fifteen variants, is interdependent in a sense. Similar to the other clusters, most of them state that a group of Jews came to the Prophet for arbitration on the case of two adulterers, and they misinformed him about the punishment for adultery. Thanks to the intervention of ʿAbdullāh b. Salām, the Prophet found the true punishment for adultery mentioned in the Torah and implemented it on the two adulterers. However, no other clusters among these variants mention ʿAbdullāh b. Salām's name and his role in the episode. Therefore, the elements related to ʿAbdullāh b. Salām's involvement in the episode can only be dated back to ʿAbdullāh b. ʿUmar's date of death, which is 73/693. Given Hirschfeld and Lecker's views that ʿAbdullāh b. Salām converted to Islam at least eight years after the Muslim emigration to Medina, this strengthens the argument that he was not involved in the incident, because the evidence suggests that the stoning episode of the two Jews occurred before the conversion of ʿAbdullāh b. Salām.

At this point, the Jews and Muslims had become bitter enemies, and it was unlikely that they would come to the Prophet for arbitration. Even if he had converted to Islam earlier than Hirschfeld's suggestion, his involvement could only be traced back to ʿAbdullāh b. ʿUmar's date of death (73/693).

This element was possibly interpolated into the text to make the case more dramatic and theologically charged.[123] Some narrators would embellish prophetic reports by adding theological ingredients to make them more attractive for the audiences. It additionally emphasises that the Jews distorted their Torah by not implementing its explicit ruling, as ʿAbdullāh b. Salām was made to testify to this flagrant violation of Jewish law. This interpolation of the ʿAbdullāh b. Salām element into the text was surely a 'retrojecting'.

123 Stafford, 'Constructing Muḥammad's Legitimacy', p. 136 and *passim*, asserts that the Muslim 'accounts of Ibn Salām's life and career reflect the transmitters' evolving conception of Muḥammad's status as a prophet'. In this chapter, it became evident that at least one of these reports was heavily manipulated, potentially for use in polemical debates with the Jews. However, this evidence does not support Stafford's thesis.

The interpolation of this event could be related to the interreligious debates between Muslims and Jews that might have emerged in the late first/seventh and early second/eighth centuries after the invasion of Iraq and Palestine, where there was a sizable Jewish population. The aim may have been to further vilify and embarrass the Jewish scholars, as had been the practice of Christian scholars.[124] Or, it could be related to the legal school's assertion of the existence of the stoning penalty. The existence of such an element that vilifies Jewish scholars would have supported their case that the removal of the stoning penalty was tantamount to the Jewish practice of distorting the meaning or implementation of the verses of the Torah. This would have placed their opponents, who perhaps suggested the alternative punishment of lashing, in a defensive position, as no Muslim would have wanted to make the blunder of 'distorting' the Qur'an. This was the same shameful charge levelled against the Jews and Christians in the Qur'an.[125]

However, other common elements of the variant clusters can be successfully dated back to the Prophet. The study of the variants has reconstructed the original text of the hadith that a group of Jews asked the Prophet to arbitrate on the punishment of two adulterers. It is also clear that the Jews did not ask the Prophet to issue a pronouncement of guilty verdict for the offenders as he exerted no effort to investigate the occurrence of the offence. Instead, as an arbitrator, Muhammad focused on finding the correct punishment according to the Torah. The only exception to this is the twenty-sixth variant, which was likely tampered with. In response to the arbitration request, the Prophet launched an investigation and either located the relevant punishment in the Torah, or some Jewish scholars confessed to the correct punishment for adultery. The Prophet then ordered the implementation of the Jewish punishment on the offenders, which was the stoning penalty. The core elements of the variants can be dated back to the lifetime of the Prophet, probably within the first couple of years from when Muslim emigrated from Mecca to Medina.

John Burton has already made the speculative argument that Muslim legal schools fabricated these types of reports to promote their legal positions. He held Shāfiʿī (d. 204/820) responsible for developing this particular report around the unreliability of Jewish scholars and their proclivity towards distorting their holy text.[126] He further compared the stoning penalty narrative in Islamic sources with the episode about Jesus Christ, an

124 Knust, 'Early Christian Re-writing and the History of the *Pericope Adulterae*'.

125 Nickel, *Narratives of Tampering in the Earliest Commentaries on the Quran*; Reynolds, 'On the Qur'anic Accusation of Scriptural Falsification (*Taḥrīf*) and Christian Anti-Jewish Polemic'.

126 Burton, *An Introduction to the Ḥadīth*, pp. 86–7.

adulteress and a group of Jews mentioned in the Gospel of John.[127] Burton alluded to the possibility that the idea of embarrassing and vilifying Jewish scholars and 'scoring points' against them was already extant in the Christian tradition. It was only natural hence that Muslim scholars enjoined such an undertaking. Therefore, similar to early Gospel scholars, Muslim scholars of hadith fabricated a similar story to press for their agenda both theologically and legally.[128] I will delve more into this episode mentioned in the Gospel of John below.

However, this investigation cannot alone establish Shāfiʿī's culpability. It is more probable that the reports had already been embellished with appealing details and widely circulated by the third/ninth century. Shāfiʿī had the luxury of choosing the most suitable reports to strengthen his view on the stoning penalty. These reports were also particularly important to his legal theory surrounding abrogation.[129] The Qur'anic verse on the stoning penalty was missing from the Qur'an, yet it endured a long existence in hadith literature. Thus, they were perfectly legitimate for the theory of abrogation that Shāfiʿī ardently supported.

The successful dating of these variants to the lifetime of the Prophet makes it possible to confirm the dating of the 'Constitution of Medina', as the variants indicate that the Prophet's arbitration of the episode took place in accordance with the terms of this document. It is also clear that the Prophet was not enforcing an Islamic ruling for adultery, and it is probable that if he had ever implemented this practice afterwards, he was acting on the Jewish tradition, not on the Qur'anic injunction, which clearly defines the appropriate punishment as lashing:

> The woman and the man guilty of adultery or fornication (*zinā*) – lash each of them with a hundred lashes. Let not compassion move you in their case, in a matter prescribed by God, if ye believe in God and the Last Day, and let a party of the Believers witness their punishment. (Q. 24:2)

It is possible that the Prophet implemented the stoning penalty on the arbitration request of the Jews, and may very well have implemented it on Muslims thereafter based on Jewish rulings, which would be prior to the Lashing Verse being revealed. However, as discussed above, the other episodes of the stoning penalty, which was supposedly implemented on Muslim offenders, could only be dated back to Zuhrī at the earliest. Therefore, it is not certain whether the Prophet ever stoned Muslims. Even if

127 Burton, 'Law and Exegesis', pp. 269–84.
128 Burton, 'Law and Exegesis', pp. 282–3.
129 See Burton, *The Collection of the Qur'ān*.

he did, it seems he temporarily borrowed the punishment from the Jews of Medina. Ramon Harvey has already made a compelling case for this possibility.[130] Once the Prophet pressed with the creation of an independent Muslim identity and Q. 24:2 was also revealed, he must have abandoned this practice, along with other practices,[131] as it was not found in the Qur'an. It seems implausible that Muhammad was eager to change the direction of the prayer and turned away from other forms of Jewish laws and practices[132] to detach from Jewish tradition, yet remained loyal to stoning despite the clear Qur'anic injunction of the lashing for offenders. Furthermore, the variants indicate that the stoning penalty was an issue of debate among the Jews, as members of society found it too harsh.

In this vein, following the connection Burton made about the use of the stoning penalty in Christian and Muslim contexts, Jennifer Wright Knust investigated the origins of the episode mentioned in the Gospel of John (John 7:53–8:11). A group of apparent Jews urged Jesus to stone an adulteress, which was the prescribed punishment according to the Law of Moses. However, Jesus purportedly retorts, 'Let anyone among you who is without sin be the first to throw a stone at her,' thus, embarrassing the Jews and implying that it was a harsh penalty and therefore refused to implement it. Knust notes that the Jewish element of the episode is added to the text later on. Still, the actual episode could have been extant from the second century. 'Though the *pericope adulterae* was not necessarily or inherently about the hypocrisy and culpability of "the Jews", it came to be reread, and rewritten, in this way.'[133]

There could be a similarity with the Muslim narrative that the 'Abdullāh b. Salām elements were later interpolated into the text to consolidate the vilification of the Jewish scholars who tried to hide the stoning penalty in the Torah. The kernel of the story is possibly a genuine historical event, however, in that a group of ordinary Jews asked the Prophet to arbitrate the matter, and the Prophet enquired about the existing ruling in the Torah.

Suppose the episode mentioned in the Gospel of John (John 7:53–8:11) was circulated from the second century. In that case, it is evident that even the early Christians found such a punishment too harsh as they interpolated Jews or Jewish scholars into the story to vilify them for suggesting such a penalty. In any case, there seems to be an understanding that the punishment was perceived as too harsh.

130 Harvey, *The Qur'an and the Just Society*, p. 187.

131 For a detailed study of these practices, see Kister, '"Do Not Assimilate Yourselves"', pp. 321–71; Kister, *Concepts and Ideas at the Dawn of Islam*, pp. 354–71.

132 Mazuz, *The Religious and Spiritual Life of the Jews of Medina*, pp. 41–84.

133 Knust, 'Early Christian Re-writing and the History of the *Pericope Adulterae*'.

Another critical point is that in the al-Barāʾ b. ʿĀzib cluster, a Jewish man also informs the Prophet that the Jews had lightened the punishment because the noble Jews found it too harsh, and when they did not see it implemented on the noble ones, the ordinary Jews protested. And so, the Jewish leaders agreed on a lighter punishment, which was the blackening of faces and being carried out by a donkey in public. If this element could have been dated, it would have been possible to argue that the idea of implementing the penal code according to social classes entered into the Medinan Jews' law from Roman law, as it was justified in the Justinian Digest.[134] The harsher penalties were applied against the lower classes, while softer penalties were for the higher class. If this was the case, it could have provided substantial evidence about the origins of the Jews of Medina, who most probably emigrated to Medina from Palestine after the destruction of the Second Temple in 70 CE by the Romans.[135] It appears these Jews lived under Roman rule, as they knew they had adopted the class-based implementation of law from the Roman penal system. Juan Cole has even argued[136] for the influence of Roman laws in northern Arabia and the Qur'an.[137] Would it be possible that the Jews of Medina learned about the Roman laws in Arabia? As far as this case is concerned, this possibility is unlikely because it seems that only the Jews of Medina are familiar with the discriminatory implementation of Roman law.[138] In other words, in this specific instance, the Medinan Arabs appear to be unaware of the class-based implementation of the law. Only the Jews of Medina were knowledgeable about it, indicating that their understanding derived from their time in Jerusalem.

From another point of view, the Muslims who interpolated this element into the text knew about this practice and might have inserted it into the text as a brief explanation. Given that al-Barāʾ b. ʿĀzib was an early convert who lived in Medina, he could have mentioned this Jewish practice as an explanation (or interpretation) which was then interpolated into the actual text. Either way, it is not possible to have a definite opinion on this issue.

Finally, the findings of the reports attributed to the Prophet on the stoning of two adulterer Jews have led to some important discoveries about the early period of Islam. Significant information about the role of the Prophet

134 Scott, 'The Enactments of Justinian'.

135 Donner, *Muhammad and the Believers*, p.30.

136 Cole, 'Muhammad and Justinian'.

137 I agree with Cole's thesis that in its formative period, Roman law influenced Islamic law, because the context or time and place played a crucial role in the formation and development of Islamic law. Law can only make sense to people if it settles the problems, in accordance with the spirit of the society and time.

138 Cole provides a concise overview of the possibility of the influence of Roman law on Islamic law; Cole, 'Muhammad and Justinian'.

in Medina, his relations with the Jews and the formation of Islamic law can be extracted from these reports with relative certainty. There is also strong evidence of interference with the hadiths in order to make them more appealing to the public and garner support for theological and legal reasons. Most importantly of all, the findings are crucial for the study of the distortion of the Qur'an. Together with Chapter 2, this chapter demonstrated that 'the Book of God' was used interchangeably for the Qur'an and the Torah among the people of Medina. Furthermore, the Prophet could act on the Torah, and he indeed did so, and this was the implementation of the stoning penalty. This finding is critical to Chapter 4, on the study of reports attributed to 'Umar, as it will shed further light on his adamant support of the missing Stoning Verse in the Qur'an.

CHAPTER 4

Caliph ʿUmar's Sermon on the 'Missing Stoning Verse'

Among the various reports on the stoning penalty, the one attributed to the second caliph, ʿUmar, is the most important. This account, as well as attesting to the practice of stoning, also appears to support the thesis that the text of the Qur'an underwent distortion. In the report in question, ʿUmar expresses his frustration that the so-called Stoning Verse was not included in the Qur'anic codex after the Prophet's death. Verses of the Qur'an could only be abrogated by the prophetic practice, and thus any alteration that took place after the Prophet's death may be a corruption of its text. Furthermore, some ostensibly plagiarised variants of these traditions that are attributed to Shiʿi Imams appear in Shiʿi sources, such as al-Sayyārī's *Kitāb al-qirā'āt*,[1] which have been used to justify the distortion narrative.[2] I will investigate these Shiʿi reports in Chapter 5.

I have identified sixteen variants of ʿUmar's report in some of the earliest Sunni hadith collections. At the end of the chapter, I will show how these variants can be reliably dated back to ʿUmar. In other words, as I will discuss below, ʿUmar inadvertently originated the idea that the Qur'an's text had been corrupted through omission.

More importantly, however, this chapter will demonstrate that ʿUmar's statements on the Stoning Verse have greater importance for the textual history of the Qur'an than previously appreciated. Despite ʿUmar's insistence that the supposedly missing verse should be included in the Qur'anic text, the early Muslim community resisted his political and religious authority, and rejected his interference with the established codex. Therefore, ʿUmar's difference of opinion with the Muslim community (most probably with

1 al-Sayyārī, Revelation and Falsification, p. 10.

2 Amir-Moezzi has been the main advocate of this view most recently; see Amir-Moezzi, 'The Shiʿis and the Qur'an'.

Zayd b. Thābit, who led the committee for the Qur'an's collection during the caliphates of Abū Bakr and 'Uthmān) corroborates Muslim accounts of the Qur'an's textual history, namely, that its text was first compiled and fixed during the caliphate of Abū Bakr.[3]

According to reports found in early Sunni sources, 'Umar (d. 23/644) became infuriated by the people's lack of commitment to implement the stoning penalty. This led him to issue a warning to Muslims from the pulpit, during the congregational prayers in the Prophet's Mosque in Medina. In this sermon, he re-emphasised the importance of stoning and explicitly stated that a verse on it was revealed in the Qur'an. The following variant from Bukhārī's *Ṣaḥīḥ* provides the essential elements of the tradition attributed to 'Umar:

> Narrated to us by 'Abd al-'Azīz b. 'Abdullāh, narrated to me by Ibrāhīm b. Sa'd, on the authority of Ṣāliḥ, on the authority of Ibn Shihāb [al-Zuhrī], on the authority of 'Ubaydullāh b. 'Abdullāh b. 'Utba b. Mas'ūd, on the authority of Ibn 'Abbās, who said:
>
> [. . .] 'Umar sat on the pulpit. When the reciters of the call for prayer finished their call, 'Umar praised and glorified God as He deserves. 'Umar then said: 'Now then, I will tell you something that has been decreed for me to say [by God]. I do not know, perhaps it is a sign that my time of death is nearing. So, whoever comprehends it and memorises it must narrate it to others wherever he goes. But if someone fears that he does not comprehend it, it is unlawful for him to attribute a lie to me. God sent Muhammad with the truth and revealed to him the Book. In the Qur'an, God sent down the Stoning Verse. We recited it, comprehended it and memorised it. The Messenger of God stoned, and we stoned after him. I am afraid that after a long time has passed, some will claim: "By God! We cannot find the Stoning Verse in the Book of God." Therefore, they will go astray by abandoning an obligation that God has revealed. The stoning [penalty] is in the Book of God prescribed for those chaste (*uḥṣina*) men or chaste women who commit adultery, if it is established by clear evidence, or pregnancy or confession.' Then ['Umar continued]: 'We used to recite it as we read from the Book of God: "O people! Do not claim to be the offspring of other than your fathers, as it is an ingratitude from you to claim to be the offspring of other than your father."'[4]

3 Motzki provides a brief overview of Muslim accounts regarding the collection of the Qur'an. These accounts state that Abū Bakr first collected the Qur'an, and 'Umar was also involved in this project. Motzki, 'The Collection of the Qur'an', p. 6.

4 Bukhārī, *Ṣaḥīḥ*, vol. 2, pp. 168–9.

The above text is prefaced with an elaborate introduction by Ibn 'Abbās, who provides the background to what led 'Umar to deliver this sermon during the congregational prayers, possibly the day prior. Ibn 'Abbās heard this information from 'Abd al-Raḥmān b. 'Awf (d. 33/653–4), an early and influential Companion of the Prophet, who later played a crucial role in 'Uthmān's nomination as third caliph. The initial conversation occurred during a Qur'an class where Ibn 'Abbās was teaching the Qur'an to those Muslims who had emigrated from Mecca to Medina. 'Abd al-Raḥmān b. 'Awf was present, and he informed Ibn 'Abbās that when he accompanied 'Umar to his final pilgrimage, a man approached 'Umar and questioned him about the legitimacy of Abū Bakr's appointment as the successor of the Prophet at Saqīfa – an event at which 'Abd al-Raḥmān b. 'Awf was also present.

This unnamed person hinted that another individual (*fulān*) – also unnamed – would have been better suited than Abū Bakr and informed him that, when 'Umar dies, he will pledge allegiance to this person. It can be speculated that the individual who questioned 'Umar was referring to 'Alī b. Abī Ṭālib (d. 40/661), his main rival to succeed the Prophet.[5] It seems that 'Umar was vexed by this question, as he was instrumental in the nomination of Abū Bakr, and Abū Bakr had designated him his successor. Thus, questioning Abū Bakr's legitimacy meant questioning 'Umar's legitimacy. 'Umar informed people around him that he would clarify the issue of succession to the Prophet during the day, possibly in Minā.

However, 'Abd al-Raḥmān b. 'Awf intervened and advised 'Umar that the audience in Minā was not suitable for such a statement, as there was a risk that they would misunderstand him. Instead, he suggested that 'Umar wait until he returned to Medina and address the issue in front of a more receptive audience. 'Umar heeded the advice and declared that he would speak on the matter in his first sermon after returning to Medina. 'Umar arrived in Medina on Friday, Dhū al-Ḥijja 23/644, and delivered the sermon after sunset. Ibn 'Abbās seems to have a vivid memory of listening to a sermon while sitting near the pulpit with another prominent Companion, Sa'īd b. Zayd b. 'Amr b. Nufayl (d. 51/671).[6]

In anticipation of 'Umar's sermon, Ibn 'Abbās and Sa'īd b. Zayd had a brief exchange, after which the sermon commenced. 'Umar began with a dramatic opening, in which he foretells of his own imminent demise,

5 I have studied the tension between Abū Bakr and 'Alī during the early days of Abū Bakr's reign and its relevance to the textual history of the Qur'an previously; see Kara, *In Search of Ali Ibn Abi Talib's Codex*.

6 Sa'īd b. Zayd was a cousin and brother-in-law of 'Umar. According to Muslim reports, he and his wife had become Muslim before 'Umar and played an important role in 'Umar's conversion to Islam.

making this sermon one of his last significant public statements. In it, he addressed two matters that he deemed central to his legacy: the stoning penalty and the legitimacy of Abū Bakr's succession to the Prophet. While the part dealing with the matter of succession is not directly relevant to the study at hand, it is curious that 'Umar saw these two matters as most pressing, especially that of stoning.

There are, in total, sixteen variants of this report. These are recorded in the oldest Sunni collections, including the canonical ones: two exist in Mālik's *Muwaṭṭa'*, two in 'Abd al-Razzāq's *Muṣannaf*, three in Ibn Abī Shayba's *Muṣannaf*, three in Bukhārī's *Ṣaḥīh*, one in Ibn Mājah's *Sunan*, two in Tirmidhī's *Sunan*, one in Abū Dāwūd's *Sunan* and two in Muslim's *Ṣaḥīh*. These variants are all reported through two separate individuals – Ibn 'Abbās and Sa'īd b. al-Musayyab – who received the account from its primary source, 'Umar, and narrated them to multiple transmitters.

Two independent transmission lines, one from Ibn 'Abbās and one from Sa'īd, transmitted the variants via various well-known collectors until they were recorded in writing. Based on an initial observation of these lines of transmission, I can identify 'Umar as the Common Link and the source since the report spreads out from him immediately by Ibn 'Abbās and Sa'īd b. al-Musayyab, who can be considered the Partial Common Links (PCLs). Given the existence of two PCLs, I have divided the variants into two groups.

Aside from the Common Link and PCLs, there are important individuals who play a crucial role in the distribution of the report, such as 'Ubaydullāh b. 'Abdullāh, Zuhrī, Ma'mar, Ibn Abī Shayba, Dāwūd b. Abī Hind and Ibn Jud'ān. It is important to note that the Ibn 'Abbās and Sa'īd b. al-Musayyab clusters rejoin via collectors such as Mālik, Ibn Abī Shayba, Tirmidhī and Muslim. This presents a risk of forgery, as it is possible for these four individuals to tamper with the two independent transmission lines. However, the *isnād-cum-matn* analysis does not accept an a priori assumption of systematic forgery in the absence of a clear motive on the part of the forger and actual evidence of forgery. Furthermore, if an individual collector transmits two different versions of the same report, it would be a strong indication that he did not tamper with the text himself, although this does not exclude the possibility of a previous transmitter tampering with it.

The Ibn 'Abbās Cluster

Chain of Transmission Analysis

The Ibn 'Abbās variants spread out via two main transmission lines from 'Ubaydullāh b. 'Abdullāh and Yūsuf b. Mihrān. Both transmit the report to the next two individuals: Zuhrī and Ibn Jud'ān. From this point, the transmission lines fan out. Zuhrī transmits the report through six different lines while Ibn Jud'ān transmits it via two. The Zuhrī and Ibn Jud'ān transmissions converge through Ma'mar, which affords Ma'mar the opportunity to tamper with Yūsuf b. Mihrān's variant to make it look like 'Ubaydullāh b. 'Abdullāh's. However, Ibn Jud'ān transmits another variant to Ash'ath, which is then independently transmitted by Ibn Idrīs and Ibn Abī Shayba. This second transmission line allows us to detect any potential forgery through textual comparison. Assuming there is no apparent problem with the texts of these transmission lines, it is possible to reliably date this group of variants to Ibn 'Abbās. Having identified the possible problems with the chain of transmission map, I will now proceed to analyse individual chains of transmission.

The first variant of the report was recorded in Mālik's *Muwaṭṭa'*,[7] who reported it from Zuhrī. The sound relationship between Mālik and Zuhrī has been well documented.[8] Therefore, I can move beyond Zuhrī and investigate other narrators in the chain. The chain of transmission map points to Zuhrī as the most likely culprit for any forgery, as many transmission lines fan out from him. He could have invented this tradition and given it a reliable-looking chain. This would lure later collectors such as Mālik, Ma'mar and Sufyān b. 'Uyayna into transmitting it. The main problem with a forgery thesis in this case is the existence of Yūsuf b. Mihrān's transmission line. According to the Schachtian approach, Zuhrī could have collaborated with his student Ma'mar to forge an additional chain to pre-empt any suspicions of forgery via the Ibn Jud'ān chain, yet it is highly improbable that he also forged the Ash'ath transmission from Ibn Jud'ān's chain. Ma'mar also reported from Ibn Jud'ān, and they both lived in Basra, but it would have been difficult for Ma'mar to forge the report and attribute it to Ibn Jud'ān without the latter's collaboration due to the existence of the Ash'ath chain. I cannot think of any motive which would bring Zuhrī, Ma'mar and Ibn Jud'ān to collaborate in forging this report. Also given Ibn Jud'ān's known Shi'i tendencies, Zuhrī and Ma'mar could have chosen a more credible narrator for their forgery.

Zuhrī reported the traditions from 'Ubaydullāh b. 'Abdullāh [b. 'Utba b. Mas'ūd] (d. 98/716–17), a second-generation Muslim who lived in Medina and visited Basra[9] and was also the brother of the hadith collector 'Awn b. 'Abdullāh b. 'Utba. 'Ubaydullāh was born during 'Umar's caliphate, or shortly thereafter. Mālik and Zuhrī both reported from him directly, and

7 Mālik, *Muwaṭṭa'*, vol. 5, p. 824.

8 Motzki et al., Analysing Muslim Traditions.

9 al-Mizzī, *Tadhīb al-kamāl fī asmā' al-rijāl*, vol. 6, pp. 416–17.

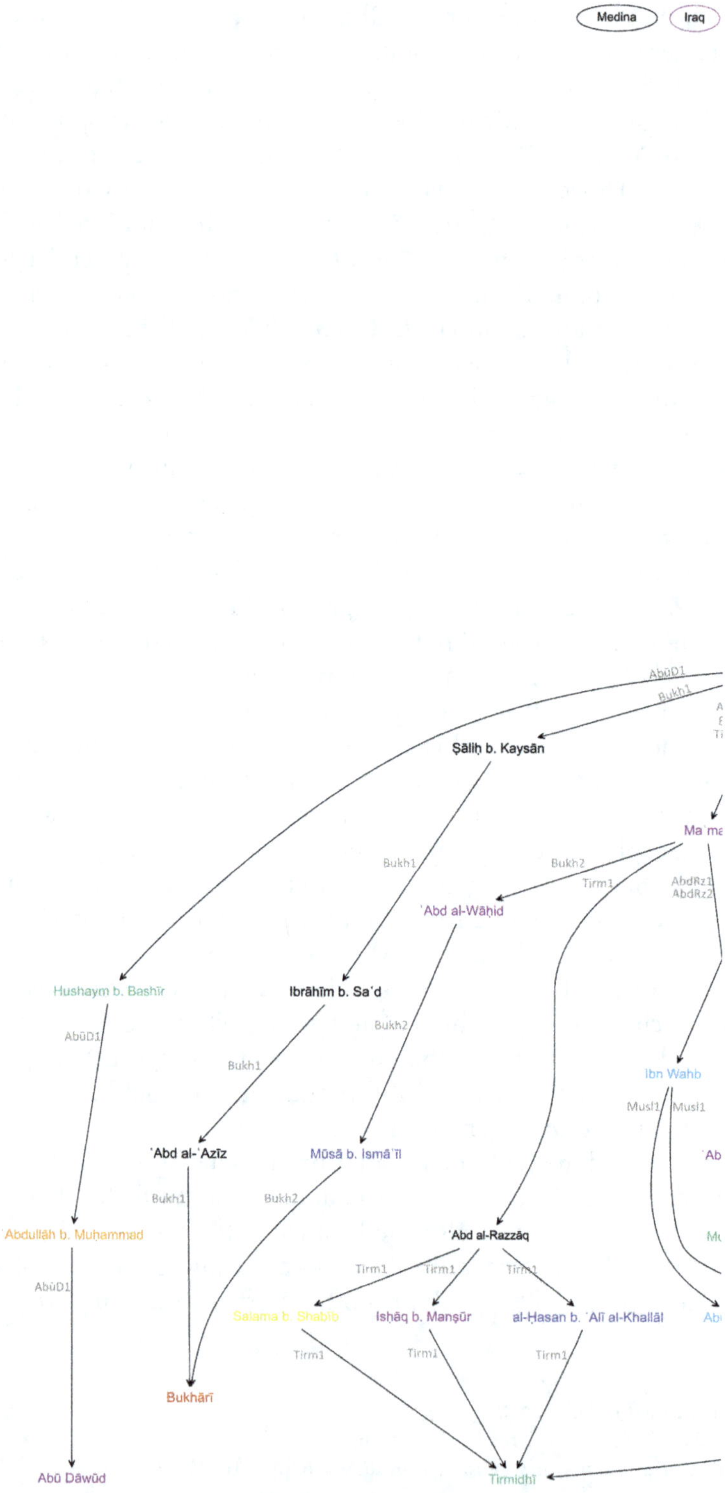

Diagram 4 Available online at: https://edin.ac/4a04vST

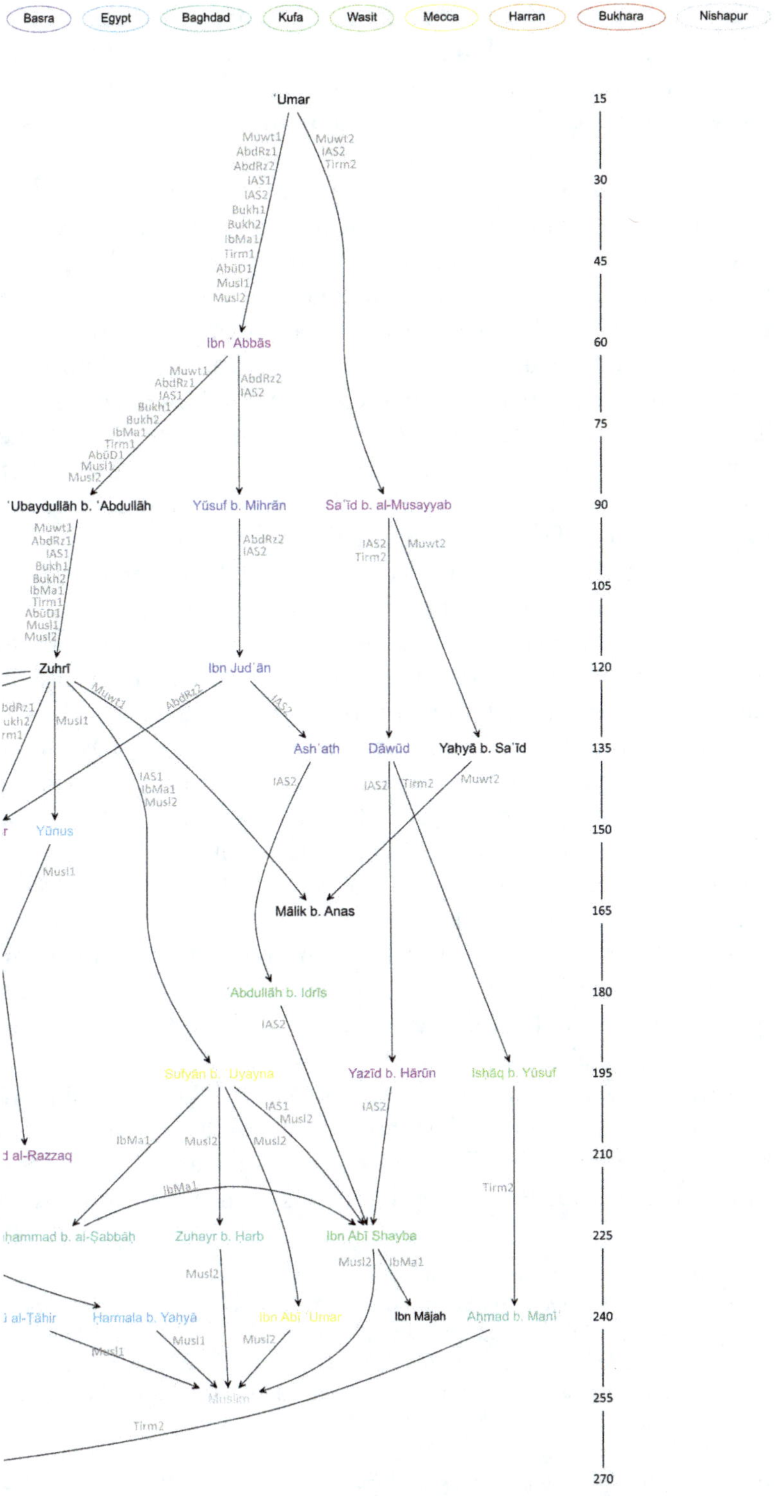

Basra
Egypt
Baghdad
Kufa
Wasit
Mecca
Harran
Bukhara
Nishapur
ʿUmar
Muwt1 AbdRz1 AbdRz2 IAS1 IAS2 Bukh1 Bukh2 IbMa1 Tirm1 AbūD1 Musl1 Musl2
Muwt2 IAS2 Tirm2
Ibn ʿAbbās
Muwt1 AbdRz1 IAS1 Bukh1 Bukh2 IbMa1 Tirm1 AbūD1 Musl1 Musl2
AbdRz2 IAS2
ʿUbaydullāh b. ʿAbdullāh
Yūsuf b. Mihrān
Saʿīd b. al-Musayyab
Muwt1 AbdRz1 IAS1 Bukh1 Bukh2 IbMa1 Tirm1 AbūD1 Musl1 Musl2
AbdRz2 IAS2
IAS2 Tirm2
Muwt2
Zuhrī
Ibn Judʿān
Muwt1
AbdRz2
IAS2
Musl1
IAS1 IbMa1 Musl2
Ashʿath
Dāwūd
Yaḥyā b. Saʿīd
Yūnus
Mālik b. Anas
ʿAbdullāh b. Idrīs
Sufyān b. ʿUyayna
Yazīd b. Hārūn
Isḥāq b. Yūsuf
Ibn Abī Shayba
Zuhayr b. Ḥarb
Harmala b. Yaḥyā
Ibn Abī ʿUmar
Ibn Mājah
Aḥmad b. Manīʿ
Muslim
Tirm2
15
30
45
60
75
90
105
120
135
150
165
180
195
210
225
240
255
270

Mālik also reported from him via Zuhrī.[10] Given the proximity of the two scholars in terms of both time and location, Zuhrī, who was from Medina, could have reported this variant from 'Ubaydullāh. Meanwhile, the existence of Yūsuf b. Mihrān's transmission line rules out the possibility of a forgery on the part of 'Ubaydullāh.

'Ubaydullāh reported the variant from Ibn 'Abbās (d. 68/687–8), a cousin of the Prophet and one of the foremost early scholars and authorities on the Qur'an. Ibn 'Abbās was active in Mecca, Medina and Iraq. Due to his outstanding religious knowledge, Ibn 'Abbās served as an adviser to the second and third caliphs and was a strong supporter of the fourth. 'Umar took a particular liking to Ibn 'Abbās and revered him in the presence of other prominent Companions.[11] Ibn 'Abbās heard his variant from 'Umar (d. 23/644). Could Ibn 'Abbās have forged the report? The pro-'Alī stance he adopted towards the end of his life could be grounds for suspicion. If he had political motives, this report would have given him the opportunity to defame 'Umar by attributing a report to him that portrayed him as questioning the integrity of the Qur'an. However, his pro-'Alī stance alone is not sufficient grounds for him to forge the report. Furthermore, 'Alī's major political rival during his reign was Mu'āwiya (d. 60/680) rather than 'Umar, who had died years earlier. Therefore, there is little reason to suspect that Ibn 'Abbās forged this report to defame 'Umar.

The second variant[12] is recorded in 'Abd al-Razzāq's *Muṣannaf*.[13] 'Abd al-Razzāq received it from Ma'mar, and, thereafter, the chain is identical to Mālik's variant: Zuhrī ← 'Ubaydullāh b. 'Abdullāh ← Ibn 'Abbās. Zuhrī also transmitted it to Ma'mar, who reported it to 'Abd al-Razzāq. I have discussed the veracity of this chain previously. However, due to this chain's similarity to that of Mālik, a Schachtian assumption would have been that Mālik forged this well-known chain to substantiate his strongly held view that the Qur'an prescribed stoning. However, the existence of several other transmission lines and collectors would render any such endeavour extremely difficult.

The third variant[14] in this group is also from 'Abd al-Razzāq's *Muṣannaf*. It is attributed to Ibn 'Abbās, but via a different chain. 'Abd al-Razzāq heard it from one of his favourite sources, Ma'mar b. Rāshid (d. 153/770). Motzki has provided an in-depth analysis of the connection between 'Abd

10 al-Dhahabī, *Siyar a'lām al-nubalā'*, vol. 4, pp. 475–9.

11 Ibn Sa'd, *al-Ṭabaqāt*, vol. 9, pp. 314–20; al-Dhahabī, *Siyar a'lām al-nubalā'*, vol. 3, pp. 332–41; al-Mizzī, *Tahdhīb al-kamāl fī asmā' al-rijāl*, vol. 15, pp. 154–62.

12 I have excluded ten other variants that mention the word 'stoning' in 'Abd al-Razzāq's *Muṣannaf*. They are either not directly related to the stoning or the texts are too short or peculiar.

13 al-Ṣan'ānī, *Muṣannaf*, vol. 7, p. 315.

14 al-Ṣan'ānī, *Muṣannaf*, vol. 7, pp. 329–30.

al-Razzāq and Maʿmar.[15] Maʿmar heard it from Ibn Judʿān (d. 131/749), who was originally from Mecca but was active in Basra. Ibn Judʿān was born blind from a slave mother and there are conflicting reports about his knowledge and reliability in Sunni works of *rijāl* (biographical evaluation), but he was generally perceived as unreliable, an assessment which may be related to his pro-ʿAlī inclinations.[16] Along with Ibn ʿAbbās, he is the second narrator to have had Shiʿi inclinations. However, being Shiʿi is not itself grounds for assuming a forgery. It was not uncommon for some ‘extremist’ Shiʿis to tamper with the existing reports attributed to the Shiʿi Imams,[17] but it is highly unlikely that they would forge a report from scratch and attribute it to Sunni transmitters. In any case, neither Ibn Judʿān nor Ibn ʿAbbās were known to harbour extremist tendencies. Furthermore, ʿUbaydullāh b. ʿAbdullāh and Zuhrī transmit variants of the same report independently of Ibn Judʿān. Hence, unless something is brought to light during our textual analysis, Ibn Judʿān’s pro-ʿAlī leanings alone do not indicate a forgery.

On the face of it, Maʿmar, who also lived in Basra, could have received the tradition from Ibn Judʿān, who received the variant from Yūsuf b. Mihrān, who also lived in Basra and is known to have reported traditions from Ibn ʿAbbās.[18] Works of biographical evaluations state that only Ibn Judʿān was known to report from Yūsuf b. Mihrān. There is no date of death mentioned for him, but given that he was between Ibn ʿAbbās (d. 68/687–8) and Ibn Judʿān (d. 131/749), it is possible that he died around the year 100/719. Because he was active in Basra and may have lived at the same time as the other two, one might suggest that Ibn Judʿān received the variant from Yūsuf b. Mihrān, who heard it from Ibn ʿAbbās. While studying the first variant above, I discussed the connection between Ibn ʿAbbās and ʿUmar. Hence, it appears that this variant spread in Basra around the mid-first/seventh century and, theoretically, Ibn ʿAbbās could have heard it from ʿUmar directly, as there was both a geographical and generational proximity between the two transmitters.

The fourth variant was recorded in Ibn Abī Shayba’s *Muṣannaf*.[19] He received it from Sufyān b. ʿUyayna (d. 198/813–14), who was active in Iraq and the Hijaz, and then Zuhrī ← ʿUbaydullāh ← Ibn ʿAbbās. I have discussed this chain in different combinations previously and have established its veracity. It is important to note that after Zuhrī, Sufyān b. ʿUyayna is the second-most prolific transmitter of the report, as he transmits it to

15 Motzki et al., *Analysing Muslim Traditions*, pp. 5–11.

16 al-Mizzī, *Tahdhīb al-kamāl fī asmāʾ al-rijāl*, vol. 20, pp. 434–4; al-Dhahabī, *Siyar aʿlām al-nubalāʾ*, vol. 5, pp. 206–8.

17 Kara, ‘The Collection of the Qurʾān in the Early Shīʿite Discourse’, pp. 375–406.

18 Ibn Saʿd, *al-Ṭabaqāt*, vol. 5, p. 221; Bukhārī, *al-Tārīkh al-kabīr*, vol. 8, pp. 375–6.

19 Ibn Abī Shayba, *Muṣannaf*, vol. 5, p. 539.

five other individuals. This variant travels from Medina to Basra and then returns to Medina, probably via Zuhrī.

The fifth variant is also in Ibn Abī Shayba's *Muṣannaf*.[20] He received it from ʿAbdullāh b. Idrīs (d. 192/808), a prominent scholar based in Kufa. He moved to Baghdad briefly but then returned to Kufa.[21] ʿAbdullāh b. Idrīs heard it from Ashʿath b. ʿAbd al-Malik (d. 142/759–60),[22] a client of the Ḥumrān tribe and resident of Basra.[23] Like the fourth variant, Ashʿath b. ʿAbd al-Malik heard it from the PCL Ibn Judʿān (d. 131/749), who received it from Yūsuf b. Mihrān, who received it from Ibn ʿAbbās, who heard it from ʿUmar. I have studied the connection from ʿAlī b. Zayd b. Judʿān onwards above and noted that the transmission line seems genuine. The fifth variant is found in Bukhārī's *Ṣaḥīḥ*.[24] He received it from Sufyān b. ʿUyayna ← Zuhrī ← ʿUbaydullāh ← Ibn ʿAbbās. The veracity of this chain has been established previously.

The sixth variant is found in Bukhārī's *Ṣaḥīḥ*,[25] and is reported from ʿAbd al-ʿAzīz b. ʿAbdullāh (d. circa 220/835–6), a prominent hadith collector from Medina. He reported many traditions that appear in the canonical Sunni collections.[26] He heard it from Ibrāhīm b. Saʿd (d. circa 184/800–1), who was related to Zuhrī. Ibrāhīm b. Saʿd was also active in Medina and Baghdad[27] and heard it from Ṣāliḥ b. Kaysān (d. 140/757–8), who was a colleague of Zuhrī.[28] Ṣāliḥ b. Kaysān was born and lived in Medina.[29] He heard the variant from Zuhrī, who heard it from ʿUbaydullāh b. ʿAbdullāh (d. 94/712–13). He too was a well-known hadith collector, as well as a long-time teacher of Zuhrī. ʿUbaydullāh b. ʿAbdullāh heard it from Ibn ʿAbbās, who narrated it from ʿUmar. Based on the chain of transmission analysis, I conclude that there is no apparent problem with this Medinan chain of transmission.

20 Ibn Abī Shayba, *Muṣannaf*, vol. 5, p. 540.

21 al-Baghdādī, *Tārīkh Baghdād*, vol. 11, pp. 69–75; al-Dhahabī, *Siyar aʿlām al-nubalāʾ*, vol. 9, pp. 42–8.

22 Bukhārī states the date of death as 146; however, the majority of sources seem to have accepted the year 142 as the correct date of death. See Bukhārī, *al-Tārīkh al-kabīr*, vol. 1, p. 432.

23 al-Mizzī, *Tahdhīb al-kamāl fī asmāʾ al-rijāl*, vol. 3, pp. 277–86; Bukhārī, *al-Tārīkh al-kabīr*, vol. 1, pp. 431–2.

24 Bukhārī, *Ṣaḥīḥ*, vol. 8, p. 168.

25 Bukhārī, *Ṣaḥīḥ*, vol. 2, pp. 168–9.

26 al-Dhahabī, *Tadhhīb al-kamāl fī asmāʾ al-rijāl*, vol. 6, p. 112; al-Dhahabī, *Siyar aʿlām al-nubalāʾ*, vol. 10, p. 389.

27 al-Baghdādī, *Tārīkh Baghdād*, vol. 6, pp. 601–8.

28 al-Dhahabī, *Tadhkirat al-ḥuffāẓ*, vol. 1, pp. 148–9; Bukhārī, *al-Tārīkh al-kabīr*, vol. 4, p. 288; al-Mizzī, *Tahdhīb al-kamāl fī asmāʾ al-rijāl*, vol. 18, pp. 73–84.

29 al-Dhahabī, *Tadhkirat al-ḥuffāẓ*, vol. 1, pp. 148–9; Bukhārī, *al-Tārīkh al-kabīr*, vol. 4, p. 288; al-Mizzī, *Tahdhīb al-kamāl fī asmāʾ al-rijāl*, vol. 18, pp. 73–84.

The seventh variant is in Bukhārī's *Ṣaḥīḥ*.[30] He heard it from Mūsā b. Ismā'īl (d. 223/837–8), who was active in Basra and Tabuk.[31] Mūsā b. Ismā'īl heard it from 'Abd al-Wāḥid b. Ziyād (d. circa 176/792–3), who was active in Basra and Kufa.[32] 'Abd al-Wāḥid heard it from Ma'mar b. Rāshid, who was active in Basra and received the variant from Zuhrī. The rest of the chain transmitted via 'Ubaydullāh b. 'Abdullāh ← Ibn 'Abbās ← 'Umar, which has been examined above.

The eighth variant is recorded in Ibn Mājah's *Sunan*,[33] and he received it from Ibn Abī Shayba. Ibn Mājah probably copied this variant directly from Ibn Abī Shayba's *Muṣannaf*, as it is well known that Ibn Mājah quotes from that work often. However, I could not find this variant in Ibn Abī Shayba's *Muṣannaf*, which may indicate that it was lost due to an editorial mishap. In any case, Ibn Abī Shayba heard it from Muḥammad b. al-Ṣabbāḥ (d. 227/841), who was born in Rayy but active in Baghdad.[34] He heard it from Sufyān b. 'Uyayna (d. 198/813–14), who was active in the Hijaz and Iraq. The rest of the chain continues with Zuhrī ← 'Ubaydullāh b. 'Abdullāh ← Ibn 'Abbās ← 'Umar.[35]

The ninth variant is found in Tirmidhī's *Sunan*[36] and he received it from several transmitters, including Salama b. Shabīb (d. 247/861), Isḥāq b. Manṣūr (d. 251/865) and al-Ḥasan b. 'Alī al-Khallāl (d. 242/857). All of them could have received this variant from 'Abd al-Razzāq (d. 211/826) and informed Tirmidhī of it thereafter. Salama b. Shabīb was an itinerant collector who was active in Mecca, Khorasan and Egypt.[37] Isḥāq b. Manṣūr was also a well-travelled hadith collector. He was born in Merv and moved to Iraq, the Hijaz and Syria.[38] Al-Ḥasan b. 'Alī al-Khallāl was active in Basra and Mecca.[39] They could also have received the variant from 'Abd al-Razzāq, who had recorded two versions of the tradition in his *Muṣannaf*, both via his informant Ma'mar. He recorded the third variant (see above) with transmissions through Ma'mar ← Zuhrī ← 'Ubaydullāh b. 'Abdullāh ← Ibn 'Abbās ← 'Umar, which is the same chain that Tirmidhī transmitted. Therefore, it can be safely assumed that Salama b. Shabīb, Isḥāq b. Manṣūr and al-Ḥasan b. 'Alī al-Khallāl either read the variant in 'Abd al-Razzāq's *Muṣannaf* or heard it directly from him. Either case may

30 Bukhārī, *Ṣaḥīḥ*, vol. 9, pp. 103–4.
31 al-Mizzī, *Tahdhīb al-kamāl fī asmā' al-rijāl*, vol. 29, pp. 21–30.
32 al-Dhahabī, *Tadhhīb tahdhīb al-kamāl fī asmā' al-rijāl*, vol. 6, p. 179.
33 Ibn Mājah, *Sunan*, vol. 1, p. 853.
34 al-Dhahabī, *Siyar a'lām al-nubalā'*, vol. 10, pp. 671–2.
35 I have already discussed the connection between these individuals above.
36 Tirmidhī, *Sunan*, vol. 2, p. 90.
37 al-Dhahabī, *Siyar a'lām al-nubalā'*, vol. 12, pp. 257–8.
38 al-Baghdādī, *Tārīkh Baghdād*, vol. 7, pp. 385–7.
39 al-Dhahabī, *Siyar a'lām al-nubalā'*, vol. 11, p. 399.

be plausible, and the chain of the variant can be tentatively traced back to Ibn ʿAbbās.

The tenth variant was recorded in Abū Dāwūd's *Sunan*.[40] He travelled and collected traditions in Iraq, Egypt, Syria, the Hijaz, Nishapur and Merv. He reports the variant from ʿAbdullāh b. Muḥammad al-Nufaylī (d. 234/848–9), who was from Harran[41] and served as one of Abū Dāwūd's main sources.[42] Al-Nufaylī reports it from Hushaym b. Bashīr (d. 183/799), who was active in Wasit and Baghdad,[43] and received it from Zuhrī. Upon first glance, there seems to be a gap between the two, but Hushaym was born in 104/722 and enjoyed a long life.[44] Therefore, he could have heard the variant from Zuhrī. There seems to be no interruption from Zuhrī until Abū Dāwūd, and the chain is transmitted via ʿUbaydullāh b. ʿAbdullāh b. ʿUtba ← Ibn ʿAbbās ← ʿUmar.

The eleventh variant in the Ibn ʿAbbās cluster was recorded in Muslim's *Ṣaḥīh*.[45] He received it from both Abū al-Ṭāhir and Ḥarmala b. Yaḥyā. Abū al-Ṭāhir (also known as Ibn al-Sirḥ, d. 250/864) was a reputable scholar from Egypt. He reported traditions from Ibn Wahb and commented on Ibn Wahb's edition of the *Muwaṭṭaʾ*.[46] Ḥarmala b. Yaḥyā (also known as Abū Ḥafṣ al-Tūjībī, d. 243/858) was also a well-known scholar in Egypt and primarily reported traditions from Ibn Wahb. Both received the variant from [ʿAbdullāh] Ibn Wahb (d. 197/813) of Egypt. He had an impeccable reputation for narrating hadith.[47] He heard the variant from Yūnus [b. Yazīd] (d. 159/776) of Egypt, who was praised for mastering and widely transmitting Zuhrī's traditions.[48] He also reports this variant from Zuhrī in Medina and then ʿUbaydullāh b. ʿAbdullāh ← Ibn ʿAbbās ← ʿUmar. According to this chain, Yūnus b. Yazīd received it in Medina and transmitted it in Egypt. There is nothing in this chain to suggest forgery.

Finally, the twelfth variant is recorded in Muslim's *Ṣaḥīh*.[49] He heard it from Ibn Abī Shayba, Zuhayr b. Ḥarb and Ibn Abī ʿUmar. The chain is identical to that of the fourth variant, which is in Ibn Abī Shayba's *Muṣannaf*. Hence, it is certain that Muslim's source is Ibn Abī Shayba, and there is no need to investigate this transmission further.

40 al-Dhahabī, *Siyar aʿlām al-nubalāʾ*, vol. 4, pp. 144–5.
41 Northern part of Mesopotamia or Jazira.
42 al-Dhahabī, *Siyar aʿlām al-nubalāʾ*, vol. 10, pp. 634–7.
43 al-Dhahabī, *Siyar aʿlām al-nubalāʾ*, vol. 8, pp. 287–94.
44 al-Dhahabī, *Siyar aʿlām al-nubalāʾ*, vol. 8, p. 288.
45 Muslim, *Ṣaḥīḥ*, vol. 2, p. 1317.
46 al-Dhahabī, *Siyar aʿlām al-nubalāʾ*, vol. 12, pp. 62–3.
47 al-Dhahabī, *Siyar aʿlām al-nubalāʾ*, vol. 9, pp. 224–34.
48 al-Dhahabī, *Siyar aʿlām al-nubalāʾ*, vol. 6, pp. 224–34.
49 Muslim, *Ṣaḥīḥ*, vol. 2, p. 1317.

In summary, no issues appear with the chains of transmission outlined above, and they suggest a genuine process of transmission. The main line was spread out from Ibn ʿAbbās via two collectors, namely, Zuhrī and Ibn Judʿān. They then disseminated the variants widely with Zuhrī playing a crucial role in this process. The chain of transmission analysis also suggests that variants of this report circulated in Medina, Basra, Kufa and Egypt in the second/eighth century. If not for the Ibn Judʿān ← Yūsuf b. Mihrān transmission line, I could have only traced these variants back to Zuhrī, but the existence of an alternative transmission means I can date the Ibn ʿAbbās cluster as far back as his death in 68/687–8.

Textual Analysis

This group of variants provides an account of ʿUmar publicly maintaining that a Stoning Verse was revealed to the Prophet, and that the penalty was implemented. He further expressed his displeasure at the fact that Muslims had omitted this verse from the official Qur'anic codex and then denied its existence altogether. The variants state that ʿUmar delivered this statement immediately following his return from, what would come to be, his final Hajj. It is well known that ʿUmar died in either Dhū al-Ḥijja or Muḥarram, in the year 23/644. The tenth day of Dhū al-Ḥijja marks the end of the Hajj and the Eid of al-Aḍḥā, so this sermon probably took place during the first ten days of Dhū al-Ḥijja 23/644, while the Hajj rituals were ongoing. Therefore, unlike many historical events from Islam's early history, we can pinpoint a specific date and time in which this episode is said to have occurred. If the dating process of these variants is successful, then the event they describe took place in the year 23/644.

Following his discussion of the Stoning Verse, ʿUmar's sermon turns to the issue of Abū Bakr's nomination as the Prophet's successor or caliph. This is not relevant to the present discussion, but it suggests that these were two sources of controversy that ʿUmar felt strongly about and wished to address publicly before his death, thereby saving future Muslims from going astray.

In the case of the Stoning Verse, ʿUmar was adamant that it was revealed in the Qur'an and that the Muslims recited and memorised it during the Prophet's lifetime. He even provided the wording of the verse and stated that the early Muslims implemented the punishment it prescribed. However, he did not explain why the verse was omitted when the Qur'an was compiled after the Prophet's death – a process in which ʿUmar had been involved.[50] He

50 John Burton makes a good case for this point and discusses some traditions in which ʿUmar makes unsuccessful attempts to have the Stoning Verse included in the Qur'an, but Zayd b. Thābit rejects it. Burton, *The Collection of the Qur'ān*, pp. 68–104.

was worried that later Muslims would be reluctant to accept the validity of such a punishment given its absence from the Qur'an, which made him fear that the punishment would be forgotten and, consequently, that the Muslim community would deviate from the path of God.

What makes the account even more remarkable is that 'Umar reportedly recited a second verse also not found in the Qur'an: 'O people! Do not claim to be the offspring of other than your fathers, as it is an ingratitude from you to claim to be the offspring of other than your father.' How could 'Umar recite two different 'verses' of the Qur'an which were absent from the Qur'anic text? I will investigate the variants of the tradition to see if it is possible to trace an original version back to 'Umar.

The two variants in Mālik's *Muwaṭṭa'* appear to recount the same assembly in the Prophet's Mosque in which 'Umar maintained the existence of a Stoning Verse. These variants, however, differ from one another in several ways. The first variant, narrated through Ibn 'Abbās, is a simplified two-sentence abstract of 'Umar's claims regarding stoning. He stated that the Stoning Verse was revealed in the Qur'an and that stoning was prescribed for male and female adulterers if their guilt was established by evidence, pregnancy[51] or confession:

> I have heard 'Umar b. al-Khaṭṭāb saying that the stoning [penalty] is surely included in the Book of God for those men and women who commit adultery, if they are married. It is clearly established with evidence, pregnancy or confession.[52]

The second variant, found in 'Abd al-Razzāq's *Muṣannaf* and reported through Ibn 'Abbās, resembles Mālik's first, which is also reported through Ibn 'Abbās. However, it is slightly longer and contains some additional information. Furthermore, some elements in the third variant resemble those found in the first, such as 'God the Exalted appointed Muhammad with the truth and sent with him the Book in which there was revealed the Stoning Verse'. The first variant included the phrase 'I have heard 'Umar b. al-Khaṭṭāb saying that stoning is surely included in the Book of God'. Also, similar terminology was used for the adulterers. The first variant refers to them as 'those men and women who commit adultery' (*man zanā min al-rijāli wa-l-nisā'i*), while the second says 'whoever commits adultery' (*man zanā*). Finally, both the first and second variants include the same requirements for conviction: evidence, pregnancy or confession.

51 Kecia Ali points out the condition of pregnancy 'places women disproportionately in jeopardy of punishment'. Ali, *Sexual Ethics and Islam*, 63.

52 Mālik, *Muwaṭṭa'*, vol. 5, p. 823.

However, the second variant includes some additional details not found in the first, such as the phrase 'God the Exalted appointed Muhammad with the truth' and

> The Messenger of God stoned, and we stoned after him. I am afraid that a time will come, in which some people will say: 'By God! We do not find stoning in the Book of God!' They will go astray by abandoning an injunction that was sent down by God.[53]

These additional elements can be summarised under three categories: (1) affirming the prophethood of Muhammad; (2) the Prophet Muhammad and the Muslims after him stoning adulterers; and (3) 'Umar's concern about later generations' denial of the Stoning Verse and, therefore, their breach of a divine injunction. The second and third elements are also found in the Saʿīd b. al-Musayyab cluster, albeit paraphrased, which may suggest this passage was part of the original version of the report but omitted in the first variant.

Furthermore, although this variant is about the Stoning Verse, the locus of concern in the second variant appears to be the Prophet's authority as lawmaker and his practice of stoning. A similar reference exists in Saʿīd b. al-Musayyab's variants too, but there is more emphasis on the Prophet in the second variant. This could be because in the absence of a verse about stoning in the codified Qur'an, transmitters opted to emphasise the Prophet's implementation of stoning to strengthen its legitimacy. In this vein, Maʿmar and Zuhrī, who transmit the second variant from 'Ubaydullāh b. 'Abdullāh from Ibn 'Abbās, may have paraphrased some of the wordings of the variant to reflect such an emphasis. However, such interference seems to be minor and has little effect on the overall meaning.

The text of the third variant[54] may corroborate the idea that the emphasis on the Prophet's *sunna* was asserted in these texts as a result of paraphrasing by either Maʿmar or Zuhrī. The variant recorded in Ibn Abī Shayba's *Muṣannaf* is transmitted through Maʿmar ← Ibn Judʿān ← Yūsuf b. Mihrān ← Ibn 'Abbās, but not by Zuhrī, and it does not emphasise the *sunna* of the Prophet. Instead, this variant emphasises Abū Bakr's implementation of the stoning penalty. Therefore, it could be argued that Zuhrī inserted his *sunna*-centric view into the text. The text of the third variant includes extra information, such as the sermon taking place during a congregational prayer and 'Umar delivering it from the pulpit. He warned people by saying, 'O people! Do not be deceived about the Stoning Verse. It was revealed in the Book of God the All-powerful and Almighty, and we

53 al-Ṣanʿānī, *Muṣannaf*, vol. 7, p. 315.
54 al-Ṣanʿānī, *Muṣannaf*, vol. 7, pp. 329–30.

have read it.'[55] Like the previous variants, the third asserts the inclusion of a Stoning Verse in the Qur'an and the continuing validity of its ruling. The variant also adds: 'However, many [verses] have been lost from the Qur'an when Muhammad died. One of these verses that the Prophet had was the stoning [verse].' The variant does not only claim that the Stoning Verse was lost from the Qur'an but many other verses along with it following the Prophet's death. The previous variants do not mention the fate of the Stoning Verse, but this variant clearly states that it was lost (*dhahaba*). The earlier variants are also silent about when the verse was lost from the Qur'anic canon, while this one says it occurred after the death of the Prophet.

These details create further problems for those who claim that the Stoning Verse was abrogated.[56] If the verse was lost after the death of the Prophet, it goes against the Qur'an's insistence that, as the Messenger of God, the Prophet in his lifetime provided the normative standard for the Qur'an alone. Anything that happened after his death, such as the omission or insertion of verses, may therefore be a corruption of the text. Even if it were true that the doctrine of abrogation existed in the Qur'an and the Stoning Verse was abrogated, only the Prophet had the authority to enact this. Therefore, according to this account, the Stoning Verse does not qualify as a case of abrogation, but rather as a case of textual distortion.

Furthermore, instead of the practice of the Prophet, the third variant asserts that it was Abū Bakr's *sunna* to stone: 'Abū Bakr stoned, and we have stoned after him.' This element is problematic and can only be explained by the fact that in the third variant (and the fourteenth variant of Saʿīd b. al-Musayyab) 'Umar says: 'The Messenger of God stoned, and we stoned after him.' So, by saying 'we', 'Umar refers to the reigns of Abū Bakr and himself. However, it seems that in this variant, the name of Abū Bakr has replaced that of Muhammad, while retaining the phrase 'we have stoned after him'. There may be two reasons for this: either the transmitters made an error, or there was a deliberate effort to move the focus from the Prophet to the caliphs. It is impossible to verify either of these options at this point. Finally, the variant expresses concern that a future generation may deny the existence of the stoning penalty, along with other religious teachings because they do not find them in the Qur'an.[57]

55 al-Ṣanʿānī, *Muṣannaf*, vol. 7, pp. 329–30.

56 Khadduri, *al-Shāfiʿī's al-Risālā*, pp. 123–45. Burton deals with this issue in great detail and exposes the apologetic Muslim writing to deal with the problem. Burton, *The Collection of the Qur'an*, pp. 96–100.

57 'A faction will arrive from this nation (*umma*) who will deny the stoning [penalty] and they will deny the sunset from the west, and they will deny the intercession, the Day of Judgement and they will deny Dajjāl (the false messiah), they will deny the torment of purgatory and they will deny a faction who exit hellfire after entering into it.'

The fourth variant[58] is mentioned in Ibn Abī Shayba's *Muṣannaf* and resembles the second variant recorded in the *Muṣannaf* of 'Abd al-Razzāq. Both are reported through Zuhrī and go back to Ibn 'Abbās. This variant opens with 'Umar worrying that future generations will deny the stoning penalty and thereby deviate from the right path. Like the second variant, the fourth explains how the charge of adultery may be established, which is either by evidence, pregnancy or confession. However, the fourth variant omits the introductory sentence of the second, namely, 'God the Exalted appointed Muhammad with truth and sent him with the Book'. However, it still invokes the *sunna* of the Prophet to legitimise the stoning penalty, as it states, 'The Messenger of God stoned, and we stoned after him.'

In addition to this, before invoking the Prophet's practice, the fourth variant provides the exact wording of the Stoning Verse, 'The verse reads: "If an old man and woman commit adultery, stone both of them unconditionally."' This wording is found only in the Sa'īd b. al-Musayyab cluster since Ibn 'Abbās's cluster does not contain it. Therefore, it is odd to find the verse's wording included in this variant, which belongs to the cluster from Ibn 'Abbās. One possibility is that Ibn Abī Shayba, who recorded both the Ibn 'Abbās and Sa'īd b. al-Musayyab variants, mixed up the chains.[59] It could also be that this information was included in the text as an explanatory gloss but later became fully integrated into it.

This variant ends with Sufyān b. 'Uyayna being asked, 'did the Messenger of God stone?' He said, 'Yes.' This last element was certainly included by Ibn Abī Shayba, who heard the variant from Sufyān b. 'Uyayna. Perhaps Ibn Abī Shayba heard it in a lecture delivered by Sufyān b. 'Uyayna and the students questioned him if the Prophet stoned too. Nevertheless, this anecdote sparks some curiosity. If the students questioned Sufyān b. 'Uyayna (d. 198/813–14) about the Prophet's execution of the stoning penalty, it might imply that the penalty was not an established norm in Mecca during the third/ninth century.

The fifth variant is found in Ibn Abī Shayba's *Muṣannaf*[60] and comes through Ibn 'Abbās, as a paraphrased version of the longer variants.[61] It does not explicitly mention the Stoning Verse, and instead emphasises that 'Stoning is one of God's punishments; it is not to be circumvented. The Messenger of God implemented the stoning, Abū Bakr stoned and I stoned

58 Ibn Abī Shayba, *Muṣannaf*, vol. 5, p .539.

59 I wish to thank Jens Scheiner for suggesting this probability.

60 Ibn Abī Shayba, *Muṣannaf*, vol. 5, p. 540.

61 Donner considers this a 'compression' and notes that through compression, an account is condensed or made smaller by communicators who were solely interested in the overall essence of the account or a specific aspect or detail of it (Donner, *Narratives of Islamic Origins*, p. 263). Donner also attributes this view to Zaman, 'The Evolution of a Hadith', pp. 146–82; and Lecker, 'The Death of the Prophet Muḥammad's Father'.

as well.' Although there is no mention of the Stoning Verse directly, the phrase 'Stoning is one of God's punishments' suggests that this variant's transmitters reworded it. Furthermore, the variant seems to support the hypothesis that the Prophet and Abū Bakr's names were both mentioned in the variants as those who practised the penalty. Still, in some of the transmissions, at least one of them was mistakenly omitted. This variant includes the names of both the Prophet and Abū Bakr.

The sixth variant is in Bukhārī's *Ṣaḥīḥ* and narrated through Ibn 'Abbās. This text is similar to that of the second (in 'Abd al-Razzāq's *Muṣannaf*) and fourth (in Ibn Abī Shayba's *Muṣannaf*) variants, both of which are reported through Zuhrī. However, a closer resemblance exists between the fourth and sixth variants. For example, like the fourth variant, the sixth begins with 'Umar expressing his concern that later generations would deviate from God's path by denying that a Stoning Verse was revealed in the Qur'an. It stresses the appropriateness of stoning adulterers when their crime is established by unambiguous evidence, pregnancy or confession. Finally, the sixth variant also says that the Prophet implemented the stoning penalty and that the Muslims – an apparent reference to Abū Bakr – followed him in this. Therefore, even though they both appear like paraphrases, these two variants display a great deal of textual affinity and share several elements in common. However, they differ insofar as the fourth includes the wording of the Stoning Verse, while the sixth does not. Until now, no variant reported from Ibn 'Abbās had such information except for the fourth, which suggests that it was either not part of the original report or that Ibn Abī Shayba mixed up the chains.

The seventh variant was recorded in Bukhārī's *Ṣaḥīḥ* and is the lengthiest by far. I have already quoted and briefly examined a segment of it above. It is remarkable that such a politically sensitive account found its way into arguably the most important Sunni hadith collection, especially considering it also implicated individuals such as 'Abd al-Raḥmān b. 'Awf and Sa'īd b. Zayd b. 'Amr b. Nufayl, who were known to be 'Umar's relatives and supporters. It would be interesting to pursue the topic further, but other variants of the tradition do not include the section on Abū Bakr's succession. It is unlikely that Bukhārī fabricated this segment as he was a fervent Sunni, and his collection was highly selective in supporting Sunni orthodoxy.

Could it be that one of the narrators had a hidden Shi'i tendency and seized the opportunity by interpolating this portion of the text? I have already noted the presence of two pro-Shi'i individuals in the chains of these variants – Ibn 'Abbās and Ibn Jud'ān – but Ibn Jud'ān did not narrate this report, and the other variants of Ibn 'Abbās do not include this element. On the face of it, therefore, two possibilities remain. The first is that the narrators – possibly after Zuhrī, who was known for his close relations with the Umayyad court – interpolated the section about the succession to the text. The second is that the section related to the succession was censored in the other variants, and that this variant evaded censorship due to Bukhārī's impeccable reputation. Bukhārī's motivation to include it in the collection may be to support 'Umar's point of view in his own words. A final note on this matter is that one of the variants[62] reported by Mālik from Sa'īd b. al-Musayyab (discussed below) includes an incident at al-Abṭaḥ. It is possible that two separate incidents led 'Umar to address the two issues together upon the completion of his final Hajj. These incidents would include a person questioning 'Umar about the legitimacy of the succession, followed by 'Umar remembering the stoning penalty when he struggled to collect pebbles to stone the Devil as part of the sacred ritual.

The first section of this variant, which exclusively concerns stoning, appears identical to the second variant recorded by 'Abd al-Razzāq. The structure and elements of both are similar, and the two are interdependent and display a textual affinity with one another. Both begin by invoking God's appointment of the Prophet and the revelation of the Book, which they say included the Stoning Verse. They then state that the Prophet stoned and 'we' – an apparent reference to Abū Bakr and 'Umar – stoned after him. The first section then continues with 'Umar's worry that future generations will deny the stoning penalty and deviate from God's path. Finally, both variants state that the punishment is for men and women whose adultery has been established by unambiguous evidence, pregnancy or confession. The only significant difference between the two variants is that the present one includes a sentence missing from the third, namely, 'We recited it, comprehended it and memorised it'. Although there are slight differences in wording, both variants appear very similar. Given that their chain of narrators is similar until Zuhrī ← 'Ubaydullāh b. 'Abdullāh ← Ibn 'Abbās ← 'Umar, the differences in their texts may be explained by Zuhrī paraphrasing them when narrating. I will only include these common elements, which are also available in the previous variants, in any 'original report' attributable to 'Umar.

The eighth variant[63] is in Bukhārī's *Ṣaḥīḥ* and is almost identical to the seventh. It begins with a preamble in which Ibn 'Abbās was teaching the Qur'an to 'Abd al-Raḥmān b. 'Awf in Minā. On this occasion, 'Abd al-Raḥmān told Ibn 'Abbās that a man approached 'Umar and questioned him about the legitimacy of Abū Bakr's succession to the Prophet. He also informed 'Umar that when 'Umar dies, he would pledge allegiance to a specific man, probably referring to 'Alī. 'Umar seems to have been irritated by the man's impertinence and told those around him that he would deliver a speech addressing the issue of the succession that evening. However, as in

62 Mālik, *Muwaṭṭa'*, vol. 5, p. 824.
63 Bukhārī, *Ṣaḥīḥ*, vol. 9, pp. 103–4.

the previous variant, 'Abd al-Raḥmān b. 'Awf advised 'Umar against such a move on the grounds that most of the people there were common folk who might not understand his speech and its context.

Therefore, he advised 'Umar to wait until they had returned to Medina. Up until this point, despite slight differences in wording, the two variants seem similar. This may be explained by the similarity in their chains, which are identical up to Zuhrī and then diverge, with the ninth variant being narrated by Ibrāhīm b. Sa'd ← Ṣāliḥ ← 'Abd al-'Azīz b. 'Abdullāh and the eighth variant by Mūsā b. Ismā'īl ← 'Abd al-Wāḥid ← Ma'mar. The slight differences in wording, then, seem attributable to the narrators of each variant.

However, interestingly, the eighth variant continues with a brief statement that 'Umar made in Medina. 'Ibn 'Abbās said: when we arrived in Medina, 'Umar said: "Indeed, God sent Muhammad with the truth and revealed the Book to him and the Stoning Verse was revealed in it."' No other details were given on the stoning penalty and there is no mention of 'Umar addressing the question of succession. It is unlikely that Bukhārī shortened the variant, as he did not hesitate to include a lengthy and controversial variant of the same tradition. However, it is possible that the shortening of the variant took place with Zuhrī as in the eighth variant 'Umar explicitly claimed that the Qur'an contained a Stoning Verse. Secondly, the introductory section of the variant comprises elements that challenge the official Sunni account of the succession issue, as they call attention to the fact that some Muslims clearly disputed the legitimacy of Abū Bakr's succession. However, unlike the elements concerning stoning, the elements concerning succession may only be dated to Zuhrī's death, 224/742. Therefore, they may or may not have been part of the original report.

The ninth variant is in Ibn Mājah's *Sunan* and appears to be an identical copy of the fourth variant in Ibn Abī Shayba's *Muṣannaf*. Ibn Mājah included the name of Ibn Abī Shayba in the chain of transmission. Therefore, it is almost certain that he obtained it directly from his *Muṣannaf*. In addition, these are the only two variants to provide the actual text of the Stoning Verse, which suggests that, for all practical purposes, they are a single variant: 'if an old man and woman (*al-shaykh wa-l-shaykha*) commit adultery, they are to be stoned unconditionally.'[64] Therefore, it is highly unlikely that the original report included such wording.

Furthermore, in some other variants, such as the eighth variant of the Ibn 'Abbās cluster and the fourteenth of the Sa'īd b. al-Musayyab's cluster, the wording of the Stoning Verse is included as a comment of the author or redactor. So, it is possible that it was inserted in this variant as an explanatory gloss by the author. The prime suspect for this is Ibn Abī Shayba, as

64 Burton notes Nöldeke's observation that the term *shaykha* is alien to Qur'anic vocabulary. See Burton, *The Collection of the Qur'ān*, p. 80.

the variant appears to have been copied directly from his *Muṣannaf*. Ibn Abī Shayba was probably aware of the verse's wording based on some other reports, and he thus continued to include it in the text. This would indicate that the verse's wording was not a part of the original report and that, along the way, the wording of the verse was fully integrated into the variant through editorial redactions without malicious intent, and thus remained in the text thereafter.

The tenth variant is in Tirmidhī's *Sunan* and appears identical to the second variant recorded in ʿAbd al-Razzāq's *Muṣannaf* and the seventh recorded in Bukhārī's *Ṣaḥīḥ*. It contains all the elements included in both variants except for the additional phrase included in Bukhārī's version, 'We recited, comprehended and memorised it'. The second variant also did not include this element.

The eleventh variant is in Abū Dāwūd's *Sunan* and is again similar to the tenth variant. Aside from the elements 'we read and memorised the verse' and 'I swear by God, if it was not for the fact that people would claim that ʿUmar added it to the Book of God Almighty, I would have written it down in the Qur'an', it includes the same elements as found in the other variants reported in the Ibn ʿAbbās cluster. ʿUmar's claim that he memorised and recited the verse is also found in the third, seventh and eleventh variants. As I will discuss, ʿUmar's unrealised wish to insert the Stoning Verse into the Qur'anic codex is also referenced in the fourteenth and sixteenth variants of the Saʿīd b. al-Musayyab cluster. This makes it possible to date this element back to ʿUmar along with the other common elements of the Ibn ʿAbbās and the Saʿīd b. al-Musayyab clusters.

The twelfth variant is in Muslim's *Ṣaḥīḥ* and resembles the one in Abū Dāwūd's *Sunan*, except for the mention of ʿUmar's unrealised wish to insert the Stoning Verse into the codex. The thirteenth variant – also from Muslim's *Ṣaḥīḥ* – has the exact same text as the twelfth variant. Having studied all the textual variants in this group, I can now propose a reconstruction of the original text that is attributable to Ibn ʿAbbās, and possibly even to ʿUmar.

The account of the incidents that took place in Mecca relates to questions being asked about Abū Bakr's succession and Umar's difficulty in collecting pebbles for the ritual stoning of the Devil. These elements could only have been heard by Ibn ʿAbbās from a third party – ʿAbd al-Raḥmān b. ʿAwf – as Ibn ʿAbbās did not directly witness them. These, therefore, cannot be traced back to ʿUmar. Consequently, they cannot be part of the original report. However, the following elements could be considered from the original text:

1. The claim that a Stoning Verse was revealed in the Book of God.
2. The claim that the Prophet and early Muslims stoned adulterers.

3. ʿUmar's concern that later generations might deny the existence of the stoning penalty.
4. ʿUmar's unrealised wish to insert it into the Qur'anic text.

These four elements may be part of the original report and thus dated back to ʿUmar. Finally, the second missing verse cannot be dated back to ʿUmar as it only exists in one variant:

> O, people! Do not claim to be the offspring of other than your fathers, as it is an ingratitude from you to claim to be the offspring of other than your father.

Because of the similarity of the verse that ʿUmar mentioned to a Qur'anic verse that played an important role in Chapter 1 about breastfeeding, it was tempting to think that ʿUmar's memory failed him. Therefore, he misquoted an existing verse of the Qur'an mistakenly. Here is the existing verse of the Qur'an:

> Call them (adopted children) after their [biological] fathers, that is more just in the eyes of God. If you do not know their fathers' [names, call them] your brothers in religion and your clients (*mawālīkum*). (Q. 33:5)

But such a line of thinking is not verifiable, and therefore speculative. One of the narrators might have included this 'missing verse' as an explanatory gloss to strengthen ʿUmar's position on the stoning verse.

The Saʿīd b. al-Musayyab Cluster

Chain of Transmission Analysis

There are three variants in the Saʿīd b. al-Musayyab cluster. The fourteenth variant, reported in Mālik's *Muwaṭṭa'*,[65] reaches Mālik via Yaḥyā b. Saʿīd (d. 143/760–1), who was one of the foremost scholars of Medina. He was a third-generation Muslim and a major source for Mālik.[66] It is important to note that Mālik also heard one of the Ibn ʿAbbās variants, but the chain by which he received Saʿīd b. al-Musayyab's variant is completely different, and thus there is no risk of prior cross-contamination. If there are any distortions or corruptions to the text, it would more likely be the fault of Mālik, because he had heard both variants. The same can also be said for Ibn Abī Shayba and Tirmidhī, and I have already noted above that Ibn Abī

65 Mālik, *Muwaṭṭa'*, vol. 5, p. 824.
66 al-Dhahabī, *Siyar aʿlām al-nubalā'*, vol. 5, pp. 467–81.

Shayba might have mixed up the chains of the above-mentioned variant. This does not necessarily mean that the other collectors did not have access to both clusters, but we only have direct evidence in the case of these three collectors.

Yaḥyā b. Saʿīd heard the variant from Saʿīd b. al-Musayyab (d. 94/712), a prominent scholar and one of the leading jurists among the second generation of Muslims. Saʿīd b. al-Musayyab was married to the daughter of Abū Hurayra, the famous transmitter of prophetic traditions. He notably refused to pledge alliance to 'Abdullāh b. Zubayr and al-Walīd I (d. 96/715) when the latter's father, the Umayyad caliph 'Abd al-Malik (d. 86/705), ordered him to pledge allegiance to his son. As a result, he was tortured daily by the Umayyad officials for some time, yet he did not yield.[67] Perhaps due to his resistance to the Umayyad rulers or his genuine affinity for Zayn al-'Ābidīn (d. 94/712 or 95/713), the fourth Shiʿi Imam, some Shiʿi scholars – including al-Shaykh al-Mufīd (d. 413/1022) – considered him to be a Shiʿi.[68] Saʿīd b. al-Musayyab narrated the variant from 'Umar (d. 23/644). The obvious problem with this chain is that Saʿīd b. al-Musayyab was born towards the end of 'Umar's caliphate. Therefore, it is impossible for him to have directly witnessed the event he related. The events in the report took place towards the end of 'Umar's caliphate, when Saʿīd b. al-Musayyab would most likely have been an infant. Therefore, there must be another person in the chain that links 'Umar to Saʿīd b. al-Musayyab. Given that Saʿīd b. al-Musayyab was married to the daughter of Abū Hurayra, who narrated a group of variant traditions from the Prophet about the stoning penalty, it is possible that Saʿīd b. al-Musayyab heard[69] the tradition from his father-in-law but did not mention his name in the chain since it was a family chain.[70] An important piece of evidence that corroborates this is that Saʿīd b. al-Musayyab heard another prophetic tradition from Abū Hurayra on the stoning penalty, and hence there is some precedence here.[71] There are also other examples of Saʿīd b. al-Musayyab reporting traditions from Abū Hurayra.[72]

Furthermore, at no point does Saʿīd b. al-Musayyab claim to have heard the tradition directly from 'Umar and, given that they are of different

67 Ibn Saʿd, *al-Ṭabaqāt*, vol. 2, pp. 325–9.

68 al-Shaykh al-Mufīd, *al-Ikhtiṣāṣ*, p. 8.

69 Syed Atif Rizwan suggests that Saʿīd b. al-Musayyab's informant could be Ibn 'Abbās instead of 'Umar; however, the linguistic distinction and textual evidence refute his thesis. Rizwan, 'The Resurrection of Stoning as Punishment', pp. 290–301.

70 While Schacht considers family *isnād*s a priori untrustworthy, Motzki considers them 'especially reliable because of the longer and more intimate contact that existed between the transmitters and his informant'; Motzki et al., *Analysing Muslim Traditions*, pp. 22–3.

71 al-Ṣanʿānī, *Muṣannaf*, vol. 7, pp. 316–18.

72 Bukhārī, *Ṣaḥīḥ*, vol. 6, p. 2688; Muslim, *Ṣaḥīḥ*, vol. 4, p. 2148; Ibn Mājah, *Sunan*, vol. 1, p. 69.

generations, it is evident that he did not directly hear it from him. It is unlikely that he forged this variant because of the generational gap, as it would have been easy to detect such a forgery. However, without any additional evidence, this theory remains an inference. One piece of evidence for such a connection may be the textual affinity and interdependence between the Saʿīd b. al-Musayyab and Ibn ʿAbbās variants. The similarly paraphrased elements found in the texts that come down through these two transmission lines may suggest that they both had a common source. Until then, I can preliminarily date the chain of transmission of this variant to Saʿīd b. al-Musayyab's date of death, which was 94/712.

The fifteenth variant is found in the *Muṣannaf* of Ibn Abī Shayba,[73] who received the variant from Yazīd b. Hārūn (d. 206/821) – a well-regarded hadith collector, who was originally from Bukhara but active in Iraq.[74] Yazīd b. Hārūn is one of Ibn Abī Shayba's most recurrently cited informants, as he includes eighty-seven traditions from him in the *Muṣannaf*. Consequently, it is possible that Ibn Abī Shayba received the variant from him. Yazīd b. Hārūn received the variant from Dāwūd b. Abī Hind (d. 139–40/757–8), a reputable scholar who first lived in Transoxiana and then Basra. He was a client of the Banū Qushayr and was a student of Saʿīd b. al-Musayyab, and also reported traditions from him.[75] There seems to be an age gap between Yazīd b. Hārūn and Dāwūd b. Abī Hind, but sixty-six years is still within reason as Yazīd b. Hārūn could have heard the variant while he was very young. Dāwūd b. Abī Hind received the variant from Saʿīd b. al-Musayyab and, as with the previous variant, narrated it from ʿUmar.

The sixteenth variant is in Tirmidhī's *Sunan*.[76] Tirmidhī, who was active in Transoxiana, Iraq and the Hijaz, received it from Aḥmad b. Manīʿ (d. 244/859), who lived first in the region of Khorasan before moving to Baghdad.[77] Aḥmad b. Manīʿ received it from Isḥāq b. Yūsuf al-Azraq (d. 195/811), a reputable scholar from Wasit.[78] Isḥāq b. Yūsuf heard it from Dāwūd b. Abī Hind, who, as noted earlier, lived in Transoxiana before moving to Basra. There appears to be an age gap between Isḥāq b. Yūsuf and Dāwūd b. Abī Hind. However, sources state that Isḥāq b. Yūsuf was born in 117/735–6, which means that Isḥāq b. Yūsuf could have heard the variant from Dāwūd b. Abī Hind while a young student. Dāwūd b. Abī

73 Ibn Abī Shayba, *Muṣannaf*, vol. 5, p. 539.

74 al-Dhahabī, *Siyar aʿlām al-nubalāʾ*, vol. 9, pp. 358–71; al-Baghdādī, *Tārīkh Baghdād*, vol. 10, pp. 493–505; al-Dhahabī, *Tadhkirat al-ḥuffāẓ*, vol. 1, pp. 317–20.

75 Bukhārī, *al-Tārīkh al-kabīr*, vol. 2, pp. 231–2; al-Dhahabī, *Siyar aʿlām al-nubalāʾ*, vol. 6, pp. 376–8.

76 Tirmidhī, *Sunan*, vol. 2, p. 90.

77 al-Dhahabī, *Siyar aʿlām al-nubalāʾ*, vol. 11, pp. 483–4.

78 Ibn Saʿd, *al-Ṭabaqāt*, vol. 9, p. 317; al-Dhahabī, *Tadhkirat al-ḥuffāẓ*, vol. 1, p. 320; al-ʿAsqalānī, *Tahdhīb al-tahdhīb*, vol. 1, pp. 340–1.

Hind, a prominent scholar of hadith, received the variant from Saʿīd b. al-Musayyab, who narrated it from ʿUmar. As I discussed in regard to the second variant, it is impossible for Saʿīd b. al-Musayyab to have heard it directly from ʿUmar. Thus, the chain of transmission of this cluster seems to be interrupted, but I will suspend drawing a definitive conclusion until I have studied the textual variants. Finally, unlike the widespread Ibn ʿAbbās clusters, it is evident that the Saʿīd b. al-Musayyab cluster was mostly confined to Basra and Kufa.

Textual Analysis

Mālik's variant from the Saʿīd b. al-Musayyab cluster – and the fourteenth overall – offers a less detailed account and provides a different context. The second variant begins with ʿUmar's performance of his last Hajj in 23/644 and probably took place on the ninth day of Dhū al-Ḥijja, when the pilgrims often collect pebbles to perform the stoning of the Devil (*ramī al-jamarāt*) on the tenth, eleventh, twelfth and thirteenth[79] of Dhū al-Ḥijja in Minā. Pilgrims throw seven stones for three days; each day at one of the three pillars situated in Minā. They may extend the ritual for one extra day. This ritual signifies Abraham's defiance of the Devil's temptations. In the variant, it appears that ʿUmar collected pebbles in al-Abṭaḥ[80] to perform the ritual. However, he struggles with this due to either his old age, ill health or both. Upon collecting the pebbles, he drops down on his knees and prays to God about his ill health and asks not to be left to go on like this for too long, meaning he asks God to hasten his death.

This introductory section of the tradition is curious; the narrator seems to be drawing a connection between the ritual stoning of the Devil on Hajj and the stoning penalty. The mention of ʿUmar's collection of the pebbles for stoning the Devil and his subsequent prayer seems to be setting the scene for ʿUmar's sermon on the Stoning Verse in the Qur'an. There is a subtle connection between ʿUmar's prayer and his sermon, in which he also raises concerns about the Stoning Verse being forgotten:

> Beware! Lest you destroy the Stoning Verse, and some may say 'we cannot find it in the Book of God'. The Messenger of God stoned and we did too. By He in whose hand is my soul, if I was not afraid that people might say "Umar b. al-Khaṭṭāb added it to the Book of God, the Exalted', I would have written it [in the Qur'an] – 'the old man and old woman stone them both unconditionally' – for we have definitely recited it.[81]

79 The thirteenth of Dhū al-Ḥijja is only for those who do not leave Minā on the twelfth.

80 A place around 6 km outside of Mecca, en route to the city Medina.

81 Mālik, *Muwaṭṭa'*, vol. 5, p. 824.

'Umar is adamant that a Stoning Verse was revealed, and he feels religiously bound to remind people of its existence.

Abrogation of the Qur'anic Verses

'Umar's statement raises two questions. Firstly, if the verse was not included in the Qur'anic codex at the time, why was 'Umar so adamant about its existence as well as its implementation? And secondly, why was his audience reluctant to implement it? Given that 'Umar was the caliph at the time, he could have implemented it forcefully.

As to the first question, traditional Sunni scholarship raised the idea that a verse's wording can be abrogated, while its meaning remains intact, such that its implementation continues to be in force. John Burton scrutinises this notion in detail and concludes that it was introduced to give legitimacy to the view of Muslim legal schools.[82] In support of his theory on the origins of abrogation, Burton meticulously examines the intense rivalry among Muslim legal schools.[83] His assertion about the prevalence of rivalry between Muslim legal schools emphasised the creation of fabricated traditions to reinforce each school's perspective. This process, Burton argued, led to the inclusion of legal schools' opinions alongside the Qur'an and Sunna as sources of Islamic law.[84] To establish the credibility of these traditions and discredit rival schools, the proponents introduced the practice of *isnād* criticism. This involved categorising traditions based on the historical reliability of the narrators.[85]

In cases where legal schools' verdicts contradicted Qur'anic verses, the proponents devised the concept of the occasions of revelation (*asbāb al-nuzūl*) to contextualise the verses and align them with their perspectives.[86] However, this technique alone was insufficient to manipulate the Qur'an, which posed a significant challenge to the legal schools' authority. Thus, the method of abrogating and abrogated (*al-nāsikh wa-l-mansūkh*) emerged as a convenient tool to nullify certain verses conflicting with their opinions and legitimise their positions in the Qur'an.

Burton emphasised the critical role of the concepts of abrogating and abrogated in his thesis, closely intertwined with the issue of the compilation of the Qur'an. He raised pertinent questions regarding the significance of the principles of abrogation in shaping the Muslim accounts of the Qur'an's history and the circumstances surrounding its initial

82 Burton, *The Collection of the Qur'ān*, pp. 225–39.

83 I provided a more detailed analysis of Burton's views in *In Search of Ali Ibn Abi Talib's Codex*, pp. 30–2.

84 Kara, *In Search of Ali Ibn Abi Talib's Codex*, p. 13

85 Kara, *In Search of Ali Ibn Abi Talib's Codex*, pp. 14–15.

86 Kara, *In Search of Ali Ibn Abi Talib's Codex*, p. 15.

compilation.[87] He supported this argument by examining various hadiths, demonstrating how different legal rulings stemmed from the diverse interpretations of Qur'anic verses.[88]

Burton's final conclusion emphasised a consensus among legal schools that the Qur'an was 'incomplete'. The tools employed, particularly the concept of abrogation, implicitly suggested the 'incompleteness' of the Qur'an. As abrogation was a common practice during the Prophet's lifetime, with some verses omitted and replaced by others, the Qur'an could not have been completed during that time, therefore remaining open to changes. While not all of Burton's hypotheses are convincing, particularly his overarching conclusions about Muslim scholars' mass fabrication of hadith, his meticulous examination of abrogation and the related literature remains compelling. Burton offers sound arguments about the untenability of this notion. However, the second part of the question, why 'Umar was eager to remind his audience of the verse's existence, needs further discussion.

There are at least two possible explanations for 'Umar's insistence. He may have made a connection between the stoning of the Devil (*ramī al-jamarāt*) in Hajj and the stoning penalty (*rajm*), as they both involve collecting stones. It seems reasonable that while collecting stones to stone the Devil, 'Umar recalled the collecting of stones to carry out the stoning penalty. If this is the case, it indicates that the penalty had not been practised for a long time and, when 'Umar's memory was triggered by the experience of collecting stones, he felt the urge to remind others. It is possible that stoning was only implemented on a couple of occasions during the Prophet's life and that the practice was effectively abandoned afterwards. There is an important point to the story, however, that 'Umar struggles to collect the stones for the ritual due to his old age and/or ill health. If he is in such bad shape, so far as to pray to God to hasten his death, he might also be suffering age-related issues affecting his memory in the months before his death. The second possibility is that the tradition is a forgery, and the forger devised a dramatic scene for its opening.

Following the incident in al-Abṭaḥ, the variant continues with 'Umar's sermon at the Prophet's Mosque in Medina. There is no mention of the mosque, and so the variant simply states that 'Umar entered Medina. However, the language of the variant is in the style of a sermon, as if 'Umar is addressing an audience. Be that as it may, it appears that this variant differs from the account of Ibn 'Abbās. The textual elements show that Ibn 'Abbās's text is more detailed and complete, but Sa'īd b. al-Musayyab's

87 Kara, *In Search of Ali Ibn Abi Talib's Codex*, p. 17.

88 Kara, *In Search of Ali Ibn Abi Talib's Codex*, p. 34.

context is different from Ibn ʿAbbās's context, in that it is brief and omits some important details:

> When ʿUmar b. al-Khaṭṭāb came out of Minā, he paused at al-Abṭaḥ. He gathered a pile of gravel. He then threw his cloak over the gravel. But he dropped down [on his knees]. He then raised his hands to the sky and said: 'O God! I have grown old and my strength has weakened. My pasture is scattered. Take me to You without stinting anything and without exceeding.' ʿUmar then entered into Medina and addressed the people, he said: . . .[89]

Nevertheless, they both share elements in common, which points to a common source – namely, ʿUmar. Ibn ʿAbbās's account provides a different context to ʿUmar's sermon because he was only informed about the event in Minā and did not know about what happened in al-Abṭaḥ. But, as the text of this variant states, ʿUmar went to al-Abṭaḥ – possibly after the episode in Minā – and then the event with the pebbles took place. However, this was only witnessed by or reported to Saʿīd b. al-Musayyab's informant, Abū Hurayra. It is possible that Abū Hurayra was unaware of the incident in Minā too. Given the major differences between the contexts of the variants, it is highly unlikely that Saʿīd b. al-Musayyab heard it from Ibn ʿAbbās. But could Saʿīd b. al-Musayyab have forged his variant and attributed it to ʿUmar? One of the most common ways of forging reports is by creating variants from a master copy and forging a line of transmission. However, the textual analysis precludes this possibility as, if Saʿīd b. al-Musayyab had forged the report, he would have certainly included more identical elements and the same context in his variant, unless he wanted to avoid controversy by replacing the politically charged encounter in Minā with the less controversial experience in al-Abṭaḥ.

However, this is also highly unlikely given that Saʿīd b. al-Musayyab was considered to be pro-ʿAlī. Conversely, the variants provide such different contexts for ʿUmar's sermon that they may be viewed as two separate reports. Therefore, the most likely explanation is that Saʿīd b. al-Musayyab heard about the same event from a different informant,[90] in this case a close family member who could have been ignored or dropped in the chain, namely, his father-in-law, Abū Hurayra. The famous legal scholar Shāfiʿī also reached the same conclusion that the actual source of Saʿīd b. al-Musayyab was Abū Hurayra.[91]

89 Mālik, *Muwaṭṭa'*, vol. 5, p. 824.

90 Motzki makes an excellent case for such a possibility in Motzki, 'The Prophet and the Cat', pp. 18–83.

91 Brown, *Hadith*, p. 92.

Furthermore, the note of Mālik at the end of the text, which reads ‘Mālik said: Yaḥyā b. Saʿīd heard Saʿīd b. al-Musayyab say: “Dhū al-Ḥijja had not passed before ‘Umar was murdered, may God have mercy on him”’, indicates that the text refers to the same sermon which took place just after ‘Umar’s last pilgrimage. In the sermon, he warned people about forgetting the Stoning Verse by neglecting to implement its ordinance and reminded people that the Prophet stoned adulterers and that ‘we’ (perhaps referring to Abū Bakr and himself) stoned the adulterers: ‘Be careful lest you destroy the Stoning Verse, and some may say “we cannot find it in the Book of God.” The Messenger of God stoned and so did we.’[92] This may mean that they stoned during the lifetime of the Prophet. He then made the crucial statement in the variant, that ‘If I was not afraid that people would say “‘Umar b. al-Khaṭṭāb added it to the Book of God, the Exalted,” I would have written it [in the Qur’an] – that is, the old man and old woman, stone them both unconditionally – we have definitely recited it.’

First of all, ‘Umar’s expression of frustration is evidence that there was a written codex of the Qur’an at the time of the caliphate of ‘Umar, which Muslims referred to. The existence of such an authoritative codex confirms the early Muslim accounts that the collection of the Qur’an took place immediately after the death of the Prophet. Furthermore, it shows that they referred to it for guidance, but that this codex did not include the Stoning Verse. Even though ‘Umar was caliph at the time and had a formidable reputation, he could not insert the supposedly missing verse into the Qur’anic codex. This specific element is present in both the Ibn ‘Abbās and Saʿīd b. al-Musayyab clusters. Therefore, the textual evidence supports my hypothesis that Saʿīd b. al-Musayyab heard the report from Abū Hurayra. This enables us to date it back to the year 23/644.

Evidence from Hadith for Closure of the Qur’anic Canon during or before ‘Umar’s Reign

Furthermore, the overall gist of the variants is that ‘Umar claimed to know that a verse of stoning exists, but he was not able to insert it into the Qur’anic codex. This implies that there was a strong consensus among the early Muslim community against the existence of the Stoning Verse in the Qur’an and perhaps even against its legitimacy as the practice of the Prophet. Therefore, they were reluctant to implement the stoning penalty, which is why ‘Umar decided to re-emphasise its significance.

The section in question also provides a possible wording for this Stoning Verse: ‘the old man and old woman, stone them both unconditionally’ (*al-shaykh wa-l-shaykha fa-arjumūhumā al-battata*). The wording of

92 Mālik, *Muwaṭṭa’*, vol. 5, p. 824.

the first variant is different from the second: 'For those men and women who commit adultery (*'alā man zanā min al-rijāli wa-l-nisā'i*) if they are chastised.' The latter correlates with the difference in the chains of transmission. By contrast, the first variant in the Ibn 'Abbās cluster refers to the offender as '*man zanā min al-rijāli wa-al-nisā'i*', while the thirteenth variant in the Sa'īd b. al-Musayyab cluster refers to the offender as '*al-shaykh wa-l-shaykha*', which becomes the term for married people who commit adultery. It is likely that the term became part of legal parlance during the second/eighth century when Mālik was active, as Mālik adds a comment to the first variant to say that 'Yaḥyā said: I heard Mālik saying "the meaning of old man and old woman (*al-shaykh wa-al-shaykha*) is married man and married woman, stone them both unconditionally."'[93]

The last sections of both variants confirm the difference between the texts and thus correlate with the divergent chains of the two variant clusters. The variants must have come from two different lines of transmission, thus they are paraphrased. Even the alleged Stoning Verse was paraphrased, and these paraphrases do not match what we know about the development of the Qur'an's canon. As mentioned earlier, Sadeghi and Goudarzi, in their study of the Ṣan'ā' palimpsests, concluded that there exist minor distinctions among the Companion codices and the 'Uthmānic codex. They noted that, 'With only a few exceptions, the differences among the codices are at the level of morphemes, words, and phrases – not at the level of sentences or verses.'[94] A comprehensive follow-up study of the Ṣan'ā' palimpsests by Éléonore Cellard affirmed Sadeghi and Goudarzi's findings.[95] Furthermore, Marijn van Putten, in his significant study, demonstrated that there was even a unity in the spelling of the verses of the Qur'an in various early manuscripts.[96]

However, there are two different variants of this allegedly missing verse. This suggests that it was not a verse of the Qur'an after all but rather a saying of the Prophet and that 'Umar's memory failed him due to old age or health issues. For this very reason, it was not included in the Qur'anic codex and 'Umar was not able to accurately remember it.

The text of the fifteenth variant[97] is in Ibn Abī Shayba's *Muṣannaf* and contains a short text which reads that 'on the authority of 'Umar, who said:

93 Mālik, *Muwaṭṭa'*, vol. 5, p. 824.

94 Sadeghi and Goudarzi, 'Ṣan'ā' 1 and the Origins of the Qur'ān', p. 8. See also Sadeghi and Bergmann, 'The Codex of a Companion of the Prophet and the Qur'ān of the Prophet', p. 347.

95 Cellard, 'The Ṣan'ā' Palimpsest', pp. 27–8.

96 van Putten, '"The Grace of God" as Evidence for a Written Uthmanic Archetype', pp. 271–88.

97 Ibn Abī Shayba, *Muṣannaf*, vol. 5, p. 539.

"The Messenger of God stoned, Abū Bakr stoned and I stoned myself."' The text is short but noteworthy, as discussed above. While some of the variants reported through Zuhrī focus on the *sunna* of the Prophet, the third variant in the Ibn ʿAbbās cluster shifts the question of legitimacy to Abū Bakr's custom of stoning adulterers. However, in the fifteenth variant, all three names are mentioned to have implemented the penalty: Muhammad, Abū Bakr and ʿUmar. Aside from the possibility that there have been rival interpretations in the Islamic tradition by different scholars which influenced the wording of the texts, it is also possible that there was a genuine error of transmission that led to different names being given to those who implemented the stoning penalty. As transmission took place orally, it would not be overly conspicuous to confuse names or take some names for granted, such as the Prophet's, and assume that listeners would understand what the speaker meant. It is possible that when ʿUmar delivered the sermon, he meant that the Prophet and Muslims (i.e. Abū Bakr and himself) implemented the penalty at the time of the Prophet, but the transmitters were either negligent or forgetful in conveying this. It is tempting to consider it to be a textual contradiction, but it is more plausible to justify such problematic elements as genuine mistakes.[98]

The sixteenth variant is recorded in Tirmidhī's *Sunan*. Like the fifteenth, it includes the name of Abū Bakr along with the Prophet and the pronoun 'I' (referring to ʿUmar) for those who practised the stoning penalty. Furthermore, it includes ʿUmar's expression of concern that future generations would deny the existence of the stoning penalty because of its omission from the Qur'an. This variant also includes the element 'Were it not for the fact that I dislike adding it [the Stoning Verse] to the Book of God, I would have written it in the *muṣḥaf* (the codex)'.[99] Understandably, ʿUmar's concern might have led him to contemplate the effects of such a drastic undertaking. Despite that, by this time the Qur'anic codex had already been fixed, so he was probably concerned about the reaction of the early Muslims, who would oppose such a move and perhaps even question the legitimacy of Umar's caliphate.

Summary and Conclusion

Two separate transmission lines come down from ʿUmar via Ibn ʿAbbās and Saʿīd b. al-Musayyab. Each of them disseminates the tradition independently. Although Saʿīd b. al-Musayyab's variants are sound transmissions, there is a gap between Saʿīd b. al-Musayyab and ʿUmar. Saʿīd b. al-Musayyab was an infant during the reign of ʿUmar, so it is impossible that he heard

98 See Motzki et al., *Analysing Muslim Traditions*, pp. 10, 32, 143, 357, 367 and *passim*.

99 Tirmidhī, *Sunan*, vol. 2, p. 90.

'Umar's sermon directly. However, the textual analysis provides further evidence that the reports of Ibn 'Abbās and Sa'īd b. al-Musayyab are interdependent. The texts of these variants included common elements, such as 'Umar's firm conviction that the Stoning Verse was revealed in the Book of God; that the early Muslims recited and memorised it; that the Prophet, Abū Bakr and 'Umar all stoned adulterers (perhaps at the time of the Prophet); 'Umar's expression of concern that later generations would forget about the penalty along with his reflection that he could not insert the Stoning Verse into the already codified Qur'an; and that the crime of adultery can only be established through unambiguous evidence, pregnancy and confession. These linguistically different common elements allow us to date the variants to the common source, who is 'Umar, a few weeks or months prior to his death on the 31 Dhū al-Ḥijja 23 /1 October 644.

This textual information further suggests that 'Umar's physical condition in the last year of the caliphate was deteriorating and, as a result, he may have confused a prophetic tradition for a Qur'anic verse. Furthermore, the wording of the Stoning Verse clearly marks it as not being originally part of the report. It is probably a later interpolation into the text in the form of an explanatory gloss. In light of this, I may conclude that there was no missing Stoning Verse in the Qur'an that was preached by the Prophet and, hence, the tradition cannot be used as an argument for the textual corruption of the Qur'an.

More importantly, based on the textual evidence, the dating of the compiled codex of the Qur'an can be traced to 'Umar's date of death, which is 23/644, with certainty. However, because 'Umar could not interfere with the Qur'anic codex, it is possible to move the date event earlier, namely, to the reign of Abū Bakr (d. 13/634). The overall content of the texts suggests that 'Umar's inability to interfere with the Qur'anic codex is the result of an early process of codification of the codex – one that predated his reign. Hence, this codification must have taken place during his predecessor's time. This finding brings the dating of the Qur'anic codex nearer to the death of the Prophet. This date corresponds with traditional Muslim accounts of the textual history of the Qur'an that state that it was first collated during the reign of Abū Bakr.

PART III

Distortion Narratives in Shi‘i Hadith

CHAPTER 5

Transition of the Distortion Narrative into Shiʿi Reports

As discussed in the previous chapters, the stoning penalty is one of most debated topics in Sunni jurisprudence, but it received lesser attention in Shiʿi jurisprudence. A limited number of reports attributed to the Shiʿi Imams ostensibly warranted implementing the stoning penalty on adulterers. However, because of political and theological issues, Shiʿis were not in a position to deliberate the implementation of the penalty during the classical period. Therefore, it was a matter of theoretical discussion for them.

For political reasons, aside from ʿAlī's turbulent caliphate between 35/656 and 40/661, Twelver Shiʿis did not have an official state until the Safavid dynasty (906/1501–1148/1736). Some reports in Sunni and Shiʿi sources show that ʿAlī implemented the stoning penalty during his caliphate, but these reports are scarce.[1] I have located nine reports in the earliest Sunni hadith collections[2] that state ʿAlī stoned an adulteress on a Friday. There may be, nonetheless, merit in studying these reports to attain the whole picture about the stoning penalty. Still, since these reports are not directly related to the distortion, I have not examined them in this book.

Be that as it may, Shiʿi reports are remarkably similar to relevant Sunni reports on the distortion, despite the differences in their chains of transmission. The Shiʿi reports on the distortion of the Qur'an are attributed to two Shiʿi Imams, Muḥammad al-Bāqir and Jaʿfar al-Ṣādiq. However, there is only one report[3] attributed to the fifth Imam, Abū Jaʿfar Muḥammad al-Bāqir[4] (d. 114/733). I have studied some other reports attributed to

1 Eltantawi mentions some Shiʿi reports from al-Ṭuṣī's works. She also notes the similarity of these reports to the relevant Sunni reports but opts out of examining the chains of these traditions. Eltantawi, 'Ṭūsī Did Not "Opt Out"', pp. 312–32.

2 For example, Ibn Abī Shayba, *Muṣannaf*, vol. 5, p. 541; al-Ṣanʿānī, *Muṣannaf*, vol. 7, p. 326.

3 al-Sayyārī, *Revelation and Falsification*, p. 110.

4 Pierce, *Twelve Infallible Men*, pp. 96–105.

al-Bāqir, which are ostensibly related to the distortion of the Qur'an. The study revealed that the traditions attributed to al-Bāqir on the distortion of the Qur'an are deliberately tampered with by ʿAmr b. Abī al-Miqdām, an 'extremist' Shiʿi, who used it for his anti-Sunni sectarian campaign.[5] However, this single report differs from these traditions, and the report is in fact attributed to the sixth Imam, Jaʿfar al-Ṣādiq (d. 148/765). But, because it is a single report, it is impossible to study here.

The reports attributed to Jaʿfar al-Ṣādiq can be found in the following Twelver and Ismaili sources: Sulaym b. Qays al-Hilālī's (d. mid-second/eighth century) *Kitāb*, ʿAlī b. Ibrāhīm al-Qummī's (d. 307/980) *Tafsīr*, Aḥmad b. Muḥammad al-Sayyārī's (d. mid-third/ninth century) *Kitāb al-qirāʾāt*, Muḥammad b. Yaʿqūb al-Kulaynī (d. 329/941) *al-Kāfī*, al-Shaykh al-Ṣadūq's (d. 381/991) *Kitāb man lā yaḥḍuruhu al-faqīh* and *ʿIlal al-sharāʾiʿ*, al-Shaykh al-Ṭūsī's (d. 460/1067) *Tahdhīb al-aḥkām* and finally the Ismaili scholar al-Qāḍī al-Nuʿmān's (d. 363/973) *Daʿāʾim al-islām*.

According to one of the variants, Jaʿfar al-Ṣādiq, who is referred to as Abū ʿAbdullāh, informs one of his trusted companions, Abū Yaʿqūb [Isḥāq b. Yazīd b. Ismāʿīl al-Ṭāʾī] (d. mid-second century), about the omission of certain verses from Sūrat al-Aḥzāb, indicating an apparent distortion of the Qur'an. Upon questioning the authenticity of al-Aḥzāb, which consists of 73 verses in the standard Qur'an, it states that the *sūra* was longer than Sūrat al-Baqara, which consists of 286 verses. Thus, it implies that a considerable chunk of the *sūra* has gone missing:

> Ibn Sayf, on the authority of his brother, on the authority of his father, on the authority of ʿĪsā b. Aʿyan, on the authority of Abū Yaʿqūb and al-Barqī, on the authority of ʿUthmān b. ʿĪsā, on the authority of Abū Yaʿqūb, who said: 'Abū ʿAbdullāh (Imam Jaʿfar al-Ṣādiq) said: "Did you read the Qur'an?" I replied: "I have read only whatever we have of it." He said, "But I ask you, as for what you have; how many [verses] do you find in the *sūra* that is known as al-Aḥzāb?" I said: "[More than] seventy verses." He said: "Yet it was longer than the *sūra* which was called al-Baqara before. There was the Stoning Verse: 'the old man and woman, if they commit adultery, stone both of them unconditionally for they had satisfied their lust, as a punishment from God Almighty.'"'[6]

Furthermore, it also relates the wording of one of the missing verses in the *sūra*, namely, the so-called Stoning Verse: 'the old man and woman, if they commit adultery, stone both of them unconditionally for, they had satisfied

5 Kara, 'The Collection of the Qurʾān in the Early Shīʿite Discourse', pp. 375–406.
6 al-Sayyārī, *Revelation and Falsification*, p. 110.

their lust, as a punishment from God Almighty.' This text is remarkably similar to the traditions attributed to 'Umar, which were studied in Chapter 4.

The texts of these reports are strikingly similar to two reports recorded in 'Abd al-Razzāq's *Muṣannaf* and Bukhārī's *Ṣaḥīh*. The report mentioned in 'Abd al-Razzāq's *Muṣannaf*[7] is attributed to Ubayy b. Ka'b, one of the scribes of the Prophet who held his own copy of the Qur'an. The second report,[8] recorded in Bukhārī's *Ṣaḥīh*,[9] is attributed to Zayd b. Thābit, who was also a scribe of the Prophet and oversaw the collection of the Qur'an on two occasions. Out of these two similar reports,[10] the text of the report attributed to Ubayy b. Ka'b is almost identical to the report recorded in al-Sayyārī's *Kitāb al-qirā'āt*:

> 'Abd al-Razzāq, on the authority of al-Thawrī, on the authority of 'Āṣim b. Abī al-Najūd, on the authority of Zirri b. Ḥubaysh, who said, Ubayy b. Ka'b told me: 'How many [verses] do you read in Sūrat al-Aḥzāb?' He said, I said: 'Either seventy-three or seventy-four.' He said: 'No, it was around Sūrat al-Baqara or longer than it. And there was the Stoning Verse in it.' He said, I said: 'Abū al-Mundhir, what is the Stoning Verse?' 'If the old man and woman commit adultery, stone them unconditionally as a punishment from God, surely God is Mighty and Wise.' Al-Thawrī said: 'We heard from some of the Companions of the Prophet who would read the Qur'an that the Qur'an was afflicted on the day of [war with] Musaylama, and some verses were lost from the Qur'an.'[11]

It is very suspicious that similar texts are attributed to Sunni and Shi'i authorities with different chains. This applies especially so to the inclusion of the so-called missing Stoning Verse that I studied in Chapter 4, which gives the impression that the Shi'i variants may have been plagiarised

7 al-Ṣan'ānī, *Muṣannaf*, vol. 7, pp. 329–30.

8 'Narrated to us by Abū al-Yamān, reported to us by Shu'ayb, on the authority of Zuhrī, also, narrated to us by Ismā'īl who said, narrated to me by my brother, on the authority of Sulaymān, who saw it, on the authority of Muḥammad b. Abī 'Atīq, on the authority of Zuhrī, on the authority of Khārija b. Zayd; Zayd b. Thābit said: "When we collated the codex from loose pages, I missed a verse from *Sūra al-Aḥzāb* which I would hear the Messenger of God reading it. I could not find the verse with anyone except for with Khuzayma b. Thābit al-Anṣārī whose witness was considered by the Messenger of God equal to two men: 'Among the believers are men who are truthful to their covenant with God.'" Bukhārī, *Ṣaḥīḥ*, vol. 3, p. 1033.

9 Bukhārī, *Ṣaḥīḥ*, vol. 3, p. 1033.

10 Kohlberg and Amir-Moezzi discuss some other similar reports, but these two reports are not mentioned. Further, astonishingly, they take the reports on the distortion of *al-Aḥzāb* granted without analysing them. See al-Sayyārī, *Revelation and Falsification*, pp. 198–9.

11 al-Ṣan'ānī, *Muṣannaf*, vol. 7, pp. 329–30.

copies of Sunni reports. Although reliable historical research should start from 'zero point' without any assumptions, I kept this principle in mind in Chapters 3–4.

However, my findings up to this point increased my suspicion of forgery. The main reason for my suspicion is that I have already dated 'Umar's reports to slightly before his date of death, in the year 24/644. Therefore, I established that the earliest reports on the missing Stoning Verse originated from him. Taking this finding for granted, it is feasible to reach the assumption that some Shi'i hadith collectors were aware of these reports and for obvious theological reasons, decided to tamper with these reports by forging an entire new chain of narration to attribute these reports to the Shi'i Imams. The similarity between the texts gives further credit to this hypothesis. It should not be surprising that Shi'is were aware of these reports being attributed to 'Umar since they contain crucial pieces of information regarding the succession issue. The reports indirectly acknowledge the tension during the appointment of Abū Bakr as the Prophet's successor and call it a *falta* or 'rushed decision' from the mouth of 'Umar himself. This must have been a valuable propaganda tool for early Shi'is who were familiar with this report.[12] Therefore, it might have inspired some sectarian Shi'is to use other sections of these reports to their advantage by developing and instigating the idea of the distortion of the Qur'an.

The Qur'anic Codex as Part of the Sectarian Discourse

Within a sectarian context, it could be well argued that some Shi'is were troubled by the lack of apparent proof from the Qur'an in support of the succession and authority of the Imams, and they thus felt obliged to take matters into their own hands. If Sunnis could interfere with the 'divine will' in the appointment of 'Alī as the successor of the Prophet, they could also tamper with the supporting Qur'anic evidence on the succession and merits of 'Alī and his offspring. To achieve their objective, they started by tampering with those Sunni reports which were already in circulation, both textually and in relation to their chains of transmission. This was done in order to cast doubt on the textual integrity of the Qur'an. Andreas Görke confirms the occurrence of this kind of corruption in Sunni reports:

> The third kind of change would be the deliberate change of the meaning – or the *isnād* – to make it sound better for the audience,

12 Even Madelung, who has no stake in the dispute, could not resist the temptation to acknowledge such a controversial report in the most revered canonical Sunni hadith collection; therefore he begins his opening arguments with this report, taking its veracity for granted. Madelung, *The Succession to Muhammad*, pp. 28–31.

make it fit a special situation, etc. Finally, a tradition may be completely reworked to change the meaning and give the opposite sense, counter *aḥādīth* can be invented, duplicate traditions can be produced with completely new *asānīd*. All of these changes can be shown to have happened in Muslim traditions, but not all traditions underwent the same changes.[13]

I have also illustrated in my previous monograph[14] an example of where such corruption occurred in Shi'i reports. I found that 'Amr b. Abī al-Miqdām, through reworking a variant ascribed to the fifth Imam, Abū Ja'far Muḥammad al-Bāqir, manipulated the meaning of the report to attribute the collection of the Qur'anic codex to the Imams. There seems to have been a concerted effort to use the Qur'anic codex as part of the sectarian discourse during the early period of Islam. The ultimate authority of the Qur'an among Muslims may explain this phenomenon and, therefore, Muslims desired to justify their positions from within the Qur'an itself. This desire went so far as to inspire the forging of narrations to claim that the Qur'an had been distorted, in order to justify their particular views.

In a sense, this campaign is similar to commentaries of the Qur'an. Certain theological schools have cherry-picked and interpreted verses of the Qur'an to legitimise their own creedal positions.[15] Various schools of thought interpreted the Qur'anic verses to justify their own theological, legal and political positions, and some of the fabricated traditions supplemented these views. This was because for an idea to gain legitimacy, it needed to be ascribed to the Qur'an. The religious authority of the Qur'an

13 Görke, 'Eschatology, History, and the Common Link', p. 182.

14 Kara, *In Search of Ali Ibn Abi Talib's Codex.*

15 Burton also demonstrated this attitude in the works of Muslim legal schools. He, despite acknowledging the authenticity of the Qur'an as the work of Muhammad, went on to claim that the entire hadith corpus on the collection of the Qur'an by the Companions – and the Muslim hadith corpus in general – was a product of 'projecting-back' efforts. Thus, the hadiths were all fabricated. However, Burton was mistaken to generalise his views without overwhelming proof. He had some circumstantial evidence which backed up his theory to some extent. But his argument that labelled major Sunni hadith collectors as liars or forgers would not hold before an impartial court. Because he issued his verdict without proof beyond a reasonable doubt, he was merely pointing out inconsistencies in the relevant Sunni hadith literature. Such inconsistencies are a natural process of oral transmission that he failed to consider. In a sense, historical enquiries are similar to court procedures in their objective to find 'what really happened' in the past. They should seek the same kind of compelling evidence to reach definite conclusions. This is where *isnād-cum-matn* analysis provides the most crucial input; it gives a systematic and orderly method to reach convincing conclusions with compelling evidence, of course in the presence of hadith variants to work with. Harald Motzki, in implementing this methodology, already disproved Burton's thesis by dating Muslim traditions on the collection of the Qur'an to the first quarter of the second century.

was firmly established in the first century of Islam. Hence, although no other authority could ignore it, they were forced to gain legitimacy by it. This notion that individuals forged hadiths to gain legitimacy or interpreted verses as per their theological views indicates the pressing need for Muslim elites to make themselves relevant in the light of the Qur'an. This intense urge among early Muslims 'to gain legitimacy from the Qur'an' in itself casts doubt on theories against the originality of the Qur'an that the Prophet preached. The Qur'anic codex must have existed from the very early times of the nascent religion, so that it could have accumulated such a sacred status and yielded authority and legitimacy to the early Muslims.

But what if their idea did not exist in the Qur'an? This did not stop some fervent supporters of certain schools of thought. If they did not have their desired proof in the Qur'an, they still attributed these ideas to the Qur'an by means of a false concept that enabled them to claim their evidence was missing from the Qur'an. In a way, those who were desperate to find legitimacy for their views did not hesitate to attack the textual integrity of the Qur'an.

In this specific case, it was helpful for some Shiʿi groups as they had a precedent for the idea of distortion in the Qur'an. Because of the significance of 'Umar's report for 'Alī's claim to succession, most Shiʿis must have been acquainted with this well-distributed report in Muslim lands. As I have studied in Chapter 4, the reports attributed to 'Umar were in circulation in Kufa, a major Shiʿi centre in the second/eighth century. A genuine slip of memory committed by 'Umar, who adamantly defended the existence of the Stoning Verse in the Qur'an, was exploited by some Shiʿi groups to enable them to argue for the legitimacy of the Imams in the Qur'an.

But why did these Shiʿis adopt these specific reports? This question arises because there are some other reports in the Sunni hadith corpus, such as traditions attributed to 'Ā'isha which I studied previously. There might be an innocent and straightforward explanation for this, namely, that they simply did not know about them. Although these reports were in circulation in the first quarter of the second century, Shiʿi scholars did not pay much attention to them. They would not, however, miss essential reports on 'Umar's reported testimony regarding the succession issue, including his position on the stoning penalty which is a major punishment. This was because these very reports also related to the succession of Abū Bakr and 'Umar. No specialist Shiʿi scholar would have missed these reports, as they were also recorded in the earliest Sunni hadith collections and perhaps widely circulated at the time by pro-'Alī figures like Ibn 'Abbās and Saʿīd b. al-Musayyab. While some Shiʿis must have been contemplating these reports to justify 'Alī's succession, some others might have been inspired by these reports and thus made their own versions of them. This would fix the most crucial problem in Shiʿi theology, namely, the lack of *naṣṣ* or divine decree for the concept of imamate. The solution was to claim that they were purged from the Qur'an, just as the so-called Stoning Verse was purged from it.

This hypothesis sounds promising at the start of the analysis, but I will see if the investigation of the material at hand will support this hypothesis. However, I cannot analyse the two Sunni variants because two variants are not suitable for carrying out *isnād-cum-matn* analysis. These two variants may come in handy when I examine the texts of the Shiʿi reports because they were recorded in some of the earliest Sunni hadith collections. On the other hand, there are fourteen Shiʿi variants, including one Ismaili variant. Therefore, I will continue with my analysis of them.

The Jaʿfar al-Ṣādiq Cluster

Chain of Transmission Analysis

Out of the fourteen variants attributed to Jaʿfar al-Ṣādiq, three have no chains of transmission; they are directly quoted in Sulaym b. Qays al-Hilālī's *Kitāb*, ʿAlī b. Ibrāhīm al-Qummī's *Tafsīr* and al-Qāḍī al-Nuʿmān's *Daʿāʾim al-islām.* In addition, one of the variants recorded in Aḥmad b. Muḥammad al-Sayyārī's *Kitāb al-qirāʾāt* is a duplicate.

Abū Yaʿqūb [al-Asadī] seems to have played an important role in the transmission of the report. He transmits it to three different individuals but with an identical text recorded by al-Sayyārī. No name was given in one of these chains except for Abū Yaʿqūb. Thus, I may identify him as a possible Common Link. Hishām b. Sālim and ʿAbdullāh b. Sinān also transmit the report to multiple individuals. Therefore, they are also Common Links. The rest of the transmission occurs in the form of single strand narrations.

The first variant is found in al-Sayyārī's *Kitāb al-qirāʾāt.*[16] His full name is Abū ʿAbdullāh Aḥmad b. Muḥammad b. al-Sayyār. Kohlberg and Amir-Moezzi provide a detailed biography which notes that information about his date of activity is unreliable. Still, they are confident that he was active in the middle of the third/ninth century.[17] Furthermore, based on his teachers and students, he lived in Qom. He was known to be among the disciples of the tenth Imam, ʿAlī al-Hādī (d. 254/868), and the eleventh Imam, al-Ḥasan al-ʿAskarī (d. 260/873).

Undoubtedly, the book was authored by him and included the variant; however, certain charges levelled against him may make it difficult to consider a genuine transmission process. Shiʿi biographers heavily criticised

16 al-Sayyārī, *Revelation and Falsification*, p. 109.
17 al-Sayyārī, *Revelation and Falsification*, pp. 31–2.

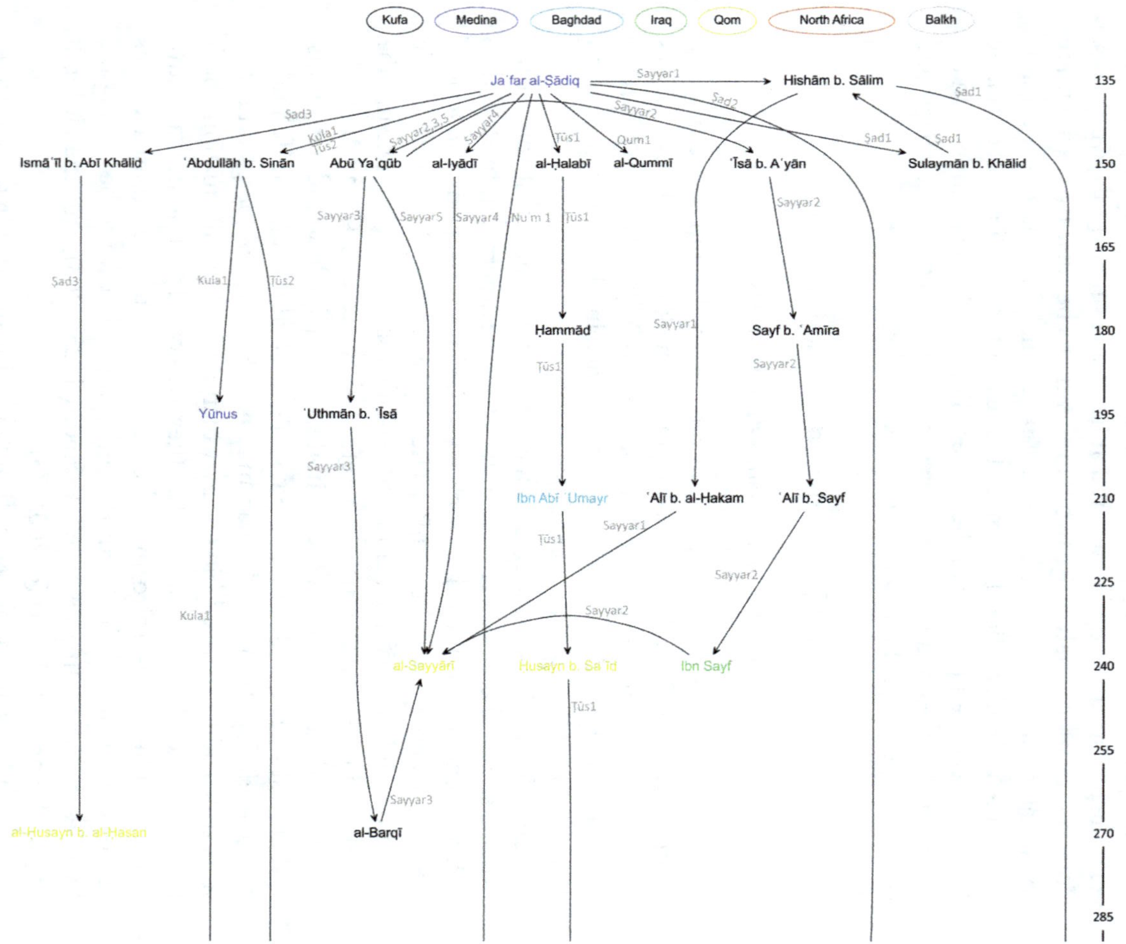

Kufa
Medina
Baghdad
Iraq
Qom
North Africa
Balkh
Ja῾far al-Ṣādiq
Hishām b. Sālim
Ismā῾īl b. Abī Khālid
῾Abdullāh b. Sinān
Abū Ya῾qūb
al-Iyādī
al-Ḥalabī
al-Qummī
῾Īsā b. A῾yān
Sulaymān b. Khālid
Ḥammād
Sayf b. ῾Amīra
Yūnus
῾Uthmān b. ῾Īsā
Ibn Abī ῾Umayr
῾Alī b. al-Ḥakam
῾Alī b. Sayf
al-Sayyārī
Ḥusayn b. Sa῾īd
Ibn Sayf
al-Ḥusayn b. al-Ḥasan
al-Barqī
Sayyar1
Sayyar2
Sayyar2,3,5
Sayyar3
Sayyar4
Sayyar5
Ṣad1
Ṣad2
Ṣad3
Kula1
Ṭūs1
Ṭūs2
Qum1
Nu῾m 1
135
150
165
180
195
210
225
240
255
270
285

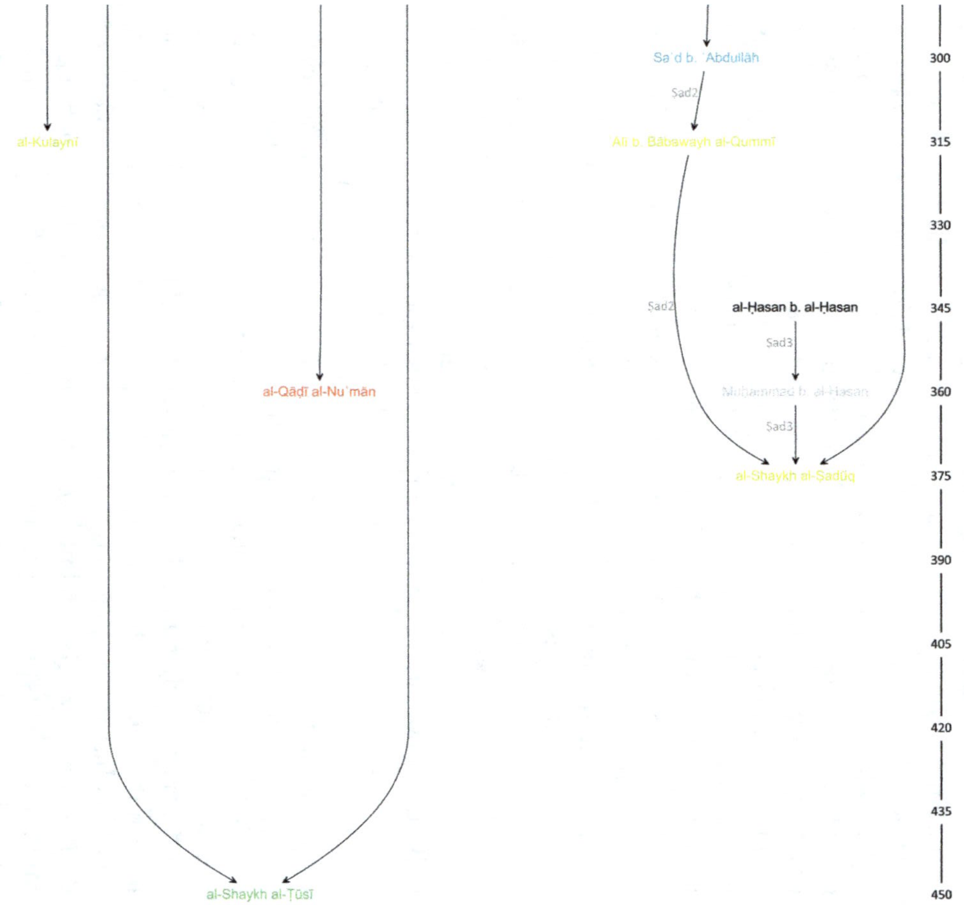

Diagram 5 Available online at: https://edin.ac/4comjcg

him for being an 'extremist', who believed in metempsychosis or the transmigration of the soul, particularly its reincarnation after death. Therefore, he was considered to be a deviant by Twelver Shi'is. They also state that his transmissions were unreliable as he habitually transmitted incomplete chains. Furthermore, there is a specific charge of lying and fraud levelled against him by Imam al-Ḥasan al-'Askarī. In an epistle attributed to Imam al-Ḥasan al-'Askarī, while responding to a question about al-Sayyārī, he urged his followers, 'He does not occupy the position he claims for himself; do not pay him any attention.'[18] Kohlberg and Amir-Moezzi rightly suggest that the Imam's statement might have been a response to al-Sayyārī's claim to be a financial agent (*wakīl*) of the Imam.[19] The Imam reportedly wanted to prevent him from collecting religious taxes, which amount to 20 per cent of the annual surplus income Shi'i's accumulate in a year.

These accusations against al-Sayyārī make it problematic for the sake of the chain of transmission analysis, especially due to the charges of lying, fraud and extremism. He seems to thus have a motive and precedent for backing this idea of distortion. Needless to state that these kinds of accusations, on their own, may not have direct relevance to the *isnād-cum-matn* analysis, but they become useful when anomalies arise in the study of the chain and text. In such cases, we can use them as supporting arguments, indicating a potential motive for forgery or manipulation.

Nevertheless, there are other variants of the tradition, so it may be possible to verify whether al-Sayyārī fabricated this report by examining the remaining variants and their texts in the next section. In any case, al-Sayyārī received the variant from 'Alī b. al-Ḥakam, a prominent Shi'i hadith collector based in Kufa.[20] He was known to be a companion of the eighth Imam, 'Alī b. Mūsā al-Riḍā (d. 203/818), and his son and the ninth Imam, Muḥammad b. 'Alī al-Jawād (d. 220/835).[21] As a prolific transmitter, he reported around 1,462 reports in the four most important Shi'i hadith compilations,[22] or the Four Books. There is no date of death for 'Alī b. al-Ḥakam but given the reports from both the eighth and ninth Imams, it is probable that he was active until the first quarter of the third/ninth century. As he did not report from the tenth Imam, he must have stopped his scholarly activities (or perhaps died) before 220/835 or soon thereafter.

18 Tafrīshī, *Naqd al-rijāl*, vol. 1, p. 609.
19 al-Sayyārī, *Revelation and Falsification*, pp. 32–3.
20 al-Ṭūsī, *al-Fihrist*, vol. 1, p. 87.
21 Tafrīshī, *Naqd al-rijāl*, vol. 7, p. 446.
22 al-Lajna al-'Alamiyya fī Mu'assasat al-Imām al-Ṣādiq, *Mawsū'a ṭabaqāt al-fuqahā'*, vol. 3, p. 393.

There seems to be a minor issue with al-Sayyārī receiving the variant from ʿAlī b. al-Ḥakam. As noted above, Kohlberg and Amir-Moezzi suggest that he was active in the mid-third/ninth century and possibly died by the end of that century. However, to receive this report from ʿAlī b. al-Ḥakam, he must have been active in the first quarter of the third/ninth century. Theoretically, it is possible, since as a young student he visited ʿAlī b. al-Ḥakam in Kufa and later recorded it in his book. Although this may be theoretically viable, in order for this to have occurred, al-Sayyārī must have either enjoyed a very long life or died earlier than what Kohlberg and Amir-Moezzi suggested. It is believed that al-Sayyārī lived in Qom, but there was an organic connection between the Shiʿi centres of Qom and Kufa along with occasional travels, especially for education and visiting.[23]

ʿAlī b. al-Ḥakam received the variant from Hishām b. Sālim, who was a prominent jurist, hadith collector and companion of the sixth Imam, Jaʿfar al-Ṣādiq (d. 148/765), and seventh Imam, Mūsā b. Jaʿfar al-Kāẓim (d. 183/799). He resided in Kufa and reportedly played a crucial role in the succession of Imam al-Kāẓim. He was a client of Bishr b. Marwān (d. 74/694),[24] the Umayyad governor of Iraq. He travelled to Medina to learn from Jaʿfar al-Ṣādiq, and several books were attributed to him,[25] including an *ʾAṣl*.[26] Some allegations are levelled against him, but Shiʿi scholars usually consider him to be a reliable transmitter.[27] There is no date of death for him, but it is possible that he died or became inactive a few years after Jaʿfar al-Ṣādiq's death. There seems to be no major problem with this chain reaching up to Jaʿfar al-Ṣādiq.

The second variant is in al-Sayyārī's *Kitāb al-qirāʾāt*.[28] He received the variant from Ibn Sayf, who is al-Ḥusayn b. Sayf b. ʿAmīra.[29] He was from Baghdad but active in Basra and Kufa as well.[30] He was the author of two hadith collections, one of which he narrated from his brother ʿAlī b. Sayf.[31] There is no date of death for him, but he was probably active in the first half of the third/ninth century. I came to this view based on the knowledge that his father, Sayf b. ʿAmīra al-Nakhaʿī, who is also mentioned in this chain, was a companion of Imams Jaʿfar al-Ṣādiq (d. 148/765) and al-Kāẓim (d. 183/799).

23 See Newman, *The Formative Period of Twelver Shīʿism.*
24 al-Najāshī, *Rijāl*, p. 414.
25 al-Ṭūsī, *al-Fihrist*, vol. 1, p. 174.
26 *ʾAṣl* is a collection of the sayings of the Imams and the hadiths which are reported directly from an Imam.
27 al-Khoei, *Muʿjam rijāl al-ḥadīth*, vol. 15, pp. 324–9.
28 al-Sayyārī, *Kitāb al-qirāʾāt*, p. 110.
29 Kuzudişli provides a detailed study on Ibn Sayf. Kuzudişli, 'Sunnī–Shīʿī Interaction'.
30 al-Amīn, *Aʿyān al-shīʿa*, vol. 6, p. 34.
31 al-Najāshī, *Rijāl*, p. 56; al-Sayyārī, *Revelation and Falsification*, p. 58.

Ibn Sayf narrated the variant from his brother ʿAlī b. Sayf, who was a respected Shiʿi scholar and companion of the eighth Imam, ʿAlī b. Mūsā al-Riḍā (d. 203/818). He was based in Kufa and reported from al-Riḍā.[32] Above, I mentioned that Ibn Sayf also reported a book from his brother ʿAlī b. Sayf, and thus this variant may have been from that book, or by means of an oral transmission. ʿAlī b. Sayf then received the variant from his father, Sayf b. ʿAmīra al-Nakhaʿī, who was based in Kufa and reported from the sixth and seventh Imams.[33]

Sayf also reportedly has a book and is considered to be a reliable transmitter.[34] Kohlberg and Amir-Moezzi note that this family line occurs over forty times in *Kitāb al-qirāʾāt*. Given that Sayf b. ʿAmīra al-Nakhaʿī reported from Jaʿfar al-Ṣādiq, he could have received the variant from him and reported it to his sons. He did not, however, hear it from Jaʿfar al-Ṣādiq directly. He received it from ʿĪsā b. Aʿyan, who also narrated from Jaʿfar al-Ṣādiq, and was possibly Jaʿfar al-Ṣādiq's companion.[35] He was a client of the al-Asadī tribe based in Kufa and is considered reliable.[36] He seems to have a book as well.[37]

ʿĪsā b. Aʿyan received the variant from Abū Yaʿqūb [al-Asadī], who was a resident of Kufa[38] and companion of Jaʿfar al-Ṣādiq. The connection between the two is probably due to the al-Asadī tribe. While ʿĪsā b. Aʿyan was a client of the tribe, Abū Yaʿqūb was its member. There is no date of death for them, but since they were both companions of Jaʿfar al-Ṣādiq, they were active in the mid-second/eighth century. Abū Yaʿqūb then received the variant from Jaʿfar al-Ṣādiq without interruption.

In the chain of transmission of the same variant, al-Sayyārī mentioned that he received the exact text through a different chain of transmission. I will also briefly examine the third chain. The third chain starts with [Aḥmad b. Muḥammad b. Khālid] al-Barqī (d. 274/887–8 or 280/893–4). He was a well-known Twelver hadith collector and historian based in Kufa.[39] Although he was considered reliable, he was banished from Qom temporarily for transmitting reports from unreliable transmitters, or reports without chains or missing transmitters (*mursal*).[40] He authored numerous

32 al-Khoei, *Muʿjam rijāl al-ḥadīth*, vol. 13, p. 61.

33 Modarressi, *Tradition and Survival*, vol. 1, p. 371; al-Sayyārī, *Revelation and Falsification*, p. 58.

34 al-Khoei, *Muʿjam rijāl al-ḥadīth*, vol. 3, p. 382.

35 al-Tustarī, *Qāmūs al-rijāl*, vol. 8, p. 303.

36 al-Najāshī, *Rijāl*, p. 296.

37 al-Ṭūsī, *al-Fihrist*, vol. 1, p. 117; Qahpāyī, *Majmaʿ al-rijāl*, vol. 4, p. 299.

38 al-Ṭūsī, *Rijāl*, p. 326; Burūjardī, *Ṭarāʾif al-maqāl fī maʿrifat ṭabaqāt al-rijāl*, vol. 1, p. 649.

39 al-Najāshī, *Rijāl*, pp. 76–7.

40 al-Khoei, *Muʿjam rijāl al-ḥadīth*, vol. 3, pp. 49–54.

books, most importantly *al-Maḥāsin* and *Rijāl*, and was one of the most cited authorities by al-Sayyārī.[41]

Al-Barqī received the variant from ʿUthmān b. ʿĪsā [al-Rawwāsī] (d. after 203/818–19). A controversial figure among Twelver Shiʿis, he was known to be a representative of Imam al-Kāẓim (d. 183/799) in Kufa, and was initially held in high esteem. ʿUthmān b. ʿĪsā received both cash and property on behalf of al-Kāẓim when the latter was in prison. However, when al-Kāẓim died, he refused to accept Imam al-Riḍā's succession to his father and did not hand over the cash and property that he had received on behalf of Imam al-Kāẓim. He went so far as to deny the death of Imam al-Kāẓim to avoid returning inheritance to his son and hence became one of the heads of Waqfiyya who refused to accept the succession of Imam al-Riḍā.[42]

This taint might put the chain in a precarious position because he was possibly ostracised by those who continued to follow al-Riḍā. However, this is the second chain that reports the exact text. Thus, it is possible that al-Barqī received this report from ʿUthmān b. ʿĪsā, who then heard it from Abū Yaʿqūb. He, in return, received it from Jaʿfar al-Ṣādiq. The variants of this report emerged in Medina, where Jaʿfar al-Ṣādiq was a resident and were transmitted to Kufa, and from Kufa to Qom through various individuals. Abū Yaʿqūb seems to be one of the Common Links that transmitted the report to more than one transmitter. It is difficult to ascertain the original text ascribed to Jaʿfar al-Ṣādiq, however. I can only attempt to recover the original report in the textual analysis section.

The fourth chain of transmission is in al-Sayyārī's *Kitāb al-qirāʾāt*,[43] which only includes the name of a certain al-Iyādī who reports it from Jaʿfar al-Ṣādiq. Al-Iyādī is an unknown person; Kohlberg and Amir-Moezzi speculate[44] his identity as either Abū al-Qāsim al-Iyādī who was mentioned only in one chain in al-Shaykh al-Mufīd's (d. 413/1022) *al-Ikhtiṣāṣ*[45] or al-Qāsim b. Ismāʿīl al-Anbārī. However, it is pure speculation and, in any case, mentioning one person in the chain is not enough to attribute it to Jaʿfar al-Ṣādiq. The fifth chain[46] in al-Sayyārī's *Kitāb al-qirāʾāt* includes Abū Yaʿqūb, but only his name is given on its own. The other individual is not identified. The text section also states 'the same of it'. Therefore, there is no need to examine this chain.

The sixth chain of transmission[47] under examination is reported in Muḥammad b. Yaʿqūb b. Isḥāq al-Kulaynī's (d. 328/939 or 329/940)

41 al-Sayyārī, *Revelation and Falsification*, p. 32.
42 al-Khoei, *Muʿjam rijāl al-ḥadīth*, vol. 15, pp. 129–32.
43 al-Sayyārī, *Revelation and Falsification*, p. 109.
44 al-Sayyārī, *Revelation and Falsification*, p. 199.
45 al-Mufīd, *al-Ikhtiṣāṣ*, vol. 1, p. 10.
46 al-Sayyārī, *Revelation and Falsification*, p. 110.
47 al-Kulaynī, *al-Kāfī*, vol. 14, p. 16.

al-Kāfī.[48] Al-Kulaynī is known to be one of the most outstanding Shi'i scholars as he authored the most crucial Shi'i hadith collection. He was active in Rayy, Qom and Baghdad.[49] He received the variant from Yūnus [b. 'Abd al-Raḥmān] (d. 208/823–4), who was a client based in Medina and companion of Imams al-Kāẓim and al-Riḍā.[50] He was born during the reign of the Umayyad caliph Hishām b. 'Abd al-Malik (r. 105/724–125/743). Yūnus authored many books and was known to have supported al-Riḍā during the internal uproar caused by Waqfiyya's refusal to accept his imamate.[51] However, there is a considerable time gap between al-Kulaynī and Yūnus. Al-Kulaynī could have received the variant directly from Yūnus, but he probably received it from one of Yūnus's books. There is no evidence for either of these, however.

In any case, Yūnus received it from 'Abdullāh b. Sinān, who was known to be a companion of Imam Ja'far al-Ṣādiq. He was referred to as a client and thought to be a resident of Kufa, and was considered reliable. There is no date of death for him, but he might have lived during al-Kāẓim's (d. 183/799) imamate, but there is no compelling evidence. In any case, it appears that he became inactive in the mid-second/eighth century. He authored a book and transmitted more than 1,146 reports from Ja'far al-Ṣādiq.[52] There is no problem with Yūnus receiving the variant from 'Abdullāh b. Sinān and him receiving it from Ja'far al-Ṣādiq. The time gap between al-Kulaynī and Yūnus only makes it possible to date this variant back to al-Kulaynī at this stage, though it might be possible to revise this date during the analysis of the text.

The seventh variant is recorded in 'Alī b. Ibrāhīm al-Qummī's (d. 307/980) *Tafsīr* (known as *Tafsīr al-Qummī*).[53] *Tafsīr al-Qummī* is one of the oldest Shi'i sources, written in the third/ninth century. The author, 'Alī b. Ibrāhīm al-Qummī, is a contemporary of al-Sayyārī and a teacher of al-Kulaynī. Most classical Shi'i scholars consider it a genuine work by 'Alī b. Ibrāhīm al-Qummī. Some modern Shi'i scholars such as Āghā Buzurg al-Tihrānī[54] (d. 1970) and Muḥammad Hādī Ma'rifat[55] (d. 2007) argue that some of it was not taught by 'Alī b. Ibrāhīm al-Qummī, but rather the editor of the book, Abū al-Faḍl al-'Abbās b. Muḥammad (d. fourth/tenth century), who was a possible student of al-Qummī. He remains unknown, however, as no information is available about him.

48 See Lawson, 'Note for the Study of a Shīʿī Qur'ān', pp. 279–95.

49 al-Khoei, *Mu'jam rijāl al-ḥadīth*, vol. 19, pp. 54–8.

50 al-Ṭūsī, *Rijāl*, p. 368; al-Khoei, *Mu'jam rijāl al-ḥadīth*, vol. 21, pp. 209–28.

51 al-Najāshī, *Rijāl*, pp. 446–8.

52 al-Najāshī, *Rijāl*, p. 214; al-Khoei, *Mu'jam rijāl al-ḥadīth*, vol. 11, pp. 224–8.

53 al-Qummī, *Tafsīr al-Qummī*, vol. 2, p. 95.

54 Tihrānī, *al-Dharīʿa ilā taṣānīf al-shīʿa*, vol. 4, pp. 302–4.

55 Ma'rifat, *Ṣiyānat al-Qur'ān min al-taḥrīf*, pp. 197–8.

Abū al-Faḍl combined[56] his teacher's notes with the *Tafsīr* of Abū al-Jārūd (d. between 150/767 and 160/777), who was a controversial Zaydi figure. He was unpopular among Twelver scholars due to his disagreement with Imams al-Bāqir and Ṣādiq. Because this variant does not have a chain, I cannot analyse it any further.

The eighth chain[57] was recorded in Ibn Bābawayh, or al-Shaykh al-Ṣadūq's[58] influential (d. 381/991) *al-Faqīh*.[59] Al-Ṣadūq is known to be one of the greatest Shi'i hadith scholars of the fourth/tenth century. He lived in the Buyid era and resided in Qom but travelled to Rayy, Mashhad, Nishapur, the Hijaz, Iraq and Transoxiana.[60] These travels enabled him to learn many Shi'i reports. His *al-Faqīh*, together with al-Kulaynī's *al-Kāfī*, is considered among the four fundamental books in Shi'i creed.[61] It also contains jurisprudential reports ascribed to the Prophet and the Imams. Ibn Bābawayh received the variant from Hishām b. Sālim, who was a prominent jurist and hadith collector and companion of the sixth Imam, Ja'far al-Ṣādiq (d. 148/765), and the seventh Imam, Mūsā b. Ja'far al-Kāẓim (d. 183/799). As I have noted above, Hishām b. Sālim transmits the same variant to al-Sayyārī ← 'Alī b. al-Ḥakam ← Hishām b. Sālim ← al-Ja'far. However, in this variant Hishām b. Sālim received it from Sulaymān b. Khālid, who received it from al-Ja'far.

The apparent issue with this chain is the time gap between al-Ṣadūq and Hishām b. Sālim; al-Ṣadūq lived in the fourth/tenth century and Hishām b. Sālim lived in the second/eighth century. One explanation may be that al-Ṣadūq read the variant from one of the books of Hishām b. Sālim, but there is no indication of that in the chain. The second possibility is that al-Ṣadūq read it from al-Sayyārī's *Kitāb al-qirā'āt* but did not want to mention al-Sayyārī in the chain. This may be plausible, but the existence of the extra transmitter, Sulaymān b. Khālid, makes this possibility improbable. Sulaymān b. Khālid was a client who reported from al-Ja'far. He died during the lifetime of Imam al-Ja'far and could have heard the report. He was also based in Kufa.[62] Because of the time gap between al-Ṣadūq and Hishām b. Sālim, however, I can only date this variant to al-Ṣadūq's date of death, in the year 381/991.

56 Ma'rifat notes the similarity of the introduction of the book with *Tafsīr al-Nu'mānī*. Therefore, he argues against the single authorship of the book by al-Qummī. Ma'rifat, *Ṣiyānat al-Qur'ān min al-taḥrīf*, p. 197. See also al-Nu'mānī, *Tafsīr al-Nu'mānī*.

57 Ibn Bābawayh, *Man lā yaḥḍuruhu al-faqīh*, vol. 4, p. 36.

58 Warner, *The Words of the Imams*.

59 Warner provides useful information about *al-Faqīh*. Warner, *The Words of the Imams*, 22–3 and *passim*.

60 al-Khoei, *Mu'jam rijāl al-ḥadīth*, vol. 17, pp. 340–51.

61 See, Ehteshami, 'The Four Books of Shi'i Hadith'.

62 al-Najāshī, *Rijāl*, p. 183.

The ninth chain of transmission[63] is found in another work of al-Shaykh al-Ṣadūq, namely, *'Ilal al-sharā'i'*.[64] The book contains reports from the Prophet and Imams about the reasonings behind religious rulings. Despite the similarity in the text, the chain of this report is different from the previous variant. Al-Ṣadūq received it from his father, 'Alī b. Bābawayh al-Qummī (d. 329/940–1), who was a reliable Qom jurist, and several books have been attributed to him.[65] He received the variant from the prominent hadith collector and scholar Sa'd b. 'Abdullāh [al-Ash'arī] (d. 301/913), who was active in Baghdad and Qom and wrote many books, including a biography.[66] There is a problem with this chain as there is a one- or two-generation gap between Sa'd b. 'Abdullāh (d. 301/913) and Ja'far al-Ṣādiq (d. 148/765). Sa'd b. 'Abdullāh admits that this is a *marfū'* (elevated) chain, meaning that Sa'd b. 'Abdullāh omitted his source(s) either intentionally or unknowingly. Yet he reported it as if he heard it directly from al-Ja'far. According to *isnād-cum-matn* analysis, this chain has historical source value only up until Sa'd b. 'Abdullāh, and thus can only be dated back to his date of death, in the year 301/913.

The tenth chain of transmission is also recorded in al-Shaykh al-Ṣadūq's *'Ilal al-sharā'i'*. He received it from his well-known informant and friend, Muḥammad b. al-Ḥasan [b. Isḥāq]. According to various sources, Muḥammad b. al-Ḥasan encouraged al-Ṣadūq to write his famous *al-Faqīh* in the region of Ilaq near Balkh.[67] There is no date of death for him, but he was a contemporary of al-Ṣadūq (d. 381/991). Therefore, he was likely active in the second half of the fourth century and possibly died around the same time, or slightly earlier. Muḥammad b. al-Ḥasan received it from al-Ḥasan b. al-Ḥasan b. Abān, indicating a typographical error in the chain as it should refer to al-Ḥusayn b. al-Ḥasan b. Abān, who was active in Qom and thought to be a companion of Imam Ḥasan al-'Askarī (d. 260/874), but interestingly did not report from him. It is possible that this was a mistake and he lived later than al-'Askarī, possibly dying towards the end of the third/ninth century. Nevertheless, he could have transmitted this variant to Muḥammad b. al-Ḥasan without interruption.[68]

Al-Ḥusayn b. al-Ḥasan received the variant from Ismā'īl b. Khālid, but there is no such person in Shi'i sources. He is actually Ismā'īl b. Abī Khālid,[69] who was a companion of Imams al-Bāqir and Ja'far al-Ṣādiq, a resident of

63 Ibn Bābawayh, *'Ilal al-sharā'i'*, vol. 2, p. 540.
64 Warner provides details about *'Ilal al-sharā'i'*. Warner, *The Words of the Imams*, p. 24 and *passim*.
65 al-Najāshī, *Rijāl*, p. 68.
66 al-Najāshī, *Rijāl*, pp. 177–8; al-Ṭūsī, *al-Fihrist*, vol. 1, pp. 75–6.
67 al-Khoei, *Mu'jam rijāl al-ḥadīth*, vol. 16, p. 222.
68 al-Khoei, *Mu'jam rijāl al-ḥadīth*, vol. 6, p. 231.
69 al-Amīn, *A'yān al-shī'a*, vol. 3, pp. 310, 322.

Kufa and considered reliable.[70] Given that he lived during Jaʿfar al-Ṣādiq's lifetime (d. 148/765) and his father's, it is very probable that Ismāʿīl b. Abī Khālid died before or soon after Jaʿfar al-Ṣādiq. This makes it difficult for him to transmit this variant to Muḥammad b. al-Ḥasan, who most probably died towards the end of the third/ninth century. There is a gap of at least one generation in this chain. Consequently, I can only date this chain to Muḥammad b. al-Ḥasan's date of death, which is in the third/ninth century.

The eleventh chain is found in Muḥammad b. al-Ḥasan b. ʿAlī b. al-Ḥasan's *Tahdhīb al-aḥkām*. The author is better known as al-Shaykh al-Ṭūsī (d. 460/1067), one of the greatest Twelver jurists and hadith compliers. He was born in Khorasan but lived in Baghdad and Najaf during the Buyid dynasty and briefly under the Seljuks. He studied with Sunni scholars, more specifically those of the Shāfiʿī legal school. Therefore, it is probable that Shāfiʿī legal doctrines influenced him.[71] A very influential scholar of his time, he shaped the intellectual and scholarly landscape of Twelver Shiʿism for at least two centuries. His work *Tahdhīb al-aḥkām* is considered one of the four most important Twelver sources. He received the variant from al-Ḥusayn b. Saʿīd [al-Ahwāzī], a well-known Twelver jurist and hadith collector. He first lived in Kufa but then moved to Qom. There is no definite information about his date of death, but he is thought to have died in the mid-third/ninth century, which makes it impossible for al-Shaykh al-Ṭūsī to have received the variant from him as between them there is a gap of around two centuries. However, it is possible that al-Shaykh al-Ṭūsī read the variant in one of al-Ḥusayn b. Saʿīd's books, as the latter was a prolific writer, having authored over thirty works.[72] There is no information in the chain to reflect this, however.

Al-Ḥusayn b. Saʿīd received the variant from Ibn Abī ʿUmayr (d. 217/832–3), a prominent Shiʿi hadith narrator. He was a companion of Imams al-Kāẓim, al-Riḍā and al-Jawād. He was considered among the 'people of consensus' (*aṣḥāb al-ijmāʿ*), a group of hadith transmitters whose reliability is regarded highly by Twelver biographical evaluation scholars. Most traditional Shiʿi scholars consider the reports that they transmit as reliable.[73] He originated from Baghdad and lived therein during the reign of Hārūn al-Rashīd (r. 170/786–193/809) and was persecuted and imprisoned for a considerable time for being a Shiʿi.[74] It is possible that al-Ḥusayn b. Saʿīd

70 al-Ṭūsī, *al-Fihrist*, vol. 1, p. 10; Tafrīshī, *Naqd al-rijāl*, vol. 7, p. 26.

71 Stewart, *Islamic Legal Orthodoxy*.

72 al-Najāshī, *Rijāl*, pp. 77–8; al-Ṭūsī, *Rijāl*, p. 385; al-Khoei, *Muʿjam rijāl al-ḥadīth*, vol. 6, pp. 265–7.

73 However, this view has come under scrutiny thanks to modern-era *rijāl* scholars like al-Khoei (d. 1992). He rejected such blanket reliability attributed to the 'people of consensus'. See al-Khoei, *Muʿjam rijāl al-ḥadīth*, vol. 1, pp. 57–61.

74 al-Najāshī, *Rijāl*, pp. 326–7.

received the report from Ibn Abī 'Umayr as they lived around the exact location and during the same time.

Ibn Abī 'Umayr received it from Ḥammād. He might have been either Ḥammād b. 'Uthmān (d. 190/805–6) or Ḥammād b. 'Īsā al-Juhanī (d. 209/824–5), both of whom are transmitters to Ibn Abī 'Umayr and considered reliable. It is more likely that he received this variant from Ḥammād b. 'Uthmān as Ibn Abī 'Umayr received over a hundred reports from Ḥammād b. 'Uthmān. Furthermore, between both Ḥammāds, Ḥammād b. 'Uthmān has a higher standing as he was considered among the 'people of consensus', similar to Ibn Abī 'Umayr. Ḥammād b. 'Uthmān was a companion of Ja'far al-Ṣādiq and was based in Kufa.[75] He did not, however, receive the variant directly from Ja'far al-Ṣādiq, but rather al-Ḥalabī, which often refers to Muḥammad b. 'Alī b. Abī Shu'ba al-Ḥalabī, a distinguished member of the Shi'i community in Kufa and a companion of Ja'far al-Ṣādiq. He received the praise of Ja'far al-Ṣādiq for authoring *al-Jamī'*, which gained prominence among Ismailis. However, it is more likely that the Ḥammād in this chain refers to his brother 'Ubaydullāh b. 'Alī al-Ḥalabī, as this is the usual path by which he narrates: Ibn Abī 'Umayr ← Ḥammād ← al-Ḥalabī. He died in the mid-second century.[76]

Although the lower end of this chain is problematic, the higher end is highly reliable, including two 'people of consensus' and prominent companions of Ja'far al-Ṣādiq. This may be suspicious because it increases the possibility of forgery. If it is forged, by forming an impeccable chain, the forger convinced prominent scholars like al-Ṭūsī to record or transmit it. This theory needs further proof, which I may find during the textual analysis. Nevertheless, it is very problematic that al-Shaykh al-Ṭūsī received the variant from al-Ḥusayn b. Sa'īd as there is a gap of almost two centuries between the two. It is improbable that al-Shaykh al-Ṭūsī forged the chain and attributed it to al-Ḥusayn b. Sa'īd because it would have been evident to scholars, given the time gap between the two. It could have been a book written by al-Ḥusayn b. Sa'īd from which al-Ṭūsī recorded this report, but there is no indication for this. Even if it was a copy, it is also difficult to ascertain if al-Ṭūsī was reading it from a genuine copy written by Ḥusayn b. Sa'īd, but that is not improbable. In any case, this chain is dubious, as *isnād-cum-matn* analysis can only date it back to al-Ṭūsī. However, the textual analysis might have given an earlier date if it has textual affinity and interdependence with the other variants.

Al-Ṭūsī narrated another variant, the twelfth chain, in his *Tahdhīb al-aḥkām* from 'Abdullāh b. Sinān, who also transmitted another variant to

75 Modarressi, *Tradition and Survival*, vol. 1, p. 239; al-Tustarī, *Qāmūs al-rijāl*, vol. 3, pp. 650–5; al-Najāshī, *Rijāl*, p. 143; al-Ṭūsī, *al-Fihrist*, vol. 1, pp. 60–1.

76 Modarressi, *Tradition and Survival*, vol. 1, pp. 338, 380–2.

al-Kulaynī. As I have noted above, ʿAbdullāh b. Sinān died around the mid-second/eighth century. However, al-Ṭūsī died in 460/1067, thus there is a three-century gap between the two. Therefore, he did not receive it personally from ʿAbdullāh b. Sinān. He may have received it from one of his books and decided not to mention it. If this is the case, there should have been a more remarkable textual similarity between the two reports transmitted through ʿAbdullāh b. Sinān and recorded in *al-Kāfī* and *Tahdhīb al-aḥkām*. Or, he might have copied it from *al-Kāfī* but he did not indicate it, which was the usual style of al-Ṭūsī. In this case, the text needs to be verbatim to the text recorded in *al-Kāfī*. Until verified through textual analysis, I can only date this variant to al-Ṭūsī.

The last and thirteenth variant was recorded by al-Nuʿmān b. Muḥammad, known as al-Qāḍī al-Nuʿmān, in his *Daʿāʾim al-islām* (d. 363/973). He was one of the greatest Ismaili jurists and theologians who lived during the Fatimid era and held key positions in the Fatimid state. *Daʿāʾim al-islām* is a significant source for the Ismailis. Al-Qāḍī al-Nuʿmān omitted the chains in the reports mentioned in this book, and for this reason, Twelver Shiʿi scholars considered this book unreliable. He did not cite any chain for this variant; therefore, it is impossible to study it.

Among the thirteen variants, only the first two chains reach al-Jaʿfar, and because these two chains are independent of each other, it may have been possible to date them back to Jaʿfar al-Ṣādiq provisionally. However, because both are recorded in al-Sayyārī's *Kitāb al-qirāʾāt* and al-Sayyārī is known to have 'extremist' views, he has a strong motive to forge these reports. Nevertheless, I can only reach a definitive conclusion after studying the texts of the variants.

Textual Analysis

The text of the first variant was recorded in al-Sayyārī's *Kitāb al-qirāʾāt*. According to the short text, Hishām b. Sālim questions Jaʿfar al-Ṣādiq about Sūrat al-Aḥzāb, 'I asked Abū ʿAbdullāh' (*saʾaltu Abā ʿAbdullāh*). Although it does not mention the nature of the question, the reply gives the impression that the question was about the length of the *sūra*. In Jaʿfar al-Ṣādiq's response to the question, he states that 'Sūrat al-Aḥzāb was like al-Baqara, and the like of it, and two-thirds of it'. According to the chain of transmission analysis, this is an uninterrupted transmission, yet al-Sayyārī has a motive to forge or manipulate it. It is also questionable if he received it from his stated informant, but I concluded that it was probable.

This concise statement challenges the current Qur'anic codex, according to which Sūrat al-Aḥzāb consists of 73 verses. However, Sūrat al-Baqara consists of 286 verses in the present Cairo edition of the ʿUthmānic codex. Thus, al-Aḥzāb being similar to al-Baqara, plus the like of it, makes it double

286 verses, which would be 572 verses. In addition, two-thirds of it, which is 190, resulting in 762 verses. According to this report, Sūrat al-Aḥzāb initially consisted of 762 verses.

Consequently, this short report makes a major statement about the textual integrity of the Qur'an. It implies that a major section of Sūrat al-Aḥzāb was removed or lost. It implies that the verses were lost after the death of the Prophet. Because it seems to be comparing the existing *sūra* in the second/eighth century with a previous version, it could technically be possible that a considerable chunk of the verses of the *sūra* was revealed to the Prophet, and then it was abrogated. On the other hand, what was the point of revealing around 700 verses and then abrogating them? This possibility does not make much sense. The dialogue is not clear, but there is a slight hint which may mean the question and answer were about the verses allegedly removed from the Qur'an, after the death of the Prophet.

Theology of Distortion

Furthermore, the chapter of the Qur'an in question, Sūrat al-Aḥzāb, makes this query more interesting and supports the suspicion that the question was about what was lost from the Qur'an after the death of the Prophet. Sūrat al-Aḥzāb[77] was believed to be revealed in Medina and discusses some of the most controversial topics related to the life of the Prophet, including his wives, household and the Companions. The early section of the chapter was believed to be revealed during the Battle of the Trench, which also gave its name to the verse al-Aḥzāb (the Confederates), referring to the confederation that was built against the Prophet and his followers. Wanting to finish off the Muslims completely, the polytheists of Mecca assembled a sizable army consisting of various Arab and Jewish tribes while the outnumbered Muslims decided to remain in a defensive position. Therefore, Muhammad ordered his followers to dig trenches around Medina and fortify the city entrances. The confederate army laid siege against the Muslims in the years 5/627. Although the Muslims gained a strategic victory in the end, it was a difficult battle for them.[78] Some wavered under the difficult condition of hunger and fear of an overwhelming enemy.

In line with these challenging times, the *sūra* first describes the fear and doubts of some of the Companions of the Prophet in the face of the siege. It criticises, rebukes and warns Muslims about their thoughts of fear, doubt, desertion and rebellion (Q. 33:9–27). It then moves on to the Prophet's

77 David Powers noted the shortening of al-Aḥzāb narratives for his thesis on Zayd b. Ḥāritha, the adopted son of the Prophet, in Powers, 'Sinless, Sonless and Seal of Prophets', pp. 406–7.

78 Kennedy, *The Prophet and the Age of the Caliphates*, pp. 38–9.

wives. It rebukes them harshly and warns them against desiring the worldly life over the Hereafter, by means of committing misconduct and unbecoming communication with others. (Q. 33:28–32, 59). Q. 33:32 refers to the term Household of the Prophet (*ahl al-bayt*):

> stay at your houses, and do not display yourselves as they used to in the pagan past; keep up the prayer, give the alms, and obey God and His Messenger. God wants to keep impurity away from you, Household of the Prophet, and purify you thoroughly. (Q. 33:32)

This verse is particularly important for Shiʿis because it is used as the 'Qur'anic evidence' for the infallibility of the Shiʿi Imams and Fāṭima, the daughter of the Prophet. Despite the context of the verse which addresses the Prophet's wives explicitly, Shiʿis believe that this last section of the verse, 'God wants to keep impurity away from you, Household of the Prophet, and purify you thoroughly', does not refer to the wives of the Prophet but to the Shiʿi Imams and Fāṭima. There is a compelling grammatical argument that Shiʿis put forward which is that the initial parts of the verse which refer to the Prophet's wives use feminine pronouns. However, the last section uses masculine pronouns (*ʿankum* and *yuṭahhirakum* instead of *ʿankunna* and *yuṭahhirakunna*). Arabic grammar justifies the Shiʿi position: feminine pronouns can only refer to females, but masculine pronouns can refer to males as well as males and females together. Therefore, the last section of the verse does not refer to Prophet's wives but Fāṭima, ʿAlī and their children, Ḥasan and Ḥusayn. On the other hand, the contextual evidence suggests that the verse may refer to the Prophet's wives.[79]

Therefore, Shiʿis claim that this verse is either misplaced or should form an individual verse. Alternatively, some marginal views claimed that the verses that supposedly elaborate on the merits of the major Shiʿi figures, mentioned before and after Q. 33:32, were omitted from the Qur'an. In a sense, this marginal view eliminated the contextual evidence with a drastic solution, ultimately making a case for the distortion of the Qur'an. The chapter then continues with the censuring of believers about entering the Prophet's home and their communication with his wives (Q. 33:53–4).

Given the controversial nature of the chapter, it is understandable why some Shiʿis expected to see more in the *sūra*. It explicitly censured the Companions of the Prophet, who, according to Sunni theology, are held in high esteem and were guaranteed Paradise regardless of their deeds. Therefore, for Shiʿis the *sūra* points out a major flaw in Sunni theology. Second, it took on the Prophet's wives, some of whom had counterclaims to be the Prophet's Household, against Fāṭima, ʿAlī and their children,

79 Madelung, *The Succession to Muhammad*, pp. 13–15.

Ḥasan and Ḥusayn. Furthermore, during the caliphate of ʿAlī, ʿĀ'isha, whom Sunnis consider the favourite wife of the Prophet, launched a rebellion against ʿAlī, which led to the Battle of the Camel in 36/656. More importantly, the verse commands the wives of the Prophet to not leave their houses, something which ʿĀ'isha violated in the Battle of the Camel. Thus, she attracted the displeasure of the Shiʿis, and they believed the verses were criticising ʿĀ'isha.[80]

Nevertheless, although the verses are unequivocal in their criticism of the Prophet's wives, they still fall short of some Shiʿis expectations. Similar to the verses that censure the Companions, their names are not mentioned specifically. It is not clear which Companions of the Prophet were overtaken with doubts and fears and which wives of the Prophet desired a glittery life, thus pressuring the Prophet. Finally, the names which are included in the Household of the Prophet are not mentioned. Therefore, it is fathomable that for some Shiʿis, there was something 'wrong' with Sūrat al-Aḥzāb and its distortion remained a close possibility. The short text of the variant at hand may seem to carry this theological baggage, but it is impossible to reach such a conclusion based on the analysis of one variant.

The text of the second variant was also recorded in al-Sayyārī's *Kitāb al-qirāʾāt*. According to the text, instead of Hishām b. Sālim, Abū Yaʿqūb engages in a dialogue with Jaʿfar al-Ṣādiq. In this variant, the dialogue is initiated by Jaʿfar al-Ṣādiq, whereas in the previous variant it was initiated by Hishām b. Sālim. This difference in the texts may tentatively suggest that these texts are not variants but rather two different texts narrating two independent events. If such distortion of the Qur'anic text had occurred, he could have taught it to his followers on various occasions. But it could have also been possible that one statement took different forms due to the oral transmission process or was distorted deliberately through interpolations. But if it was an actual transmission, it is curious that Jaʿfar al-Ṣādiq compared al-Aḥzāb against al-Baqara on two occasions. Including this element makes it more likely that this text is a variant of the report at hand, but likely not an original saying of Jaʿfar al-Ṣādiq.

Forgery Culture in Hadith Narrations

Nevertheless, this report contains similar information about Sūrat al-Aḥzāb included in the first text, namely, that it was considerably longer than the

80 For a detailed overview of the Shiʿi account of the events mentioned here, see Madelung, *The Succession to Muhammad*, 1–56; Jafri, *Origins and Development of Shiʿi Islam*, 1–70.

present version. It was the length of al-Baqara, which is 286 verses in its current version, but the text also claims that the original al-Baqara was distorted through omission. The original al-Baqara was equal in length to al-Aḥzāb, both of which were considerably longer. More importantly, these variants mention one of the missing verses from the original al-Aḥzāb: 'the old man (*al-shaykh*) and woman (*al-shaykha*), if they commit adultery, stone them unconditionally for they had satisfied their lust, as a punishment from God Almighty.'

According to the previous report, just under 700 verses were missing from Sūrat al-Aḥzāb, yet only the Stoning Verse was mentioned. The addition of the so-called missing Stoning Verse to this variant makes it remarkably interesting because the section '*al-shaykh wa-l-shaykha idhā zanayā fa-arjumūhumā al-battata*' ('the old man and woman, if they commit adultery, stone them unconditionally') is the exact copy of the Stoning Verse reports attributed to 'Umar. More specifically, it is identical to the group of reports transmitted through Saʿīd b. al-Musayyab. I noted that these reports were in circulation in Basra and Kufa in Chapter 4 and the Saʿīd b. al-Musayyab reports predate the reports under examination in this chapter. In the chain of transmission analysis section of this chapter, al-Sayyārī's source for this variant was Ibn Sayf. Ibn Sayf and his family (his brother and father), who report the variant, were from Baghdad but active in Basra and Kufa. It cannot be mere coincidence that the exact wording of a tradition attributed to 'Umar ends up in a Shiʿi report attributed to Jaʿfar al-Ṣādiq via a Shiʿi chain, and both reports were in circulation in Basra and Kufa. It was either a case of interpolating the wording of the so-called Stoning Verse in the form of an explanatory gloss to the report or a deliberate effort of forgery. Ibn Sayf and his family could be responsible for this interpolation, as I cannot trace these reports back to al-Ṣādiq.

There is another chain (the third chain) given with this same text in al-Sayyārī's *Kitāb al-qirāʾāt*. This chain is different from the other texts coming through the Common Link Abū Yaʿqūb. Both the second and third chains come through Abū Yaʿqūb, therefore it could be theoretically possible that Abū Yaʿqūb is responsible for this interpolation. However, since the text is identical, it is impossible to extract additional information. There is thus no evidence to hold Abū Yaʿqūb responsible and since no separate text is available, al-Sayyārī or someone else might have invented this chain.

The fourth text, which was also found in al-Sayyārī's *Kitāb al-qirāʾāt*, is terse and only states, 'Sūrat al-Aḥzāb was 700 verses.' This text apparently contradicts the first text that I studied, according to which al-Aḥzāb consisted of 762 verses. However, it is evident that there is the element of rounding up in the first text, and it is possible that this text also may not give an accurate number, meaning that it could be around 700 verses. Because it is too short, it is impossible to gather any other meaningful information from this text. The fifth text is the last variant recorded in al-Sayyārī's book and briefly states that the text is 'the same as', referring to the text of the second variant I studied above. Again, it is not possible to extract textual information from this variant.

The text of the sixth variant was recorded in al-Kulaynī's *al-Kāfī*. There is no mention of Sūrat al-Aḥzāb in this text. It starts with a statement by Ja'far al-Ṣādiq, who said:

> The stoning [penalty] is in the Qur'an, [it is the] word of Almighty: 'If the old man and woman (*shaykh* and *shaykha*) commit adultery stone both of them unconditionally. For they have quenched lust.'

The text is partially similar to the second section of the second text recorded by al-Sayyārī. The text confirms that the stoning penalty was in the Qur'an as the Word of God, and it includes the wording of the Stoning Verse. It is possible that in the case of al-Sayyārī's first variant, two separate reports were merged into one, meaning thereby the reports on the shortening of al-Aḥzāb along with the Stoning Verse. This is a strong possibility because a similar version of the text is narrated as an independent text in *al-Kāfī*.

Such a possibility becomes even more palpable in another text, the seventh, which was recorded in 'Alī b. Ibrāhīm al-Qummī's (d. 307/980) *Tafsīr*.[81] As mentioned when analysing the chain of transmission, modern Shi'i scholars contend that the text has multiple authors. It is unclear which part of the book this variant belongs to as there is no chain. It is possible that it belongs to the part of the book reported or dictated by al-Qummī because it is similar to the variant recorded in *al-Kāfī*. Al-Kulaynī could have received it from his teacher al-Qummī, with its chain, and recorded it. However, the text is more similar to al-Sayyārī's version because the introductory sentences, before the wording of the verse in both al-Sayyārī and al-Qummī's versions, start with inflections of the verb *kāna* (to be). More importantly, the wordings of both verses start with 'the old man and woman' (*al-shaykh wa-l-shaykha*), yet in al-Kulaynī's version, there is no introductory sentence at all. It right away narrates the wording of the verse which starts with the conditional clause 'if they commit adultery' (*idhā zanā*). Aside from these minor differences, the texts are similar as the changes are mainly in the form of slight paraphrasing by changing the words' location in the sentence. This indicates that there is a common source for these variants. It is doubtful, however, if the common source is Imam Ja'far al-Ṣādiq. Of course, there is the additional element about Sūrat al-Aḥzāb being included in al-Sayyārī's variant, which makes it plausible

81 al-Qummī, *Tafsīr al-Qummī*, vol. 2, p. 95.

that this section is a later addition to the original text of the report by way of merging two different texts.

Given the more remarkable textual similarity between al-Qummī and the second part of al-Sayyārī's second variants, it is conceivable that they had a common transmitter. It is not possible to know this transmitter from the study of these texts alone, however. Either al-Sayyārī or one of his close informants likely merged the two reports. As suggested above, it appears that these reports were forged out of the Sunni reports attributed to 'Umar, as their origins could also be traced back to Basra and Kufa. When analysing the chain of transmission, I also traced one of al-Kulaynī's informants, 'Abdullāh b. Sinān, to Kufa. It becomes clear that the text of this report travelled from Basra and Kufa.

Nevertheless, textually I cannot date these before al-Qummī and al-Sayyārī because they are contemporaneous; they might have even been received/copied from one another. The very similar nature of these reports indicates a written transmission rather than an oral transmission. It is a possibility that al-Sayyārī recorded it from al-Qummī or Ibn Jārud's *Tafsīr*, which seems to be the reference for al-Qummī's *Tafsīr*. It was then merged with the report about the shortening of al-Aḥzāb and finally redacted. The chain attached to the text might belong to the report about al-Aḥzāb. Regardless, I can only date this report back to al-Qummī.

On the other hand, it may be possible to date al-Kulaynī's variant to an earlier date because he shares a common source with al-Ṭūsī, as they both recorded their texts through 'Abdullāh b. Sinān. As I noted above, al-Kulaynī's text differs from his teacher's, thus it is obvious that he did not receive it from his teacher. However, al-Ṭūsī's text, which I study as the twelfth chain in the previous section, is certainly not a different variant. It is verbatim to al-Kulaynī's text, hence he must have copied it from *al-Kāfī* while excluding the chain. There is no way of dating these last three variants before the late third/ninth century. As I cannot trace these reports back to Ja'far al-Ṣādiq, it was more likely the case that these reports were forged in third-century Iraq, under the influence of the Sunni reports about the so-called missing Stoning Verse that was attributed to 'Umar. Because of the section of the report attributed to 'Umar on the succession narrative, this report must have become popular among the early Shi'i communities[82] of Kufa and Basra. Therefore, some sub-Shi'i factions or individuals who had a motivation to justify the fundamental Shi'i concepts of imamate and the succession of the Household of the Prophet forged these reports by way of attributing these texts to Imam Ja'far al-Ṣādiq via Shi'i transmitters.

82 For the existence of the early Shi'i communities in Kufa, see Haider, *The Origins of the Shī'a*.

Al-Shaykh al-Ṣadūq's *al-Faqīh* records the eighth text. Although this text is transmitted through Hishām b. Sālim, who also transmits one of the first reports of al-Sayyārī, the text of both variants differs. While al-Sayyārī's text is about the shortening of al-Aḥzāb, al-Ṣadūq's text is about the Stoning Verse. Al-Ṣadūq's text is almost like al-Kulaynī's version:

> I have said to Abū ʿAbdullāh (Jaʿfar al-Ṣādiq): is there stoning [penalty] in the Qur'an? He said 'yes.' I asked, 'how?' He said: 'The old man and woman (*al-shaykh wa-l-shaykha*) are to be stoned unconditionally. Indeed, they had quenched lust.'

However, unlike al-Kulaynī's version, 'if they commit adultery' (*idhā zanayā*) is dropped from the beginning of the sentence. Furthermore, this version includes a conversation between Sulaymān b. Khālid and Imam Jaʿfar al-Ṣādiq. It is possible that ʿAbdullāh b. Sinān, who reported this from Jaʿfar al-Ṣādiq, witnessed the dialogue between Sulaymān b. Khālid and Jaʿfar al-Ṣādiq. Or it could be that this section was redacted. Since the wording of the verse does not include 'if they commit adultery', it may have been dropped mistakenly or deliberately to make it appear like a different report. It does not make sense linguistically to omit the condition of stoning and only mention the punishment. If it is a case of forgery, this may also be the purpose of the inclusion of the dialogue between Sulaymān b. Khālid and Jaʿfar al-Ṣādiq, namely, to give it a context.

There would have been more deliberation on these issues but knowing that this text originally belongs to the report attributed to ʿUmar, it is almost certainly a forgery, making these considerations pointless. At the moment, it is not possible to establish the culprit for this forgery. It is improbable that the forger was al-Sayyārī because he genuinely records various reports. He could have unified them to make them more convincing, but he did not. Also, he was from Qom, but these reports originated in Kufa and Basra. It is more likely that he was genuinely interested in the subject and compiled them. It is questionable whether these collectors are responsible for the forgeries and due to the gaps in the chain of narrations, it is difficult to establish who the culprits are.

Al-Ṣadūq recorded another text, which is the ninth variant, in *ʿIlal al-sharāʾiʿ*. This text is similar to al-Qummī and the second part of al-Sayyārī's first texts. Although it does not mention the term 'Stoning Verse', it gives the wording of the verse. This wording is verbatim to al-Qummī's text and al-Sayyārī's first text. This is an interesting find because the exact wording of the verse was mentioned as the statement of Jaʿfar al-Ṣādiq. It is peculiar that Jaʿfar al-Ṣādiq did not mention that this was the missing Stoning Verse on this occasion. The chain of transmission of this variant was elevated (*marfūʿ*), meaning it did not reach the Imam. The chain of transmission analysis concurs with the textual analysis, namely, that this variant can only be traced back to Qom where *Tafsīr al-Qummī* and *Kitāb al-qirā'āt* were authored and the last traceable transmitter of this report, Sa'd b. 'Abdullāh (d. 301/913), was active.

It also reinforces the earlier position that these collectors were not responsible for the redaction or forgery. They recorded textually different variants of the same report, which works against the intent of a forger, as they would want to have textual unity in their plot. In this specific case, al-Ṣadūq recorded two textual variations of the same report because he genuinely received these varying reports.

Al-Ṣadūq's third text, which is the tenth variant, is recorded in *'Ilal al-sharā'i'*. This text is also very similar to the text al-Ṣadūq recorded in *al-Faqīh*, but there are three notable differences: (1) instead of Sulaymān b. Khālid, Ismā'īl b. Abī Khālid questions al-Ja'far; (2) the conditional clause and verb 'if they commit adultery' (*idhā zanayā*) in this variant is not dropped, and comes after '*al-shaykh wa-l-shaykha*'; and (3) there is the particle *qad* (certainly) that comes before 'Indeed, they had quenched lust' (*fa-innahumā qad qaḍayā al-shahwata*). Because *qad* is only included in *'Ilal al-sharā'i'*, the editor of the work likely interpolated it into the text.

Although the names of the individuals who questioned Ja'far al-Ṣādiq are different, the questions are the same and the responses are very similar. It is either that this topic was a hotly debated issue in the first half of the second/eighth century, hence people often questioned Ja'far al-Ṣādiq about it, or they are variants of the same report. Given the textual similarities, it is probable that this is the same variant. There may, however, be an error in the name of Ismā'īl b. Abī Khālid. This name was mentioned as Ismā'īl b. Khālid in the original text but because there was no hadith transmitter with such a name, I concluded that he must have been Ismā'īl b. Abī Khālid.

However, it could also have been Sulaymān b. Khālid, meaning that instead of Sulaymān, Ismā'īl was recorded. Since the rest of the name is the same, this is probable, especially given the fact that both variants were recorded by al-Ṣadūq, and he might have committed an editorial slip. The textual similarities in these texts also support this possibility. Be that as it may, both Sulaymān b. Khālid and Ismā'īl b. Abī Khālid lived in Kufa, and both were contemporaries. From the perspective of the chain of transmission analysis, such a possibility would have made Sulaymān b. Khālid a Common Link. However, the evidence is inconclusive, and therefore I cannot date it to earlier than the result of the chain of transmission analysis which was Muḥammad b. Ḥasan's date of death in the third/ninth century.

Following from that, because the conditional clause and verb 'if they commit adultery' (*idhā zanayā*) in this variant is not omitted, it is almost certain that this was from the original report. Hence, al-Ṣadūq made an error by omitting it. It seems it would be more of an editorial error on al-Ṣadūq's part, as it is normal to forget a word or two in the recording. Also, since it does not make sense to omit the condition of the punishment, it may not have occurred by means of oral transmission. Lastly, the addition of *qad* seems to be an error as well, since the sentence already includes *inna* for emphasis. The inclusion of an additional *qad* is doubling, therefore, it must have occurred due to an editorial error.

The eleventh text is recorded in al-Ṭūsī's *Tahdhīb*. This text is peculiarly different from other variants:

> Al-Husayn b. Saʿīd reported from Ibn Abī ʿUmayr, who reported from Ḥammād, who reported from al-Ḥalabī, who reported from Abū ʿAbdullāh, who said: 'If a man accuses his wife of adultery, he cannot call her to a mutual act of swearing (*yulāʿinuhā*) until he says, "I saw a man committing adultery with her between her legs." And if a man says to his wife, "I did not find you a virgin," and he has no evidence, he is lashed in accordance with the Islamic punishment, and is separated from his wife.'
>
> He also said, 'The Stoning Verse (*rajm*) was in the Qur'an, and the old man and old woman must be stoned to death as they fulfilled their desires.'
>
> And I asked him about the mutual act of swearing that a husband throws at his wife, denies her children and divorces her, then after that he claims that the child is his, and he disavows his previous accusations. He said, 'As for the woman, she never goes back to him, and as for the child, I would return [the child] to him (the father) should he claim him, and I do not leave his child with no inheritance. In this case, the son would inherit from the father but the father would not inherit the son, and his heritage would be for his maternal uncles. And if his father does not claim him, his maternal uncles inherit him but he does not inherit them. And if someone calls him "O son of a fornicator", he is punished with the lashing.'

It first discusses the punishment for a man who accuses his wife of adultery without evidence. It then mentions that there was the Stoning Verse in the Qur'an and then continues with the initial discussion on the husband's accusation of a wife without evidence and the status of the child in such a case. It is clear that the mentioning of the Stoning Verse is out of place, in the text: 'He said, There was the Stoning Verse in the Qur'an: old man and old woman stone them unconditionally since they had quenched their lust.' There is an interpolation in this text. The main topic of the text is about the false accusation of a wife by her husband, thus it is not related to the Stoning Verse. Yet Jaʿfar al-Ṣādiq purports to mention it out of the blue.

Furthermore, the wording of the verse is similar to the text recorded in al-Ṣadūq's *al-Faqīh* because, in both versions, *idhā zanayā* is omitted. It also continues to confirm the existence of the Stoning Verse in the Qur'an in a reworded style. However, the only difference is that this text includes 'since' (*bi-mā*) in the place of 'they are' (*fa-innahumā*) in al-Ṣadūq's text. Therefore, one possibility is that al-Ṭūsī redacted this text by a deliberate interpolation of the wording of the verse. Since he studied with Sunni scholars, especially Shāfiʿī legal scholars whose school supports the idea of a missing Stoning Verse in the context of abrogation, he might have been influenced by these ideas. Therefore, he made a deliberate effort to insert the readily available wording of the Stoning Verse in a distantly related report.

However, although this is plausible, it is not probable because there is another text also included in al-Ṭūsī's *Tahdhīb* which has a slightly different wording. Therefore, the inclusion of the different variants of the Stoning Verse in the same book makes it clear that al-Ṭūsī is not the culprit.

Either his narrator(s) or the later editors of *Tahdhīb* made this interpolation. Among the two possibilities, the former is more likely because, if it had been the later editors of *Tahdhīb*, then they would have included the same text existing in another report in *Tahdhīb*. Given that there is a two-century gap between al-Ṭūsī and his narrator, it is most probable that his narrator is the culprit. According to the chain of transmission, the narrator is deemed to be al-Ḥusayn b. Saʿīd [al-Ahwāzī] and there is a 200-year gap between the two. It is not certain how al-Ṭūsī received the variant from al-Ḥusayn b. Saʿīd. It seems to be the case that al-Ṭūsī received it in the form of a written record, not an oral transmission, and during this written transmission, the interpolation occurred. Therefore, it can only be dated to al-Ṭūsī's date of death, in the year 460/1067.

The thirteenth and last text is included in al-Qāḍī al-Nuʿmān's (d. 363/973) *Daʿāʾim al-islām*. There is no chain for this text, but the first section of it is similar to the variants in *Tafsīr al-Qummī* and the tenth variant in *Tahdhīb al-aḥkām* (*kānat Āyat al-Rajm fī al-Qurʾān*), and the ending is similar to *ʿIlal al-sharāʾiʿ* because of the inclusion of the element of '*fa-innahumā qad qaḍayā*' at the end. It is more probable that al-Qāḍī al-Nuʿmān recorded the text from al-Qummī because al-Qummī lived a generation earlier than al-Qāḍī al-Nuʿmān while al-Ṣadūq was his contemporary. Hence, there is no conclusive evidence in this regard.

The study of the textual evidence combined with the chain of transmission analysis has demonstrated that these variants can only be dated to the third/ninth century. Thus, they cannot be dated back to Imam Jaʿfar al-Ṣādiq, who died in 148/765, since there are multiple occasions of forgery, redactions and merging. Most importantly, there is an unmistakable similarity between the Sunni and Shiʿi reports related to the missing Stoning Verse. It is almost certain that Shiʿi reports were plagiarised versions of Sunni reports, similar to the report recorded in 'Abd al-Razzāq's (d. 211/827) *Muṣannaf* that I quoted at the beginning of the chapter. It may be that the Shi'i reports were based on 'Abd al-Razzāq as he lived before all the major Shi'i collectors who recorded these variants, or it may be that their sources were similar since 'Abd al-Razzāq spent time in Iraq and collected reports there. Nevertheless, it is astonishing that no pre-modern Shi'i scholar made such a connection. They ignored the outstanding textual similarities between the Sunni and Shi'i reports and even used[83] the Sunni concept of abrogation to explain the reports on the missing Stoning Verse. The only modern scholar who noticed the specific connection is al-Sayyid Abū al-Qāsim al-Khoei (d. 1992). In his *Tafṣīl al-sharī'a fī sharḥ taḥrīr al-wasīla*,[84] al-Khoei studies al-Ṣadūq's ninth variant recorded in *'Ilal al-sharā'i'* and al-Ṭūsī's tenth variant recorded in *Tahdhīb al-aḥkām*. While he considers both chains sound, he contends that Imam al-Ṣādiq must have been practising dissimulation (*taqiyya*). In other words, he gave false religious opinions because of political persecution. He acknowledges that the idea originated from the reports attributed to 'Umar and outrightly rejects the idea of a missing Stoning Verse as it amounts to the distortion of the Qur'an.[85] Yet, he falls short of considering that the Shi'i reports were deliberate forgeries that were plagiarised from Sunni reports. The dissimulation theory is not workable in this case, however, as I have noted above, since there are deliberate forgery efforts with these reports. Most importantly, it is impossible to date them back to al-Ṣādiq. As mentioned in the Introduction, Modarressi vaguely made such a connection as well. Given Modarressi's extensive traditional Islamic seminary training, it is possible that he attained his views from the prominent Shi'i scholar al-Khoei, or even from his predecessor and highly influential figure of the twentieth-century Shi'i seminary Husayn Ali Borujerdi (d. 1961).[86] However, he likely did not want to cite them as academia did not merit the scholarship of traditional Muslim scholars.[87]

83 For example, the great Twelver hadith scholar Muḥammad Bāqir Majlisī (d. 1110/1699) argues that the Stoning Verse was abrogated; the wording of this verse was removed from the Qur'an while its meaning remains intact (al-Kulaynī, *al-Kāfī*, vol. 14, p. 16).

84 al-Khoei, *Tafṣīl al-sharī'a fī sharḥ taḥrīr al-wasīla*, p. 163.

85 I discovered this information after I concluded this chapter. When I realised that there was an obvious connection between the reports attributed to 'Umar and Shi'i reports, I assumed that other scholars must have also noticed the connection and I felt obliged to reach out to some Shi'i scholars in Qom. In response to my enquiry, Sayyed Ali Reza Sadr directed me to al-Khoei's *Tafṣīl al-sharī'a*, for which I am grateful to him.

86 Burūjardī, *Nihāyat al-uṣūl*, pp. 481–5.

87 I express my gratitude to Hassan Ansari for informing me about Burūjardī's book and bringing to my attention the possibility of Burūjardī's influence over Modarressi. This occurred when I had already completed the first draft of the book.

Summary and Conclusion

The study established an uninterrupted transmission in the first and second chains of narration and suggested that the report emerged in Medina, then travelling to Kufa and Qom. In the third chain, there was a controversial figure, thus he had the motive for promoting unconventional views about the Qur'an. I considered the remaining chains defective because of the time gap between transmitters. Based on the study of the thirteen chains, only the first two chains reach Jaʿfar al-Ṣādiq. Furthermore, because these two chains are independent, it may have been possible to date them back to Jaʿfar al-Ṣādiq. However, because both were recorded in al-Sayyārī's *Kitāb al-qirāʾāt* and al-Sayyārī was known to have 'extremist' views, he has a motive to forge these reports. Therefore, based on the chain of transmission analysis alone, I could not date the variants earlier than the books they were recorded in, which is the third/ninth century.

As for the textual analysis, the first five texts were recorded in al-Sayyārī's *Kitāb al-qirāʾāt.* The first text was related to the shortening of Sūrat al-Aḥzāb after the death of the Prophet. Although this report is not directly related to the Stoning Verse, it is related indirectly since the report suggests that the missing Stoning Verse was part of Sūrat al-Aḥzāb. Furthermore, I noted cases of where two separate reports merged, namely, the shortening of Sūrat al-Aḥzāb and the Stoning Verse.

The second text was a combination of the shortening of Sūrat al-Aḥzāb, thus partially a variant of the first report, and the wording of the Stoning Verse. The reports contained contradictory information, such as the number of verses in the 'original' Sūrat al-Aḥzāb. Also, the second variant suggested that Sūrat al-Baqara was shortened, and this information was not available in the first variant. The wording of the Stoning Verse was identical to the reports attributed to 'Umar. More specifically, they were identical to the Saʿīd b. al-Musayyab clusters studied in Chapter 4. I dated those reports to death of 'Umar, which is 26/644, and these reports were in circulation in Basra after that. Al-Sayyārī's source for this variant was Ibn Sayf, who was active in Basra. Therefore, this particular report is a forgery, and was plagiarised from the reports attributed to 'Umar. The third text does not have an independent chain. The fourth text was again about the shortening of Sūrat al-Aḥzāb, but the number of the 'original' verses was 700, less than the previous numbers, thus contradicting the earlier texts.

The sixth text, recorded in *al-Kāfī*, together with the rest of the variants, only included the element of the Stoning Verse and there was no mention of the shortening of Sūrat al-Aḥzāb. Therefore, it became more convincing that these two elements were deliberately merged into a single report. The wording of the *Kitāb al-qirā'āt* variant is structurally more similar to the seventh variant in *Tafsīr al-Qummī*, which may suggest a common source. However, because the authorship of *Tafsīr al-Qummī* is debated, there was no chain for this variant. For these reasons, I could not date these variants to any earlier date than the books in which they were recorded.

In the eighth text in al-Ṣadūq's *al-Faqīh*, Hishām b. Sālim, who transmits this report, also transmits one of the reports recorded by al-Sayyārī. The texts, however, are not similar. Thus, no textual interdependence could have enabled me to date these variants to his date of death.

Al-Ṣadūq's other variant, that is, the ninth variant in *'Ilal al-sharā'i'*, did not mention the term 'Stoning Verse'. Instead, it provided the wording of it, and the wording followed al-Qummī's text and al-Sayyārī's first text verbatim. The chain of narration analysis concurred with the textual analysis, that this variant could only be traced back to Qom, where *Tafsīr al-Qummī* and *Kitāb al-qirā'āt* were authored, and the last traceable transmitter of this report, Sa'd b. 'Abdullāh (d. 301/913), was active. The tenth text recorded in *'Ilal al-sharā'i'* was similar to the text in al-Ṣadūq's *al-Faqīh*.

In the eleventh text, I uncovered a blatant case of interpolation. The text of the variant is about a case of unsubstantiated accusation levelled by a husband against his wife. In the middle of this text, the Stoning Verse was implanted. This version is similar to the text in al-Ṣadūq's *al-Faqīh* because 'if they commit adultery' (*idhā zanayā*) is omitted from the text. This forgery must have been committed before the text reached al-Ṭūsī, but I could only date it to al-Ṭūsī's date of death, in the year 460/1067.

Al-Ṭūsī's text, which studied as the twelfth variant, was the same as Kulaynī's text. Therefore, he copied it from *al-Kāfī* while excluding the chain. The thirteenth and last text in al-Qāḍī al-Nu'mān's *Da'ā'im al-islām* did not have a chain, but I studied it in the textual analysis section. Based on the similarities between this version and al-Qummī's version, and because al-Qummī was a generation older than al-Qāḍī al-Nu'mān, he received the variant from al-Qummī.

Based on the study of all variants, it is impossible to date these variants before the late third/ninth century. As I cannot trace these reports back to Ja'far al-Ṣādiq, it was more likely the case that these reports were forged in third/ninth-century Iraq, under the influence of the Sunni reports about the so-called missing Stoning Verse that was attributed to 'Umar. The only common element in these variants is the wording of the Stoning Verse. Because of the element of the report attributed to 'Umar on the succession narrative, this report must have become popular among early Shi'i communities of Kufa and Basra. Therefore, some sub-Shi'i factions or individuals who had a compelling motivation to justify the fundamental Shiʿi concept of imamate and the succession of the Household of the Prophet forged these reports by way of attributing these texts to Imam Jaʿfar al-Ṣādiq via Shiʿi transmitters.

CHAPTER 6

Distorting the Book of God

On the Nature of Shiʿi Reports on the Distortion Narrative

A common challenge in the study of Shiʿi reports on distortion, like the ones in al-Sayyārī's book, lies in the lack of any variants. Despite the considerable attention given to Shiʿi narratives concerning the Qur'an's distortion, most of the existing reports lack any workable variations. Unlike the reports I studied in the previous chapters, the number of Shiʿi variants on the distortion is limited. For example, there are some reports of the alleged distortion of the Qur'an in al-Sayyārī's book, but it is difficult to locate them in other Shiʿi sources such as al-Kulaynī's *al-Kāfī* or al-ʿAyyāshī's *Tafsīr*. Most of these reports are in the form of an addition of the names of the Imams and the daughter of the Prophet to the existing verses of the Qur'an, but they have no variants in other Shiʿi collections. The lack of variants may be related to the usual problem with Twelver Shiʿi reports, that because of their minority status, Shiʿis were mainly an underground movement until the reign of the Buyids. Only after the rise of pro-Shiʿi Buyids in 333–4/945 did Shiʿi scholars have the opportunity to express their religious views more openly and teach their understanding of Islam to their followers freely until 447/1055.[1] Therefore, the lack of political protection and support might have hindered the collection and preservation of their reports. Furthermore, the minority status afforded to Shiʿis also affected their circulation of reports as they could not widely distribute their reports simply because they lacked the numbers.

Given the vast number of reports in Shiʿi hadith collections, however, this may not be the only reason. Although Shiʿis only found the opportunity to teach, widely circulate and record their reports in the fourth/tenth

1 Baker, *Medieval Islamic Sectarianism*, ch. 4.

century, more than a century later than Sunnis, they still preserved their reports in secret and transmitted them in major Shiʿi centres such as Kufa and Qom. Therefore, it is possible that the lack of any variants of the relevant reports may be indicative of a forgery, especially given my conclusion in Chapter 5 that some Sunni reports were plagiarised and then tampered with by some Shiʿis in pursuit of a sectarian agenda. Once the precedence was set, it was only natural that others would follow in order to achieve the desired objective.

The textual evidence strongly supports this possibility since most claims about the distortion of the Qur'an involves the insertion of the names of ʿAlī and the other Imams within the existing verses. There just so happens to be no change in the rest of the verses of the Qur'an. Indeed, if there had been such tampering with the verses of the Qur'an, there should have been more textual evidence. This evidence should have been in the form of paraphrasing the Qur'an's verses.

Simply inserting the names of the Household of the Prophet in some of the verses of the Qur'an, and keeping the rest of the verses intact, raises a great deal of suspicion. In addition, the lack of variation between the reports increases the doubt that, rather than a distortion of the Qur'an, there was a process of fabrication of reports carried out both individually and collectively for sectarian reasons. Most of those reports, which are included in Shiʿi commentaries[2] as verses referring to Imams, give an important indication of the source of such fabrications. In other words, Shiʿi commentaries were presented as reports attributed to the Imams. These commentaries inspired some sectarian Shiʿis to turn them into reports by editing and integrating the commentaries into the main body of the verses of the Qur'an. There is no certainty, however, that the source of these commentaries were the Imams.

The Connection between Hadith Forgery and Shiʿi Identity

Also, it is dubious whether al-Sayyārī forged all these traditions himself. It is more probable that he collected them from some Shiʿis of Kufa who were trying to preserve their Shiʿi identity in the third/ninth century as such unconventional views were rampant in Kufa during this period.[3] This hypothesis is based on my findings from Chapter 5, that al-Sayyārī had a genuine interest in these types of reports. He probably collected these reports from Kufa, where there must have been a sectarian attempt to preserve and promote a certain version of Shiʿi identity.

Thanks to Najam Haider's significant findings,[4] it is clear that from as early as the second/eighth century, a distinct Shiʿi identity emerged

2 For example, see al-Kulaynī, *al-Kāfī*, vol. 1, pp. 412–17.

3 Modarressi, *Crisis and Consolidation in the Formative Period of Shīʿite Islam.*

4 Haider, *The Origins of the Shīʿa.*

in Kufa. Edmund Hayes and Mushegh Asatryan[5] have debated on the nature of the Shi'i community.[6] Asatryan argued that the Shi'i community consisted of a loose unity, and was therefore more imagined than real. Hayes, building upon Etan Kohlber's work,[7] made a convincing case for the Imami Shi'i community 'not just as an imagined, symbolic community (which they certainly were), but also as a community defined, structured[8] and bounded by concrete social interactions, and, crucially, by certain institutions, which developed over time'.[9] The research at hand seems to be furthering Hayes's argument, which was also confirmed by Haider, namely, that Shi'is had a distinct identity and were a community in the sense that Hayes defines it. They were propagating their theological views and even resorting to forgery to make a stronger case for their cause.

It is only natural for some Shi'is to think that one of the ways to preserve and promote this identity was to legitimise the succession of the Shi'i Imams along with the concept of imamate. Therefore, towards the third/ninth century, these reports emerged and were promoted among some sections of the Shi'i community in Kufa. As Hossein Modarressi demonstrated, these were not only the 'extremist' (*ghulāt*) Shi'is, but also the traditionists who paid great importance to the reports attributed to the Imams.[10]

In a similar vein, in al-Kulaynī's *al-Kāfī*, the style of these types of reports transforms into commentarial form. These reports often include the expression 'I asked Abū 'Abdullāh or Imam Ja'far al-Ṣādiq about the Word of God that . . .' (*sa'altu Abā 'Abdullāh 'an qawli Allāh . . .*). The expression is followed by the verse in question, which in this example is 'Among those, We created a group of people who guide with the truth and act justly according to it' (Q. 7:181), along with the response of the Imam, such as 'he said, they are the Imams' (*qāla hum al-a'immatu*).[11] Some traditions include the expression 'this is how it was revealed' (*hākadhā nazalat*)[12] and others do not include any explanation except the addition of the names of the Imams in the verses of the Qur'an.[13]

5 Asatryan, 'The Good, the Bad, and the Heretic in Early Islamic History'.
6 On the Imami community, see also Newman, *The Formative Period of Twelver Shī'ism*; Bar-Asher, *Scripture and Exegesis in Early Imāmī Shiism.*
7 Kohlberg, 'Imam and Community in the Pre-Ghayba Period'.
8 See also Hayes, *Agents of the Hidden Imam*, p. 18 and *passim.*
9 Hayes, 'The Institutions of the Shīʿī Imāmate', p. 189.
10 Modarressi, *Crisis and Consolidation in the Formative Period of Shī'ite Islam*, p. 129 and *passim.*
11 al-Kulaynī, *al-Kāfī*, vol. 1, p. 414.
12 al-Kulaynī, *al-Kāfī*, vol. 1, p. 414.
13 al-Kulaynī, *al-Kāfī*, vol. 1, p. 414.

Some other reports include the distinct expression that Gabriel revealed this verse to Muhammad as such (*nazala Jibrāʾīl bi-hādhihi al-āyati ʿalā Muḥammadin hākadhā*)[14] followed by the Qur'anic verse (in this case Q. 2:90) with the inclusion of the name of the Imam (*fī ʿAlī*). These kinds of reports are only recorded in al-Kulaynī's *al-Kāfī*, however. As we know, the main transmitter to al-Kulaynī is al-Sayyārī, thus they return to him. As there are no alternative variants it seems that only al-Sayyārī was interested in these kinds of reports, or that the other transmission lines did not survive. It is meaningful to note that al-Kulaynī included these reports in the section on reports proving the imamate in Qur'anic commentary. Since he assumed that they are part of the same commentary genre, as a seasoned traditionalist, he might have also assumed that they were authentic reports ascribed to the Imams. Al-Sayyārī believed, however, that they were not commentaries but genuine reports about the distortion of the Qur'an, and he thus collected them from various reporters.

Isnād-cum-matn analysis cannot analyse these types of reports due to two significant issues. Firstly, the verses mentioned in these reports are textually identical versions of the verses included in the standard Qur'anic codex. The only additions are the names of the infallibles, mainly referring to ʿAlī's name, along with the words of guardianship (*wilāya*) and leadership (*imāma*). The remaining sections of the verses are identical, without even the slightest alteration. Secondly, the transmission lines do not differ. In other words, aside from the variants transmitted via al-Sayyārī, there are no other variants of the same reports with different chains of narration. These kinds of reports are attributed to either Imams al-Bāqir or Jaʿfar al-Ṣādiq, and the style of the reports indicate that they delivered lectures on the Qur'an to their students. Therefore, other students should have heard the same reports and then transmitted them.

It is also important to notice that if it is the case, these reports were not forged out of nothing, but rather seem to be replicas of other existing reports which explicitly state that they are the commentaries by the Imams. In any case, I found two reports about the distortion that may be suitable for *isnād-cum-matn* analysis. As noted above, although several reports are related to the distortion of the Qur'an, the variants are scarce. Aside from reports collected by al-Kulaynī and al-Sayyārī, which are not suitable for *isnād-cum-matn* analysis for the reasons stated above, two explicit reports may be analysed using *isnād-cum-matn* analysis since these reports have some sort of independent texts that do not contain lengthy amounts of Qur'anic verses.

14 For example, see al-Kulaynī, *al-Kāfī*, vol. 1, p. 417.

The Imam al-Bāqir Cluster

One such report is attributed to the fifth Imam, Muḥammad al-Bāqir. The report seems to be based on a hadith about the legacy of the Prophet, which is basically an interpretation of the famous prophetic report about the 'hadith of the two weighty things' (*ḥadīth al-thaqalayn*). The original report is widely attested through Sunni and Shi'i chains. It refers to the legacy of the Prophet and urges his followers to follow the Qur'an and his descendants (*ahl al-bayt*) after him. However, in some versions recorded in later sources, the words 'tradition' (*sunna*)[15] replaced *'itratī ahl baytī*. Still, in other canonical Sunni works, the expression *'itratī ahl baytī* is mentioned:

> I saw the Messenger of God during the Pilgrimage, on the Day of 'Arafa (the ninth day of Dhū al-Ḥijja). He was mounted on his camel al-Qaṣwā' and giving a sermon. He said: 'O people! I have left two things among you, which if you hold fast to, you shall not go astray: The Book of God and my family, the people of my house.'[16]

This report seems to support the claim of 'Alī and his descendants, through his only daughter, Fāṭima, for the succession of the Prophet. Despite its religious and political implications, it made it into the canonical Sunni sources through several different chains. The report attributed to al-Bāqir seems to be a commentary on this report as it cites the original report and then states how Muslims fail to follow these two important sources that the Prophet left behind for the guidance of the Muslim community. However, the report attributed to al-Bāqir also includes additions to this seemingly original report:

> It was narrated to us by 'Alī b. Muḥammad, on the authority of Qāsim b. Muḥammad, on the authority of Sulaymān b. Dāwūd, on the authority of Yaḥyā b. Ādam, on the authority of Sharīk, on the authority of Jābir, who said: 'Abū Ja'far (Imam al-Bāqir) said, The Messenger of God announced to his Companions at Minā that 'O people! I am leaving among you two weighty things (*thaqalayn*). If you follow them, you will never go astray. The Book of God and my progeny; my family. These two will never separate until they return to me by the pool [in Paradise].' He then said, 'O people! I am leaving among you the sanctities of God: The Book of God,

15 al-Hindī, *Kanz al-'ummāl fī sunan al-aqwāl wa-l-af'āl*, vol. 1, p. 187. As a matter of fact, on the same page, al-Hindī also mentions a variant of the report, which includes the expression *'itratī ahl baytī*.

16 Tirmidhī, *Jāmi'*, vol. 5, p. 621.

> my progeny and the Kaaba, the Sacred House.' Abū Ja'far then said: 'As for the Book of God, they have distorted (*ḥarrafū*) it; as for the Kaaba, they destroyed it; and as for the progeny, they killed them. They have abandoned these trusts of God.'[17]

It seems that al-Bāqir combined the two separate hadiths of the Prophet and added his comments to them. The study of the reports attributed to the Prophet about his legacy is critical, but not directly related to the discussion. What is most relevant is the last section of the report, in which al-Bāqir seemingly claims that the early Muslims abandoned the legacy of the Prophet by killing his progeny, destroying the Kaaba and distorting the Qur'an. There is no historical dispute about the occurrence of the first two events, namely, the killing of the progeny of the Prophet and the destruction of the Kaaba soon after the death of the Prophet.

The soldiers of the Umayyad ruler Yazīd b. Mu'āwiya (r. 60/680–64/683) massacred Ḥusayn, the grandson of the Prophet, and most of his family in 60/680 at the Battle of Karbala. The Umayyads then attacked Medina and Mecca in 64/683–4 to subdue the Medinans and Meccans who had pledged allegiance to 'Abdullāh b. al-Zubayr (r. 63/683–73/692). In the heat of the siege of Mecca, Yazīd's army targeted the Kaaba with catapults and burnt it.[18] It is almost certain that the reports refer to these two events. Therefore, this strengthens the argument that al-Bāqir was commenting on the tradition of the Prophet in light of important historical events. The distortion of the Qur'an is more problematic, however. There is no specific historical event he could have referred to as the alteration of the Quran. It may refer to the third caliph 'Uthmān's standardisation of the Qur'anic codex wherein the committee led by Zayd b. Thābit produced the official version, and 'Uthmān ordered the destruction of alternative copies, which were held by other scribes of the Prophet.

The text here is specific. It does not say that the Qur'an was burnt or destroyed, rather it states that the Qur'an was distorted. Given that the Shi'i Imams did not dispute the authenticity of 'Uthmān's standard version,[19] it is difficult to discern whether the reports refer to this particular event. It seems that the report does not refer to a specific event but to a process in which the meaning or the wording of the Qur'an was tampered with.

Moreover, it is also possible that al-Bāqir's reference alludes to al-Ḥajjāj b. Yūsuf's redaction of the Qur'an under 'Abd al-Malik. The events of Ḥusayn's killing and the attacks on Mecca and Medina occurred at the outset of the 680s. The rhetorical parallelism within this context suggests

17 al-Qummī, *Baṣā'ir al-darajāt*, p. 414.

18 Donner, *Muhammad and the Believers*, pp. 178–81.

19 Kara, 'Suppression of 'Alī Ibn Abī Ṭālib's Codex'.

that the distortion of the Qur'an, as mentioned by al-Bāqir, transpired within a corresponding timeframe.[20] Al-Bāqir, who lived 57/677–114/733, likely had access to first-hand information about these events.[21] However, Sinai provides a detailed analysis of al-Ḥajjāj b. Yūsuf's redaction of the Qur'an wherein he downplays the hype surrounding it.[22] Therefore, the account of al-Ḥajjāj b. Yūsuf's redaction is subject to dispute and seems to pertain primarily to the addition of diacritical vowels in the codex. In any case, I would need to examine the variants closely to understand these reports better, especially what they mean, and if they can be traced back to al-Bāqir.

Chain of Transmission Analysis

There are four reports attributed to the fifth Imam, al-Bāqir, suggesting that the Qur'an was distorted. These numbers are less than the number of variants studied in previous chapters, and I have already made a case that it may be more rewarding to work with reports with many variants. However, if extracting meaningful historical information is possible, it is also feasible to work with fewer.[23]

Three of these reports were recorded in Muḥammad b. al-Ḥasan al-Ṣaffār's (d. 290/903) *Baṣā'ir al-darajāt.* One of them is recorded in 'Allāma Majlisī's (d. 1110/1699) *Biḥār al-anwār.* Although the latter is a much later hadith collection, he might have collected an undetected variant. Therefore, there is merit in including this variant in the chain of transmission analysis. According to the variants, three narrators received the variants from al-Bāqir, and then these reports reached a written source. These transmitters were Sa'd al-Iskāf and Jābir. The third informant was mentioned as 'a man', thus he was an unknown person. Furthermore, there seems to be no Common Links or Partial Common Links (PCLs). Jābir seems to transmit it to two different transmitters, but it is not certain if this chain is the same as what al-Ṣaffār recorded in *Baṣā'ir al-darajāt.* The textual analysis should be able to reach a definitive conclusion on this. There are only two transmitters between Jābir and

20 I wish to express my gratitude to the anonymous reviewer for bringing this possibility to my attention.

21 Kohlberg and Amir-Moezzi investigated this prospect, aided by circumstantial evidence, aiming to present a potential scenario of Qur'anic distortion in al-Sayyārī, *Revelation and Falsification*, pp. 18–23. Further, Powers previously made a similar case about al-Ḥajjāj b. Yūsuf's redaction in Powers, 'Sinless, Sonless and Seal of Prophets', pp. 406–8.

22 Sinai, 'When Did the Consonantal Skeleton of the Quran Reach Closure? Part I', pp. 278–85.

23 I make a case for working with fewer variants in Kara, 'The Collection of the Qur'ān in the Early Shī'ite Discourse', pp. 375–406.

Majlisī, and it is known that Majlisī often quotes from *Baṣā'īr al-darajāt* in his *Biḥār al-anwār*, sometimes without even mentioning his source.[24] I will only be able to confirm if Jābir is a Common Link at the end of our study. Lastly, the chain of the second variant included the name of Jābir and the Prophet in its chain, but it is obvious in this set of variants that al-Bāqir narrated a prophetic tradition and added his commentary at the end. Because of my focus on the part of the report that al-Bāqir relates, I treat him as the source of the report.

The first chain[25] was recorded in Muḥammad b. al-Ḥasan al-Ṣaffār's (d. 290/903) *Baṣā'īr al-darajāt.*[26] Al-Ṣaffār was one of the most prominent Shi'i scholars of Qom, and he was a companion of the eleventh Imam, Ḥasan al-'Askarī (d. 260/874), along with having taught the famous Shi'i hadith collector al-Kulaynī. He was a client of the famous Ash'arī tribe, whose members were influential in Kufa and Qom.[27] He received the variant from 'Alī b. Muḥammad [b. 'Abdullāh al-Bandār] of Qom.[28] He was also a teacher of al-Kulaynī and transmitted reports from al-Sayyārī.[29] There is no date of death for him, but because he narrated reports to al-Sayyārī (d. mid- or late third/ninth century) and taught al-Kulaynī (d. 329/941), he might have been a contemporary of both. Therefore, it is possible that he transmitted the report to al-Ṣaffār, who died in 290/903.

He received the variant from Qāsim b. Muḥammad [al-Iṣfahānī or al-Qummī].[30] There is little information about him in biographical evaluations, but al-Najāshī considered him reliable.[31] He was active in Isfahan and Qom and it appears that 'Alī b. Muḥammad was also active in Qom. Thus, he could have transmitted the report to 'Alī b. Muḥammad. He reported the variant from Sulaymān b. Dāwūd [al-Munqarī] of Basra, who reportedly used the nickname al-Shāzakūnī. He was evaluated differently in Shi'i sources, and was considered reliable by al-Najāshī, but al-Najāshī also noted that he did not investigate Sulaymān b. Dāwūd thoroughly. He was active in Basra and narrated reports from the companions of the sixth Imam, Ja'far al-Ṣādiq.[32] However, his activities in Basra were related to his studies and

24 Kara, *In Search of Ali Ibn Abi Talib's Codex*, pp. 97–8.

25 al-Qummī, *Baṣā'ir al-darajāt*, p. 413.

26 Amir-Moezzi was one of the earliest scholars to study the work and its reports; see Amir-Moezzi, *The Divine Guide in Early Shi'ism*. Andrew Newman also examined the work at length; see Newman, *The Formative Period of Twelver Shī'ism*, pp. 67–93.

27 Newman, *The Formative Period of Twelver Shī'ism*, p. 67; Kara, *In Search of Ali Ibn Abi Talib's Codex*, p. 99.

28 Al-Khoei undertakes a lengthy and compelling study in this regard; al-Khoei, *Mu'jam rijāl al-ḥadīth*, vol. 13, pp. 126–35.

29 al-Khoei, *Mu'jam rijāl al-ḥadīth*, vol. 13, pp. 140–1.

30 al-Khoei, *Mu'jam rijāl al-ḥadīth*, vol. 15, pp. 35–7.

31 al-Najāshī, *Rijāl*, p. 315.

32 al-Najāshī, *Rijāl*, pp. 184–5.

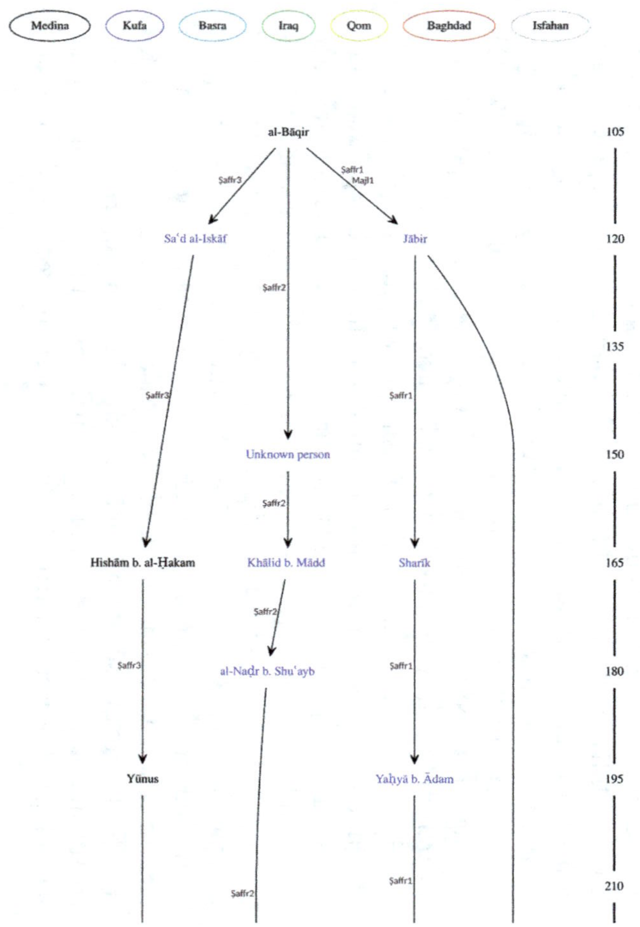
Medina
Kufa
Basra
Iraq
Qom
Baghdad
Isfahan
al-Bāqir
Ṣaffr3
Ṣaffr1
Majl1
Sa'd al-Iskāf
Jābir
Ṣaffr2
Ṣaffr3
Ṣaffr1
Unknown person
Ṣaffr2
Hishām b. al-Ḥakam
Khālid b. Mādd
Sharīk
Ṣaffr2
Ṣaffr3
al-Naḍr b. Shu'ayb
Ṣaffr1
Yūnus
Yaḥyā b. Ādam
Ṣaffr2
Ṣaffr1
105
120
135
150
165
180
195
210

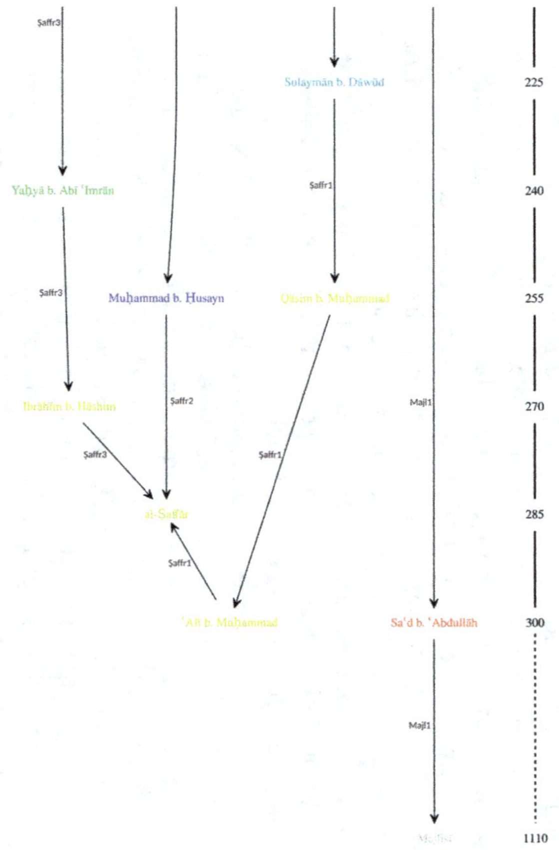

Diagram 6 Available online at: https://edin.ac/4aj8FVJ

he eventually settled in Isfahan.[33] According to Ibn al-Ghaḍā'irī (d. fifth/eleventh century), he was a weak narrator.[34] Majlisī also echoed this position, that Sulaymān b. Dāwūd was a weak transmitter,[35] possibly under the influence of al-Ghaḍā'irī. However, modern-era Shi'i scholars suspect the authenticity of Ibn al-Ghaḍā'irī's *Rijāl* or *al-Ḍu'afā'*. They argue that he was not the author of this book, but it was later attributed to him.[36] Further, al-Khoei also refutes Ibn al-Ghaḍā'irī's evaluation of Sulaymān b. Dāwūd; the former considered him reliable but rejected the idea that he used the nickname al-Shāzakūnī.[37] As he reported from the companions of Ja'far al-Ṣādiq, he might have been active in the second half of the second century. Up to this point, this report was probably circulating in Basra and Qom.

Sulaymān b. Dāwūd received it from Yaḥyā b. Ādam (d. 203/818),[38] who was based in Kufa but also travelled to Baghdad for learning. He was a prominent scholar and hadith collector, and reportedly died at the age of seventy. According to Sunni and Shi'i sources, he did not follow a particular school of thought. Because Sunni scholars considered him reliable, it was unlikely that they thought he was Shi'i; even Shi'i sources do not claim him to be a Shi'i. He was known to have criticised the opinions of Abū Ḥanīfa and Mālik.[39] He is quite an unusual person to report such a pro-Shi'i narration, but because he was a resident of Kufa, it is probable that he heard it from Shi'i transmitters and reported it to Sulaymān b. Dāwūd. In this case, the report could be traced back to Kufa.

Yaḥyā b. Ādam received it from Sharīk [b. 'Abdullāh al-Nakha'ī] (d. 177/794), who was a resident of Kufa. There were conflicting reports about his affiliations – some considered him Sunni, while others held that he was pro-'Alī.[40] Nevertheless, he lived in Kufa at the time and could have transmitted the variant to Yaḥyā b. Ādam. Sharīk received the variant from Jābir [b. Yazīd al-Ju'fī] (d. 128/756), who was one of the second-generation Muslims, as well as a great Shi'i scholar and hadith narrator of his time. He was one of the most prominent companions of the fifth and sixth Imams. He was born in Yemen but resided in Kufa. He would travel to Medina to learn from

33 al-Baghdādī, *Tārīkh Baghdād*, vol. 9, p. 42.

34 al-Ghaḍā'irī, *Rijāl Ibn al-Ghaḍā'irī*, p. 89.

35 Majlisī, *al-Wajīza fī al-rijāl*, p. 89; al-Khoei, *Mu'jam rijāl al-ḥadīth*, vol. 9, p. 269.

36 See Kara, *In Search of Ali Ibn Abi Talib's Codex*, pp. 135–6.

37 al-Khoei, *Mu'jam rijāl al-ḥadīth*, vol. 9, pp. 268–70.

38 In the text, he was mentioned as Yaḥyā b. Adīm; however, this seems to be a typographical error.

39 Kallek, 'YAHYÂ b. ÂDEM', p. 234; al-Khoei, *Mu'jam rijāl al-ḥadīth*, vol. 19, p. 21; al-Dhahabī, *Siyar a'lām al-nubalā'*, vol. 9, pp. 523–5.

40 al-Dhahabī, *Siyar a'lām al-nubalā'*, vol. 8, pp. 200–5; al-Khoei, *Mu'jam rijāl al-ḥadīth*, vol. 4, pp. 27–9.

the sixth Imam, al-Bāqir, but despite his prominence among Shiʿi scholars, some have criticised him for harbouring extremist views.[41]

Finally, Jābir received it from al-Bāqir. Given the strong connection between the two, as mentioned in the biographical literature, along with the time and locations wherein Jābir lived, there is no problem with him having received the report from al-Bāqir. Based on this chain, it seems that this variant originated in Medina, where al-Bāqir resided, and was then spread in Kufa through Jābir, Sharīk and Yaḥyā b. Ādam, and then finally travelled to Basra and Qom.

The second chain[42] was also found in al-Ṣaffār's *Baṣāʾir al-darajāt*. He was a resident of Qom. He received the report from Muḥammad b. Ḥusayn [b. Abī al-Khaṭṭāb] (d. 262/875), who was a prominent Shiʿi scholar and resided in Kufa. He was also a prolific hadith transmitter and was graded as reliable.[43] There is no reason to be suspicious of al-Ṣaffār having received the report. Muḥammad b. Ḥusayn received it from one of his informants, al-Naḍr b. Shuʿayb. I studied Naḍr b. Shuʿayb elsewhere,[44] and determined that he was an unknown (*majhūl*) person as there is only indirect information available on him, which is based on his position in the chains of transmission. His reports are present in some of the major Shiʿi sources. Muḥammad b. Ḥusayn often reported from Naḍr b. Shuʿayb, who reported from ʿAbd al-Ghaffār al-Jāzī and Khālid b. Mādd al-Qalānisī. Based on his relations with other transmitters, he might have lived between 140/757 and 210/825.

He narrated the tradition from Khālid b. Mādd al-Qalānisī, who was a well-reputed companion of the sixth and seventh Imams. He was a resident of Kufa and had a book of hadith compilation although some objected to his reliability.[45] Since Naḍr b. Shuʿayb's connections were from Kufa, he might have been a resident of Kufa. Nevertheless, as he is an unknown person, it is pointless to further analyse. The fact that Khālid b. Mādd al-Qalānisī's source was also an unknown person (*rajulin*) makes this chain even more problematic. Therefore, this chain can only be dated back to Muḥammad b. Ḥusayn's date of death, in the year 262/875.

The third chain[46] was also found in al-Ṣaffār's *Baṣāʾir al-darajāt*. He received the variant from Ibrāhīm b. Hāshim [al-Qummī], who was the father of the famous ʿAlī b. Ibrāhīm al-Qummī, the author of *Tafsīr al-Qummī*. Ibrāhīm b. Hāshim was born in Kufa but then moved to Qom and he was

41 al-Khoei, *Muʿjam rijāl al-ḥadīth*, vol. 4, pp. 336–46.
42 al-Qummī, *Baṣāʾir al-darajāt*, p. 414.
43 Kara, *In Search of Ali Ibn Abi Talib's Codex*, p. 108.
44 Kara, *In Search of Ali Ibn Abi Talib's Codex*, pp.110–13.
45 al-Najāshī, *Rijāl*, p. 149.
46 al-Qummī, *Baṣāʾir al-darajāt*, p. 414.

considered reliable and narrated numerous reports. Some believed he was the first transmitter who disseminated Kufan reports in Qom.[47] He was also a companion of the ninth Imam, al-Jawād (d. 220/835).[48] No date of death was mentioned for him, but his son lived through the second half of the third/ninth century and died around the first half of the fourth/tenth century.

Therefore, he probably lived in the first half of the third/ninth century and possibly died towards the end of the second half of the century. This possibility is strengthened because he was a companion of the ninth Imam, al-Jawād, who was assassinated in 220/835. Thus, Ibrāhīm b. Hāshim was a contemporary of al-Ṣaffār. Because they both lived in Qom, al-Ṣaffār probably received this report from Ibrāhīm b. Hāshim. If this can be established, Ibrāhīm b. Hāshim should then also be responsible for spreading this report from Kufa to Qom.

Ibrāhīm b. Hāshim received the report from Yaḥyā b. Abī 'Imrān, whom al-Khoei identifies as [al-Yaḥyā b. Abī 'Imrān] Ḥamadānī. He was a reliable transmitter and thought to be an agent of Imam al-Jawād.[49] He was active in Iraq, where he could have transmitted the report to Ibrāhīm b. Hāshim. Although there is no information about his date of death, the knowledge that he was a companion of Imam al-Jawād provides an important clue as to his activity date, which was probably in in the first half of the third/ninth century. Therefore, he might have been a contemporary of Ibrāhīm b. Hāshim and could have received the report from him. Yaḥyā b. Abī 'Imrān also received the report from Yūnus [b. 'Abd al-Raḥmān] (d. 208/823–4).

Interestingly, Yūnus transmitted another report on the same subject, which I discussed in Chapter 5. Al-Kulaynī (d. 328/939 or 329/940) recorded the sixth variant of Chapter 5 on the authority of Yūnus, but because of the time gap between the two, I remain cautious with that chain. The chain at hand, however, seems to be a healthier one. As I noted, Yūnus was a client based in Medina and a companion of Imams al-Kāẓim and al-Riḍā. He authored many books and was known to have supported al-Riḍā during the internal uproar caused by Waqfiyya's refusal to accept al-Riḍā's imamate and he was among the 'people of consensus'. Yaḥyā b. Abī 'Imrān could have received the variant during his visits to Medina for pilgrimage or simply for seeking knowledge and tradition.

Yūnus received the variant from Hishām b. al-Ḥakam (d. 179/795–6), who was one of his teachers. Hishām was a famous theologian and companion of Imams al-Ṣādiq and al-Kāẓim. He possessed well-known debating skills in theology and was active in Medina, Kufa, Baghdad and Basra.[50]

47 al-Najāshī, *Rijāl*, p. 16.

48 al-Khoei, *Mu'jam rijāl al-ḥadīth*, vol. 1, pp. 289–91.

49 al-Khoei, *Mu'jam rijāl al-ḥadīth*, vol. 21, pp. 28–30.

50 al-Khoei, *Mu'jam rijāl al-ḥadīth*, vol. 20, pp. 297–323; al-Najāshī, *Rijāl*, pp. 433–4.

He received the variant from Sa'd al-Iskāf, who was a resident of Kufa and a client. It was believed that he was a companion of Imam al-Bāqir; however, some scholars debated his reliability. In his evaluation, al-Najāshī perplexingly stated that 'he knows and denies'.[51] However, al-Khoei explains what al-Najāshī meant, 'he reports traditions which contradict common sense',[52] meaning he reports some extremist reports. According to al-Khoei, however, this statement does not contradict Sa'd al-Iskāf's reliability. There is no date of death for him, but because he was a companion of al-Bāqir, who died in 114/732, he was likely active in the first quarter of the second/eighth century, and possibly even before. Because he was a companion of al-Bāqir, he might have heard the report from him. The analysis of the third chain shows that this particular variant originated in Medina, travelled between Medina and Kufa and was finally transmitted to Qom by Ibrāhīm b. Hāshim.

Majlisī's (d. 1110/1699) *Biḥār al-anwār* recorded the fourth chain.[53] Given the date of his death, it is obvious that he did not receive the reports personally but compiled them from more than 400 older Shi'i and Sunni works. *Biḥār al-anwār* was a response to the Safavid-era needs of the Shi'i society, which was forming a factional Shi'i identity under powerful political patronage. Therefore, the religious sources needed to respond to many aspects of life from a Shi'i perspective, and this was one of the motivations for Majlisī to compile his massive 25-volume work (contemporary prints published as many as 110 volumes) that included around 100,000 reports.

Majlisī receives the report from the third/ninth-century scholar Sa'd b. 'Abdullāh [al-Ash'arī] (d. 301/913), who was discussed in Chapter 5. He was a very prominent hadith collector and scholar, being active in both Baghdad and Qom. He was a contemporary of al-Ṣaffār and wrote many books, including a biographical work. Majlisī probably copied this variant from one of his books. His statement 'with his chain of transmission'[54] makes this possibility palpable. However, he did not express his source clearly. Furthermore, the chain Majlisī cited contains only one person before reaching al-Bāqir: Jābir [b. Yazīd] al-Ju'fī (d. 128/756). The time gap between Sa'd b. 'Abdullāh and Jābir al-Ju'fī is almost two centuries, hence it is impossible for the former to have received it from the latter. It may have been the case that Majlisī knew the other individuals in the chain and summarised it by removing other names, but there is no evidence for this. Therefore, there is no way to date this chain further than Sa'd b. 'Abdullāh's date of death, 301/913.

51 al-Najāshī, *Rijāl*, p. 178.
52 al-Khoei, *Mu'jam rijāl al-ḥadīth*, vol. 9, p. 72.
53 Majlisī, *Biḥār al-anwār*, vol. 97, pp. 140–1.
54 Majlisī, *Biḥār al-anwār*, vol. 97, pp. 140–1.

Out of the four chains of transmission, three of them were recorded in al-Ṣaffār's *Baṣā'ir al-darajāt*, and one of them was recorded in Majlisī's *Biḥār al-anwār*. Out of the three reports recorded in al-Ṣaffār's *Baṣā'ir al-darajāt*, two of them, namely, the first and third reports, can be dated back to al-Bāqir. If this is confirmed in the textual analysis, then al-Bāqir becomes both a Common Link and the source of this report. On the other hand, the chain of transmission analysis could not establish Jābir al-Ju'fī as a Common Link or PCL.

Textual Analysis

There are four texts to analyse. The first variant was included in Ṣaffār's *Baṣā'ir al-darajāt*, which was quoted above.[55] There is a similar report attributed to the Prophet and recorded in 'Alī b. Ibrāhīm al-Qummī's *Tafsīr al-Qummī*. The content is identical to the reports attributed to al-Bāqir, yet the chain of this report goes back to the Prophet Muhammad through his prominent Companion Abū Dharr:

> Narrated to me by my father, on the authority of Ṣafwān b. Yaḥyā, on the authority of Abū Jārūd, on the authority of 'Imrān b. Haytham, on the authority of Mālik b. Ḍamra, on the authority of Abū Dharr, who said: 'When the verse ("On the Day [some] faces will turn bright and [some] faces will turn dark . . ." Q. 3:106) was revealed, the Messenger of God said: "My community will return to me on the Day of Resurrection under five banners." He will then ask one of these groups about what they did with the two weighty things (*thaqalayn*) after him. The first group will say: "As for the greater one (the Qur'an), we have distorted and disregarded it behind our backs. As for the smaller one (the Household of the Prophet), we antagonised, hated and oppressed it."'[56]

Given its prophecy about the distortion of the Qur'an, and the oppression of the Household of the Prophet, this report might have influenced other reports attributed to the Prophet. According to the text of the report ascribed to al-Bāqir, he narrated it from the Prophet and then commented on it. Even this commentary, however, seems to be coming from the Prophet. This report only has one variant, which is mentioned in *Tafsīr al-Qummī*. Therefore, it is not possible to examine this report. Because of the similarity of it to the report ascribed to al-Bāqir, the latter part of the report might have been a forgery.

55 al-Qummī, *Baṣā'ir al-darajāt*, p. 414.
56 al-Qummī, *Tafsīr al-Qummī*, vol. 1, p. 109.

According to the first report, al-Bāqir narrated the famous tradition of the Prophet about the *thaqalayn*, or two weighty things. The event reportedly occurred in Minā, which is visited by Muslim pilgrims as a part of the Hajj ritual. Hence, it is probable that the Prophet made this statement during Hajj. Since this is one of the most widely attested reports of the Prophet and al-Bāqir was a second-generation Muslim based in Medina, where this report originated from, it was probable that he was well aware of this report. Therefore, he did not need to cite any informants. However, in the chain of the second variant of this report, al-Bāqir cites the name of Jābir b. ʿAbdullāh al-Anṣārī (d. 78/697), one of the prominent Companions of the Prophet, as his source, thus filling the gap between himself and the Prophet. Jābir was one of the narrators of the report of *thaqalayn*, along with many other important reports for the Shiʿis, and he was a loyal supporter of ʿAlī and the family of the Prophet.[57]

It is probable that the report at hand included the same source in the chain, but it was dropped during the transmission or redaction process. There may have been a theological motivation for such an omission, which is the ability afforded to Shiʿi Imams to cite reports from the Prophet without a chain due to their special knowledge. In any case, there is no serious problem with al-Bāqir's narrating of this report. In the rest of the text, al-Bāqir stated the tradition about the *thaqalayn* and then reported that 'He [the Prophet] then said, "O people! I am leaving among you the sanctities of God: the Book of God, my progeny and the Kaaba, the Sacred House."' This section of the report is not part of the *thaqalayn* tradition. Therefore, it is likely that al-Bāqir combined two different traditions of the Prophet which are related to each other. Both reports reassert the significance of the Qur'an and the family of the Prophet. However, the second statement includes an additional element which is the Kaaba, the House of God. After this point, al-Bāqir asserts his own comment: 'Abū Jaʿfar then said: "As for the Book of God, they have distorted (*ḥarrafū*) it; as for the Kaaba, they destroyed it; and as for the progeny, they killed them. They have abandoned these trusts of God."'

Based on the reading of the text, it consists of three components; two separate reports of the Prophet and the commentary of al-Bāqir. The last section, which contains al-Bāqir's comments, is the part which has prime importance for our investigation. Because the parts attributed to the Prophet do not mention the distortion of the Qur'an, and stick to al-Bāqir's commentary, this last section includes such information. It is not clear, however, what kind of distortion (*fa-ḥarrafū*) al-Bāqir refers to – is it the distortion of the wording of the Qur'an or the distortion of the meaning?

57 al-Dhahabī, *Siyar aʿlām al-nubalāʾ*, vol. 3, pp. 190–3; al-Khoei, *Muʿjam rijāl al-ḥadīth*, vol. 4, pp. 330–7.

It is clear from the verses of the Qur'an that the original meaning may refer to the distortion of the meaning or interpretation of the Qur'an, as well as to its text. The primary evidence for this should come from the textual analysis of the variants. The study of the remaining three variants will potentially give a more convincing result. In the chain, I managed to trace this report back to al-Bāqir, therefore if I find the element of distortion in multiple variants, it may be possible to date the notion of distortion to Imam al-Bāqir. But even if this is the case, it is not clear what kind of distortion he was referring to.

The text of the second variant was also recorded in al-Ṣaffār's *Baṣā'ir al-darajāt.* In the chain analysis, I noted two problems, which were the inclusion of al-Naḍr b. Shu'ayb, who was an unknown person, along with another second unknown person in the chain. The textual analysis may help overcome some of the deficiencies found when analysing the chain of transmission. As I noted above, this variant included the name of Jābir and the Prophet in its chain, but it is obvious in this set of variants that al-Bāqir narrated a prophetic tradition and added his commentary in the end. Because my focus is the part of the report that al-Bāqir uttered, I indicate him to be the source of the report. It was probably the case for the other three variants as well because al-Bāqir repeats the same prophetic report in these variants, but the names of the Prophet and Jābir might have been dropped due to theological reasons.

In the text of the second variant, there is no mention of Minā or the location where the Prophet made his statement. Al-Bāqir narrates the prophetic tradition from the start of the text, but this section of the text is a heavily paraphrased version of the first text as it states, 'I am leaving among you two weighty things (*thaqalayn*): the greater weight and the lesser weight (*al-thaqala al-akbara wa-l-thaqala al-aṣghara*). If you adhere to them, you will not go astray, nor will you change.' While the first sentence, 'I am leaving among you two weighty things (*thaqalayn*)', is identical, the second text includes the elements of 'the greater weight and the lesser weight' (*al-thaqala al-akbara wa-l-thaqala al-aṣghara*). Thus, it makes a value statement about the two weighty things without mentioning what they are. In the first section of the text, al-Bāqir narrated the prophetic tradition. Therefore, this part where the value judgement was made is ascribed to the Prophet. Al-Bāqir, in the last section of the report, explained what the greater weight and the lesser weight meant and the reasoning for it.

After this statement, the second text includes the common element of 'If you adhere to them, you will not go astray, nor will you change'. This section is similar to the previous text except for adding 'nor will you change' (*lā tabaddalū*). The text then continues with a question that the unknown narrator puts to al-Bāqir about the prophetic statement: 'I then asked [about the Prophet's words] "These two will never separate from each other until they return to me by the pool [in Paradise]". [He replied:] "This was given to me like that."' This statement was included in the first section of the first text; however, in this second text, it was included in the commentarial section of al-Bāqir. By responding, 'This was given to me like that,' it appears that al-Bāqir affirms that this element was also included in the original report.

The man then questions him about the meaning of the expressions 'the greater weight' and 'the lesser weight'. Al-Bāqir then commented that '[Abū Ja'far] said: "the greater weight is the Book of God because a side of it is at the hand of God and the other side of it is at the hand of man. The lesser weight is my progeny and my family."' The last element was included in the text of the first version, but the meaning of the two weights was given at an earlier stage.

The analysis of the two texts suggests that this report might have originated in al-Bāqir's study circle. He was the first Shi'i Imam who established organised study circles to teach his students about the Qur'an, hadith, Islamic law and theology. He was based in Medina but had a very strong following in Kufa and to a lesser extent in Basra.[58] It seems likely that he narrated this report in one of these study circles, and multiple people heard him and then narrated this report. The second text was received from al-Bāqir by an unknown person, and one more person was involved in its transmission. Yet two texts show the characteristics of textual interdependence. The core of the text is the same, and both texts contain the same textual elements, such as the Prophet leaving two weighty or precious things for people to follow, namely, the Qur'an and his Household. He urged believers to follow these two guides to avoid going astray, and the text also states that the Qur'an and the Household of the Prophet bonded together eternally.

However, there is no mention of the prophetic tradition 'O people! I am leaving among you the sanctities of God: the Book of God, my progeny and the Kaaba, the Sacred House. Abū Ja'far then said: "As for the Book of God, they have distorted (*ḥarrafū*) it; as for the Kaaba, they destroyed it; and as for the progeny, they killed them. They have abandoned these trusts of God."' The exclusion of this section of the report strengthens my thesis that these were two separate reports which were put together either by al-Ṣaffār or one of the other transmitters. It is probable that al-Ṣaffār was not the culprit, for he had access to the other variants, and thus must have known about the other variants of the same report. But because he recorded the other reports as they were, he must have recorded this text as he received it, assuming that this was a different variant of the report.

58 Lalani, *Early Shi'i Thought*, pp. 96–113.

Because I can detect the paraphrased common elements in the two textual variants, these common elements may potentially be dated back to al-Bāqir, despite the deficiency in the second chain. This is because both texts arrive at *Baṣā'ir al-darajāt* from al-Bāqir (and before him, the Prophet) through two independent chains. These two chains carry two similar texts, which indicates interdependence along with some common elements which are paraphrased to the extent that there does not seem to be a sign of forgery. It may be possible to date these common elements back to al-Bāqir at the end of the investigation. However, so far, it is impossible to date the last section of the report, which includes the narrative on distortion, back to al-Bāqir.

The text of the third report was recorded in al-Ṣaffār's *Baṣā'īr al-darajāt*, through an uninterrupted chain from al-Bāqir to al-Ṣaffār. However, this chain did not include the part after al-Bāqir, reaching up to Muhammad. This text is in the form of questions, meaning that Sa'd al-Iskāf questions al-Bāqir about the prophetic tradition on the weighty things. In this version, instead of al-Bāqir, Sa'd al-Iskāf recited the report. Al-Bāqir makes the following commentary: 'The Book of God and our proof will continue to point to it until they return to the pool [in the Paradise].'

This text contains the core elements included in previous texts, namely, the prophetic report on the weighty things (*thaqalayn*) and for people to follow them, and that he urged believers to follow these two guides which are bonded together eternally. There is no mention of the meaning of the two weighty things. In other reports, these were mentioned as the Qur'an and the Household of the Prophet. Furthermore, the warning that if people do not follow the two weighty things, that they will go astray, is missing from the third text. Finally, the crucial part about the distortion of the Qur'an is also missing from this text.

As the chain of this report is uninterrupted and independent of the other two chains, it is more plausible to trace the common elements mentioned therein, which are the two weighty things. Though some other common elements existed in the previous two reports, it is safer to trace the common themes mentioned in all three of these reports. Taking such an approach will further overcome the deficiency of the second variant's chain. However, the study of the fourth variant's text should be completed before finalising the textual analysis.

The fourth and last text is included in Majlisī's *Biḥār al-anwār*. I have noted, in the chain of transmission analysis, the fact that the chain of this variant only has two transmitters before it reaches Majlisī. Additionally, I speculated that because of one of the transmitters, Jābir, it is probable that Majlisī copied it from al-Ṣaffār's *Baṣā'ir*, just as he copied many other reports from there. However, he stated that he received it from Sa'd b. 'Abdullāh (d. 301/913), who was a contemporary of al-Ṣaffār. The first part of the fourth report gives the impression that Majlisī's variant is almost identical to al-Ṣaffār's first variant:

> On the authority of Abū Jaʿfar, who said: 'The Messenger of God, announced in Minā and said: "O people! I am leaving among you two weighty things (*thaqalayn*). If you adhere to them, you will never go astray: the Book of God and my progeny, my family."'[59]

Both the first and fourth variants include the location of the prophetic tradition, Minā, which is a piece of crucial evidence to show that the sources of these two reports could be the same, since variants two and three do not have this information in their texts. Both variants also verbatim include all the common elements. There are only two differences in these variants. The first is that the fourth variant omits the phrase 'his companions' (*aṣḥābahu*). This may result from the redaction process, as there is no change to the previous and latter words, rather only the phrase 'his companions' is dropped from the text. The omission of 'his companions' may be explained as a genuine editorial mishap, or a deliberate effort of either Saʿd b. ʿAbdullāh or Majlisī to purge a Shiʿi report of the names of the 'companions'.

Second is the omission of the section on the distortion of the Qur'anic text. I noted earlier that this section on the distortion of the Qur'an is a separate report which was joined together at some point in the transmission process. The text of the fourth variant increases the likelihood this assessment because, despite its identical textual structure to the text of the first variant, it does not include this section as they were two separate reports.

Based on the analysis of the chain of transmission and text, it is possible to suggest that the first and fourth variants had the same chain of transmission going through Jābir. Because both al-Ṣaffār and Saʿd b. ʿAbdullāh are contemporaneous, Saʿd b. ʿAbdullāh received it from al-Ṣaffār but did not include the second section of the report as he knew that they were two separate reports. Or the source of al-Ṣaffār and Saʿd b. ʿAbdullāh was the same. This is because of the identical nature of both texts, but al-Ṣaffār deliberately or inadvertently combined the text of the two reports.

Based on the textual analysis of the four variants in conjunction with the chain of transmission analysis, I can date certain elements back to al-Bāqir: (1) A prophetic report on the two weighty things (*thaqalayn*) and that the Prophet left two weighty or precious things for people to follow, and (2) that al-Bāqir urged believers to follow these two guides, which are eternally bonded together. These common elements likely made up the original report attributed to al-Bāqir. However, it is certain that the element of the distortion of the Qur'an is not from the original part of the report, meaning

59 Majlisī, *Biḥār al-anwār*, vol. 97, pp. 140–1.

al-Bāqir never uttered those comments. They were later interpolated into the existing report.

Summary and Conclusion

Three out of four reports were recorded in Muḥammad b. al-Ḥasan al-Ṣaffār's *Baṣā'ir al-darajāt*. One of them is recorded in 'Allāma Majlisī's *Biḥār al-anwār*. The chain of transmission analysis of the first chain revealed that it was an uninterrupted chain, meaning it can be dated back to al-Bāqir. Thus, this suggests that it originated in Medina, where al-Bāqir resided, and was spread in Kufa and then travelled to Basra and Qom. However, the second chain was problematic, therefore I could date this chain back to Muḥammad b. Ḥusayn's date of death, in the year 262/875. The third chain was recorded in al-Ṣaffār's *Baṣā'ir al-darajāt*, with an uninterrupted chain. The analysis of the third chain indicates that this variant can also be dated back to al-Bāqir. It hence originated in Medina, travelled between Medina and Kufa and was finally transmitted from Kufa to Qom.

The final chain recorded in Majlisī's *Biḥār al-anwār* was problematic due to a significant time difference between Majlisī and his sources. Therefore, I could only date this chain to Sa'd b. 'Abdullāh's date of death, in the year 301/913. Out of the four variants, two of them, namely, the first and third reports, could be dated back to al-Bāqir, based on the chain analysis alone.

In the textual analysis of the variants, I found it difficult to reach a definitive conclusion on what the word *taḥrīf* meant in the reports ascribed to al-Bāqir. The original meaning could refer to the distortion of the meaning or interpretation of the Qur'an and/or its text. In any case, I noted that the report recorded in *Baṣā'ir al-darajāt* is a synthesised report which combines two different prophetic reports, followed by al-Bāqir's commentary on them. While the prophetic reports do not mention the distortion, the commentary attributed to al-Bāqir does.

In the text of the second variant recorded in al-Ṣaffār's *Baṣā'ir al-darajāt*, there was no mention of the location where the Prophet uttered the statement. Al-Bāqir narrated the prophetic tradition from the start of the text. This section of the text is a heavily paraphrased version of the first text. Two texts showed the characteristics of textual interdependence. The core of the texts is the same as both texts contain the same textual elements, such as the Prophet left two weighty or precious things for people to follow, the Qur'an and his Household. He urged believers to follow these two guides to avoid going astray. The text also states that the Qur'an and the Household of the Prophet are bonded together eternally.

However, there was no mention of the prophetic tradition 'O people! I am leaving among you the sanctities of God: the Book of God, my progeny and the Kaaba, the Sacred House. Abū Ja'far then said: "As for the Book of

God, they have distorted (*ḥarrafū*) it; as for the Kaaba; they destroyed it; and as for the progeny, they killed them. They have abandoned these trusts of God."' The exclusion of this section of the report strengthened my thesis that these were two separate reports which were put together, either by al-Ṣaffār or one of the transmitters.

As I could detect the paraphrased common elements in the two textual variants, these common elements could potentially be dated back to al-Bāqir, despite the deficiency of the second chain. This was because both texts arrive at *Baṣā'ir al-darajāt* from al-Bāqir (and before him the Prophet) in two independent chains. These two chains carry two similar texts, which show signs of interdependence. There were some common elements which were paraphrased to the extent that there does not seem to be a sign of forgery. It was possible to date these common elements back to al-Bāqir. However, it remains impossible to date the last section of the report, which includes the narrative on distortion back to al-Bāqir.

This third text, recorded in al-Ṣaffār's *Baṣā'ir al-darajāt*, contained the core elements included in the previous texts. These are the prophetic report on the two weighty things and him having left two weighty things for people to follow, which are bonded together eternally. There was no mention, however, of the meaning of the two weighty things. In other reports, these were mentioned as the Qur'an and the Household of the Prophet. Furthermore, the warning, that if people do not follow the two weighty things, they will go astray, is missing from the third text. Finally, the crucial part about the distortion of the Qur'an is also missing from this text. Because the chain of this report was uninterrupted and independent of the other two chains, it is more plausible to trace the common elements mentioned in all these reports.

The fourth and last text was recorded in Majlisī's *Biḥār al-anwār* and was identical to the text of the first variant. Both variants include the common elements, and only two differences. The first is that the fourth variant omits the phrase 'his companions' (*aṣḥābahu*). Second is the omission of the section on the distortion of the Qur'anic text. The text of the fourth variant reinforced my assessment that despite its similarity to the text of the first variant, it does not include the element of distortion, because they were two separate reports.

Based on the comparative study of the chains and texts, it becomes clear that only some elements can be dated back to al-Bāqir, which were part of the original report. These elements are the prophetic report on the two weighty things (*thaqalayn*) and the element that the Prophet left two weighty or precious things for people to follow. Al-Bāqir urged believers to follow these two guides which are eternally bonded together. The remaining elements are later additions to the report and most probably forgeries, especially the element of the distortion of the Qur'an, whether referring to its meaning or text.

CHAPTER 7

The Return of the Avenger and Teaching the Correct Qur'an

One of the aspects of the distortion of the Qur'an is related to al-Qā'im[1] (the Avenger or the Restorer), or the twelfth Imam, al-Mahdī. A group of reports claim that when the last Imam, al-Mahdī, or al-Qā'im, returns from his Occultation, he will set up tents to teach people the correct Qur'an. Within the group of reports related to the distortion narrative, the previous reports were about the time of the Prophet, soon after his death and several years after his death. In other words, these reports were about past events. However, this particular report is apocalyptic. According to Twelver theology, the twelfth Imam, al-Mahdī, has gone into Major Occultation in the year 329/941 and will return before the Day of Judgement to fill the earth with justice and avenge the injustice that the previous infallibles were made to suffer. His mission will include teaching people about the correct reading of the Qur'an, and in this sense, it is an essential manifestation of the theological background of the narrative about the distortion of the Qur'an.

Apocalypse in the Distortion Narrative

Building upon the previous findings in this book, a sceptical position would entail that for some Twelvers, the confirmation by earlier Imams on the distortion was insufficient, and so they decided to include the twelfth Imam, al-Mahdī, in the narrative and make a stronger case. Combining the distortion with the return of the awaited Imam would enhance the credibility of the narrative on the distortion and reinforce the significance of

1 The messianic Shi'i figure who is expected to return before the Day of Judgement to fill the earth with justice. Twelver Shi'is believe that he is the twelfth Imam, al-Mahdī.

the mission of the Avenger. Aside from establishing justice in this world, he would also deal with the injustice committed against the Qur'an:

> It was narrated to us by Abū Sulaymān Aḥmad b. Hawdha, who said, it was narrated to us by Ibrāhīm b. Isḥāq al-Nahāwandī, who said, it was narrated to us by 'Abdullāh b. Ḥammād al-Anṣārī, on the authority of Ṣabbāḥ al-Muzanī, on the authority of al-Ḥārith b. Ḥaṣīra, on the authority of al-Aṣbagh b. Nubāta, who said, I heard 'Alī saying, "it is as if I were with the Persians, in their tents, in the Mosque of Kufa, teaching people the Qur'an as it was revealed." I asked the Commander of the Faithful ('Alī): "Is it not as it was revealed?" He said: "No, the names of seventy [people] from Quraysh were erased from the Qur'an and the names of their fathers. Abū Lahab's name was left only in contempt of the Messenger of God; because he was his uncle."'[2]

One cannot miss the connection between the narrative on 'Alī b. Abī Ṭalib's collection of the first Qur'anic codex[3] and its rejection by the Muslim community's elites during Abū Bakr's reign. In the narratives, when he presented his codex to the people in the Prophet's Mosque, some individuals in the crowd censured him, and consequently prompted him to take an oath that no one would see his codex again.

It seems that certain Shi'i factions built a secondary narrative around this possible historical event to argue that 'Alī's codex was the correct Qur'an and all the other codices were distorted. This theory is used as one of the supporting arguments for the distortion of the Qur'an. If the reports on Imam al-Mahdī's teaching of the correct Qur'an are placed next to these reports, it becomes evident that there is a concentrated effort to build a theology around the events related to 'Alī's collection of the Qur'an. The Avenger, who is the heir of the Imams, would come to restore what his great ancestor could not achieve.

There is a gap in the reports regarding how the Avenger would restore the correct reading of the Qur'an after such a long time. He would not receive a second revelation from God as the Qur'an is clear that the Prophet was the final individual to receive revelation from God, and thus the path of the revelation was closed after his death (Q. 33:40). However, within the context of the existing narrative on Imam 'Alī's codex, the Avenger is to reinstate 'Alī's correct Qur'an. In other words, he would not receive a second edition of the Qur'an from God. This idea was perhaps built around the understanding

2 al-Nu'mānī, *Kitāb al-ghayba*, p. 318.

3 Kara, *In Search of Ali Ibn Abi Talib's Codex*.

that 'Alī's codex remained in the possession of his progeny,[4] and the Avenger would return with that codex.

It may be possible to make a stronger case for the alterations to the Shi'i narrative driven by theological concerns. I already have examined some of the reports attributed to the sixth Imam, al-Ja'far, in this regard;[5] here is a sample indicating that possibility:

> We have been told by Muḥammad b. al-Ḥusayn from 'Abd al-Raḥmān b. Abī Najrān from Hāshim from Sālim b. Abū Samala [*sic.* Salama], who said: 'A man was reading [the Qur'an] in the presence of Abū 'Abdullāh [who is Ja'far al-Ṣādiq] and I heard a word from the Qur'an which was not part of the Qur'an that people used to read. Abū 'Abdullāh said, "*mah mah*! Stop it; do not utter this recitation and read it (the Qur'an) as other people are reading it until the rise of al-Mahdī (al-Qā'im). And when he rises, he will recite the Book of God as it should be recited and will take out the *muṣḥaf* which 'Alī wrote." He (Abū 'Abdullāh) said 'Alī presented it to people because he had finished and written it, and he told them: 'Here is the Book of God as He revealed it to Muhammad, and I have collected it between the two covers.' They said, 'we already possess the *muṣḥaf* in which the Qur'ān is collected, so we do not need it ('Alī's *muṣḥaf*).' He ['Alī] said: 'Henceforth, by God! You will never see this after this for I have discharged my duty by informing you about it (my *muṣḥaf*) when I collected it so that you recite it.'[6]

In studying these reports, I found that only two elements could be dated back to al-Ṣādiq. After the death of the Prophet, 'Alī self-isolated at home until he collated the Qur'an. After that, he presented it to some of the people, but they rejected it.[7] According to *isnād-cum-matn* analysis, it is not possible to date anything else back to Ja'far al-Ṣādiq, including the narrative that when the Avenger returned, he would recite the Qur'an in the correct format, as 'Alī preserved it:

> A man was reading [the Qur'ān] in the presence of Abū 'Abdullāh (Ja'far al-Ṣādiq) and I heard a word from the Qur'ān which was not part of the Qur'ān that people used to read. Abū 'Abdullāh said, '*mah mah*! Stop it; do not utter this recitation and read it (the Qur'ān) as other people are reading it until the rise of Mahdi (al-Qā'im).

4 Ibn al-Nadīm, *Kitāb al-fihrist*, p. 390.

5 Kara, *In Search of Ali Ibn Abi Talib's Codex*, p. 156.

6 al-Qummī, *Baṣā'ir al-darajāt*, p. 193.

7 Kara, 'The Collection of the Qur'ān in the Early Shī'ite Discourse'.

> And when he rises, he will recite the Book of God as it should be recited and will take out the *muṣḥaf* which ʿAlī wrote.'

There is relative certainty that this part of the report is a later interpolation and perhaps an attempt to embellish ʿAlī's collection of the Qur'an into the formation of Shiʿi theology, which had been building its identity around the Occultation and return of the last Imam, al-Mahdī. Nevertheless, the study of the variants will reveal whether it is possible to substantiate the theory of theological interpolations and forgery in these reports relating to the Avenger and the correct reading of the Qur'an.

The report at hand has seven variants: two variants in Ibn Jaʿfar al-Nuʿmānī's (d. 360/970–1) *Kitāb al-ghayba*, one variant in Shaykh al-Mufīd's *al-Irshād* (d. 413/1022), one variant in al-Fattāl al-Nayshābūrī's (d. 508/1114) *Rawḍat al-wāʿiẓīn wa-baṣīrat al-muttaʿiẓīn*, one report in Bahāʾ al-Din al-Irbilī's (d. 692/1293) *Kashf al-ghumma fī maʿrifat al-aʾimma* and two variants in Majlisī's (d. 1110/1698) *Biḥār al-anwār*. While four variants were attributed to ʿAlī b. Abī Ṭālib (d. 40/661), three variants were attributed to the fifth Imam, al-Bāqir (d. 114/733). I could have investigated these two sets of reports separately because they are attributed to two different sources. However, due to the similarity of the texts, I chose to treat them as the same variant. This is based on the Shiʿi understanding that the Imams could narrate the reports without citing their ancestors or the previous Imams. There are many occasions in which a Shiʿi Imam mentions a report without mentioning his source. Though it did not always happen, it was often the case that they narrated directly from previous Imams. In Chapter 6, there was an instance where the source of the Imam was edited out from the report, but in another source, it was still present, and the person was not infallible. It was most probably due to theological motivations that the Imams did not need to rely on others to transmit knowledge, as they were the inheritors of God-given knowledge. This idea likely emerged later on as per the formation of the theology of imamate, as there are instances in which the Imams narrate reports from Companions of the Prophet, or the companions of the previous Imams.[8] Regardless, if the study eventually demonstrates that these are distinct reports, I can treat them as separate reports.

Chain of Transmission Analysis

Due to the textual similarities, if I consider the al-Bāqir variants of the report as attributed to ʿAlī, then there are seven variants. These variants spread out from ʿAlī into three lines via al-Bāqir, Ḥabbata al-ʿUranī and

8 Modarressi attributes the origins of the divine knowledge of the Imams to the extremist Shiʿi group Mufawwiḍa, which became influential in third/ninth-century Iraq. Modarressi, *Crisis and Consolidation in the Formative Period of Shīʿite Islam*, p. 27 and *passim*.

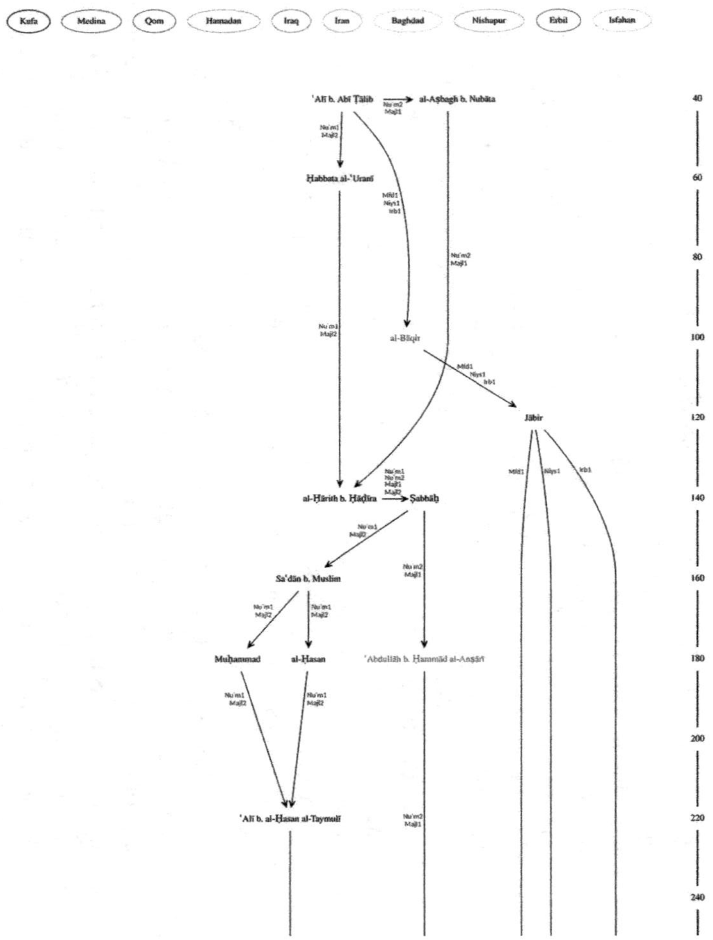
Kufa
Medina
Qom
Hamadan
Iraq
Iran
Baghdad
Nishapur
Erbil
Isfahan
ʿAlī b. Abī Ṭālib
al-Aṣbagh b. Nubāta
Ḥabbata al-ʿUranī
al-Bāqir
Jābir
al-Ḥārith b. Ḥaḍīra
Ṣabbāḥ
Saʿdān b. Muslim
Muḥammad
al-Ḥasan
ʿAbdullāh b. Ḥammād al-Anṣārī
ʿAlī b. al-Ḥasan al-Taymulī
40
60
80
100
120
140
160
180
200
220
240

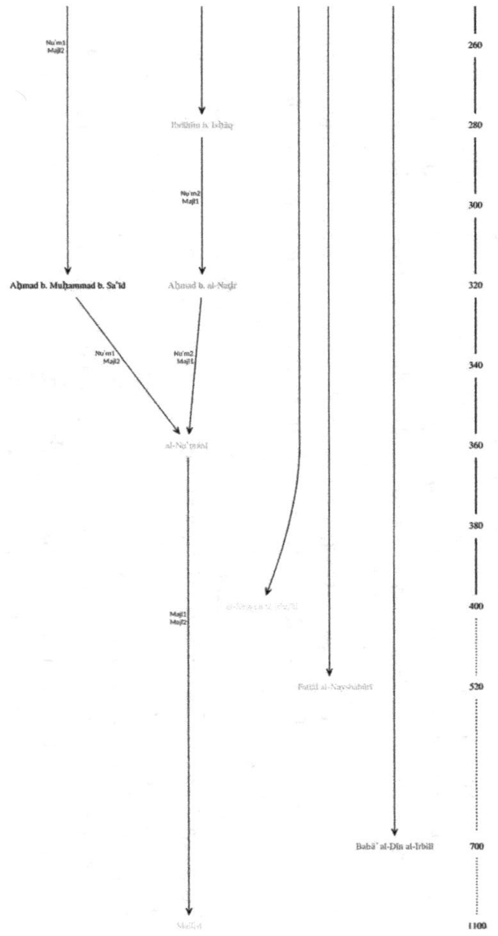

Diagram 7 Available online at: https://edin.ac/4ckpgKO

al-Aṣbagh b. Nubāta. This tentatively makes 'Alī the Common Link and source of the reports. However, the variants recorded by Majlisī were quoted from al-Nu'mānī's *Kitāb al-ghayba*, thus in reality there are five variants. The al-Bāqir line continues with Jābir, who seems to be a Partial Common Link (PCL). The other two lines spread separately but then immediately reconnect at al-Ḥārith b. Ḥaṣīra and then separate after the next person, Ṣabbāḥ al-Muzanī, who seems to be the second PCL. They then continue as a separate line until they reach Ibn Ja'far al-Nu'mānī's *Kitāb al-ghayba*. I will therefore be dealing with two independent lines of transmission. Though the two lines reconnect twice, this might expose their text to alteration and restrict my chances of accurately dating it back to its source.

I start my analysis with the two variants recorded in Ja'far al-Nu'mānī's *Kitāb al-ghayba*. Al-Nu'mānī (d. 360/970–1) was a respected Shi'i theologian and hadith scholar who was praised by fellow Shi'i scholars. He was a prominent student of al-Kulaynī[9] and was active in Iran, Iraq and Syria. He reportedly authored numerous books, including *Kitāb al-ghayba* and died in Syria[10] in 360/970–1. Al-Nu'mānī authored *Kitāb al-ghayba* (*The Book of Occultation*) in 342/953–4, thirteen years after the twelfth Imam, al-Mahdī, went into the Major Occultation in 329/941, and it was the first known book written on the subject.[11] In that sense, it was an important work for Twelver Shi'is to make sense of the new status quo, since Shi'is had to deal with the absence of their Imam while waiting for his return. This must have created an immense theological vacuum which needed to be clarified and explained for Shi'i scholars to keep the community's commitment and devotion to the Household of the Prophet intact.

In this framework, al-Nu'mānī collects all the accessible reports about al-Mahdī and his return in *Kitāb al-ghayba*, which therefore becomes a precious source for later Shi'i theologians. Al-Nu'mānī recorded two reports about the return of al-Mahdī and his teaching of the correct Qur'an. He received the first report from Aḥmad b. Muḥammad b. Sa'īd, who was a very prominent scholar of hadith. He adhered to the Jārūdī branch of Zaydism until the end of his life and resided in Kufa. Twelver Shi'i scholars had great respect and trust for him, and he authored several books on hadith and the lives of Twelver and Zaydi Imams. He died in 333/944–5 in Kufa,[12] making him a contemporary and teacher of al-Kulaynī.[13]

9 al-Khoei, *Mu'jam rijāl al-ḥadīth*, vol. 15, p. 232.

10 al-Najāshī, *Rijāl*, pp. 383–4.

11 Khawānsārī, *Rawḍāt al-jannāt*, vol. 6, pp. 127–9.

12 al-Najāshī, *Rijāl*, pp. 94–5.

13 Al-Nu'mānī highly praised Aḥmad b. Muḥammad b. Sa'īd in the introduction to his *Kitāb al-ghayba*, which provides written evidence of their connection. The fact that Aḥmad b. Muḥammad b. Sa'īd was a Zaydi, yet highly regarded by the Twelvers, indicates that he had an impeccable reputation. He then transmitted the report to al-Nu'mānī (al-Nu'mānī, *Kitāb al-ghayba*, p. 25).

Aḥmad b. Muḥammad b. Saʿīd received the report from ʿAlī b. al-Ḥasan al-Taymulī (d. 224/839), who was a resident of Kufa and generally considered to be a reliable transmitter. He was a companion of the seventh Imam, al-Riḍā. The only blemish on his reputation was that after the death of the sixth Imam, al-Ṣādiq, he shifted his loyalties from the Twelvers to the Faṭaḥiyya by believing in the imamate of ʿAbdullāh al-Afṭaḥ (d. 149/766), instead of his younger brother and the seventh Imam, al-Kāẓim (d. 183/799). However, it appears that he repented and returned to the ranks of the Twelvers after the death of ʿAbdullāh al-Afṭaḥ, which occurred two months after his bid for the imamate.[14]

Al-Taymulī received the variant from al-Ḥasan and Muḥammad, who were the sons of ʿAlī b. Yūsuf. Al-Ḥasan b. ʿAlī b. Yūsuf was al-Ḥasan b. ʿAlī b. Baqāh.[15] He was a reputable Kufan scholar. He reported from the companions of the sixth Imam, al-Jaʿfar, and he had a book called *Nawādir*.[16] His brother was also a scholar from Kufa. There is no date of death for al-Ḥasan b. ʿAlī, but if he reported from the companions of the sixth Imam, he was likely active in the second half of the second/eighth century. Therefore, both he and his brother could transmit the variant to al-Taymulī.

Al-Ḥasan b. ʿAlī b. Yūsuf and his brother received the report from Saʿdān b. Muslim [al-ʿĀmirī], who was a client. There is limited information about him in the early sources.[17] Later sources note that he was a companion of the sixth Imam, al-Ṣādiq, and he had an *ʿAṣl*. He seems to be a resident of Kufa and was considered a reliable and prominent hadith collector.[18] There is no date of death for him in the sources, but because he was believed to be a companion of the sixth Imam, he was likely active in the second/eighth century. Therefore, it is possible for him to have transmitted the report to al-Ḥasan and Muḥammad.

Saʿdān b. Muslim received the variant from Ṣabbāḥ al-Muzanī, who is Ṣabbāḥ b. Yaḥyā al-Muznī. He seems to be a reliable scholar based in Kufa and reported from both Imams al-Bāqir and Jaʿfar al-Ṣādiq.[19] Although he does not have a date of death, because he reported from the fifth and sixth Imams, he was likely active in the first half of the second/eighth century in Kufa. Thus, it is possible for him to have transmitted the report to Saʿdān b. Muslim.

Ṣabbāḥ b. Yaḥyā al-Muznī received it from al-Ḥārith b. Ḥaṣīra [al-Asadī or al-Azdī], who was thought to be a companion of the sixth Imam, al-Ṣādiq.[20]

14 al-Najāshī, *Rijāl*, pp. 34–6.
15 al-Khoei, *Muʿjam rijāl al-ḥadīth*, vol. 6, pp. 30, 67.
16 al-Najāshī, *Rijāl*, p. 40.
17 al-Najāshī, *Rijāl*, pp. 192–3; al-Ṭūsī, *al-Fihrist*, vol. 1, pp. 140–1.
18 al-Amīn, *Aʿyān al-shīʿa*, vol. 7, p. 232; al-Khoei, *Muʿjam rijāl al-ḥadīth*, vol. 9, pp. 104–8.
19 al-Najāshī, *Rijāl*, p. 104; al-Khoei, *Muʿjam rijāl al-ḥadīth*, vol. 10, p. 104.
20 al-Khoei, *Muʿjam rijāl al-ḥadīth*, vol. 5, pp. 168–9.

Sources have scarce information about him but he reported from some of the prominent Shi'i figures such as Jābir al-Juʿfī (d. 128/756).[21] Because Ṣabbāḥ b. Yaḥyā al-Muznī lived in the first half of the second/eighth century in Kufa, al-Ḥārith b. Ḥaṣīra likely died some time in the first half of the second/eighth century too. Therefore, it is probable that al-Muznī received the report from al-Ḥārith b. Ḥaṣīra.

Al-Ḥārith b. Ḥaṣīra received it from Ḥabbata al-ʿUranī, who was a companion of ʿAlī and was possibly also with Imam Ḥasan.[22] He was from Kufa and died around 76/695–6, and there are various reports about his personality in Sunni and Shiʿi sources. According to historian Khaṭīb al-Baghdādī, he was weak, and according to Shiʿi sources, he was praised at best but not trusted.[23] It is possible for him to have heard the report from ʿAlī (40/661) and transmitted it to al-Ḥārith b. Ḥaṣīra. The upper chain of this report can be traced back to ʿAlī. The individuals in the chain might have been motivated to forge or alter this report, but there is no strong evidence for that. Therefore, it seems that this report emerged in Kufa and remained there for generations and then spread out of Kufa when al-Nuʿmānī authored *Kitāb al-ghayba*.

The second chain is recorded in al-Nuʿmānī's *Kitāb al-ghayba*. He received it from Abū Sulaymān Aḥmad b. Hawdha, who is Aḥmad b. al-Naḍr (d. 333/945).[24] He is known as Ibn Abī Harāsa and was active in Nahrawan, Iraq. Given that al-Nuʿmānī died in 360/970–1, it is possible that he received the report from Aḥmad b. al-Naḍr, who received it from Ibrāhīm b. Isḥāq al-Nahāwandī. He was considered weak in his reports and believed to have had doubts about his faith, meaning he was a *ghālin* or extremist Shiʿi. He authored several books and was active in the year 269/883.[25] He seems to have originated from Nahawand, a city in the Hamadan Province of Iran, but he was active in Iraq too. His being weak and having extremist views may mean he had the motive to forge or tamper with reports. The textual analysis will provide more to this end. Nevertheless, it seems possible that he transmitted the report to Aḥmad b. al-Naḍr.

Ibrāhīm b. Isḥāq al-Nahāwandī received the report from ʿAbdullāh b. Ḥammād al-Anṣārī, who was a prominent Shiʿi narrator and author of two books.[26] He was believed to be a companion of the seventh Imam, al-Kāẓim (d. 183/799), or the eighth Imam, al-Riḍā (d. 203/818), but these possibilities remain speculative as he never reported from either Imam.[27]

21 al-Mizzī, *Tahdhīb al-kamāl fī asmāʾ al-rijāl*, vol. 5, pp. 224–5.
22 al-Khoei, *Muʿjam rijāl al-ḥadīth*, vol. 5, pp. 192–3.
23 al-Amīn, *Aʿyān al-shīʿa*, vol. 4, pp. 387–8.
24 al-Khoei, *Muʿjam rijāl al-ḥadīth*, vol. 3, p. 156.
25 al-Najāshī, *Rijāl*, p. 19; al-Amīn, *Aʿyān al-shīʿa*, vol. 2, p. 111.
26 al-Najāshī, *Rijāl*, p. 217; al-Ṭūsī, *al-Fihrist*, p. 170.
27 al-Khoei, *Muʿjam rijāl al-ḥadīth*, vol. 11, pp. 186–9.

Furthermore, it was known that despite his perceived reputation, he narrated weak reports. He seems to be active in Qom, and it was more likely that he transmitted the report to Ibrāhīm b. Isḥāq al-Nahāwandī in Iran. And so he was responsible for the distribution of the report to Qom. There is no date of death for him, but he was probably active in the second half of the second/eighth century. This possibility makes his connection to Ibrāhīm b. Isḥāq al-Nahāwandī problematic, as he was still alive and active in the year 269/883. Al-Nahāwandī might have lived another decade or so but if this is the case, he might have died towards the end of the third/ninth century, creating a gap of a century between the two transmitters. Although it is not uncommon for some people to enjoy a considerably long life, this age gap and the blemished reputation of both transmitters raise considerable doubts about this chain.

However, given that this chain reconnects the transmission line at Ṣabbāḥ al-Muzanī, it may be possible to examine the connection between al-Nahāwandī and al-Anṣārī in the textual analysis. Upon re-joining at Ṣabbāḥ al-Muzanī, similar to the first chain, the line goes up to al-Ḥārith b. Ḥaṣīra but disjoins at al-Aṣbagh b. Nubāta, who received the report from ʿAlī. Al-Aṣbagh b. Nubāta was a very close companion of ʿAlī b. Abī Ṭālib and among his elite warriors and commanders. For Shiʿis, he was renowned for his impeccable reputation as a transmitter and passionate advocate of ʿAlī. He reported some of the most famous sayings of ʿAlī. On the other hand, due to his fervent devotion to ʿAlī, Sunni sources considered him weak. He probably lived a little while after ʿAlī but perhaps died during Imam Ḥasan's (d. 50/670) era.

Some reports suggest that he also reported from Imam Ḥusayn, including the account of his murder in Karbala, but these accounts were based on chains that included several unknown individuals, hence difficult to verify.[28] Weighing the available information, it is probable that he died before the year 50/670. As I noted in the study of the previous chain, al-Ḥārith b. Ḥaṣīra should have been active around that time. Hence, he could have received the report from al-Aṣbagh b. Nubāta. Al-Aṣbagh b. Nubāta then heard the report from ʿAlī directly.

The third chain was recorded in al-Shaykh al-Mufīd's (d. 413/1022) *al-Irshād*. He is one of the greatest Shiʿi scholars who deeply influenced Shiʿi theology, history and jurisprudence. He played a crucial role as the leader of the Buyid-era Shiʿi community in Karkh, the major Shiʿi centre at the time. Because of the less Shiʿi hostile environment that the Buyids had created by exerting political pressure on the Abbasids, he had the freedom to preach Shiʿi teachings. Although, at this point, he was mostly

28 al-Najāshī, *Rijāl*, p. 7; al-Ṭūsī, *al-Fihrist*, p. 85; al-Khoei, *Muʿjam rijāl al-ḥadīth*, vol. 4, pp. 132–6; Ishkevari, 'Al-Aṣbagh b. Nubāta'.

immune to Abbasid persecution, he and other Shi'is nevertheless came under attack from a group of Ḥanbalīs. As a result, the city of Karkh, rife with sectarianism, was subject to numerous burnings, including that of al-Mufīd's house.[29]

Al-Mufīd authored his *al-Irshād* in a relatively free yet turmoiled environment in the year 411/1020, two years before his death. The book gives a historical account of the lives of the infallible Imams and is considered the most reliable history of the Imams. Before analysing the chain further, a point of interest to note is that al-Mufīd mentions al-Nuʿmānī's *Kitāb al-ghayba* in his *al-Irshād*,[30] which shows he was familiar with the narrations in the book. He did not, however, cite the same reports of al-Nuʿmānī's chains. He rather opts for the chain that ends at Imam al-Bāqir. Considering his impeccable reputation, it is improbable that he forged a new chain. It is more likely the case that he did not trust the chain of the reports attributed to Imam ʿAlī and opted for a safer option that was attributed to al-Bāqir by one of his closest companions.

Al-Mufīd narrated the variant from Jābir [b. Yazīd al-Juʿfī]. As I discussed in the previous chapters, Jābir was a second-generation Muslim, and a great Shi'i scholar and hadith narrator of his time. He was one of the most prominent companions of the fifth and sixth Imams and also narrated the report on the so-called missing Stoning Verse discussed previously. The main problem with this chain is the obvious time gap between al-Mufīd (d. 413/1022) and Jābir (d. 128/756), which consists of three hundred years. Obviously, al-Mufīd must have been aware of this time gap, yet he did not quote one of the reports recorded in al-Nuʿmānī's *Kitāb al-ghayba* which have longer chains and go back to ʿAlī. Instead, he opted for the report which has a massive time gap and goes back to al-Bāqir.

One of the reasons for al-Mufīd's decision might have been that he deliberately avoided quoting a report from al-Nuʿmānī because he either did not trust the reports in *Kitāb al-ghayba*, since some of the individuals in the chain were problematic, or he had figured out that the reports were similar, and consequently opted for the safer option: a report could that be traced back to another Imam through a transmitter with an impeccable reputation. Given that it was acceptable at the time to have such a gap in the chains, especially at the lower levels since such reports might have been well known to the scholars, they seem a safer choice than reports that contained deficient transmitters at higher levels. In a way, they had to decide between either quoting a report that contained problematic transmitters in the chain or reports that contained reliable chains yet had a gap at the lower levels. Apparently, al-Mufīd felt obliged to include a report in his

29 Stewart, *Islamic Legal Orthodoxy*, pp. 118–25.

30 al-Mufīd, *al-Irshād*, vol. 2, p. 350.

book on the return of al-Mahdī to make a stronger case for his return and thus went with the second option.

Nevertheless, it is important to study the rest of the chain, because I initially speculated that Jābir's source, Imam al-Bāqir, might have received the same report from his great-grandfather ʿAlī b. Abī Ṭālib through the family chain, or through his source. This source might not have been an infallible, and therefore was removed from the chain for theological reasons that were developed later on; namely, that the Imams did not need to report from those who were not Imams. The third option may be that he had a different source. When analysing the text, it may be possible to verify if Imam al-Bāqir narrated the same report, which was attributed to ʿAlī or another source. Jābir was a prominent companion of al-Bāqir, but he was criticised for having extremist views.[31] Nevertheless, it was possible that he received the report from al-Bāqir.

The fourth chain was recorded in Muḥammad b. Aḥmad Fattāl al-Nayshābūrī's *Rawḍat al-wāʿiẓīn* (d. 508/1114), which is about the life of the Prophet Muhammad and the Imams. He is the teacher of the well-known Shiʿi scholar Ibn Shahrāshūb (d. 588/1192) and apparently a prominent scholar in Nishapur.[32] He was reportedly killed on order of the Seljuk governor of the city and given the title of martyr. However, there are reservations about his identity as his name and work are not mentioned in major Shiʿi sources.[33] He appears to have published the book, nonetheless. He reported it from Jābir, who then reported it from Imam al-Bāqir. There is even a greater time gap between Jābir and Muḥammad b. Aḥmad Fattāl al-Nayshābūrī. The same possibilities are valid for this variant too. It could be that Fattāl al-Nayshābūrī quoted it from al-Mufīd's *al-Irshād*, though this can only be further investigated in the textual analysis.

The fifth variant was recorded in Bahāʾ al-Dīn al-Irbilī's (d. 692/1293) *Kashf al-ghumma fi maʿrifat al-aʾimma*. He was a prominent Twelver who lived in Erbil. His father was the city governor, and Bahāʾ al-Dīn al-Irbilī served the Ilkhanids as a government official. He trained many students and gained prominence in the region. *Kashf al-ghumma* contains the biographies of the Imams. He was buried near Baghdad and reportedly authored the book in the year 687/1144.[34]

Bahāʾ al-Dīn al-Irbilī reported it again from Jābir, who then received it from al-Bāqir. The time gap between Bahāʾ al-Dīn al-Irbilī, who died in 692/1293, and Jābir (d. 128/756) is vast. It is obvious that he quoted a

31 al-Khoei, *Muʿjam rijāl al-ḥadīth*, vol. 4, pp. 336–46.

32 Tehrānī, *Ṭabaqāt aʿlām al-shīʿa*, vol. 2, pp. 236–7; al-Tustarī, *Qāmūs al-rijāl*, vol. 9, p. 74.

33 al-Khoei, *Muʿjam rijāl al-ḥadīth*, vol. 16, p. 19.

34 al-Khoei, *Muʿjam rijāl al-ḥadīth*, vol. 13, p. 114; Tihrānī, *Ṭabaqāt aʿlām al-shīʿa*, vol. 5, p. 390; Tihrānī, *al-Dharīʿa ilā taṣānīf al-shīʿa*, vol. 18, pp. 47–8.

well-known report, thus it was acceptable to record a report that the author could not hear directly. Even if he had copied it from a written book, he did not mention his source. He could have read it from al-Mufīd's *al-Irshād* or Fattāl al-Nayshābūrī's *Rawḍat al-wāʿiẓīn*. It could have even been another book, but nevertheless, it remains impossible to know his real source.

The remaining two variants were recorded in Majlisī's (d. 1110/1699) *Biḥār al-anwār*. Both variants' chains are the same as the chains recorded in al-Nuʿmānī's *Kitāb al-ghayba*. Therefore, there is no need to analyse the chains. The analysis of the chains of transmission has shown that there are two sets of chains of transmission in these variants. The first are the ones recorded in al-Nuʿmānī's *Kitāb al-ghayba*, which seemingly originate from ʿAlī and are then transmitted by two separate individuals, Ḥabbata al-ʿUranī and al-Aṣbagh b. Nubāta. After that, they re-join with al-Ḥārith b. Ḥaṣīra and then disjoin after Ṣabbāḥ b. Yaḥyā al-Muznī, and continue thereafter as two separate reports until they reach al-Nuʿmānī's *Kitāb al-ghayba*. This set of variants may be traced back to ʿAlī, but one of the variants included a problematic individual in the chain, namely, Ḥabbata al-ʿUranī, who may have had a motive to forge the report. However, an alternative transmission line includes al-Aṣbagh b. Nubāta, who was more reliable and could thus make up for this deficiency in the chain. Nevertheless, because of this line of transmission in frequent interaction, it is difficult to treat them as two separate transmission lines before Ṣabbāḥ al-Muzanī.

The second set of variants seemingly originate from al-Bāqir, but it is possible that they could be the variants of the report attributed to ʿAlī due to the textual similarities. However, these variants include massive time gaps in their transmission lines, and they are thus problematic. Textual analysis may clarify these problems.

Textual Analysis

Due to the complexity of the chains of transmission, textual analysis becomes more crucial in this chapter. The primary focus of the textual analysis is to examine the possible connection between two partially independent transmission lines that were recorded in al-Nuʿmānī's *Kitāb al-ghayba*, and then seek to determine whether the reports attributed to ʿAlī and al-Bāqir originated from the same base. While making these primary enquiries, I will also be able to compare and contrast the analyses of the chains of transmission with the text, in order to date these variants to the earliest date possible.

In the text reported in al-Nuʿmānī's *Kitāb al-ghayba* – attributed to ʿAlī via Ḥabbata al-ʿUranī – ʿAlī reportedly saw a vision about the apocalyptical return of his great progeny, the twelfth Imam, al-Mahdī:

> It was reported to us by Aḥmad b. Muḥammad b. Sa'īd, who said, it was narrated to us by 'Alī b. al-Ḥasan al-Taymulī, who said, it was narrated to us by al-Ḥasan and Muḥammad, the sons of 'Alī b. Yūsuf, on the authority of Sa'dān b. Muslim, on the authority of Ṣabbāḥ al-Muzanī, on the authority of al-Ḥārith b. Ḥaṣīra, on the authority of Ḥabbata al-'Uranī, who said, the Commander of the Believers ('Alī b. Abī Ṭālib) said: 'It is as if I am looking at our Shi'is in the Mosque of Kufa, wherein they have set up tents to teach people the Qur'an as it was revealed. When our Avenger (Qā'im) rises up, he will break it and reinstate its original.'[35]

According to 'Alī's vision, the followers of the Avenger (referred to as *Shī'ātinā*) set up tents in the Mosque of Kufa to teach people the so-called original Qur'an since the Avenger had already restored the correct form of the Qur'an. The reference to setting up tents to teach the correct Qur'an is the common element included in these variants, which prompted me to also include them in the study even though they were attributed to al-Bāqir. Furthermore, the variants note that the correct teaching of the Qur'an will occur upon al-Mahdī's rise or return, and provided a specific location, namely, the Mosque of Kufa.

The second text was also found in al-Nu'mānī's *Kitāb al-ghayba* – attributed to 'Alī via al-Aṣbagh b. Nubāta – and quotes the exact text of the report above. Again, 'Alī saw a vision of the rise of the Avenger and his teaching of the correct Qur'an to people in the Mosque of Kufa. There are some additional elements in this text, and some elements are seemingly different. Firstly, the element of 'with the Persians' (*bi-l-'Ajami*) is replaced with 'the followers of the Avenger' (*Shī'ātinā*). Secondly, the first variant includes 'When our Avenger (Qā'im) rises up, he will break it up and reinstate its original', but the second variant misses this element. In other words, there is no reference to the Avenger or Qā'im in the second variant. Thirdly, there is a follow-up question to the statement, which was put to 'Alī by al-Aṣbagh b. Nubāta:

> I asked the Commander of the Faithful: 'Is it not as it was revealed?' He said: 'No, the names of seventy [people] from Quraysh were erased from the Qur'an and the names of their fathers. Abū Lahab's name was left only in contempt of the Messenger of God, because he was his uncle.'[36]

This unusual statement is reportedly coming from 'Alī's mouth, and it clearly states that the Qur'an was distorted. It also gives an interesting

35 al-Nu'mānī, *Kitāb al-ghayba*, pp. 317–18.
36 al-Nu'mānī, *Kitāb al-ghayba*, p. 318.

justification for Sūrat al-Masad, in which Abū Lahab, who was an uncle of the Prophet, was explicitly cursed along with his wife.

Starting from the first different element, the replacement of 'with the Persians' (*bi-l-ʿAjami*) with 'the followers of al-Mahdī' is highly suspicious and seems to be either an oral or written redaction because it would have been unusual for ʿAlī to pinpoint a certain group of Muslims as the sole supporters of al-Mahdī in his statement. Aside from a few exceptions like Maytham al-Tammār (d. 60/692), who was a staunch supporter of ʿAlī and his sons, Persians only became a significant religious and political actors after political turmoil, or the so-called second civil war, which ensued from the murder of Ḥusayn b. ʿAlī.[37] Persians, who were the majority of freed slaves, converted to Islam and remained under the protection of a host Arab tribe. They had been discriminated against by Arabs under Umayyad rule and consequently lent considerable support to al-Mukhtār b. Abī ʿUbayd al-Thaqafī's (d. 67/687) pro-ʿAlid rebellion.[38] Therefore, it would have been highly improbable that ʿAlī would single out the Persians as the sole supporters of the Avenger. This seems rather to be a sign of local interference with the text. The second difference was mentioned in the first variant, namely, 'When our Avenger (Qā'im) rises up, he will break it up and reinstate its original', but the second variant is missing this element. This is the most crucial part of the report as it affords the report with an apocalyptical theme by connecting it to the Avenger's return. In addition, it further emphasises that there is an 'original' Qur'an which is unknown to people, and al-Mahdī will thereby restore this original Qur'an. Nevertheless, the second variant included the element 'teaching people the Qur'an as it was revealed', which already gives the meaning that the Qur'an at hand was not the original and it will be addressed on that day.

There may be a couple of explanations as to why this crucial element is missing in the second text. It is possible that a transmitter or redactor dropped this element from the text because it was obvious to them that the context was the return of the Avenger. Thus, they did not feel that it was necessary to repeat what was self-evident and thus this element was lost inadvertently. Another possibility is that the element of the Avenger was dropped intentionally, and I will discuss the second possibility further below.

Umayyads' Erasure of the Prophet's Enemies from the Qur'an

The variant becomes more interesting in the follow-up section. ʿAlī reportedly stated that 'the names of seventy [people] from Quraysh were erased from the Qur'an and the names of their fathers'. He ostensibly referred to

37 al-Khoei, *Muʿjam rijāl al-ḥadīth*, vol. 20, pp. 103–12.

38 See Haider, *The Rebel and the Imām in Early Islam*, pp. 26–114.

the leaders of the rival Banū ʿAbd Shams clan, who were the bitter enemies of the Prophet until the conquest of Mecca in 8/630. These enemies of the Prophet then embraced Islam but were always accused of being hypocrites by the Shiʿis because Banū ʿAbd Shams's Umayyad branch later plotted and fought against ʿAlī, and forced his son Ḥasan to abdicate the caliphate and finally murdered Ḥusayn.[39] This variant claims that the Qur'an included the names of these leaders not in a pleasant or natural way, but rather in the same manner in which the Qur'an damns Abū Lahab, the paternal uncle of the Prophet.

The variant implies that the Umayyads distorted the Qur'an by purging these names from the Qur'an. The only name of the enemy of the Prophet left untouched in the Qur'an was his uncle Abū Lahab. The Umayyads did this consciously to humiliate the Prophet, by editing out his other arch-enemies and leaving only his uncle's name. Thus they, in a way, humiliated the Prophet because it appeared that according to the Qur'an, only his uncle objected to his messengership. In the context of Arabian tribalism, this could have been perceived as a major insult to the Prophet.

Due to the controversial nature of this statement, ʿAlī Akbar al-Ghaffārī, the editor of *Kitāb al-ghayba*, felt obliged to insert a footnote to express his opinion that this report is not genuine. He noted that al-Ḥārith b. Ḥaṣīra was an unknown person (*majhūl*), and Ṣabbāḥ al-Muzanī was Zaydi, and both of them were weak according to Ibn al-Ghaḍā'irī's (d. 411/1020) *Rijāl*. As I have studied elsewhere,[40] Ibn al-Ghaḍā'irī's book is controversial and not taken seriously by modern-era Shiʿi scholars of hadith, therefore the argument does not seem to have a strong basis. Nevertheless, the text of the variant is problematic too. It gives the impression of a later embellishment of the text as some elements were interpolated into the text to explain why the distortion of the Qur'anic text took place. Since the transmission line joins at Ṣabbāḥ al-Muzanī, it may be difficult to trace this additional element before his date of death in the second/eighth century in Kufa. It could be either him or ʿAbdullāh b. Ḥammād al-Anṣārī, who received the report from Ṣabbāḥ al-Muzanī, and would thus be responsible for its embellishment. Ṣabbāḥ al-Muzanī could have reported this text to two different individuals, and on this occasion, he might have added this additional element. Or, it could have been added by ʿAbdullāh b. Ḥammād al-Anṣārī or anybody else in the chain before it reached *Kitāb al-ghayba*. If I had taken al-Ghaḍā'irī's allegations against Ṣabbāḥ al-Muzanī for granted, it could have been easy to spot the weakness in the chain and blame him for the interpolation. Due to the questions about al-Ghaḍā'irī's book, this may not be possible.

39 Jafri, *The Origins and Early Development of Shiʿa Islam*, pp. 1–17.

40 See Kara, *In Search of Ali Ibn Abi Talib's Codex*, pp. 135–6.

Nevertheless, Isḥāq al-Nahāwandī, who was active in the year 269/883, could also be the real culprit because he was considered an extremist. The transmission line is problematic before him, too, but he seems to be the first problematic person. There is a gap of a century between him and his narrator, 'Abdullāh b. Ḥammād al-Anṣārī. Because of the fact that he was from Nahawand, a city in the Hamadan Province of Iran, he might have interpolated both elements into the text, which would be the element of 'with the Persians' (*bi-l-'Ajami*) and the follow-up question to the statement which was supposedly put to 'Alī by al-Aṣbagh b. Nubāta. As a person of Persian origin and/or residency, he might have wanted to popularise this report in the region by relating it to the Persians and embellishing it with a further follow-up story to promote it.

Although I cannot be sure as to why he might have omitted the element of the Avenger from the text, it would be simply that the context was clear to the audience, and so he did not feel the need to repeat it. Or, there might have been a local reason due to which he did so deliberately. It may be that the local context was Iran and that these Persian Muslims hoped the Avenger would rise from within their region. It was only natural for Imam 'Alī to have a vision of the Mosque of Kufa since it was his base during his time, but the Avenger was not expected to come to the same place to teach the correct Qur'an. Thus, he might have removed the element on the return of the Avenger but kept the element on the teaching of the correct Qur'an because that was the central topic of discussion at the time. Whether this is true or not, these three additional elements could only be dated back to the second half of the third century when Isḥāq al-Nahāwandī was active.

In terms of the common elements, there are four: (1) the vision that a group of people are together (either the followers of the Avenger or the Persians); (2) the existence of the tents – in the first version it states that 'they set up the tents' and in the second version 'in their tents'; (3) that the occasion is taking place 'in the Mosque of Kufa'; and (4) a group of people try 'to teach people the Qur'an as it was revealed'.

Among these common elements, I have already discussed the first common element. In terms of the second common element, there is a sign of paraphrasing. In the first version it read 'they set up the tents', and in the second version 'in their tents'. This is normal in oral transmission as it indicates that the narrator retells the same story that he had heard. It may not be a redaction by the book's author because both versions appear in the same book.

The existence of tents, which signify a military encampment, seems to be from the original report. The followers, however, may have 'set up' these tents or been 'in their tents'. There is no conflict between these elements. Be that as it may, one issue is unclear: where would the tents be set up? Is it inside the mosque or outside of the mosque? And what would happen inside the tents? From reading the texts, it appears that the tents are for the followers of the army of the Avenger. When he rises, his army will camp in Kufa and then educate people on the correct Quran in the Mosque of Kufa. This report shows that the Avenger will fulfil the unfinished business of his great ancestor Imam ʿAlī on two fronts. Upon the inconclusive Battle of Siffin (37/657), Muʿāwiya continued his destabilising activities. Hence, ʿAlī raised an army in Kufa to finish off Muʿāwiya (d. 60/680) and hold him responsible for his rebellion and bloodshed before his assassination. The tents mentioned in the report may thus be referring to this army, except for when al-Mahdī rises. He will also raise an army to seek revenge against the Umayyads and their progenies.

Another incomplete objective of ʿAlī was to collect the Qur'an. When the Prophet died, ʿAlī remained in his house for a considerable period to collect the Qur'an, but when he collated it, he presented it to people in the Prophet's Mosque in Medina. Muslims, however, rejected ʿAlī's codex, which was believed to be the first Qur'anic codex.[41] Most Shiʿis believe that ʿAlī's codex was the most authentic Qur'an because he had his commentary on the margins, and it preserved the correct order of the *sūra*s. Some others, as narrated in these reports, believed, however, that it was different from the ʿUthmānic codex. Therefore, when al-Mahdī returns, he will fulfil the incomplete mission of ʿAlī, which is to take revenge on the supporters of the Umayyads and restore ʿAlī's codex.

The third element, namely, the Mosque of Kufa, is important. If it could be traced back to ʿAlī, it makes sense that ʿAlī saw a vision of the Mosque of Kufa in his military and administrative base. However, if the report is a forgery based on the chains of transmission, it is almost certain that it was forged in Kufa. Therefore, it is only natural that it contains the local elements of the city, and the mosque in Kufa is one of the most important sites.

The fourth element, 'to teach people the Qur'an as it was revealed', seems to have remained intact in both variants, thus it was not paraphrased. The two texts (variants six and seven) recorded in *Biḥār al-anwār* are verbatim copies of these two variants. Hence, I am unable to extract any information from these texts alone. Based on the study of the two variants, which could be dated back to ʿAlī, I can only date these common elements to Ṣabbāḥ al-Muzanī, who was active in the second/eighth century.

The third text is recorded in al-Mufīd's *al-Irshād.* The remaining four texts, including the text in *al-Irshād*, do not reach ʿAlī, but rather they seem to originate from the fifth Imam, al-Bāqir. Due to the textual similarities that are attributed to ʿAlī, however, I am analysing them together with these reports. It could be possible that these reports had longer chains, meaning that via al-Bāqir, and other individuals, these chains reached back to ʿAlī

41 See Kara, In Search of Ali Ibn Abi Talib's Codex, pp. 135–6.

too. Because of theological reasons, however, those chains might have been redacted. Through analysing the texts, it could be possible to determine if the chains of these reports were indeed redacted or not.

The text recorded in al-Mufīd's *al-Irshād* contains some common elements with the previous variants. It includes the elements of the rise of the Avenger, and the setting up of tents for teaching the correct Qur'an. However, the elements of the Mosque of Kufa and the vision of 'Alī are missing from this variant. Furthermore, there is an additional element which states that the memorisers of the Qur'an will struggle when the Avenger teaches this original Qur'an because it will contradict what they have in their memories:

> When the Avenger (al-Qā'im) of the family of the Prophet rises, he will set up tents to teach people the Qur'an as God Almighty revealed it. That day will be the most difficult [time] for those who had memorised the Qur'an, because the teachings of the Avenger will contradict what they composed in it (the Qur'an).[42]

The element of setting up the tents (*ḍaraba fasāṭīṭ*) is an important indicator that the two reports, the report attributed to 'Alī and the report attributed to al-Bāqir, were related. Since this is a very specific expression, it is curious that this expression would appear in two separate reports. Did al-Bāqir see the same vision that his great-grandfather 'Alī had seen? Or did he narrate the report he had received by way of an oral transmission, which had then been paraphrased by the time it was received? Or was it a forger who purposefully created a report for theological reasons? The forger might have used the prototype report attributed to 'Alī, redacted its text and forged a chain of transmission to fabricate a new report. The last possibility is further investigated below.

The second piece of evidence for the textual similarity is the use of the phrase 'when the Avenger (al-Qā'im) of the family of the Prophet rises'. This element was extant in the first report with a slight change: 'When our (i.e. the family of the Prophet) Avenger (Qā'im) rises'. There could be a group of reports starting with this apocalyptical expression reported from the Imams, and so the existence of the second element could be a simple coincidence. However, if the two elements are combined, the odds of there being such a coincidence decrease. The additional evidence for this possibility is that the chain of this group of reports that are attributed to al-Bāqir is interrupted due to a gap of several generations between Jābir, who heard it from al-Bāqir, and the authors of the book who recorded them. Therefore, it is probable that these reports were forged based on the report attrib-

42 al-Mufīd, *al-Irshād*, vol. 2, p. 386.

uted to ʿAlī. As they have more textual similarities or common elements with the first variant recorded in al-Nuʿmānī's *Kitāb al-ghayba*, it is possible that this version was the prototype.

The study of the remaining two texts might have provided further information, were it not for the fact that both texts recorded in Muḥammad b. Aḥmad Fattāl al-Nayshābūrī's *Rawḍat al-wāʿiẓīn* are verbatim copies of the text recorded in al-Mufīd's *al-Irshād*. Therefore, it is impossible to gather additional information from these texts.

The textual study of these reports does not change the findings of the chain of transmission analysis, namely, that the different elements can only be dated back to Isḥāq al-Nahāwandī, who was active in the year 269/883, and the common elements can only be dated back to Ṣabbāḥ al-Muzanī, who was active in the second/eighth century. The first variant recorded in al-Nuʿmānī's *Kitāb al-ghayba* seems to be the original report that can be dated back to Ṣabbāḥ al-Muzanī. The reports attributed to al-Bāqir are probably based on Ṣabbāḥ al-Muzanī's prototype. Nevertheless, these variants cannot be dated back to either Imams al-Bāqir or ʿAlī b. Abī Ṭālib.

Summary and Conclusion

Out of the seven variants of the report, four were attributed to ʿAlī b. Abī Ṭālib (d. 40/661) and three to the fifth Imam, al-Bāqir (d. 114/733). Due to the textual similarities between the two sets of reports, I decided to treat them as variants of the same report, despite them being attributed to two different sources. This was due to my initial impression that Shiʿi Imams would narrate reports without mentioning previous Imams. I also considered the second possibility that the reports attributed to al-Bāqir were fabricated based on the report attributed to ʿAlī.

Despite some problematic individuals, the first chain could reach back to ʿAlī. There were more serious issues with the second chain. The second person in the chain was an extremist, and had ulterior motives to forge or tamper with the reports. In addition, he had a gap of a century with his narrator. The two other chains recorded in *Biḥār al-anwār* are attributed to ʿAlī and are identical, therefore it was not possible to extract any further information. Based on the chain of transmission analysis alone, the two variants attributed to ʿAlī could only be dated back to the PLC Ṣabbāḥ al-Muzanī, who was active in second/eighth-century Kufa. The shorter chains that were attributed to al-Bāqir could only be dated back to the books they were found in, the earliest of which is al-Mufīd's *al-Irshād*.

The primary focus of the textual analysis was to study the possible connection between two partially independent transmission lines that were recorded in al-Nuʿmānī's *Kitāb al-ghayba*, along with investigating whether the reports attributed to 'Alī and al-Bāqir originated from the same prototype. In the textual analysis of the first two variants in al-Nu'mānī's *Kitāb al-ghayba*, I noted that there were four common elements in the first two variants. Among these common elements, despite the differences in their identity, that is, they were identified as either the followers of the Avenger or the Persians, it was clear that a group of people are undertaking the task of teaching the correct Qur'an. In terms of the second common element, there was a sign of paraphrasing: in the first version, 'they set up the tents', and in the second, 'in their tents'. Examining the texts, it seemed that the tents were intended for the followers or the army of the Avenger, who rally behind them in their march against the adversaries of the Prophet's Household and introducing the 'correct' Qur'anic codex.

The third common element, the Mosque of Kufa, was exactly the same in both variants. Similar to the third common element, the fourth element, which was 'to teach people the Qur'an as it was revealed', remained intact in both variants and thus was not paraphrased. The two texts (variants six and seven) recorded in *Biḥār al-anwār* were exact copies of these two variants. Hence, I was unable to extract any information from these texts. Based on the study of the two variants, from the chains of the transmission which could be dated back to 'Alī, I could only date the common elements to Ṣabbāḥ al-Muzanī, who was active in the second/eighth century. This was because Ṣabbāḥ al-Muzanī, the PCL, is the person that this set of chains of transmission convenes at.

Furthermore, there were some different elements in the second text, including the statement that the Qur'an was distorted. In the analysis of the different elements, I concluded that these elements were most probably the result of a forgery carried out by Isḥāq al-Nahāwandī, who was active in the year 269/883.

When studying the chains of the transmission attributed to al-Bāqir, I noted that there was a gap of a few centuries between the books that these reports were written in and the last known transmitter. In the textual analysis of the variants attributed to al-Bāqir I found that the variants recorded in Muḥammad b. Aḥmad Fattāl al-Nayshābūrī's *Rawḍat al-wā'iẓīn* are verbatim copies of al-Mufīd's *al-Irshād.* This means that they quoted the report from *al-Irshād* but did not mention their source. In al-Mufīd's text there were two common elements that were also shared by the variants attributed to 'Alī. Because of these common elements, I concluded that the variant included in al-Mufīd's *al-Irshād* is a forgery. Its text was based on the text of the report attributed to 'Alī, but with the help of a brand-new chain, it was attributed to al-Bāqir. Since they have more textual similarities or common elements with the first variant recorded in al-Nu'mānī's *Kitāb al-ghayba*, it is possible that this version was the prototype.

In conclusion, the different elements of the variants can only be dated back to Isḥāq al-Nahāwandī, who was active in the year 269/883, and the common elements could only be dated back to Ṣabbāḥ al-Muzanī, who was active in the second/eighth century. The first variant recorded in al-Nuʿmānī's *Kitāb al-ghayba* seems to be the original report that could be dated back to the aforementioned Ṣabbāḥ al-Muzanī.

Conclusion

Rethinking Narratives and Shaping Historical Discourse

The study of the history of early Islam is still incomplete, and it is crucial to re-examine existing biases to overcome any current stagnations in the field. I have made an attempt in this book to advance our understanding of the textual history of the Qur'an. As the field is still so fertile with so much left unexamined, I dealt with what I deemed to be some important issues. This study focused on only seven reports but made discoveries related to the early days of Islam and the textual history of the Qur'an. The key finding related to the distortion theory is that ʿUmar may have mistakenly believed that the stoning penalty was initially implemented as a verse of the Qur'an by the Prophet. Over time, ʿUmar appears to have confused the *sunna* of the Prophet with the verse of the Qur'an. When Muslims became hesitant to implement the penalty, he delivered a sermon on its importance and reinforced the existence of the missing Stoning Verse in the Qur'an.

ʿUmar's insistence on the existence of the stoning penalty had a ripple effect. Some variants of the report included narratives about the succession issue and ʿUmar's apologetic position, which drew particular attention from Shiʿis. They likely focused on the political implications of the report and eventually began to question whether other verses, such as those related to the succession of Imam ʿAlī and his descendants, could also have been removed from the Qur'an. The fact that ʿUmar's report was integrated into Shiʿi sources indicates that Shiʿis were familiar with the report and did not hesitate to attribute it to Imam Jaʿfar al-Ṣādiq with a forged chain of transmission. Additionally, it is worth noting that neither of the remaining Shiʿi reports could be traced back to the Imams, which strengthens the view that the Shiʿi distortion narrative did not arise from the teachings of the Shiʿi Imams but was instead developed much later.

The significance of Chapter 1 related to investigating that the number of breastfeedings required to establish the status of one who is prohibited to marry varies between five, seven and ten in different variants of Islamic texts, thereby suggesting that there was an ongoing debate on the matter. Given this diversity of views, it is highly improbable that there was a revealed verse in the Qur'an that explicitly stated the required number of breastfeedings.

The study of the texts also revealed Mālik's tendency to edit prophetic reports in accordance with his legal perspective on abrogation. This led to the conclusion that Mālik edited the texts of these variants based on his linguistic, legal and even theological views. Shāfiʿī, Mālik's student, then adopted and incorporated this approach heavily into his legal theory. Consequently, it appears that abrogation as a legal concept was adopted by Mālik and was subsequently developed and widely used by Shāfiʿī.

The chapter's most significant discovery regarding the distortion of the Qur'an was that the story of a domesticated sheep eating the folios of the Quran, including the controversial 'Breastfeeding Verse', cannot be traced back to ʿĀ'isha. This element was only found in one variant, and there were issues with the chain of that specific variant. As a result, it can only be confidently traced back to Ibn Mājah's death in 273/887.

The study of the stoning penalty narratives showed a lack of clarity about what the 'Book of God' referred to. Chapter 2, in a sense, enquired about what the two nomads meant when they came to the Prophet with the request for settlement. Did they ask the Prophet to judge according to the Qur'an or the Torah? If they meant to ask the Prophet to judge between them according to the Qur'an, and the Prophet had the Qur'an in mind when he confirmed that he was obliged to do so, the obvious problem that arises is that there is no such verse in the Qur'an. Therefore, the idea of distortion of some verses of the Qur'an is tangible.

Also, who were the 'people of knowledge' from whom they received the initial incorrect verdict? Were they Muslim scholars or Jewish scholars? I surmised that they might have been Jewish scholars because, in such an early period, the Muslim scholarly community was non-existent. If this was the case, that means the connection between rabbinic law and Islamic law was fluid during the formative period of Islam, especially in the early period of the Prophet's emigration to Medina. Consequently, the stoning penalty might have been adopted from rabbinic law.

My tentative response to these questions remains hypothetical at that point as I could not trace this hadith back to the Prophet due to the lack of solid evidence. I was, however, able to trace the hadith back to Zuhrī's date of death, in the year 124/742. Nevertheless, the study gave a possible line of enquiry to pursue in the following chapters.

Chapter 3 yielded more promising results because it was possible to date the kernel of hadith back to the Prophet's lifetime. The study of variants surrounding the arbitration between the Prophet and a group of Jews on the punishment of two adulterers highlights important aspects of the interaction between the Prophet and the Jews of Medina. It is clear that the Jews sought the Prophet's guidance as an arbitrator, rather than asking him to issue a pronouncement of guilt. The Prophet thereby focused on finding the appropriate punishment for the offence, as outlined in the Torah.

The Prophet's investigation into the appropriate punishment suggests a respect for the Jewish legal tradition and a willingness to defer to its authority. This interaction also sheds light on the early years of Muslim emigration from Mecca to Medina, as the core elements of the variants can be traced back to that period.

The study of these variants provides insight into the early history of Islam and the Prophet's relationship with other religious communities. It highlights the importance of the Torah as a legal reference for both Jews and Muslims, as the 'Book of God' could have referred to both the Qur'an and the Torah at the time. It also underscores the Prophet's role as an arbitrator in resolving disputes. By successfully dating these variants to the lifetime of the Prophet, I can also confirm the dating of the 'Constitution of Medina', as the variants suggest that the Prophet's arbitration of the episode was in accordance with the terms of this document. It is also evident that the Prophet was not enforcing an Islamic ruling for adultery at that time. If he ever implemented such a practice afterwards, it was likely based on the Jewish tradition rather than a Qur'anic injunction.

It is possible that the Prophet implemented the stoning penalty at the request of the Jews for arbitration and may have done so a few times on Muslims based on the Torah's rulings which was before the Lashing Verse was revealed. However, the stoning penalty episodes involving Muslim offenders cannot be traced back further than Zuhrī at the earliest. As a result, it is uncertain whether the Prophet ever stoned Muslims. If he did, it appears that he only temporarily borrowed the punishment from the Jews of Medina. Once the Prophet prioritised the establishment of an independent Muslim identity and Q. 24:2 was revealed, he likely abandoned this practice as it is not mentioned in the Qur'an. Otherwise, it seems implausible that Muhammad was eager to change the direction of prayer, in opposition to the Jews of Medina and distance from Jewish practices, yet he remained loyal to the practice of stoning, which goes against the clear Qur'anic injunction of lashing offenders.

An important aspect of the reports about the arbitration request of the Jews was the interpolation of the element of 'Abdullāh b. Salām into some of the variants. This interpolation points out the tension between the Jews and Muslims emerging after the takeover of Iraq and Jerusalem by the caliphs. Or, it could be an attempt to make a more forceful case for the existence of the stoning penalty. The interpolation of such an element accuses those who reject the existence of the stoning penalty of committing a similar crime as the Jews of the New Testament, namely, distortion of God's command.

Chapter 4 made intriguing discoveries about the textual history of the Qur'an. The study of the hadiths attributed to the second caliph, ʿUmar, enabled the dating of these reports back to ʿUmar – a few weeks or months before his death on 31 Dhū al-Ḥijja 23/1 October 644. Moreover, the phrasing of the Stoning Verse distinctly indicates that it was not an original part of the report but was likely added later as an explanatory gloss to the text. Based on this, it is reasonable to conclude that there was no omitted Stoning Verse in the version of the Qur'an that the Prophet taught, and as a result, nothing has been removed from the Qur'anic codex. Therefore, this tradition cannot be employed as evidence for the textual corruption of the Qur'an.

The most significant finding is that the compilation of the Qur'anic codex may have occurred earlier than previously documented, namely, during the reign of Abū Bakr (d. 13/634). The content of the texts suggests that ʿUmar's inability to modify the Qur'anic codex was due to an early process of codification that had taken place before his reign. Therefore, this process must have occurred during the time of his predecessor. This discovery moves the dating of the Qur'anic codex closer to the death of the Prophet, which is consistent with traditional Muslim accounts of the Qur'an's textual history, asserting that it was first compiled during Abū Bakr's reign.

In Chapter 5, the report attributed to ʿUmar and studied in Chapter 4 is examined, and it is found to have made its way into some key Shiʿi sources. The wording of the Stoning Verse found in Shiʿi reports was identical to the reports attributed to ʿUmar, specifically the Saʿīd b. al-Musayyab cluster, studied in Chapter 4. Since I dated those reports to the date of ʿUmar's death, which was in 26/644, and these reports were in circulation in Basra and Kufa after that, it is clear that this particular report is a forgery. The fact that these reports cannot be dated back to Imam Jaʿfar al-Ṣādiq strengthens this conclusion. The source for this variant, al-Sayyārī, cites Ibn Sayf, who was active in Basra. The forgery replaced Sunni narrators with Shiʿi ones and ascribed the report to Imam Jaʿfar al-Ṣādiq. These reports were likely forged in Iraq in the third/ninth century.

Chapters 6 and 7 examined two Shiʿi reports on the distortion of the Qur'an, and neither report could be traced back to the Imams. In Chapter 6, only some elements could be dated back to Imam al-Bāqir, namely, the narration of the prophetic report on the two weighty things (*thaqalayn*) and the Prophet leaving them for people to follow. Al-Bāqir urged believers to follow these two guides, which were eternally bonded together. However, it became apparent that the distortion elements in the report were later additions and deliberate forgeries. Yet again, forgers preferred to work with an existing report and redact it to interpolate their desired agenda instead of inventing a brand-new report.

Chapter 7 studied a report concerning the reappearance of Imam al-Mahdī, a central figure in Shiʿi eschatology. The report is attributed to ʿAlī b. Abī Ṭālib and his descendant Imam al-Bāqir, and several variants are found in different sources. My investigation found that the variants attributed to ʿAlī can only be dated back to Ṣabbāḥ al-Muzanī, a figure active in second/eighth-century Kufa, and the variants attributed to al-Bāqir are only found in later sources, with a gap of several centuries in the chain of transmission. Therefore, the variants are likely unrelated and not based on each other.

In this book sought to examine the notion of the distortion of the Qur'an through analysing hadith. By using *isnād-cum-matn* analysis, the book sought to discover the historical origins of the notions surrounding the Qur'an's distortion, identify the interaction and influence between Sunni and Shiʿi traditionalists who advocated this notion from the second/eighth to the fifth/eleventh centuries and make methodological advances in the study of early Islam by testing the boundaries of *isnād-cum-matn* analysis.

The findings demonstrated that the study of hadith could provide insight into the early history of Islam, especially with regard to the crystallisation of the Qur'anic codex, the role of the Prophet Muhammad in the early Medinan community, his relations with the Jews and the connection between Islamic law and rabbinic law. The study also sheds light on the formation of Shiʿi identity and the redaction, editing and forgery culture in the oral and written transmission of Shiʿi reports.

The use of *isnād-cum-matn* analysis revealed that there is strong evidence that Sunni legal schools redacted prophetic reports to align them with their legal views. Similarly, Shiʿi Muslims redacted some Sunni reports and forged new chains to attribute them to the Imams as part of their identity-building process. The book also identified the individuals responsible for these forgeries, which furthers our understanding of forgery culture in early Islamic history.

The study of the Stoning Verse and the missing Breastfeeding Verse demonstrates that these verses were not part of the original Qur'anic text. Instead, they were part of the oral tradition and the legal practices of early Muslims. Similarly, the study shows that the propagation of the notion of distortion of the Qur'an was primarily driven by political and sectarian motives.

These findings provide a deeper understanding of the early history of Islam and shed light on the nature of the interaction, influence, rivalry and formation between Sunni and Shiʿi denominations. Moreover, the findings demonstrate that hadiths have historical source value, and with rigorous methods, it is possible to use them in order to reconstruct the early history of Islam.

Bibliography

Ali, Aun Hasan, 'The Rational Turn in Imāmism Revisited', *Global Intellectual History* (2023), pp. 1–30.

Ali, Kecia, *Sexual Ethics and Islam: Feminist Reflections on Qur'an, Hadith, and Jurisprudence* (Oxford: Oneworld Publications, 2006).

Ali, Kecia, *Imam Shāfiʿī: Scholar and Saint* (Oxford: Oneworld Publications, 2011).

Ali, Kecia, *The Lives of Muhammad* (Cambridge, MA; London: Harvard University Press, 2016).

Altorki, Soraya, 'Milk-Kinship in Arab Society: An Unexplored Problem in the Ethnography of Marriage', *Ethnology*, 19/2 (1980) pp. 233–44.

Al-Amīn, Sayyid Muḥsin, *Aʿyān al-shīʿa*, ed. Ḥasan al-Amīn, 11 vols (Beirut: Dār al-Taʿāruf, 1983).

Amir-Moezzi, Mohammad Ali, *The Divine Guide in Early Shiʿism: The Sources of Esotericism in Islam*, trans. David Streight (Albany: State University of New York Press, 1994).

Amir-Moezzi, Mohammad Ali, *The Silent Qur'an and the Speaking Qur'an: Scriptural Sources of Islam between History and Fervor*, trans. Eric Ormsby (New York: Columbia University Press, 2016).

Amir-Moezzi, Mohammad Ali, 'The Shiʿis and the Qur'an: Between Apocalypse, Civil Wars, and Empire', *Religions*, 13/1 (2022), https://doi.org/10.3390/rel13010001.

Anthony, Sean W., *Muhammad and the Empires of Faith: The Making of the Prophet of Islam* (Berkeley: University of California Press, 2020).

Arjomand, Saïd Amir, 'The Constitution of Medina: A Sociolegal Interpretation of Muhammad's Acts of Foundation of the "*Umma*"', *International Journal of Middle East Studies*, 41/4 (2009), pp. 555–75.

Asatryan, Mushegh, 'The Good, the Bad, and the Heretic in Early Islamic History', in Majid Daneshgar and Aaron Hughes (eds), *Deconstructing Islamic Studies* (Cambridge, MA: Harvard University Press, 2020), pp. 204–52.

Al-ʿAsqalānī, Aḥmad b. ʿAlī b. Ḥājar, *Tahdhīb al-tahdhīb*, 14 vols (Beirut: Dār al-Fikr, 1984).

Al-Baghdādī, Abū Bakr, *Tārīkh Baghdād*, 23 vols (Beirut: Dār al-Kutub al-ʿIlmiyya, 1997).

Baker, Christine D., *Medieval Islamic Sectarianism* (Amsterdam: Amsterdam University Press, 2019).

Bar-Asher, Meir M., 'Variant Readings and Additions of the Imami-Shi'a to the Qur'an', *Israel Oriental Studies*, 13 (1993), pp. 39–74.

Bar-Asher, Meir M., *Scripture and Exegesis in Early Imāmī Shiism* (Leiden: Brill, 1999).

Bar-Asher, Meir M., *Jews and the Qur'an*, trans. Ethan Rundell (Princeton, NJ: Princeton University Press, 2022).

Berg, Herbert, *The Development of Exegesis in Early Islam: The Authenticity of Muslim Literature from the Formative Period* (Richmond: Curzon, 2000).

Brockopp, Jonathan, 'Ibn Lahī'a', in Kate Fleet, Gudrun Krämer, Denis Matringe, John Nawas, and Everett Rowson (eds), *Encyclopaedia of Islam*, vol. 3, http://dx.doi.org/10.1163/1573-3912_ei3_COM_30875, accessed 13 October 2021.

Brown, Jonathan A. C., *Hadith: Muhammad's Legacy in the Medieval and Modern World* (Oxford: Oneworld Publications, 2009).

Brunner, Rainer, *Die Schia und die Koranfälschung* (Würzburg: Ergon Verlag, 2001).

Brunner, Rainer, *Islamic Ecumenism in the 20th Century: The Azhar and Shiism between Rapprochement and Restraint* (Leiden: Brill, 2004).

Bukhārī, Muḥammad, *al-Tārīkh al-kabīr*, ed. 'Abd al-Raḥmān b. Muḥammad b. Abī Ḥātim, 9 vols (Beirut: Dār al-Kutub al-'Ilmiyya, 1986).

Bukhārī, Muḥammad, *Ṣaḥīḥ al-Bukhārī*, 9 vols (Beirut: Dār Ṭawq al-Najāt, 2001).

Bulliet, Richard, 'Conversion-Based Patronage and Onomastic Evidence', in Monique Bernards and John Nawas (eds), *Patronate and Patronage in Early and Classical Islam* (Leiden: Brill, 2005), pp. 246–62.

Burton, John, *The Collection of the Qur'ān* (Cambridge: Cambridge University Press, 1977).

Burton, John, 'Law and Exegesis: The Penalty for Adultery in Islam', in G. R. Hawting and Abdul-Kader A. Shareef (eds), *Approaches to the Quran* (London: Routledge, 1993), pp. 269–84.

Burton, John, *An Introduction to the Ḥadīth* (Edinburgh: Edinburgh University Press, 1994).

Burūjardī, Ḥusayn 'Alī, *Ṭarā'if al-maqāl fī ma'rifat ṭabaqāt al-rijāl*, 2 vols (Qom: Maktab Āyatullāh al-'Uḍmā al-Mar'ashī al-Najafī, 1989).

Burūjardī, Ḥusayn 'Alī, *Nihāyat al-uṣūl* (Qom: Nashr Tafakkur, 1994).

Byrskog, Samuel, *Story as History – History as Story: The Gospel Tradition in the Context of Ancient Oral History* (Leiden: Brill, 2022).

Calder, Norman, *Studies in Early Muslim Jurisprudence* (Oxford: Clarendon Press, 1993).

Campbell, Jonathan G., *Deciphering the Dead Sea Scrolls* (Oxford: Blackwell Publishing, 2008).

Cellard, Éléonore, 'The Ṣan'ā' Palimpsest: Materializing the Codices', *Journal of Near Eastern Studies*, 80/1 (2021), pp. 1–30.

Cole, Juan, 'Muhammad and Justinian: Roman Legal Traditions and the Qur'ān', *Journal of Near Eastern Studies*, 79/2 (2020), pp. 183–96.

Cole, Juan, 'Late Roman Law and the Qur'anic Punishments for Adultery', *The Muslim World*, 112/2 (2022), pp. 207–24.

Cooperson, Michael, *Classical Arabic Biography: The Heirs of the Prophets in the Age of al-Ma'mūn* (Cambridge: Cambridge University Press, 2000).

Coulson, N. J., *Succession in the Muslim Family* (Cambridge: Cambridge University Press, 1971).

Crone, Patricia, *Roman, Provincial and Islamic Law: The Origins of the Islamic Patronate* (Cambridge: Cambridge University Press, 2002).

Crone, Patricia, 'What Do We Actually Know about Mohammed?', Open Democracy, 10 June 2008, www.opendemocracy.net/en/mohammed_3866jsp/, accessed 15 November 2020.

Déroche, François, *Qur'ans of the Umayyads: A First Overview* (Leiden: Brill, 2013).

Al-Dhahabī, Shams al-Dīn, *Tadhkirat al-ḥuffāẓ*, ed. 'Abd al-Raḥmān b. Yaḥyā al-Mu'allimī, 4 vols (Hyderabad: Dā'irat al-Ma'ārif al-'Uthmāniyya, 1958).

Al-Dhahabī, Shams al-Dīn, *Tadhkirat al-ḥuffāẓ*, 4 vols (India: Osmania Oriental Publications, 1958).

Al-Dhahabī, Shams al-Dīn, *Siyar a'lām al-nubalā'*, 25 vols (Beirut: Mu'assasat al-Risāla, 2001).

Al-Dhahabī, Shams al-Dīn, *Tadhhīb tahdhīb al-kamāl fī asmā' al-rijāl*, ed. Amīn Salāma and 'Abd al-Samī' al-Bar'ī, 11 vols (Cairo: al-Fārūq, 2004).

Al-Dhahabī, Shams al-Dīn, *Tadhkirat al-ḥuffāẓ*, ed. 'Abd al-Raḥmān b. Yaḥyā al-Mu'allimī, 4 vols (Hyderabad: Dā'irat al-Ma'ārif al-'Uthmāniyya, 2009).

Donner, Fred McGraw, *Narratives of Islamic Origins: The Beginnings of Islamic Historical Writing* (Princeton, NJ: Darwin Press, 1998).

Donner, Fred McGraw, *Muhammad and the Believers: At the Origins of Islam* (Cambridge, MA: Harvard University Press, 2010).

Ehrman, Bart D., *The Orthodox Corruption of Scripture: The Effect of Early Christological Controversies on the Text of the New Testament* (New York: Oxford University Press, 2011).

Ehteshami, Amin, 'The Four Books of Shi'i Hadith: From Inception to Consolidation', *Islamic Law and Society*, 29/3 (2021), pp. 1–55.

Eliash, Joseph, 'The Shi'ite Qur'an: A Reconsideration of Goldziher's Interpretation', *Arabica Revue D'études Arabes*, 16 (1969), pp. 15–24.

Eltantawi, Sarah, 'Ṭūsī Did Not "Opt Out": Shiite Jurisprudence and the Solidification of the Stoning Punishment in the Islamic Legal Tradition', in Alireza Korangy, Wheeler M. Thackston, Roy P. Mottahedeh and William Granara (eds), *Essays in Islamic Philology, History, and Philosophy* (Berlin; Boston: De Gruyter, 2016), pp. 312–32.

Eltantawi, Sarah, *Shari'ah on Trial: Northern Nigeria's Islamic Revolution* (Berkeley: University of California Press, 2017).

Eltantawi, Sarah, 'Mysterious Legislation: 'Umar Ibn al-Khaṭṭāb's Role in the Legalization of the Stoning Punishment in the Sunni Islamic Tradition', in Nevin Reda and Yasmin Amin (eds), *Islamic Interpretive Tradition and Gender Justice* (Montreal; Kingston: McGill-Queen's University Press, 2020), pp. 288–313.

Gerhardsson, Birger, *Memory and Manuscript: Oral Tradition and Written Transmission in Rabbinic Judaism and Early Christianity with Tradition and Transmission in Early Christianity* (Grand Rapids, MI: Eerdmans, 1998).

Al-Ghaḍā'irī, Aḥmad b. al-Ḥusayn, *Rijāl Ibn al-Ghaḍā'irī* (Qum: Dār al-Ḥadīth, 2001).

Gil, Moshe, 'The Origin of the Jews of Yathrib', in F. E. Peters (ed.), *The Arabs and Arabia on the Eve of Islam* (London; New York: Routledge, 2017), pp. 145–66.

Goldziher, Ignác, *Muslim Studies*, trans. S. M. Stern and C. R. Barber (London: George Allen, 1971).

Görke, Andreas, 'Eschatology, History, and the Common Link: A Study in Methodology', in Herbert Berg (ed.), *Method and Theory in the Study of Islamic Origins* (Leiden: Brill, 2003), pp. 179–208.

Görke, Andreas, 'The Relationship between *Maghāzī* and *Ḥadīth* in Early Islamic Scholarship', *Bulletin of the School of Oriental and African Studies*, 74/2 (2011), pp. 171–85.

Görke, Andreas, Harald Motzki and Gregor Schoeler, 'First Century Sources for the Life of Muḥammad? A Debate', *Der Islam*, 89/1–2 (2012), pp. 2–59.

Haider, Najam, *The Origins of the Shīʿa: Identity, Ritual, and Sacred Space in Eighth-Century Kūfa* (Cambridge: Cambridge University Press, 2011).

Haider, Najam, *The Rebel and the Imām in Early Islam* (Cambridge: Cambridge University Press, 2019).

Hallaq, Wael B., 'The Use and Abuse of Evidence: The Question of Provincial and Roman Influences on Early Islamic Law', *Journal of the American Oriental Society*, 110/1 (1990), pp. 79–91.

Hallaq, Wael B., *An Introduction to Islamic Law* (Cambridge; New York: Cambridge University Press, 2011).

Harvey, Ramon, *The Qur'an and the Just Society* (Edinburgh: Edinburgh University Press, 2018).

Hayes, Edmund, 'The Institutions of the Shīʿī Imāmate: Towards a Social History of Early Imāmī Shiʿism', *al-Masāq*, 33/2 (2021), pp. 188–204.

Hayes, Edmund, *Agents of the Hidden Imam: Forging Twelver Shiʿism, 850–950 CE* (New York: Cambridge University Press, 2022).

Hilali, Asma, *The Sanaa Palimpsest: The Transmission of the Qur'an in the First Centuries AH* (Oxford: Oxford University Press and Institute of Ismaili Studies, 2017).

Al-Hindī, ʿAlī b. ʿAbd al-Mālik al-Muttaqī, *Kanz al-ʿummāl fī sunan al-aqwāl wa-l-afʿāl*, 18 vols (Beirut: Muʾassasat al-Risāla, 1985).

Hirschfeld, Hartwig, 'Abdallah ibn Salam', *The Jewish Encyclopedia*, vol. 1 (New York: Funk and Wagnalls, 1906), pp. 43–4.

Hock, Ronald F., 'Lazarus and Micyllus: Greco-Roman Backgrounds to Luke 16:19–31', *Journal of Biblical Literature*, 106/3 (1987), pp. 447–63.

Husayn, Nebil, *Opposing the Imām: The Legacy of the Nawāṣib in Islamic Literature* (Cambridge: Cambridge University Press, 2021).

Ibn Abī Shayba, Abū Bakr, *Muṣannaf Ibn Abī Shayba*, ed. Kamāl Yūsuf al-Ḥawt, 7 vols (Riyadh: Maktabat al-Rushd, 1988).

Ibn Abī Shayba, Abū Bakr, *Muṣannaf Ibn Abī Shayba*, 8 vols (Beirut: Dār al-Fikr, 1994).

Ibn Anas, Mālik, *Muwaṭṭaʾ* (Beirut: Dār Iḥyāʾ al-Turāth al-ʿArabī, 1994).

Ibn Anas, Mālik, *Muwaṭṭaʾ*, ed. Muḥammad Muṣṭafā al-Aʿẓamī, 8 vols (Abu Dhabi: Muʾassasat Zāyid b. Sulṭān, 2004).

Ibn Bābawayh, Muḥammad b. ʿAlī, *ʿIlal al-sharāʾiʿ*, 2 vols (Najaf: Manshūrāt al-Maktaba, 1966).

Ibn Bābawayh, Muḥammad b. ʿAlī, *Man lā yaḥḍuruhu al-faqīh*, ed. ʿAlī Akbar al-Ghaffārī, 4 vols (Qom: Daftar-i Intishārāt-i Islāmī, 1993).

Ibn Hishām, ʿAbd al-Malik, *al-Sīra al-nabawī*, ed. ʿUmar ʿAbd al-Salām Tadmurī, 2 vols (Beirut: Dār al-Kitāb al-ʿArabī, 1990).

Ibn Khalaf, Muḥammad b. Ismāʿīl, *al-ʿUlūm bi-shuyūkh al-Bukhārī wa-Muslim*, ed. ʿĀdil b. Saʿd Abū ʿAbd al-Raḥmān (Beirut: Dār al-Kitāb, 2015).

Ibn Mājah, Muḥammad b. Yazīd, *Sunan Ibn Mājah*, ed. Muḥammad Fūʾad ʿAbd al-Bāqī, 2 vols (Beirut: Dār Iḥyāʾ al-Turāth al-ʿArabī, 2010).

Ibn Mājah, Muḥammad b. Yazīd, *Sunan Ibn Mājah*, 2 vols (Beirut: al-Maktab al-ʿIlmiyya, n.d.).

Ibn al-Nadīm, Muḥammad b. Isḥāq, *Kitāb al-fihrist*, ed. Riḍā Tajaddud (Beirut: Dār al-Masīra, 1988).

Ibn al-Nadīm, Muḥammad b. Isḥāq, *Kitāb al-fihrist* (Cairo: Dār al-Īmān, n.d.).

Ibn Saʿd, Muḥammad, *Kitāb al-ṭabaqāt al-kabīr*, ed. ʿAlī Muḥammad ʿUmar, 11 vols (Cairo: Maktabat al-Khānjī, 2001).

Jafri, Syed Husain Mohammad, *Origins and Development of Shiʿa Islam* (Oxford: Oxford University Press, 2004).

Jeffery, Arthur, *Materials for the History of the Text of the Quran: The Old Codices* (Leiden: Brill, 1937).

Juynboll, G. H. A., ʻNāfiʿ, the *Mawlā* of Ibn ʿUmar, and His Position in Muslim *Ḥadīth* Literature', *Der Islam*, 70/2 (1993), pp. 207–44.

Juynboll, G. H. A., 'Some *Isnād*-Analytical Methods Illustrated on the Basis of Several Woman-Demeaning Sayings from *Ḥadīth* Literature', in Harald Motzki (ed.), *Hadith: Origins and Developments* (Aldershot: Routledge, 2004), pp. 175–216.

Juynboll, G. H. A., *Encyclopaedia of Canonical Ḥadīth* (Leiden; Boston: Brill, 2007).

Juynboll, G. H. A., *Muslim Tradition: Studies in Chronology, Provenance and Authorship of Early Hadith* (Cambridge: Cambridge University Press, 2008).

Juynboll, G. H. A., 'Mūsā b. ʿUqba', *Encyclopaedia of Canonical Ḥadīth*, http://dx.doi.org/10.1163/2590-3004_ECHO_COM_000118, accessed 12 September 2012.

Kallek, Cengiz, 'YAHYÂ b. ÂDEM', *TDV İslâm Ansiklopedisi*, vol. 43 (Istanbul: Türkiye Diyanet Vakfı İslâm Araştırmaları Merkezi, 2013), pp. 234–37.

Kara, Seyfeddin, 'The Collection of the Qurʾān in the Early Shīʿite Discourse: The Traditions Ascribed to the Fifth Imām Abū Jaʿfar Muḥammad al-Bāqir', *Journal of the Royal Asiatic Society*, 26/3 (2016), pp. 375–406.

Kara, Seyfeddin, 'Review of *The Origins of the Shīʿa: Identity, Ritual, and Sacred Space in Eighth-Century Kūfa*, by Najam Haider', *Ilahiyat Studies*, 7/2 (2016), pp. 295–99.

Kara, Seyfeddin, 'Suppression of ʿAlī Ibn Abī Ṭālib's Codex: Study of the Traditions on the Earliest Copy of the Qurʾān', *Journal of Near Eastern Studies*, 75/2 (2016), pp. 267–89.

Kara, Seyfeddin, *In Search of Ali Ibn Abi Talib's Codex: History and Traditions of the Earliest Copy of the Qur'an* (Berlin: Gerlach Press, 2018).

Kelber, Werner H., *The Oral and the Written Gospel: The Hermeneutics of Speaking and Writing in the Synoptic Tradition, Mark, Paul, and Q* (Bloomington; Indianapolis: Indiana University Press, 1997).

Kennedy, Hugh, *The Prophet and the Age of the Caliphates* (Harlow: Pearson-Longman, 2004).

Khadduri, Majid, trans., *al-Shāfiʿī's al-Risāla: Treatise on the Foundations of Islamic Jurisprudence* (Cambridge: Islamic Texts Society, 1961).

Al-Khaṭīb al-Baghdādī, Aḥmad b. ʿAlī b. Thābit, *Tārīkh Baghdād*, ed. Bashshār ʿAwwād Maʿrūf,17 vols (Beirut: Dār al-Gharb al-Islāmiyya, 2001).

Khawānsārī, Muḥammad Bāqir, *Rawḍāt al-jannāt fī aḥwāl al-ʿulamāʾ wa-l-sādāt*, 8 vols (Qom: Ismāʿīlīyān, 1991).

Al-Khoei, Abū al-Qāsim, *Muʿjam rijāl al-ḥadīth wa-tafṣīl ṭabaqāt al-ruwāt*, 24 vols (Najaf: Mu'assasat al-Khoei al-Islāmiyya, n.d.).

Kister, M. J., '"Do Not Assimilate Yourselves ...": *Lā Tashabbahū*', *Jerusalem Studies in Arabic and Islam*, 12 (1989), pp. 321–71.

Kister, M. J., *Concepts and Ideas at the Dawn of Islam* (Aldershot; Brookfield: Ashgate, 1997).

Kloppenborg, John S., *Q, the Earliest Gospel: An Introduction to the Original Stories and Sayings of Jesus* (Louisville; London: Westminster John Knox Press, 2008).

Kloppenborg, John S., 'Hirte Und Andere Kriminelle: Über Die Anwendung von Modellen', in Wolfgang Stegemann and Richard DeMaris (eds), *Alte Texte in Neuen Kontexten: Wo Steht Die Sozialwissenschaftliche Bibelexegese?* (Stuttgart: Kohlhammer, 2015), pp. 241–64.

Knust, Jennifer Wright, 'Early Christian Re-writing and the History of the *Pericope Adulterae*', *Journal of Early Christian Studies*, 14/4 (2006), pp. 485–536.

Kohlberg, Etan, 'Imam and Community in the Pre-Ghayba Period', in Saïd Arjomand (ed.), *Authority and Political Culture in Shiʿism* (Albany: State University of New York Press, 1988), pp. 25–53.

Kramers, Jan Hendrik, 'A Tradition of Manichaean Tendency ("The She-Eater of Grass")', in Harald Motzki (ed.), *Hadith: Origins and Developments* (Aldershot: Routledge, 2004), pp. 245–57.

Al-Kulaynī, Abū Jaʿfar Muḥammad b. Yaʿqūb b. Isḥāq, *al-Kāfī fī ʿilm al-dīn*, 8 vols (Tehran: Dār al-Kutub al-Islāmiyya, 1986).

Al-Kulaynī, Muḥammad b. Yaʿqūb b. Isḥāq, *al-Kāfī fī ʿilm al-dīn*,15 vols (Qom: Dār al-Ḥadīth, 2008).

Kuzudişli, Bekir, 'Sunnī–Shīʿī Interaction in the Early Period: "The Transition of the Chains of Ahl al-Sunna to the Shīʿa"', *Ilahiyat Studies*, 6/1 (2015), pp. 7–45.

Al-Lajna al-ʿAlamiyya fī Muʿassasat al-Imām al-Ṣādiq, *Mawsūʿa ṭabaqāt al-fuqahāʾ*, 14 vols (Qom: al-Lajna al-ʿAlamiyya fī Mu'assasat al-Imām al-Ṣādiq, 1997).

Lalani, Arzina R., *Early Shiʿi Thought: The Teachings of Imam Muhammad al-Bāqir* (London: I. B. Tauris, 2000).

Lawson, Todd B., 'Note for the Study of a "Shīʿī Qur'ān"', *Journal of Semitic Studies*, XXXVI/2 (1991), pp. 279–95.

Lecker, Michael, 'Muhammad at Medina: A Geographical Approach', *Jerusalem Studies in Arabic and Islam*, 6 (1985), pp. 29–62.

Lecker, Michael, 'The Death of the Prophet Muḥammad's Father: Did Wāqidī Invent Some of the Evidence?', *Zeitschrift der Deutschen Morgenländischen Gesellschaft*, 145/1 (1995), pp. 9–27.

Lecker, Michael, 'Zayd b. Thābit, "A Jew with Two Sidelocks": Judaism and Literacy in Pre-Islamic Medina (Yathrib)', *Journal of Near Eastern Studies*, 56/4 (1997), pp. 259–73.

Lecker, Michael, "Abdallāh b. Salām', in Kate Fleet, Gudrun Krämer, Denis Matringe, John Nawas and Everett Rowson (eds), *Encyclopaedia of Islam*, http://dx.doi.org.myaccess.library.utoronto.ca/10.1163/1573-3912_ei3_COM_24690, accessed 5 March 2022.

Liebesny, Herbert J., 'Comparative Legal History: Its Role in the Analysis of Islamic and Modern Near Eastern Legal Institutions', *The American Journal of Comparative Law*, 20/1 (1972), pp. 38–52.

Lucas, Scott C., *Constructive Critics, Ḥadīth Literature, and the Articulation of Sunnī Islam* (Leiden: Brill, 2004).

Lucas, Scott C., 'Where Are the Legal "Ḥadīth"?: A Study of the "Muṣannaf" of Ibn Abī Shayba', *Islamic Law and Society*, 15/3 (2008), pp. 283–314.

Lucas, Scott C., '"Perhaps You Only Kissed Her?": A Contrapuntal Reading of the Penalties for Illicit Sex in the Sunni Hadith Literature', *The Journal of Religious Ethics*, 39/3 (2011), pp. 399–415.

Madelung, Wilferd, *The Succession to Muhammad: A Study of the Early Caliphate* (Cambridge; New York: Cambridge University Press, 1997).

Majlisī, Muḥammad Bāqir, *Biḥār al-anwār*, ed. al-Sayyid Ibrāhīm al-Mayānajī and Muḥammad al-Bāqir Bahbūdī, 110 vols (Beirut: Dār Iḥyā' al-Turāth al-'Arabī, 1983).

Majlisī, Muḥammad Bāqir, *al-Wajīza fī al-rijāl* (Iran: Wazārat al-Thaqāfa wa-l-Irshād al-Islāmī, n.d.).

Ma'rifat, Muḥammad Hādī, *Ṣiyānat al-Qur'ān min al-taḥrīf* (Qom: Mu'assasat al-Tamhīd, 2008).

Ma'rifat, Muhammad Hadi, *Introduction to the Science of the Qur'an*, ed. Mohammad Saeed Bahmanpour, trans. Salim Rossier and Mansoor Limba (London: SAMT, 2014).

Mazuz, Haggai, *The Religious and Spiritual Life of the Jews of Medina* (Leiden; Boston: Brill, 2014).

Meier, John P., 'John the Baptist in Matthew's Gospel', *Journal of Biblical Literature*, 99/3 (1980), pp. 383–405.

Melchert, Christopher, 'Qur'ānic Abrogation across the Ninth Century: Shāfi'ī, Abū 'Ubayd, Muḥāsibī, and Ibn Qutaybah', in Bernard G. Weiss (ed.), *Studies in Islamic Legal Theory* (Leiden; Boston; Köln: Brill, 2002), 75–98.

Melchert, Christopher, 'The Early History of Islamic Law', in Herbert Berg (ed.), *Method and Theory in the Study of Islamic Origins* (Leiden; Boston: Brill, 2003), pp. 293–324.

Al-Mizzī, Jamāl al-Dīn, *Tahdhīb al-kamāl fī asmā' al-rijāl*, ed. Bashshār 'Awwād Ma'rūf, 35 vols (Beirut: Mu'assasat al-Risāla, 1980).

Al-Mizzī, Jamāl al-Dīn, *Tahdhīb al-kamāl fī asmā' al-rijāl*, 35 vols (Beirut: Mu'assasat al-Risāla, 1983).

Modarressi, Hossein, *Crisis and Consolidation in the Formative Period of Shī'ite Islam: Abū Ja'far Ibn Qiba al-Rāzī and His Contribution to Imāmite Shī'ite Thought* (Princeton, NJ: Darwin Press, 1993).

Modarressi, Hossein, 'Early Debates on the Integrity of the Qur'ān: A Brief Survey', *Studia Islamica*, 77 (1993), pp. 5–39.

Modarressi, Hossein, *Tradition and Survival: A Bibliographical Survey of Early Shī'ite Literature*, vol. 1 (Oxford: Oneworld Publications, 2003).

Motzki, Harald, 'The *Muṣannaf* of 'Abd al-Razzāq al-San'ānī as a Source of Authentic *Aḥādīth* of the First Century AH', *Journal of Near Eastern Studies*, 50/1 (1991), pp. 1–21.

Motzki, Harald, 'Quo Vadis, *Ḥadīṯ*-Forschung? Eine Kritische Untersuchung von G.H.A. Juynboll: Nāfi' the Mawlā of Ibn 'Umar, and His Position in Muslim *Ḥadīṯ* Literature', *Der Islam*, 73/1 (1996), pp. 40–80.

Motzki, Harald, 'The Prophet and the Cat: On Dating Mālik's *Muwaṭṭa'* and Legal Traditions', *Jerusalem Studies in Arabic and Islam*, 22 (1998), pp. 18–83.

Motzki, Harald, 'Murder of Ibn Abi l-Huqayq: On the Origin and Reliability of Some Maghazi-Reports', in Harald Motzki (ed.), *The Biography of Muhammad: The Issue of the Sources* (Leiden; Boston; Köln: Brill, 2000), pp. 170–239.

Motzki, Harald, 'The Collection of the Qur'ān: A Reconsideration of Western Views in Light of Recent Methodological Developments', *Der Islam*, 78/1 (2001), pp. 1–34.

Motzki, Harald, *The Origins of Islamic Jurisprudence: Meccan Fiqh before the Classical Schools*, trans. Marion H. Katz (Leiden; Boston; Köln: Brill, 2002).

Motzki, Harald, 'Dating Muslim Traditions: A Survey', *Arabica*, 52/2 (2005), pp. 204–53.

Motzki, Harald, Nicolet Boekhoff-van der Voort, and Sean W. Anthony, *Analysing Muslim Traditions: Studies in Legal, Exegetical and Maghāzī Ḥadīth* (Leiden; Boston: Brill, 2010).

Motzki, Harald, 'Ibn Jurayj', in Kate Fleet, Gudrun Krämer, Denis Matringe, John Nawas and Everett Rowson (eds), *Encyclopaedia of Islam*, http://dx.doi.org/10.1163/1573-3912_ei3_COM_30848, accessed 22 February 2022.

Al-Mufīd, al-Shaykh, *al-Ikhtiṣāṣ*, ed. 'Alī Akbar al-Ghaffārī (Qom: al-Mu'tamar al-'Ālamī li-Ta'līf al-Shaykh al-Mufīd, 1971).

Al-Mufīd, al-Shaykh, *al-Ikhtiṣāṣ*, ed. 'Alī Akbar al-Ghaffārī (Qom: al-Mu'tamar al-'Ālamī li-Ta'līf al-Shaykh al-Mufīd, 1992).

Al-Mufīd, al-Shaykh, *al-Irshād fī ma'rifat ḥujaj Allāh 'alā al-'ibād*, 2 vols (Qom: Kongreh-i Shaykh Mufīd, 1992).

Al-Mufīd, al-Shaykh, *Awā'il al-maqālāt fī al-madhāhib wa-l-mukhtārāt* (Beirut: Dār al-Mufīd, 1993).

Muslim, Ibn al-Ḥajjāj, *Ṣaḥīḥ Muslim*, 4 vols (Beirut: Dār Iḥyā' al-Turāth al-'Arabī, 1991).

Muslim, Ibn al-Ḥajjāj, *Ṣaḥīḥ Muslim*, ed. Muḥammad Fu'ād 'Abd al-Bāqī, 5 vols (Beirut: Dār Iḥyā' al-Turāth al-'Arabī, 2010).

Al-Najāshī, Muḥammad b. 'Abdullāh, *Rijāl al-Najāshī* (Beirut: Mu'assasat al-'Amalī li-l-Maṭbū'āt, 2010).

Nasā'ī, Aḥmad b. Shu'ayb, *Sunan al-Nasā'ī*, 8 vols (Aleppo: Maktab al-Maṭbū'āt al-Islāmī, 1994).

Nasser, Shady, *The Transmission of the Variant Readings of the Qur'ān: The Problem of Tawātur and the Emergence of Shawādhdh* (Leiden; Boston: Brill, 2012).

Newman, Andrew J., *The Formative Period of Twelver Shī'ism: Hadith as Discourse between Qum and Baghdad* (Richmond: Curzon, 2000).

Nickel, Gordon, *Narratives of Tampering in the Earliest Commentaries on the Quran* (Leiden; Boston: Brill, 2010).

Nöldeke, Theodor, Friedrich Schwally, Gotthelf Bergsträsser and Otto Pretzl, *The History of the Qur'ān*, ed. and trans. Wolfgang H. Behn (Leiden; Boston: Brill, 2012).

Al-Nu'mānī, Muḥammad b. Ibrāhīm, *Kitāb al-ghayba*, ed. 'Alī Akbar al-Ghaffārī (Tehran: Nashr-i Ṣadūq, 1977).

Al-Nu'mānī, Muḥammad b. Ibrāhīm, *Tafsīr al-Nu'mānī* (Qom: Dār al-Shabestarī al-Maṭbū'āt, n.d.).

Nūrī, Muḥaddith, *Faṣl al-khiṭāb fī taḥrīf kitāb rabb al-arbāb* (Beirut: Markaz al-Dirāsāt al-Fikriyya, 2020).

Pavlovitch, Pavel, 'Early Development of the Tradition of the Self-confessed Adulterer in Islam: An *Isnād* and *Matn* Analysis', *al-Qantara*, 34/2 (2010), pp. 371–410.

Pavlovitch, Pavel, 'The Stoning of a Pregnant Adulteress from Juhayna: The Early Evolution of a Muslim Tradition', *Islamic Law and Society*, 17/1 (2010), pp. 1–62.

Pavlovitch, Pavel, 'The Islamic Penalty for Adultery in the Third Century AH and Al-Shāfi'ī's *Risāla*', *Bulletin of the School of Oriental and African Studies*, 75/3 (2012), pp. 473–97.

Pavlovitch, Pavel, and David Powers, '"A Bequest May Not Exceed One-Third": An *Isnād*-cum-*Matn* Analysis – and Beyond', in Behnam Sadeghi, Asad Ahmed, Robert Hoyland and Adam Silverstein (eds), *Islamic Cultures, Islamic Contexts: Essays in Honor of Professor Patricia Crone* (Leiden: Brill, 2014), pp. 133–72.

Pavlovitch, Pavel, *The Formation of the Islamic Understanding of Kalāla in the Second Century AH (718–816 CE): Between Scripture and Canon* (Leiden; Boston: Brill, 2015).

Pierce, Matthew, *Twelve Infallible Men: The Imams and the Making of Shi'ism* (Cambridge, MA: Harvard University Press, 2016).

Powers, David, 'On Bequests in Early Islam', *Journal of Near Eastern Studies*, 48/3 (1989), pp. 185–200.

Powers, David, *Muḥammad Is Not the Father of Any of Your Men: The Making of the Last Prophet* (Philadelphia: University of Pennsylvania Press, 2009).

Powers, David, 'Sinless, Sonless and Seal of Prophets: Muḥammad and Kor 33, 36–40, Revisited', *Arabica*, 67 (2020), pp. 333–408.

Powers, David, 'Review of Sean William Anthony, *Muhammad and the Empires of Faith: The Making of the Prophet of Islam*, Oakland: University of California Press, 2020', *Al-Abhath*, 69/1 (2021), pp. 255–62.

Qahpāyī, 'Ināyatullāh, *Majma' al-rijāl*, 7 vols (Qom: Ismā'īlīyān, 1986).

Al-Qummī, 'Alī b. Ibrāhīm, *Tafsīr al-Qummī*, ed. Ṭayyib Mūsāwī Jazā'irī, 2 vols (Qom: Dār al-Kitāb, 1983).

Qutbuddin, Tahera, *Arabic Oration: Art and Function* (Leiden; Boston: Brill, 2019).

Rabb, Intisar, 'Simplicity, Creativity, Lucidity as "Method" in the Study of Islamic History: An Interview with Michael Cook', Islamic Law Blog, 2021, https://islamiclaw.blog/2021/01/26/14713/, accessed 1 February 2021.

Reynolds, Gabriel Said, 'On the Qur'anic Accusation of Scriptural Falsification (*Taḥrīf*) and Christian Anti-Jewish Polemic', *Journal of the American Oriental Society*, 130/2 (2010), pp. 189–202.

Rippin, Andrew, 'Literary Analysis of Qurʾān, *Tafsīr* and *Sīra*: The Methodologies of John Wansbrough', in Ibn Warraq (ed.), *The Origins of the Koran: Classic Essays on Islam's Holy Book* (Amherst: Prometheus Books, 1998), pp.151–63.

Rizwan, Syed Atif, 'The Resurrection of Stoning as Punishment for *Zinā* in Islamic Criminal Laws: From *Zinā* Flogging in the Qurʾān to *Zinā* Stoning in the Islamic Legal Tradition' (PhD diss., University of California, 2018).

Robinson, Chase F., *Islamic Historiography* (Cambridge; New York: Cambridge University Press, 2002).

Rubin, Uri, 'The "Constitution of Medina": Some Notes', *Studia Islamica*, 62 (1985), pp. 5–23.

Sadeghi, Behnam, and Uwe Bergmann, 'The Codex of a Companion of the Prophet and the Qurʾān of the Prophet', *Arabica*, 57/4 (2010), pp. 343–436.

Sadeghi, Behnam, and Mohsen Goudarzi, 'Ṣanʿāʾ 1 and the Origins of the Qurʾān', *Der Islam*, 87/1–2 (2012), pp. 1–129.

Al-Ṣaffār, Muḥammad b. al-Ḥasan, *Baṣāʾir al-darajāt fī faḍaʾil al-Muḥammad* (Qom: Āyatullāh Marʿashī Najafī Library, 1983).

Saleh, Walid A, 'Review of *Die Schia Und Die Koranfälschung*, by Rainer Brunner', *Review of Middle East Studies*, 38/2 (2004), pp. 222–4.

Al-Ṣanʿānī, ʿAbd al-Razzāq, *Muṣannaf ʿAbd al-Razzāq al-Ṣanʿānī*, ed. Ḥabīb al-Raḥmān al-Aʿẓamī, 11 vols (Beirut: al-Maktab al-Islāmiyya, 1983).

Al-Sayyārī, Abū ʿAbdullāh Aḥmad b. Muḥammad, *Revelation and Falsification: Kitāb al-qirāʾāt aw al-tanzīl wa-l-taḥrīf*, ed. Etan Kohlberg and Mohammad Ali Amir-Moezzi (Leiden: Brill, 2009).

Schacht, Joseph, *The Origins of Muhammadan Jurisprudence* (Oxford: Clarendon Press, 1967).

Scheiner, Jens, *Die Eroberung von Damaskus* (Leiden: Brill, 2010).

Scheiner, Jens, '*Isnād-cum-Matn* Analysis and *Kalāla*: Some Critical Reflections', *Journal of the American Oriental Society*, 139/2 (2019), pp. 479–86.

Schneider, Irene, 'Narrativität und Authentizität: Die Geschichte vom weisen Propheten, dem dreisten Dieb und dem koranfesten Gläubiger', *Der Islam*, 77/1 (2009), pp. 84–115.

Schoeler, Gregor, *Charakter Und Authentie Der Muslimischen Überlieferung Über Das Leben Mohammeds* (Berlin: De Gruyter, 1996).

Schoeler, Gregor, *The Biography of Muḥammad: Nature and Authenticity*, ed. James E. Montgomery, trans. Uwe Vagelpohl (New York: Routledge, 2011).

Scott, S. P., trans. 'The Enactments of Justinian: The Digest or Pandects: Book 1' (*The Civil Law*, 1932), https://droitromain.univ-grenoble-alpes.fr/Anglica/D1_Scott.htm, accessed 5 March 2022.

Serjeant, R. B., 'The "Sunnah Jāmi'ah", Pacts with the Yaṯẖrib Jews, and the "Taḥrīm" of Yaṯẖrib: Analysis and Translation of the Documents Comprised in the So-Called "Constitution of Medina"', *Bulletin of the School of Oriental and African Studies*, 41/1 (1978), pp.1–42.

Shoemaker, Stephen J., 'In Search of 'Urwa's *Sīra*: Some Methodological Issues in the Quest for "Authenticity" in the Life of Muḥammad', *Der Islam*, 85/2 (2011) pp. 257–344.

Al-Sijistānī, Abū Dāwūd, *Sunan Abī Dāwūd*, 4 vols (Beirut: al-Maktaba al-'Aṣriyya, 2011).

Sinai, Nicolai, 'When Did the Consonantal Skeleton of the Quran Reach Closure? Part I', *Bulletin of the School of Oriental and African Studies*, 77/2 (2014), pp. 273–92.

Sinai, Nicolai, 'When Did the Consonantal Skeleton of the Quran Reach Closure? Part II', *Bulletin of the School of Oriental and African Studies*, 77/3 (2014), pp. 509–21.

Stafford, Samuel A., 'Constructing Muḥammad's Legitimacy: Arabic Literary Biography and the Jewish Pedigree of the Companion 'Abd Allāh b. Salām (d. 43/633)', *Jerusalem Studies in Arabic and Islam*, 47 (2019), pp. 133–86.

Stafford, Samuel A., 'The Conversions of 'Abdallāh ibn Salām (d. 43/ 633): A Legendary Moment in the Biography of Muḥammad's Jewish Companion', *Bulletin of the School of Oriental and African Studies*, 84/2 (2021), pp. 237–61.

Stewart, Devin, *Islamic Legal Orthodoxy: Twelver Shiite Responses to the Sunni Legal System* (Salt Lake City: University of Utah Press, 1998).

Stewart, Devin, 'Reflections on the State of the Art in Western Qur'anic Studies', in Carol Bakhos and Michael Cook (eds), *Islam and Its Past: Jahiliyya, Late Antiquity, and the Qur'an* (Oxford: Oxford University Press, 2017), pp. 4–68.

Stock, Brian, *The Implications of Literacy: Written Language and Models of Interpretation in the 11th and 12th Centuries* (Princeton, NJ: Princeton University Press, 1983).

Syed, Mairaj U., 'The Construction of Historical Memory in the Exegesis of Kor 16, 106', *Arabica*, 62 (2015), pp. 607–51.

Tafrīshī, Muḥammad Taqī, *Naqd al-rijāl*, 12 vols (Qom: Jāmi' Mudarrisīn, 1990).

Takim, Liyakat, 'The Origins and Evaluations of Hadith Transmitters in Shi'i Biographical Literature', *American Journal of Islamic Social Sciences*, 24/4 (2007), pp. 26–49.

Tihrānī, Āghā Bozorg, *al-Dharī'a ilā taṣānīf al-shī'a*, 25 vols (Qom: Ismā'īlīyān and Kitābḥāne'i Islāmiyya, 1987).

Tihrānī, Aghā Bozorg, *Ṭabaqāt a'lām al-shī'a*, 6 vols (Qom: Ismā'īlīyān, n.d.).

Tirmidhī, Abū 'Īsā Muḥammad b. 'Īsā, *Jāmi' al-Tirmidhī*, ed. Bashshār 'Awwād Ma'rūf, 6 vols (Beirut: Dār al-Gharb al-Islāmiyya, 1998).

Tirmidhī, Abū 'Īsā Muḥammad b. 'Īsā, *Jāmi' al-Tirmidhī*, ed. Hafiz Abu Tahir Zubair Ali Za'i, 6 vols (Riyadh: Darussalam, 2007).

Al-Ṭūsī, Muḥammad b. al-Ḥasan, *Rijāl al-Ṭūsī*, ed. Jawad Ghayyūmī Eṣfehānī (Qom: Mu'assasat al-Nashr al-Islāmiyya, 1994).

Al-Ṭūsī, Muḥammad b. al-Ḥasan, *al-Fihrist*, ed. al-Sayyid Muḥammad Ṣādiq Baḥr al-'Ulūm (Qom: al-Sharīf al-Raḍī, n.d.).

Al-Ṭūsī, Muḥammad b. al-Ḥasan, *al-Fihrist* (Qom: Mahd Nashriyāt, n.d.).
Al-Tustarī, Muḥammad Taqī, *Qāmūs al-rijāl*,12 vols (Qom: Jāmiʿ Mudarrisīn, 1994).
ʿUṣfūrī, Khalīfa b. ʿUthmān, *Kitāb al-ṭabaqāt*, ed. Suhayl Zakkār, 4 vols (Damascus: Dār al-Fikr, 1993).
van Ess, Joseph, *Zwischen Hadit und Theologie* (Berlin: De Gruyter, 1975).
van Putten, Marijn, '"The Grace of God" as Evidence for a Written Uthmanic Archetype: The Importance of Shared Orthographic Idiosyncrasies', *Bulletin of the School of Oriental and African Studies*, 82/2 (2019), pp. 271–88.
Warner, George, *The Words of the Imams: Al-Shaykh Al-Ṣadūq and the Development of Twelver Shiʿi Hadith Literature* (London; New York; I. B. Tauris, 2021).
Webb, Peter, *Imagining the Arabs: Arab Identity and the Rise of Islam* (Edinburgh: Edinburgh University Press, 2017).
Wegner, Judith Romney, 'Islamic and Talmudic Jurisprudence: The Four Roots of Islamic Law and Their Talmudic Counterparts', *The American Journal of Legal History*, 26/1 (1982), pp. 25–71.
Yusofi Ishkevari, Hasan, 'Al-Aṣbagh b. Nubāta', *Encyclopaedia Islamica*, trans. Rahim Gholami, https://referenceworks.brillonline.com/entries/encyclopaedia-islamica/al-asbagh-b-nubata-SIM_0299, accessed 23 April 2022.
Zaman, Iftikhar, 'The Evolution of a Hadith: Transmission, Growth and the Science of *Rijal* in a Hadith of Saʿd b. Abī Waqqās' (PhD diss., University of Chicago, 1991).
Zellentin, Holger M., 'Gentile Purity Law from the Bible to the Qur'an: The Case of Sexual Purity and Illicit Intercourse', in Holger M. Zellentin (ed.), *Gentile Purity Law from the Bible to the Qur'an: The Case of Sexual Purity and Illicit Intercourse* (London; New York: Routledge, 2019), pp. 115–215.
Zellentin, Holger M., *The Qur'an's Legal Culture: The Didascalia Apostolorum as a Point of Departure* (Tübingen: Mohr Siebeck, 2013).

Index

'Abd al-A'lā, 61
'Abd al-'Azīz b. 'Abdullāh, 148
'Abd al-'Azīz b. Yaḥyā al-Ḥarrānī, 127
'Abd al-Malik b. Shu'ayb b. al-Layth, 49
'Abd al-Raḥmān b. al-Qāsim, 61
'Abd al-Ṣamad b. 'Abd al-Wārith, 61
'Abd al-Wahhāb, 60
'Abd al-Wāḥid b. Ziyād, 124
'Abd al-Wārith b. 'Abd al-Ṣamad b. 'Abd al-Wārith, 61
'Abdullāh b. Abī Bakr b. Ḥazm, 59
'Abdullāh b. Ḥammād al-Anṣārī, 236
'Abdullāh b. Idrīs, 148
'Abdullāh b. Lahī'a, 48
'Abdullāh b. Maslama al-Qa'nabī, 60, 83, 111
'Abdullāh b. Muḥammad al-Nufaylī, 149
'Abdullāh b. Murra, 123
'Abdullāh b. Numayr, 111
'Abdullāh b. Salām, 114, 121, 133
'Abdullāh b. Sinān, 186
'Abdullāh b. 'Umar, 110
'Abdullāh b. Yūsuf, 109
abrogation, 62–5, 164
Abū al-Ṭāhir, 49
Abū Bakr, 7
Abū Ḍamra, 110
Abū Ḥudhayfa, 39
Abū Hurayra, 82
Abū Lahab, 243
Abū Salama Yaḥyā b. Khalaf, 61
Abū Mu'āwiya [al-Sa'dī], 123
Abū Ṭāhir b. al-Sarḥ, 99
Abū Ya'qūb [al-Asadī], 184
Abū 'Ubayda b. 'Abdullāh b. Zam'a, 48
Ādam b. Abī Iyās, 92
adopted children, 56
ahl al-'ilm, 93
Aḥmad b. Manī', 162
[Aḥmad b. Muḥammad b. Khālid] al-Barqī, 184–5
Aḥmad b. Muḥammad b. Sa'īd, 234
Aḥmad b. al-Naḍr, 236
Aḥmad b. Sa'īd al-Ḥamdānī, 112
Aḥmad b. Ṣāliḥ, 55
Aḥmad b. Yūnus, 113
'Ā'isha, 38–9
'Alī b. 'Abdullāh, 85
'Alī b. Abī Ṭālib, 7
  'Alī's codex, 229–31
  'Alī's collection of the Qur'an, 229
'Alī b. Bābawayh al-Qummī, 188
'Alī b. al-Ḥakam, 182
'Alī b. al-Ḥasan al-Taymulī, 235
'Alī b. Muḥammad [b. 'Abdullāh al-Bandār], 213
'Alī b. Muḥammad [al-Ṭanāfisī], 111, 123
'Alī b. Sayf, 183–4
'Alī b. Yūsuf. Al-Ḥasan b. 'Alī b. Yūsuf, 235
al-A'mash, 123
'Āmir al-Sha'bī, 129
'Amr al-Nāqid, 67
'Amra bint 'Abd al-Raḥmān, 59–60
'Anbasa, 55
al-Aṣbagh b. Nubāta, 237
Ash'arī tribe, 213
Ash'ath b. 'Abd al-Malik, 148
'Āṣim b. 'Alī, 92–3
Apocalypse, 228
arbitrator, 117
authority, 178
Avenger (al-Qā'im), 228
Ayyūb [b. Abī Tamīma al-Sakhtiyānī], 44, 67

balāṭ, 121
Banū Qaynuqā', 122
al-Barā' b. 'Āzib, 123–4
Battle of the Camel, 193

Bayt al-Midrās, 122
breastfeeding, 39–75
Bukayr b. ʿAbdullāh, 49

Closure of the Qur'anic Canon, 167
common link, 20, 25
Constitution of Medina, 116–18

Dāwūd b. Abī Hind, 162
domestic sheep eating the Qur'anic folio, 65–7
dual-versus-single-penalty, 119

Faṭaḥiyya, 235
Fāṭima bint ʿUmar, 46
Fāṭima bint al-Walīd b. ʿUtba b. Rabīʿa, 56
financial agent (wakīl), 182
Forgery Culture in Hadith Narrations, 194
form criticism, 14

Gospels, 30

Ḥabbata al-ʿUranī, 236
Hadith, 12–38
Hadith Forgery and Shiʿi Identity, 207–9
Ḥafṣa's codex, 7–8
al-Ḥakam b. Mūsā, 112
al-Ḥalabī, 190
Ḥammād, 190
al-Ḥārith b. Ḥaṣīra, 235–6
Ḥarmala b. Yaḥyā, 149
Hārūn b. ʿAbdullāh, 61
Hārūn b. Saʿīd al-Aylī, 49
Hishām b. al-Ḥakam, 218
Hishām b. Sālim, 183, 187
Ḥumayd b. Nāfiʿ, 49
al-Ḥusayn b. al-Ḥasan b. Abān, 188
al-Ḥusayn b. Saʿīd [al-Ahwāzī], 189
Hushaym [b. Bashīr b. Abī Khāzim], 130
Household of the Prophet (*ahl al-bayt*), 193

Ibn ʿAbbās, 146
Ibn Abī Dhi'b, 92
Ibn Abī Mulayka, 67
Ibn Abī ʿUmar, 67, 189
Ibn Judʿān, 147
Ibn Jurayj, 45, 130
Ibn Karāma, 110
Ibn Numayr, 124
Ibn Sayf, 183
Ibn ʿUlayya, 44
Ibn ʿUyayna, 60
Ibn Wahb, 49, 99, 112
Ibrāhīm b. Ḥasan al-Miṣṣīṣī, 130
Ibrāhīm b. Hāshim [al-Qummī], 217–18
Ibrāhīm b. Isḥāq al-Nahāwandī, 236
Ibrāhīm b. al-Mundhir, 109–10
Ibrāhīm b. Saʿd, 148
Ibrāhīm b. ʿUqba, 54
ʿĪsā b. Aʿyan, 184
Isḥāq b. Ibrāhīm al-Ḥanẓalī, 67
Isḥāq b.Manṣūr, 148
Isḥāq b. Mūsā al-Anṣārī, 83, 111
Isḥāq b. Yūsuf al-Azraq, 162
Islamic law, 50
Islamic Legal Dispute, 119–20
Ismāʿīl b. Abī Khālid, 188
Ismāʿīl [b. ʿUlayya], 110
Ismāʿīl b. Mūsā [al-Fazārī], 129
isnād-cum-matn analysis, 14–18
al-Iyādī, 185

Jābir b. ʿAbdullāh, 129–30
Jābir [b. Yazīd al-Juʿfī], 216, 238
Jārūdī branch of Zaydism, 234

Khālid b. Mādd al-Qalānisī, 217
Khālid b. Makhlad, 110
Kitāb Allāh, 83

Layth b. Saʿd, 96
legitimacy, 178
like a stick penetrating into a jar, 131–2

maḥram, 38–9
Makhrama b. Bukayr, 49
Mālik, 53
Maʿmar, 54
Maʿna b. ʿĪsā al-Qazzāz, 83
marfūʿ (elevated) chain, 188
Maytham al-Tammār, 242
Minā, 163
Mughīra [b. Miqsam], 130
Muḥammad b. Abī ʿUmar, 67
Muḥammad b. al-ʿAlāʾī, 124
Muḥammad b. al-Ḥasan [b. Isḥāq], 188
Muḥammad b. Ḥusayn [b. Abī al-Khaṭṭāb], 217
Muḥammad b. Jaʿfar, 48
Muḥammad b. Isḥāq, 61, 127
Muḥammad b. al-Muthannā, 48, 60
Muḥammad b. Rāfiʿ, 68
Muḥammad b. Rumḥ, 48, 97
Muḥammad b. Salama, 127
Muḥammad b. Yūsuf al-Firyābī, 86
Mujālid [b. Saʿīd], 129
Mūsā b ʿUqba, 109

Musaddad, 86, 110, 124
Muwaṭṭa', 53

al-Nabī, 83
Naḍr b. Shu'ayb, 217
Nāfi', 44
Naṣr b. 'Alī, 87
naṣṣ, 179

occasions of revelation, 164
Occultation, 228, 234

partial common link, 22–3
people of consensus *(aṣḥāb al-ijmā')*, 189, 218
People of Knowledge, 93–5
Projecting Back, 12–14

Qāsim b. Muḥammad b. Abī Bakr, 61, 67
Qāsim b. Muḥammad [al-Iṣfahānī or al-Qummī], 213
al-Quff, 122
Qur'an
 2:75, 6
 2:113, 95
 2:114, 95
 2:144, 94
 3:106, 220
 4:46, 6
 5:13, 6
 5:41, 6
 7:181, 208
 24:2, 33
 33:32, 193
 33:5, 56
Qutayba b. Sa'īd, 96

Rabbāniyyūn, 94
Rasūl Allāh, 83
redaction criticism, 30
retrojection, 30

Ṣabbāḥ b. Yaḥyā al-Muznī, 235
Sa'd b. 'Abdullāh [al-Ash'arī], 188
Sa'd al-Iskāf, 218
Sa'dān b. Muslim [al-'Āmirī], 235
Sahla bint Suhayl, 38
Sa'īd b. al-Musayyab, 126, 161
Salama b. Shabīb, 148
Ṣāliḥ b. Kaysān, 148
Sālim b. Abī Ḥudhayfa, 38
Sālim b. 'Abdullāh b. 'Umar, 39
Ṣan'ā' palimpsests, 8, 168
Sayf b. 'Amīra al-Nakha'ī, 183–4
sectarian discourse, 176
Sharīk [b. 'Abdullāh], 129
al-shaykh wa-l-shaykha, 168
Shu'ayb b. Abī Hamza, 98
Shu'ayb b. Isḥāq, 112
Shu'ayb b. al-Layth, 49
Shu'ba, 49
single-strand hadiths, 20–4
stoning of the Devil, 163
stoning penalty, 33–4
Sufyān b. 'Uyayna, 8–5
Sulaymān b. Bilāl, 60, 110
Sulaymān b. Dāwūd [al-Munqarī], 213, 216
Sūrat al-Aḥzāb, 191–2
Ṣuriyā, 131

taḥrīf, 5–7
Theology of Distortion, 192–4
two weighty things *(ḥadīth al-thaqalayn)*, 210

'Ubaydullāh b. 'Abdullāh [b. 'Utba b.Mas'ūd], 143
'Ubaydullāh b. 'Umar [al-'Umarī], 111
Umayyads' Erasure of the Prophet's Enemies from the Qur'an, 242
Umm Kulthūm, 45
Umm Salama, 48
'Uqayl b. Khālid, 49
'Urwa b. al-Zubayr, 54
'Uthmān, 7
'Uthmān b. 'Īsā [al-Rawwāsī], 185

Wahb b. Baqiyya, 130
Wakī' [b. al-Jarrāḥ], 124
Waqfiyya, 185

Yaḥyā b. Abī 'Imrān, 218
Yaḥyā b. Ādam, 216
Yaḥyā b. Sa'īd, 160
Yaḥyā b. Yaḥyā [b. Bakr al-Tamīmī al-Naysābūrī], 124
Yazīd b. Abī Ḥabīb, 48
Yūnus, 55
Yūnus [b. 'Abd al-Raḥmān], 186

Zayd b. Aslam, 112
Zayd b. Thabit, 7
Zayn al-'Ābidīn, 161–2
Zaynab bint Abī Salama, 48
Zuhayr b. Ḥarb, 112
Zuhayr [b. Mu'āwiya], 113
Zuhrī, 48, 50, 53

EU representative:
Easy Access System Europe
Mustamäe tee 50, 10621 Tallinn, Estonia
Gpsr.requests@easproject.com

www.ingramcontent.com/pod-product-compliance
Lightning Source LLC
Chambersburg PA
CBHW050212240426
43671CB00013B/2307
* 9 7 8 1 4 7 4 4 6 2 2 4 2 *